# Private Equity and Venture Capital

# Private Equity and Venture Capital

## A practical guide for investors and practitioners

Edited by
Rick Lake and Ronald A. Lake

EUROMONEY BOOKS

Published by
Euromoney Books
Nestor House, Playhouse Yard
London EC4V 5EX
United Kingdom

Telephone: +44 020 7779 8999

ISBN 1 85564 691 9

Typeset by Julie Foster
Reprinted in 2005 by Hobbs the Printers Ltd

# Acknowledgments

The editors would like to thank all of the contributors to this volume. This includes each of the authors, as well as those unsung heroes without whom none of this would have been possible:

Stephanie Vallis, who is not only a Masterful Juggler but also a Traffic Cop extraordinaire;
Rose Montreuil, who has a sharper pencil than anyone would ever guess;
Lynn Onofrio, who, even when departing to conduct fandangos on distant shores, always finds ways to lend a hand.

As always, we owe a debt to seemingly unlikely influences, as disparate as Ganesh and the Mad Hatter, Chandler Steiner and Gerhard Rehder, and even Samuel Goldwyn, who once said, 'You should avoid cliches like the plague'.

And as always, special thanks to Pam, Ben and Emily, and the Citas.

*Rick and Ron Lake*
Lake Partners, Inc.
Greenwich, CT

# Contents

# Author biographies

## Editors

**Ronald A. Lake** and **Fredrick C. Lake** are respectively, the president and chairman of Lake Partners, Inc, an investment consulting firm located in Greenwich, Connecticut. Lake Partners advises wealthy individuals and private investment companies on asset allocation, manager selection and programme supervision.

## Contributing authors

**George P. Baker** is a professor of business administration at Harvard Business School in Boston, Massachusetts, and is an economist.

**Joseph W. Bartlett** is a partner at Morrison & Foerster, LLP in New York, and is also an adjunct professor at the New York University School of Law.

**Steve Brockman** works for Great Lakes Consulting Group in South Bend, Indiana. He is a self-described due diligence 'hired gun'.

**Daniel Burstein** is managing partner at Millennium Technology Ventures, LP. He is the co-author with Arne de Keijzer of *Big Dragon: China's Future and What It Means for Business, the Economy, and the Global Order*, (Simon & Schuster, 1998).

**Katherine A. Cattanach** is a managing principal at Sovereign Financial Services in Denver, Colorado.

**Gianluca Cicogna** is a managing partner of Zanett Lombardier Fund. Zanett is a New York-based merchant banking group that specialises in private placements to public companies.

**Jonathan E. Cole, Esq** is chair of the Venture Capital and Emerging Company Group, at the law firm of Edwards & Angell, LLC. He is based in the firm's Palm Beach, Florida office.

**Alan Doran** is principal consultant at Bannock Consulting, located in London, England. Bannock is known for consultancy and research on private equity, venture capital and related fields.

**Claudio Guazzoni** is a managing partner of Zanett Lombardier Fund. Zanett is a New York based merchant banking group that specialises in private placements to public companies.

**Donald J. Gogel** is the chief executive officer of Clayton, Dubiler & Rice, Inc, a private investment firm located in New York, New York.

**Paul A. Gompers** is an associate professor at the Harvard Business School in Boston, Massachusetts. He is also a faculty research fellow at the National Bureau of Economic Research.

**John Paul Ho** is the founder and managing director of Crimson Capital Management. Crimson is a Pacific Rim private equity/venture capital firm, focused on technology investments, especially those relating to the Internet.

**Ron Kahn** is a managing director of Duff & Phelps, LLC. Duff & Phelps is headquartered in Chicago, Illinois and provides investment banking and financial advisory services to middle market companies.

**Steven N. Kaplan** is the Leon Carroll Marshall professor of finance at the Graduate School of Business, University of Chicago, in Chicago, Illinois.

**Mary Frances Kelley** is a managing principal at Sovereign Financial Services in Denver, Colorado, and a certified public accountant.

**Bonnie Kennedy** is a principal at Ernst & Young LLP in New York, New York.

**Shiv Vikram Khemka** is a director of SUN Group and of SUN Capital Partners, a private equity fund active in Russia and the former Soviet Union.

**Josh Lerner** is a professor of business administration at the Harvard Business School in Boston, Massachusetts, and a research associate of the National Bureau of Economic Research.

**Iain Michel** is with the Lucas Group, a strategy consulting firm in Boston, Massachusetts.

**Karen Gordon Mills** is a managing director and founder of Solera Capital, LLC, a venture capital firm in New York, New York.

**Vicky Mudford** is the director of investor relations at Murray Johnstone Private Equity Limited in London, England. She was previously Executive Director of the British Venture Capital Association from 1984-1997.

**James Nelson** is the chairman of the British Venture Capital Association and is a Director of F&C Ventures Ltd. in London, England.

**Joel Press** is a senior partner of Ernst & Young, LLP in New York, New York.

**Serge Raicher** is the secretary general of the European Venture Capital Association, which is based in Brussels, Belgium. EVCA is an industry association representing the private equity and venture capital sector in Europe.

**Jesse Reyes** is the product manager of Venture Economics, a leading private equity research group, located in Newark, New Jersey.

**Betty M. Sheets** is the senior investment manager, Private Investments at the I.B.M. Retirement Fund, located in Stamford, Connecticut.

**George David Smith** is a clinical professor of economics and international business at the New York University's Stern School of Business in New York, New York. Professor Smith is an economic historian.

**Albert L. Sokol, Esq.** is a partner in the law firm of Edwards & Angell, LLC in Boston, Massachusetts. He is the chairman of the firm's International Group.

**Gail Marmostein Sweeney** is a managing principal at Sovereign Financial Services in Denver, Colorado.

**Toby Walters** is publications manager of Venture Economics, a leading private equity research group, located in Newark, New Jersey.

**Susan Wilson** is a managing director of Duff & Phelps, LLC. Duff & Phelps is headquartered in Chicago, Illinois and provides investment banking and financial advisory services to middle market companies.

# Overview and introduction

Ron Lake and Rick Lake
*Lake Partners, Inc.*

Enrico Fermi once wrote the following note to a colleague, 'Before I came here I was confused about this subject. Having listened to your lecture, I am still confused. But on a higher level.'

Private equity is not necessarily a confusing topic, but it can be highly complex. Even many of the professionals among our readers may be surprised to learn just how many nooks and crannies comprise the labyrinth that is private equity. The purpose of this collection of chapters is to provide a wide ranging set of overviews and analyses for institutional and private investors as well as venture capital and private equity professional. We believe that these chapters will prove to be more enlightening than the lecture that Fermi endured.

This book is divided into six sections:

Developed markets overview
Emerging market perspectives
Buyouts, mezzanine and specialised forms of finance
New ventures
Performance measurement
Investor perspectives

## Developed markets overview

The first section, 'Developed markets overview', gives a comprehensive summary of the major trends and developments in the major markets. It is especially interesting to note the similarities and differences between the United States, continental Europe and the United Kingdom. The United States is often considered to be the leader in the field, but it should not be forgotten that the place would not have been put on the map in the first place if an entrepreneur named Christopher Columbus had not been staked by a financial backer named Queen Isabella. The point is that private equity investing has a very long history, much of which is often forgotten or overlooked. However, in today's highly dynamic capital markets, it is true that players in America have been on the cutting edge. Private equity and venture capital in Europe and the United Kingdom are bound to experience significant change as economic and monetary unification becomes more of a reality.

## Emerging market perspectives

The section, 'Emerging market perspectives', provides a candid view of the potential and pitfalls of investing in markets as disparate as Russia, China and south-east Asia. If there is a 'quick buck' to be found in these places, it is just as likely that there is a 'quick bust' right behind. Unless, of course, you understand the essential message of our contributors in this area, which is that it is essential to understand local and regional dynamics, and learn to respond appropriately to the volatility that is inherent in markets that are changing so rapidly.

## Buyouts, mezzanine and specialised forms of finance

The section 'Buyouts, mezzanine and specialised forms of finance' is perhaps the broadest in the book, in that it covers disparate aspects of this area. What works? What doesn't? How has this changed? These are the critical questions that this group of chapters covers. The authors share important insights into 'macro' trends as well as the 'micro' motivations that drive successful deals.

## New ventures

The 'New ventures' section includes much 'nitty gritty' on the business, strategic, economic, legal and accounting aspects of venture capital. The hot IPO markets of the past few years has certainly raised the visibility of the field, including a series of Dilbert cartoons in 1999 that lampooned venture capitalists as overeager financiers showering cash on undeserving hucksters. As the chapters make clear, venture capital is very serious business that has played a critical role in the development of the high growth segments of the economy.

## Performance measurement

'Performance measurement' provides a much needed 'reality check' on how well private equity and venture capital have delivered on their promises to investors. In addition to a quantitative review of returns and risk characteristics, this section also includes several discussions on strategic issues and concerns that will be thought provoking for practitioners as well as investors. Special mention should be made of Karen Mills' chapter, which provides a forward-looking analysis of the factors that drive buyouts. As the chapter makes clear, looking at performance retrospectively is one thing, trying to look at it prospectively is very different – but perhaps even more important.

## Investor perspectives

The final section, 'Investor perspectives,' only contains two chapters, but they are among the most important in the book. Both are essentially field reports from 'battle correspondents' who have spent years in the 'trenches' of private equity. As we said at the beginning of this overview, private equity can be complex. What do you really need to know? Betty Sheet does an admirable job of laying out very clearly the essential issues for investors. Steve Brockman masterfully illustrates the real, practical aspects of doing deals. In fact, some of you may wish to start by reading these two chapters first.

Part I

# Developed markets overview

Chapter 1

# Hidden treasure: A look into private equity's history, future, and lure

Katherine A. Cattanach
*Managing principal, Sovereign Financial Services*

Mary Frances Kelley
*Managing principal, Sovereign Financial Services*

Gail Marmorstein Sweeney
*Managing principal, Sovereign Financial Services*

Individual investors looking for higher returns in a tax-efficient structure might investigate the little-known world of private equity investing. While financing business through private equity has been an important part of world commerce since the beginning of time, private equity has become part of the lexicon only relatively recently.

Although private equity is now recognised as an established asset class, it remains shrouded in at least some degree of mystery. Our purpose is to lift the veil of that mystery, trace the origins and evolution of the asset class, and discuss why investors continue to find private equity attractive.

## What constitutes a private equity investment?

The private equity sector typically makes equity or equity-linked investments in non-public companies, or in companies or parts of companies that are being taken private. These companies range from start-up enterprises to middle-market firms to public firms needing private financing for specific projects. Private equity professionals generally make direct investments in these companies, while individual and institutional investors are more likely to invest through private equity limited partnerships managed by industry professionals.

The investment focus of a limited partnership determines the characteristics of the companies in which it invests. Venture capital partnerships typically focus on high-technology companies and on companies driven by emerging and typically technology- linked markets. Buyout partnerships usually invest in more mature companies, providing funding to finance expansions, consolidations, turnarounds, and spin-offs. Special situation partnerships make investments that range more broadly to include categories such as media, which embody both venture and buyout characteristics, as well as companies in financial distress, besides equity-linked debt and other opportunities that surface from time to time rather than occur on a sustained basis.

About two-thirds of the capital committed to private equity is invested in buyouts and special situations (predominately buyouts), and one-third is invested in venture capital.

## A historical perspective

Venture capital is nearly as old as time. Queen Isabella, for example, funded Columbus's voyage to the New World, hoping to find a shorter route to the Indies. Even though Columbus was seeking a different new world from the one he found, the Queen's investment had all the major components of venture investing today: backing a visionary; investing important sums of money in an effort to push knowledge beyond existing horizons; significant downside if things don't go well, but tremendous rewards if the outcome is successful; and an illiquid investment for a significant period of time.

Private equity has only recently matured into an accepted investment option and a separate industry, moving from what was largely the purview of wealthy individuals and high net worth families in the late 1970s to an asset class dominated by institutional investors as the century draws to a close (see Exhibit 1).

As private equity began to achieve recognition as an identifiable industry, distinct market cycles also began to emerge. Exhibits 2 and 3 reveal their cycles over time, along with key events and factors that have helped shape the cycles. Special situations, as the name implies, cannot be as easily described by specific cycles because of the unique investment opportunities in this category.

As Exhibit 2 depicts, venture capital, as it is known today, got its start with the authorisation of small business investment companies (SBICs) in 1958. Two major cycles have taken place in the venture capital sector of the private equity industry since that time. The first was fuelled largely by individuals who backed venture capitalists using risk capital to fund fledgling technology companies – participating in an industrial revolution based on mass technology. That cycle peaked in 1972, then slid into the doldrums with the collapse of the initial public offering option for exit and the disastrous, then lacklustre stock market environment of the following few years.

Exhibit 1

**Sources of venture capital by limited partner type – five-year rolling average, 1983–97 (%)**

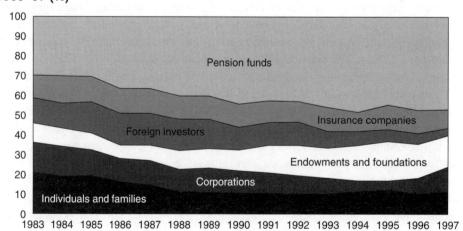

*Source: 1998 Annual Report*, Venture Economics.

Exhibit 2

## A cyclical pattern in venture capital

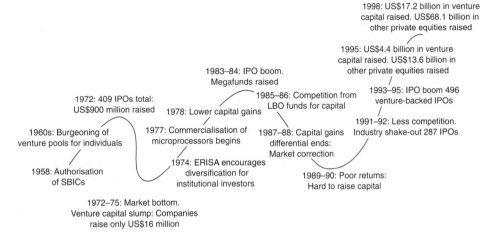

*Source:* Annual reports, Venture Economics.

Exhibit 3

## Buyouts are an identifiable sector in the second cycle

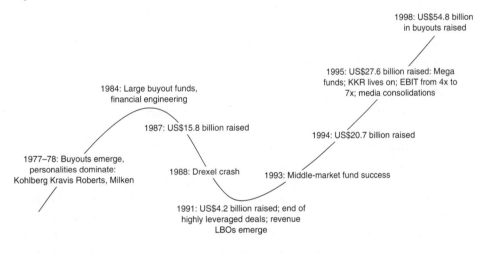

*Source:* Annual reports, Venture Economics.

The market became active again with the commercialisation of microprocessors in the late 1970s. Individuals were still the dominant backers of venture capital, joined by foundations and endowments, and a few pension funds whose farsighted boards saw the advantages of longer-term investments with enhanced returns. These early investors were amply rewarded for their willingness to take on the added risk, as venture returns soared in the late 1970s and early 1980s.

From the standpoint of the development of the private equity industry, the decade of the 1970s was also notable for two key legislative events:

- Enactment of the Employee Retirement Income Security Act (ERISA), which allowed pension funds to move out of bonds (generally government bonds) and high-quality, conservative, publicly traded stocks into more aggressive investments.
- Lowering of the capital gains tax rate, which triggered a resurgence in the stock market and made venture investing that much more attractive to wealthy individuals and high net worth families.

While most pension funds did not allocate money to private equity immediately upon ERISA's enactment, the legislation did set things in motion, as pension funds as a group proactively moved first into more diversified domestic equities, then into real estate and international equities, and finally into international bonds, venture capital, and buyout funds over the ensuing decade.

The mid- to late 1980s saw the next cyclical collapse in venture returns as the stock market corrected, and capital gains tax rate differentials ended. During the first cycle (the 1960s through the mid-1970s), venture was the only private equity option. Buyouts did not become a viable alternative option until the private equity market moved into the latter phase of its second major cycle.

As Exhibit 3 shows, the 1980s framed a period of resurgence of buyout funds, initially as financial engineering or leveraging opportunities. When the venture cycle hit bottom at the end of the 1980s, venture capitalists were not only finding it difficult to raise new funds (because of the poor returns earned by the decade's early partnerships), but were also having to compete against the exceptional returns generated by the buyout funds. As a consequence, the venture capital segment went through a shakeout, and buyout funds raised huge amounts of money from their enthusiastic sponsors, particularly among public pension funds.

Just as the switch to buyouts reached its peak, the major buyout funds ran into problems in the late 1980s, coincident with Drexel Burnham Lambert's collapse. Leverage for doing deals became considerably harder to find, as Drexel no longer provided leadership in raising the necessary junk bond capital to support highly leveraged buyout activity. In addition, potential entrepreneurs became considerably more risk-averse. Investors no longer wanted to be associated with unfriendly transactions.

As the mood of the market changed, middle-market buyout funds began to emerge as a force distinct from the huge, highly leveraged buyout funds that had heretofore dominated that segment of the market. These funds specialised in smaller deals, used decidedly less leverage, and, in most cases, provided at least some value added on the operating side of the ledger when compared to the larger buyout funds, which were focused primarily on financial engineering. The middle-market funds filled a welcome market niche both in terms of what entrepreneurs were seeking and what investors wanted – and their relative returns were compelling – which turned out to be a winning combination.

As the market cycle continued to unfold in the early to mid-1990s, venture capital regained its favour among investors. Consolidation plays, which frequently blend both venture and buyout characteristics, emerged as an important component of the private equity industry. Middle-market buyout funds continued to attract attention. To the surprise of many, the mega-buyout fund returned to prominence, although with far less leverage.

Exhibit 4

**Annual capital commitments to private equity by fund type, 1979–97 (US$ million)**

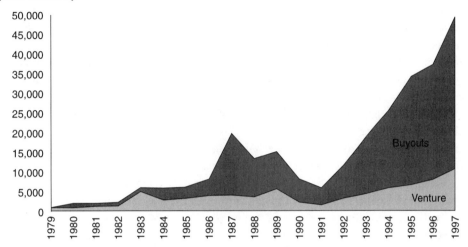

*Source: 1998 Annual Report*, Venture Economics.

Exhibit 5

**Annual commitments to private equity, 1980–98 (US$ billion)**

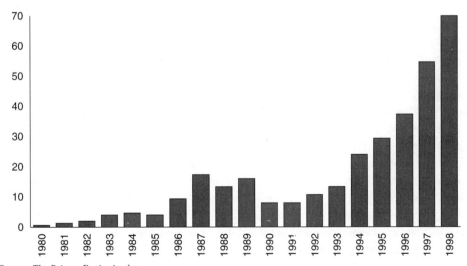

*Source: The Private Equity Analyst.*

Returns in all private equity components then skyrocketed as the IPO window remained open for an unprecedented period of time, providing an easy, rewarding exit for large numbers of portfolio companies (see Exhibit 4).

More recently, as the public markets began to look increasingly fragile, public funds, corporate pension funds, and foundations and endowments steadily increased their allocations to private equity (see Exhibit 5). Their objective: to maintain the higher levels of return to which they have become accustomed over the past 10 to 15 years even as public market returns are expected to decline.

## The mechanics of private equity partnerships

Private equity partnerships are managed by industry professionals who specialise in finding, analysing, investing in, managing, and exiting from investments in what are generally private companies. The partnerships usually have actual or effective control of their portfolio companies. The compensation structures for the partnership managers are designed to align their interests with those of their investors. Typically, the managers participate in the profits of the partnership through a performance fee, or carry, which represents a percentage of the net profit earned on the partnership's investments.

Each partnership is typically a closed-end fund with a contractual life time, or fixed term, often with a contractual investment period within that life time for commitments to new portfolio companies. The most prevalent term for private equity funds is 10 years. During that period, the investment is effectively illiquid, unless the investor is able and willing to take the risk of selling a partnership interest in a small, imperfect secondary market.

The manager's objective is to maximise investor returns from invested capital. Cash is usually taken from investors as needed, and distributions may be either in cash, if a company is sold, or in publicly traded securities, in the case of an IPO or a sale to a larger company. Each partnership tends to be specialised by type of company, stage of investment, industry, and/or source of deal.

Each investment management firm, or organisation, tends to raise a new partnership every two to four years, when the previous partnership's capital is nearly fully committed to a portfolio of companies. Of course, the ability to raise new partnerships depends to a significant degree on how successful prior partnerships have been. The new partnership is generally raised by first contacting investors who have participated in the prior partnership and institutional investors who are known to the professionals, either directly or through an intermediary. Prospective investors then investigate the fund in a process known as due diligence, which involves ascertaining whether or not the fund was successful in the past and whether it can be successful again in the future. Investors then commit one-by-one to the fund and negotiate terms with the fund's manager.

Investors in these funds anticipate higher returns than they can earn from public securities, usually a minimum of 300 to 400 basis points more. Private equity investments are considered substantially more risky than their public market equivalents. Nonetheless, sophisticated institutional investors have continued to commit increasingly more dollars to this area, especially now, when expectations for public market returns are falling. As a consequence, private equity has become an accepted component of most diversified institutional portfolios.

## Return on private equity investments

A well-executed private equity investment program can provide an internal rate of return in excess of 20 per cent. While this may not seem particularly attractive when compared to the exceptional public market returns in recent years, it is much more attractive than the historical public market return of approximately 10 per cent.

Exhibit 6

**Average annual return, 1945–97 (%)**

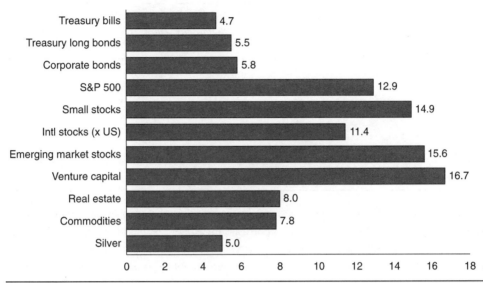

The appropriate way to measure performance in this industry is by internal rate of return (IRR), because that measure takes into account the timing of cash flows. According to Venture Economics, a leading private equity investment industry observer, the average internal rate of return for venture capital funds formed between 1969 and 1995 was 12.8 per cent. The average IRR for Venture Economics' sample of buyout and special situations funds formed between 1976 and 1995 was 17.3 per cent. Venture Economics' top-quartile pooled returns for early-stage venture capital over the last 15 years is an 18.2 per cent IRR through 30 December 1996. See histories in Exhibit 6.

Exhibit 7

**Correlations**

| Asset class | Correlation between private equity and the asset class (%) |
| --- | --- |
| Treasury bills | -25.7 |
| Treasury bonds | 16.3 |
| Corporate bonds | 14.6 |
| Large-cap stocks | 25.7 |
| Small-cap stocks | 28.7 |

*Source:* Venture Economics.

Historical venture capital returns are not available over longer periods of time because few firms reported performance earlier in the industry's history. Industry professionals generally project private equity returns at between 12 per cent and 20 per cent over the next five to ten years, compared to equity returns that are projected to be in the 9 per cent to 13 per cent range.

At the same time that a private equity programme can provide these attractive relative returns, it can also reduce total portfolio risk by damping overall volatility. This is because private equity returns have a relatively low correlation with the returns of other traditional asset classes (see Exhibit 7). They therefore may act to smooth portfolio fluctuations. As a result, the addition of private equity to an investment portfolio may increase the expected return of the total investment portfolio and reduce the variability of returns in the long term.

Exhibit 8

**Tax effects**

| Asset class | % of total return represented by long-term capital gains | Before-tax return since 1945 (%) | Effective after-tax return* (%) |
|---|---|---|---|
| Treasury bills | 1.0 | 4.7 | 2.6 |
| Corporate bonds | 15.0 | 5.8 | 3.4 |
| Large stocks | 80.0 | 12.9 | 9.7 |
| Small stocks | 66.7 | 14.9 | 10.7 |
| Non-US stocks | 66.7 | 11.4 | 8.2 |
| Venture capital | 95.0 | 16.7 | 13.2 |

* 44% tax bracket.

One additional benefit accruing to taxable investors stems from the long-term nature of private equity partnerships. Rarely will a portfolio investment be held for less than one year; the more typical holding period is two to four years. Thus, when gains are realised, such as through an IPO or the sale or merger of a portfolio company to another company, the tax effect is a long-term gain, which carries a much more attractive rate (currently 20 per cent) than ordinary income.

Exhibit 8 highlights this advantage in comparison to other traditional asset classes.

## Summary

Knowledgeable private equity investing can provide excellent absolute and relative returns that are largely long-term in nature. The major incremental risk of a well-diversified private programme over a public market portfolio is illiquidity. A well-diversified private equity portfolio can represent value investing at its best while providing excellent estate planning opportunities.

Private equity is not for everyone or every family, but it can be an excellent investment vehicle for many who are intent on wealth creation and preservation.

Reprinted with permission from:
*The Journal of Private Portfolio Management*, Volume 2, Number 1, 1999.

Chapter 2

# Overview of UK venture capital[1]

James Nelson
*Chairman of the British Venture Capital Association and Director of F&C Ventures Ltd*

Recent years have shown record amounts both invested and raised by the UK venture capital industry. For example, £4.9 billion was invested in more than 1,300 companies by UK venture capital (VC) firms in 1998. These venture capital firms also raised £5.6 billion for future investment. Seventy-three per cent of this came from sources outside the United Kingdom, mainly the United States (see Exhibit 1. For a detailed breakdown of the figures in this and later exhibits, readers are referred to the appendices at the end of this chapter).

The UK market now accounts for nearly 50 per cent of total annual European venture capital investment and is second only in size and importance to the United States.

The record amounts raised can be attributed to market maturity, the experience of UK venture capital managers and the demonstration of their success through the production of excellent annual performance figures. The 1998 WM/BVCA Performance Measurement Survey[2] showed that venture capital funds showed an outperformance compared with total UK pension fund assets over the one-, three- and five-year periods, and showed a similar performance over 10 years. Over one, three and five years, venture capital funds also outperfomed the FTSE 100 and FTSE All-Share indices. UK pension funds with a balanced exposure to UK venture capital funds will have enhanced their overall returns.

## Investing in dynamic high-growth businesses

Venture capital investment through funds managed by experienced firms enables investors to access a range of carefully selected, ambitious, quality high-growth companies before they realise their full potential, become well known or float on a stock exchange. It allows investors to participate in management buyouts (MBOs) of divisions of well established and well known companies and to benefit from the revitalisation of businesses. Each year around 40 per cent of trading company flotations on the official list of the London Stock Exchange (LSE) are VC-backed companies. Following flotation, the majority of the VC-backed companies have been shown to outperform other types of flotations[3] and VC-backed MBO flotations capitalised at over £25 million have consistently outperformed the FTSE All Share index.[4]

Companies such as William Hill (bookies), Golden Wonder (snacks), Hamleys (toy shops), and Compass Group (one of the world's largest contract catering companies) are just a few of the better-known companies to have benefited from venture capital provided to finance their MBOs since the late 1980s. Many well-known companies and consumer brands in the UK have been start-up and/or developed with venture capital backing, such as Formula One, Demon Internet, Books etc and The Covent Garden Soup Company are just a few of the names with which many people in the UK will be familiar.

Exhibit 1

**Venture capital invested by BVCA members, 1984–98 (£ million)**

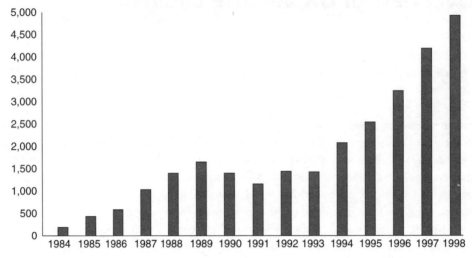

*Source:* BVCA.

## The scope and growth of UK venture capital

The US is a role model for high-technology venture capital investment, to which many countries aspire. While the US market has been established much longer than that in the UK, we can certainly learn a great deal from the US experience. In 1998, UK investment in high-technology companies, relative to GDP, was a third of that invested by the US in such companies. The gap in investment between the two countries is due to both cultural and structural differences. The US has been particularly successful in taking advantage of the effects of clustering and university spin-outs, and has found it easier to accept the risks involved in investing in high-technology companies. The 1998 UK figures for high-technology investment indicate that the UK venture capital industry is beginning to catch up. From 1996 to 1998, UK investment more than doubled (up 122 per cent) and the total number of high-technology companies backed increased by 91 per cent. The UK is now understanding and replicating the key characteristics from the US and is becoming much more experienced in the sector. Increasing commitment has, in turn, resulted in the employment of people with the necessary expertise and knowledge in the high-technology sector. This has created a more favourable environment for current and future high-technology investment.

The situation in the United Kingdom has changed dramatically over the past 15 years, bringing a stronger entrepreneurial and commercial culture that provides more attractive investment opportunities for UK venture capital firms. Legislative change allowed the structuring of MBOs and the setting up of onshore venture capital funds. Various other tax incentives encouraged business angels and entrepreneurs. The stock exchange listing rules changed to allow more biotechnology companies to float at an earlier stage in their development. The recent establishment of second-tier stock markets in most western European countries has improved the exit opportunities for the venture capital industry, benefitting valuations, shortening the holding period for investments and thereby enhancing returns. We have more role models and better-

14

Exhibit 2

**Venture capital, pension fund assets and FTSE All Share returns, to 1998 (% return per annum)**

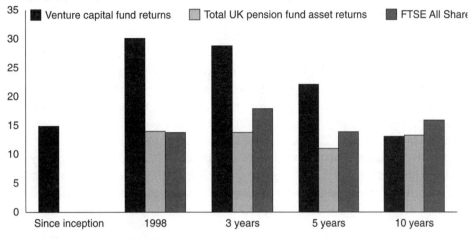

*Sources:* The WM Company and BVCA.

Exhibit 3

**Venture capital investment in high-technology companies, 1984–98 (£ million)**

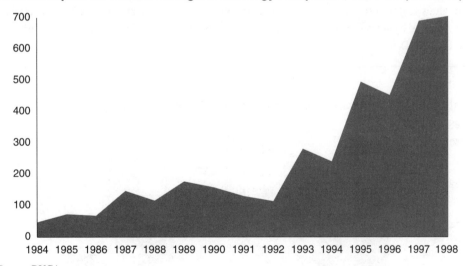

*Source:* BVCA.

quality managers for our investee companies, be they academics in research laboratories commercialising their knowledge, or well-paid, well-pensioned managers jumping ship to an MBO/MBI or start-up situation. We are beginning to get the right fiscal environment, with capital gains tax slowly being reduced, although the tax is still far too complicated. We have learned that the key to successful investing is sector expertise. Venture capital firms are increasingly concentrating on industry sectors where they can deploy expertise in depth.

As a result, venture capital investment in high-technology companies has increased by 15 times since 1984 (see Exhibit 3).

### Why should business people consider raising venture capital and what do investors look for in a company and its management team?

Venture capital provides long-term committed risk-sharing capital which helps unquoted companies grow and compete. The ability to provide capital, and experience and contacts, sets venture capital apart from other sources of business capital. Venture capital firms align their interests with the entrepreneur by taking similar equity risk. The venture capital investor makes returns from the growth and profitability of the business, whereas lenders have a legal right to interest on a loan and its repayment, irrespective of the success or failure of the business.

Ideally, venture capital investors look for a company with a good commercial product or service, and excellent potential for high growth. It is essential to have a strong management team with direct experience of the product and its market, who can demonstrate real commitment and the ambition to turn their business plan into reality.

### Venture capital helps UK companies to grow and succeed faster than others

Almost 90 per cent of VC-backed companies in a BVCA/PricewaterhouseCoopers report said that they would not have existed, or would have grown less rapidly, without venture capital. The contribution to growth was clearly quantified by the survey. On average, VC-backed companies' sales rose by 40 per cent per annum (twice as fast as FTSE 100 companies), exports grew by 44 per cent per annum and investment increased by 34 per cent per annum (see Exhibit 4).

Exhibit 4

**Venture-backed companies outperform most leading UK companies, 1993–99 (%)**

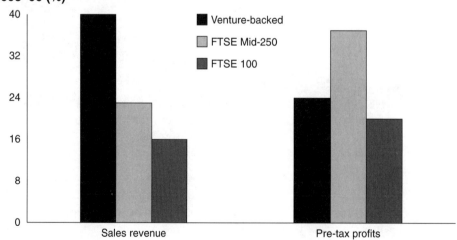

*Sources:* BVCA and FT-Extel.

## Contribution to employment

The scope of venture capital's involvement in UK companies is significant. Two million people in the United Kingdom are estimated to be employed by companies *currently* in receipt of venture capital (representing 10 per cent of private-sector employment). Over the four years to 1997/98, the number of people employed in VC-backed companies increased by 24 per cent per annum, against a national growth rate of 1.3 per cent per annum (see Exhibit 5).

## Venture capital invests more than money in companies

While the growth and success of these firms owes much to venture capital investment, the non-financial input by venture capital firms is also very important. Of the VC-backed companies analysed in the survey, 95 per cent said that they had benefited from their venture capital backers providing more than just money. In particular, they rated highly venture capital firms' advice and guidance on strategic matters, financial advice, and role in 'challenging the status quo' and as a 'sounding board for ideas'. Most venture capital investors have a wide range of experience. Many have worked in industry, others have a financial background. Most importantly, all have the specialist experience of funding and assisting companies at a time of rapid development and growth. According to this research, the venture capital firms' input was rarely seen as intrusive and the level of involvement varies from firm to firm.

However, it is not just venture capital that contributes to a company's growth. Research undertaken by PricewaterhouseCoopers has shown that very fast growth – or 'hypergrowth' – is not just a function of a company's size. It found that there were a number of similar characteristics among these companies, including; having world class products and pushing these products from the idea stage to market more quickly (within seven months as opposed to 12), in parallel (rather than sequentially), and having visionary and inspired leaders with highly ambitious employees. One of the key findings was that these companies were *not afraid to let go of some of their equity to oth-*

Exhibit 5

**Comparative average annual increase in employment in quoted and venture-backed companies, 1993–99 (%)**

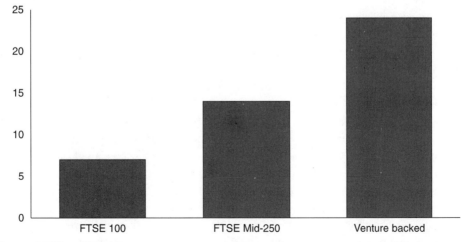

*Sources:* BVCA and FT-Extel.

*ers*. They spread their equity among institutional investors, venture capital firms, their managers and employees. To conclude, they were often small businesses behaving like big businesses.

## Outlook

The UK venture capital industry is now benefiting from the maturity and experience it has gained over the past 15 years. Venture capital managers in the United Kingdom are well positioned to offer investors their experience in investing in European unquoted companies, which should present some particularly interesting opportunities in light of European economic and monetary union. This has enabled UK managers to raise record amounts from institutional investors and offers UK and continental European companies better availability of venture capital than ever before. The UK industry will continue to change, develop and build on its experience, to ensure that it remains at the forefront of the world venture capital market.

One of the best ways to appreciate the success of the venture capital industry in the United Kingdom over recent years is to look at some examples of companies which have benefited from an input of venture capital. The BVCA, Cartier and the *Financial Times* sponsor the annual Venturer of the Year Awards, which recognise and reward the achievements, vision and enterprise of some of Britain's finest entrepreneurs. Nominations for the awards are put forward by members of the BVCA, who make up the United Kingdom's venture capital industry. The following section looks at the winners for 1999, and provides some examples of what can be achieved with the backing of venture capital.

The winner of the Venturer the Year Award was selected from the winners of seven category awards. In 1999, the tenth year of the awards, these categories included companies that raised venture capital to start-up, expand, turnaround or buy-out their businesses. They were judged for their substantial contribution to the economy, employment, innovation, their sound financial performance, return to backers and overall consistency.

## Venturer of the Year and Small MBO Award Winner – A&J Gummers Ltd

A&J Gummers is one of the top three suppliers in the UK thermostatic shower market. Ken Shaw and a partner successfully acquired the business from Pentos plc in 1985. While Shaw was determined to grow the business, his partner was more intent on reaping the financial benefits there and then, than ploughing them back into the company. With the support of Lloyds TSB Development Capital, Shaw bought out his partner in 1992. Essentially Shaw has transformed a small Birmingham-based 'metal basher' into a world-class manufacturer. He changed the product base from steam drain stopcocks and water-level gauges to shower valves and accessories and other water-control products. In 1989 A&J Gummers was the first company to introduce thermostatic valves that were compatible with all recognised plumbing systems. Shaw's track record is exceptional. He has seen seven years of uninterrupted turnover growth and his employee numbers have increased almost threefold over that period. With principles on quality of product, continuous investment in design and product development, and the creation of a secure working environment for his employees, Shaw developed the business into a clear target for acquisition by international corporate, Masco Corporation, which bought the company in early 1999. A&J Gummers is on course to continue to grow rapidly.

## Scientific research winner – Roslin Bio-Med

Roslin Bio-Med (RBM) was founded in April 1998, as a spin-out, by two scientists from the Roslin Institute in Edinburgh. They had the objective of commercialising the research performed by the institute, which led to the cloning of 'Dolly the Sheep'. Roslin Bio-Med received investment from venture capital firm 3i, which was also responsible for headhunting Simon Best, the current chief executive, formerly of Zeneca Plant, to add commercial edge to the company. The cloning of Dolly represented a major scientific breakthrough, being the first occasion that an animal had been cloned from an adult cell. This platform opened up the possibility of cloning and genetically modifying animals and human cells for medical applications. This has advanced the development of xenotransplantation, the genetic modification of pigs to allow organs such as hearts and kidneys to be used for human transplants. Best has kept the original team while changing strategy and developing a clear direction for this unique intellectual property. He has returned real value to the company and its shareholders when the biotechnology sector as a whole was experiencing a considerably rocky patch. In May of this year, RBM was acquired by Geron Corporation, which recognised the value of its technology and IP to clone human cells to treat degenerative diseases such as Parkinson's, arthritis and leukaemia.

## Small start-up winner – Pride Valley Foods Limited

Pride Valley Foods is Europe's leading supplier of speciality flat breads, producing over 40 varieties of naans, pittas, tortillas and chapatis. Pride Valley was founded in 1990 by Dr Hossain Rezaei, who first managed a business at the age of 13, when he took over his father's company. When he relocated to the UK during the Iranian revolution he had to support himself while studying for a degree at Newcastle Polytechnic and Durham University. Even then, he demonstrated considerable entrepreneurial skill by borrowing a small sum of money to buy properties to rent out to students. By the end of his degree, he owned several flats, a snooker club and some takeaway food outlets, and had noticed a difficulty in obtaining good-quality specialist breads. In 1992, venture capital firm 3i helped to fund the setting up of a modern manufacturing facility for Pride Valley Foods and funded further expansion between 1995 and 1997. Since 1992, Pride Valley has survived a price war with the competition and a fire that destroyed the whole factory, and the company is now facing a battle with the insurance company over payment for the fire damage. Despite all this, Rezaei has built a company that has consistently maintained growth at all levels in turnover, staff, product lines and factory capacity. With more than 50 per cent market share of the UK market for specialist breads, Rezaei employs over 300 staff. The company supplies Tesco, Marks & Spencer, Morrisons and other retailers, and has recently supplied 10 million pieces of naan to support the launch of McDonald's McChicken Korma Naan.

## Large start-up winner – CityFlyer Express Limited

Established in 1991, CityFlyer is an independent airline, owned by its directors and a venture capital syndicate led by 3i. CityFlyer operates services under a franchise from BA, using Gatwick airport, where it has carved out a niche for itself. Although it is not a 'no-frills' airline, in the manner of EasyJet, Ryanair or Debonair, CityFlyer operates from a lower cost structure than BA, and provides BA with a means of servicing routes it could not otherwise operate profitably. CityFlyer has always had a clear strategy to centre all its operations on Gatwick and to grow the business organically. Growth has come through detailed assessment of new routes, a focused fleet strategy and the successful acquisition of key slots at Gatwick. Tight operational control has resulted in achievement margins far higher than those of other operators. As a cost-effective short-haul feeder airline, CityFlyer has brought considerable economic and employment benefits to the Gatwick area, when many airlines were deserting it. The company has been sold to BA, subject to BA agreeing to limit its future landing rights at Gatwick.

## Expansion winner – Holmes Place plc

The first Holmes Place club was opened in Chelsea in January 1980. The business was then owned by a consortium of investors but made a loss, despite successfully attracting members. In 1988, Alan Fisher and Lawrence Alkin were brought in as joint chief executives to run the business on a full-time basis. In 1992, the company completed a reverse takeover of Barbican Health and Fitness plc and renamed the company Holmes Place plc in 1994. In 1996 they raised venture capital from NatWest Private Equity in order to fund expansion. In 1997 the company went public and has since risen three times in value to achieve a capitalisation of over £250 million. Holmes Place puts strong emphasis on creating a friendly environment at each of its clubs and, as well as its exercise facilities, offers its members restaurants, body care and beauty facilities, and an extensive calendar of social events. Holmes Place now has 37 clubs in the UK and Europe and boasts over 100,000 members. A further 16 clubs are planned for 2000 and another 21 for 2001. The company has generated enormous staff loyalty through commitment to training and development, and with a strong brand name is capable of sustaining growth in a competitive sector.

## Turnaround winner – MTL Services Limited

When Peter Coombes became chairman and chief executive of Merseyside Transport in 1990, it was probably the worst bus company in the country. That was the era of bus wars and constraints on local government spending. The company was losing both money and market share and was running a decrepit fleet of buses. Coombes was asked to do two things: stop the company going broke and buy the company on behalf of the employees. In 1992 he succeeded in buying the business through an Employee Share Ownership Plan, under which each employee was gifted 250 shares plus an additional two shares for each year of service. As a newcomer to the business, Coombes received fewer shares than the long-serving bus drivers. After severe restructuring, venture capital firm ECI Ventures came in to support an ambitious strategy to grow the business outside its core geographical area through acquisition. A strengthened management team continued to develop the existing business and explore new opportunities, and in 1997 the company took over the operation of two rail franchises, Northern Spirit and Merseyrail Electrics. Coombes has led the company from a loss-making organisation to being the largest privately-owned public transport group in the UK.

## Large MBO winner – TM Group Holdings PLC

The TM Group was formed in 1995 from the £92 million buyout from Gallagher of three businesses: Fourbuoys, the confectionery, tobacco and news (CTN) retailer; Mayfair, cigarette vending machines; and Vendpac, drinks and snack vending machines. James Lancaster had tried to get Gallagher to agree to the buyout of the vending businesses he ran some time before the deal was struck. Perversely, it was through having been given the additional responsibility to sort out Gallagher's retailing activities that he was able to engineer the decision to put both the vending and retail activities up for sale. Lancaster made the winning bid for the buyout, supported by venture capital firm HSBC Private Equity among others. Since the buyout, TM has bought four companies and consolidated its market leadership position in each of its three businesses. Under Lancaster's leadership, TM Group has almost doubled its turnover, and employee numbers have grown from 8,600 to 14,900, making it one of the largest employers in the country.

---

[1] The terms 'private equity' and 'venture capital' are synonymous in Europe and include equity investments in unquoted companies ranging from those requiring financing for start-up to those undertaking a management buy-out (MBO).

[2] This was the fifth 'Performance Measurement Survey' commissioned by the BVCA. It was produced by The WM Company, the world's leading independent performance measurer.

[3] BVCA research from 1 June 1992 to 31 December 1997.

[4] HSBC James Capel research by Sally Collier in 1997 into MBOs capitalised over £25 million with a 'significant' stake held by a venture capital firm.

Appendix 1

## Funds invested by BVCA members, 1984–98

| Year | No. of companies financed in the UK | No. of companies financed overseas | Total no. of companies financed | Funds invested in the UK (£ million) | Funds invested overseas (£ million) | Total funds invested (£ million) |
|---|---|---|---|---|---|---|
| 1984 | 350 | 129 | 479 | 140 | 50 | 190 |
| 1985 | 517 | 118 | (635) 1,185* | 277 | 47 | (324) 433* |
| 1986 | 600 | 108 | (708) 1,292* | 384 | 42 | (426) 584* |
| 1987 | 1,174 | 124 | 1,298 | 934 | 96 | 1,029 |
| 1988 | 1,326 | 201 | 1,527 | 1,298 | 96 | 1,394 |
| 1989 | 1,302 | 267 | 1,569 | 1,420 | 227 | 1,647 |
| 1990 | 1,221 | 338 | 1,559 | 1,106 | 288 | 1,394 |
| 1991 | 1,196 | 190 | 1,386 | 989 | 164 | 1,153 |
| 1992 | 1,147 | 150 | 1,297 | 1,251 | 183 | 1,434 |
| 1993 | 1,066 | 136 | 1,202 | 1,231 | 191 | 1,422 |
| 1994 | 1,101 | 107 | 1,208 | 1,668 | 406 | 2,074 |
| 1995 | 1,030 | 133 | 1,163 | 2,140 | 395 | 2,535 |
| 1996 | 1,060 | 140 | 1,200 | 2,806 | 433 | 3,239 |
| 1997 | 1,116 | 156 | 1,272 | 3,066 | 1,118 | 4,184 |
| 1998 | 1,122 | 210 | 1,332 | 3,775 | 1,144 | 4,919 |
| **Total** | **15,328** | **2,507** | **17,835** | **22,485** | **4,880** | **27,631** |

Notes

1. Figures are not strictly comparable due to annual changes in membership.

2.* Investment by 3i was not included in the 1984 figures. Final total figures in 1985 and 1986 were adjusted in 1987 to include 3i investments. Sub-totals were not altered and their final totals are in brackets.

3. BVCA investment figures are compiled from the returns from over 90 per cent of all BVCA members, and (except for 1984) include virtually every major source of venture capital in the United Kingdom.

4. 1992–97: secured debt is included where it is concurrent or alongside equity investment, or where it is rescue finance. Previously, only unsecured debt as part of an equity/quasi-equity package was included.

*Source:* BVCA.

Appendix 2

## Performance measurement survey summary results

Percentage return by investment stage

| Funds by specialisation | No. of funds surveyed | 1998 (%) | 3 years (% per annum) | 5 years (% per annum) | 10 years (% per annum) |
|---|---|---|---|---|---|
| Early stage | 23 | -27.8 | 4 | 7.3 | 8.4 |
| Development | 44 | 13.9 | 27.4 | 22.9 | 8.9 |
| Mid-MBO | 41 | 19.7 | 29.6 | 27.7 | 15.1 |
| Large MBO | 44 | 28.4 | 28.1 | 23.3 | 22.9 |
| Generalist | 37 | 64.8 | 33.8 | 20.7 | 7.1 |
| **Total** | **189** | **30.1** | **28.8** | **22.1** | **13.1** |

Notes

1. 'Early stage' includes funds that invest in seed, start-up and early-stage companies.

2. 'Development' includes expansion and small MBOs with less than £2 million of equity invested.

3. 'Mid-MBO' includes equity investments of £2–10 million.

4. 'Large MBO' includes equity investments of over £10 million.

5. 'Generalist' includes investments in a variety of stages.

Appendix 2 *continued*

## Performance measurement survey summary results *continued*

Principal sources of comparison

| UK pension funds | 1998 (%) | 3 years (% per annum) | 5 years (% per annum) | 10 years (% per annum) |
|---|---|---|---|---|
| UK equities | 12 | 17.1 | 13.4 | 15.6 |
| Overseas equities | 17.2 | 8.9 | 7.6 | 11.5 |
| UK bonds | 20.6 | 14.6 | 10.1 | 12.7 |
| Overseas bonds | 11.6 | 3.6 | 5.5 | 10.8 |
| UK index-linked | 20.3 | 13.5 | 8.5 | 10.3 |

| UK pension funds | 1998 (%) | 3 years (% per annum) | 5 years (% per annum) | 10 years (% per annum) |
|---|---|---|---|---|
| Cash | 7.3 | 6.8 | 6.9 | 9.4 |
| Property | 12.8 | 12.5 | 10.6 | 7.4 |
| **Total assets** | **16.8** | **15.5** | **13.7** | **13.3** |

| FTSE Indices | 1998 (%) | 3 years (% per annum) | 5 years (% per annum) | 10 years (% per annum) |
|---|---|---|---|---|
| FTSE All Share | 13.8 | 17.9 | 13.9 | 15.9 |
| FTSE 100 | 17.5 | 20.9 | 15.8 | 17.5 |
| FTSE Small Cap | -8.1 | 5.1 | 5.2 | 7.2 |
| FTSE Fledgling | -6.7 | 4.1 | N/A | N/A |

Note

1. From The WM Company's measurement of the 'all funds' performance of over 1,600 pension funds, with a value of £449 billion as at 31 December 1997, representing approximately three-quarters of the UK pension fund industry.

Percentage returns since inception by investment stage

| Categorisation of fund by investment specialisation | No. of funds surveyed | To December 1998 | To December 1997 | To December 1996 | To December 1995 | To December 1994 |
|---|---|---|---|---|---|---|
| Early stage | 17 | 8.3 | 8.2 | 6.5 | 4.3 | 4.0 |
| Development | 34 | 9.1 | 8.9 | 8.1 | 6.9 | 5.6 |
| Mid-MBO | 27 | 16.5 | 16.6 | 16.2 | 16.2 | 14.7 |
| Large MBO | 28 | 19.2 | 19.7 | 25.4 | 23.8 | 23.1 |
| Generalist | 30 | 13.5 | 11.7 | 9.9 | 9.7 | 7.1 |
| **Total** | **136** | **14.9** | **14.0** | **14.2** | **13.0** | **12.1** |

Appendix 2 *continued*

## Performance measurement survey summary results *continued*

Percentage returns since inception by vintage year

| Year of fund formation | No. of funds surveyed | To December 1998 | To December 1997 | To December 1996 | To December 1995 | To December 1994 |
|---|---|---|---|---|---|---|
| 1980–84 | 11 | 10.0 | 9.9 | 10.2 | 9.9 | 10.2 |
| 1985 | 12 | 18.7 | 18.7 | 18.4 | 18.8 | 19.5 |
| 1986 | 8 | 8.9 | 5.9 | 5.8 | 5.4 | 5.8 |
| 1987 | 12 | 6.8 | 6.2 | 5.0 | 3.2 | 1.1 |
| 1988 | 18 | 13.6 | 13.1 | 13.2 | 11.6 | 10.8 |
| 1989 | 18 | 14.2 | 19.4 | 18.8 | 16.7 | 14.6 |
| 1990 | 13 | 17.0 | 16.6 | 23.7 | 23.2 | 19.5 |
| 1991 | 12 | 24.2 | 23.4 | 22.4 | 18.0 | N/A |
| 1992 | 6 | 21.0 | 19.8 | 19.1 | N/A | N/A |
| 1993 | 10 | 16.6 | 10.3 | 11.3 | N/A | N/A |
| 1994 | 16 | 33.1 | N/A | N/A | N/A | N/A |
| **Total** | **136** | **14.9** | **14.0** | **14.2** | **13.0** | **12.1** |

*Source:* BVCA.

25

Appendix 3

**Average growth rates for venture-backed and quoted companies, 1993–98 (% per annum)**

|  | Venture-backed | FTSE Mid-250 | FTSE 100 |
|---|---|---|---|
| Sales revenue | 40 | 23 | 16 |
| Pre-tax profits | 24 | 37 | 20 |
| UK employment | 24 | 14 | 7 |

*Sources:* BVCA and FT-Extel.

# Chapter 3

# European private equity: reaching adulthood

Serge Raicher
*Secretary General, European Private Equity and Venture Capital Association (EVCA)*

Seventeen years ago, 43 venture capital pioneers launched EVCA, the European Venture Capital Association. These pioneers had two goals: the first was to develop a network of cooperation between the members of the young venture capital community, and the second was to promote a favourable environment for the development of the industry. Since then, the industry has evolved considerably.

## Semantics

One of the beauties of the European private equity industry is that it has many names, some of them which contradict each other, and some of them which overlap. When turning to translations, the confusion is even greater.

The fact that many European policy-makers like to refer to 'risk capital' is due to two reasons and, as is often the case in such situations, these reasons have very little to do with the industry itself. The first reason originates from international conferences and the perverse effect of translation. As French speakers refer to *'capital risque'* and Germans to *'Risiko Kapital'*, the English translation at conferences invariably becomes 'risk capital'. Thus, this terminology became widely used.

The second reason comes from political marketing. The term 'risk capital' aims at conveying the message that those providing it are willing to take *real* risks (as opposed to those who say they do, but really do not). The creativity of political advisers having flourished, we now hear reference being made to 'adventure capital' (not very encouraging for the investors …) or to 'chance capital' (which some sarcastic observers may suggest means you need luck to get it).

## Private equity and venture capital

EVCA is the European Private Equity and Venture Capital Association. Both 'private equity' and 'venture capital' terms have very well defined meanings. In France, one would talk about *'capital investissement'* on the one hand and *'capital risque'* on the other hand.

Private equity provides equity capital to enterprises that are not quoted on a stock market. Private equity can be used to develop new products and technologies, to expand working capital, to make acquisitions, or to strengthen a company's balance sheet. It can also resolve ownership and management issues. A succession in family-owned companies, or the buy-out or buy-in by experienced managers may be achieved using private equity funding.

Venture capital is, strictly speaking, a subset of private equity and refers to equity investments made for the launch, early development or expansion of a business. Among different countries, there are variations in what is meant by venture capital and private equity. In Europe, these terms are generally used interchangeably and venture capital thus includes management buy-outs (MBOs) and buy-ins (MBIs). This is in contrast to the United States, where MBOs and MBIs are not classified as venture capital.

## The economic impact of private equity

Private equity has as significant impact on a country's economy and is a major contributor to the small and medium-sized enterprise (SME) boom.

A large percentage of private equity investment is being made in micro companies. One-third of the investments are made in SMEs with less than 20 employees, and the vast majority of investment (74 per cent) goes to SMEs with fewer than 200 employees.

The Economic Impact Study of November 1996, released in association with PricewaterhouseCoopers, on venture-backed SMEs throughout Europe, shows that these companies vastly outperform Europe's top 500 companies on numerous criteria:

- *Sales:* over the five-year period in which the survey was conducted, Europe's top 500 companies saw sales growth of 14 per cent per annum. The score for the venture- backed sample was 35 per cent.
- *Pre-tax profit:* while the top 500 companies saw annual growth in pre-tax profits of 17 per cent, the score was 27 per cent for the sample.
- *Innovation:* the capacity to be innovative was measured by the ratio of research and development expenses to sales. This ratio stood at 1.3 per cent in the top 500, against 8.6 per cent in the venture-backed sample.
- *Job creation:* the contribution to Europe's biggest challenge was also measured. While employment had grown at 2 per cent per annum in the top 500, the annual employment growth was a striking 15 per cent in the venture-backed companies.

The study also revealed that 80 per cent of the venture-backed entrepreneurs said that without venture capital, their company either would not have existed, or would have grown less rapidly.

## Trends

The European private equity market is growing rapidly and may well continue to do so for a while. As Exhibit 1 reveals, the amounts raised by the European private equity industry have grown steadily through the boom of 1997 and 1998, when the level exceeded Ecu20 billion in each of those years.

Furthermore, some trends have emerged over the years:

- Internationalisation of fundraising: for the first time in 1997, a majority of the funds raised came from non-domestic sources, including a third from non-European countries. In 1998, domestic sources again accounted for the majority, but only slightly. Over 30 per cent of funds raised in 1998 still came from non-European sources.

Exhibit 1

**New funds raised, 1988–98 (Ecu million)**

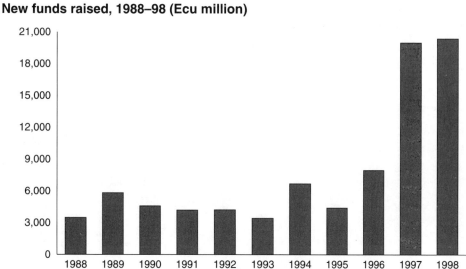

*Source:* EVCA.

- Growth of transnational funds: an increasing number of funds are being raised with a pan-European focus. The biggest funds are usually managed out of London with deal-sourcing and monitoring units scattered throughout Europe.
- Increasing interest for industry-specific funds, include numerous technology-focused funds or windows of funds.

The investment pattern also shows continued growth, with a record Ecu14.5 billion of equity poured into Europe's SMEs in 1998 (see Exhibit 2). The UK-based funds made slightly less than half of all investments, and invested an estimated Ecu1 billion in continental Europe. The next biggest countries Germany and France accounted for 13 and 12 per cent of investments respectively, the Netherlands for 7 per cent and Italy for 6 per cent.

One indicator of the various countries' potential for venture capital development is the ratio of private equity investments to gross domestic product (GDP) (see Exhibit 3). According to this criterion, and subject to a friendly economic and fiscal environment, one could expect countries such as Germany and France, as well as the Mediterranean countries, to further realise their potential for growth in private equity investment.

## Performance

We know how well private equity contributes to a country's economy. Yet for investors, the legitimate concern is to judge the capacity of fund managers to produce adequate returns.

A yearly survey conducted by Bannock Consulting and Venture Economics in co-operation with EVCA measures the performance of the private equity industry and compares its internal rate of return (IRR) with that of other asset classes. With a pooled 11.6 per cent Ecu return per annum from 1980 to 30 June 1998, European private equity performance compares

Exhibit 2

**Private equity investment, 1988–98 (Ecu million)**

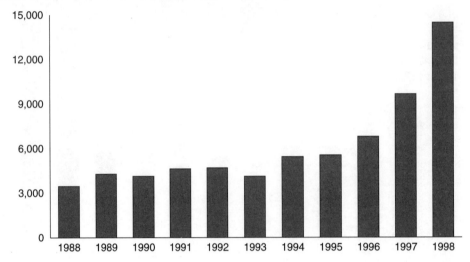

*Source:* EVCA.

Exhibit 3

**Private equity investments as a percentage of GDP (x 100), 1998**

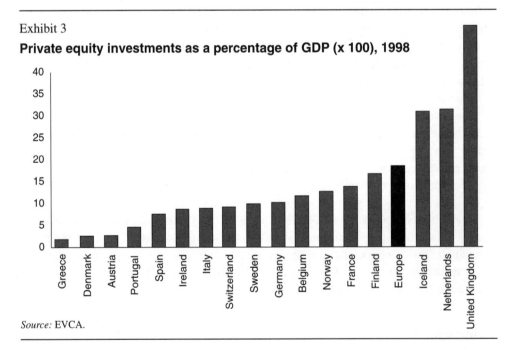

*Source:* EVCA.

favourably to other asset classes at all stages. Yet, unlike bonds and stocks, investors cannot buy 'the index' and the choice of private equity managers is therefore a crucial decision in the quest for returns.

The returns vary according to stage, fund size and possibly vintage. Yet, above all, the returns investors can achieve will be very much dependent on their ability to identify the best fund managers.

With well established performance measurement principles,[1] any venture capitalist's performance can be compared with that of others. Here again, some major trends emerge:

- Early-stage investments involve a greater risk than development-stage investments, but the median performance of the top quarter in the first category is much higher than the top quarter in the second category (22.4 per cent against 18.1 per cent).
- Buy-out funds continue to produce the highest returns over the long term.
- The top quarter of larger funds tends to outperform the top quarter of smaller funds.
- In nearly all respects, private equity compares favourably to bonds and listed stocks.[2]

An indirectly related trend should also be mentioned. According to Euro NM and Easdaq, once they are listed on stock markets, formerly venture-backed companies usually outperform those that did not receive private equity. This once again demonstrates the positive contribution of private equity to the development of these SMEs. It also shows that, subject to lock-up agreements, venture capitalists may arbitrage liquidity against valuation at the time of the IPO.

## Possible policy evolution

Irrespective of the name give to private equity, European policy-makers have recognised the positive contribution of this industry to the economic environment. Various initiatives have flourished throughout Europe at the regional, national, and transnational level. While some measures have backfired, (mainly when carried out at a regional level), most initiatives have had a positive impact, and many more public initiatives are expected for the future.

Indeed, 1998 saw the launching of two major publications: the European Commission's *Communication on Risk Capital* and the EVCA's white paper *Priorities for Private Equity*. The two documents reach similar conclusions on many issues and one can expect a positive evolution of various issues. Some of the expected developments are summarised below:

- Improved environment for entrepreneurs: The evolution should come not only from a more entrepreneur-friendly educational system, but also from more appropriate legal systems (intellectual property, company registration, labour flexibility and so on). In addition, policy-makers now understand that the transition of ownership is a crucial step for SME survival (thus preservation of jobs) and that MBOs and/or MBIs can provide a very good solution to this critical stage.
- Generalisation of tax-efficient share incentive schemes: Tax-efficient share incentive schemes will allow those who are willing to take the risk of working in smaller, riskier companies to be rewarded and taxed (for instance, through stock options that are either taxed lightly or not taxed at all) according to the entrepreneurial risk they assume.
- Further development of pension funds throughout Europe: Pension funds should be regulated according to an EC directive that is currently under discussion. One can expect that pension funds will obey they 'prudent man rule' while allocating their resources. This would have the consequence of facilitating investments in private equity.
- Possible introduction of a pan-European transparent fund structure: Today, instruments such as the FCPR in France and the Limited Partnership in the United Kingdom allow investors to be no better nor worse off when investing in SMEs via private equity funds

than if they had done it directly. Yet, as the industry becomes more international, numerous inefficiencies have emerged. These can be solved by the introduction of an international fund structure, which could have some similarities with the existing European Economic Interest Groupings (EEIG).

- Better coordination between public support and private funding: Public action in private equity has not always been very successful. It has even sometimes come into competition with private funding. Lessons have been learned from these mistakes and an increasing number of public actions are now partnered with private funding. Such partnering not only increases the credibility of a specific programme, but also serves as a shield against unwise spending of taxpayers' money.

- The emergence of a pan-European small-cap stock market: Currently, two initiatives are competing for the position of Europe's premier small-cap stock market: Easdaq and Euro NM. While their philosophies differ, the aim of providing a credible alternative to Nasdaq is the same. It can be expected that these two initiatives will not co-exist forever, and many policy-makers are already calling for increased cooperation – and possibly a merger – between the two markets.

## Beyond western Europe

European private equity has come of age. Though still somewhat smaller than its US counterpart, the gap is narrowing.

Over the next few years, one can expect the introduction of a friendly fiscal and legal environment for private equity. If the policy-makers of the various countries act in the appropriate manner, private equity should prosper and further contribute to its economic environment.

New investors are also likely to take an interest in private equity. US investors have already found their way into a market that is still far less competitive than their own. The emergence of a European investor base can also be expected. As European pension funds develop, and the awareness of private equity grows, more European investors will allocate a greater proportion of their assets to private equity (always provided venture capitalists are able to continue to produce adequate returns). It is very likely that large sums will be invested in private equity and, in turn, poured into Europe's SMEs.

The introduction of the euro should also have a very positive effect on private equity, which is, by nature, an international business. The use of the euro has removed barriers such as exchange risk, and in addition has added a key advantage, in that it greatly improves the comparability of private equity returns throughout Europe. This is true even for the United Kingdom, where an increasing number of non-sterling-denominated funds (mainly US dollars and euros) are being raised.

Finally, there are the exciting possibilities presented by central and eastern Europe and the Newly Independent States (NIS) region. Some funds rule out the possibility of any involvement beyond western Europe, but several major players in the market are raising specific regional funds dedicated to these areas. Since 1993, the EVCA has pioneered various programmes for these regions and the results are astonishingly encouraging. The question of 'if?' seems to have been replaced by that of 'when?'.

But has the train already departed? Have the US funds already cornered the relevant market? Today, the only certainty lies in the role that the European Bank for Reconstruction and Development (EBRD) plays in the region. Its strategy of partnering commercially proven investment managers is allowing many European investors to build a solid local base of experience in the region.

The various countries are evolving at very different rates and the proper timing will probably depend on the investor's long-term commitment to the region and its development. Indeed, the worst mistake that European venture capitalists could make is to have a colonial approach, and assume that business is done the same way in Poland as it is in Kazakhstan.

---

[1] EVCA has issued industry standards. More information is available at www.evca.com

[2] The *1998 Investment Benchmarks Report: European Private Equity* can be ordered from Venture Economics (+1 973 353 7178) or from Bannock Consulting (+44 171 535 0200) for US$895. Members of the EVCA and contributors to the report receive a discount.

Part II

# Emerging market perspectives

Chapter 4

# Dragon equity: thoughts on the role and future of private equity in China

Daniel Burstein
*Managing Partner, Millennium Technology Ventures, L.P.*

I'm in an off-the-beaten-track restaurant in Beijing where prosperous locals go when they want a good duck dinner. My host is Chen Ping, as clever an entrepreneur as China has yet produced. Chen is a former economic policy analyst who, in the heady days of the 1980s, developed new economic theories on a number of issues relating to China's move toward a market economy. But after Tiananmen Square, like many Chinese intellectuals, Chen gave up on working for the cherished but seemingly impossible goal of political reform and 'jumped into the sea' of business. Instead of writing economic theory, he set out to just do it.

A genuine Beijing duck dinner is a series of courses during which all parts of the duck are consumed. I've been through this many times in China, and have long wished that a genuine entrepreneur would open a Beijing duck restaurant where you could get just the good part – the succulent duck meat itself, wrapped in thin pancakes with plum sauce, scallions and cucumbers. I even have visions of a Beijing duck house of the future where you can get the duck meat prepared traditionally or, if you prefer, blackened with cajun seasonings, smothered in 'bar-b-que' sauce Texas-style, or rolled into a quesadilla with salsa, Mexican-style. We laugh about these ideas of mine – but it is clear that, even though he is a true entrepreneur Chen Ping does not think it would work in the Chinese market.

'Hello, I am a representative of the new bourgeoisie that the Chinese communists have been trying to crush for the last 50 years,' is the line Chen came up with to introduce himself to Milton Friedman. He has practised it with foreigners ever since.

As the webbed feet hors d'oeuvres arrive, we also laugh about some of the stories Chen has told me in the past about his exploits in China's emerging business world: riding elephants near the Burmese border in the 1980s in search of gems and hard woods; selling made-in-Hong Kong Christmas cards in eastern Europe the winter after the Berlin Wall fell and Czechs and Hungarians were celebrating a free Christmas; a venture into environmentally sound bathroom fixtures with the backing of a member of the Rockefeller family that did not quite work out; a variety of Internet projects; and a highly successful series of real estate deals.

As the duck soup arrives, Chen tells of his latest idea: he wants to take over a mid-sized state-owned enterprise (SOE) and run it like a private company. It is estimated there are between 100,000 and 200,000 troubled SOEs that the Chinese government authorities plan to divest. The company Chen has in mind is heavily indebted to the state banks. Because the debt is so high and the prospects so bleak, the government is willing to let entrepreneurs like Chen take over this kind of company with very little equity investment (sometimes even zero equity). There is one proviso, though: the entrepreneurs must assume the company's debts.

Sprinkling vinegar liberally into the soup, Chen explains that what can appear to foreigners as bloated, over-leveraged SOE behemoths can, in some cases, be decent companies with some high-quality assets trapped inside horrendous balance sheets. These companies may have a strong market share in the domestic market, a well known brand name, modern equipment (acquired with all those state loans), and/or real estate assets.

A kind of duck hash made out of a variety of inner organs has arrived. Chen explains that his team may not even have to assume all the debt. Instead, he will cut a deal to accept only a manageable level of red ink, perhaps a haircut of 50 per cent or so. Having assumed control of the company under these terms, Chen's team will then reduce the number of employees. This is a job the Chinese state government definitely does not want to do. Selling an SOE to an entrepreneurial group and letting the entrepreneurs do the dirty work of laying off excess employees and right-sizing the workforce provides the local political authorities with the right cosmetics to save a certain amount of face.

In the growing number of deals of this type that are being done in China, the new management may cut the workforce in half or less. It then agrees to pay unemployment compensation and welfare benefits to some of those dismissed for a certain number of years as they try to move 'from welfare to work' Chinese-style. However, getting one of these deals actually closed is not at all easy. Arranging the details of the debt haircut and the workforce dismissals typically takes many lengthy negotiating sessions between the new management and state officials. Some attempts take years to consummate; many fail altogether.

But the underlying logic is not all that different than what happened in the United States in the 1980s, when traditional captains of industry found it hard to lay off workers, even as profits were eroded and competitiveness sagged. Corporate raiders and leveraged buy-out (LBO) firms stepped in and led the downsizing, taking a lot of criticism in the process but making enormous fortunes for their trouble.

## Turning loss to profit through LBOs

I now need a good excuse to avoid the duck heart the waitress has just put on my plate. So I ask Chen a question. 'OK, after you've trimmed the debt, and dismissed unneeded workers, what else will you do to make the business profitable?'

A broad smile comes over his face as he begins to detail the rest of his business plan. 'Why do we need to own all our own equipment?' he asks rhetorically. 'Why not put it into a leasing company and lease back what we need when we need it? We can also lease it to others when it's not in use.'

Then there's the factory itself, which sits on prime real estate in a major Chinese city. 'We can move the factory out to the countryside where the land is much cheaper and convert the existing factory to residential housing,' says the man whose greatest business success has been in the housing market, profiting from the new Chinese dream of home ownership.

At last the duck meat itself arrives – my favourite part of the meal – and I raise a glass to Chen Ping and toast him. 'Congratulations,' I say. 'You have just invented the Chinese version of the leveraged buy-out.'

As we roll the duck up in the pancakes, Chen listens intently as I regale him with stories of how US LBO artists have been restructuring debts, laying off workers, disposing of assets and optimising operations for years. I tell him that this process is one of a number of secret ingredients behind the United States' renewed economic strength and global competitiveness in the 1990s. Chen is in heaven with this kind of talk; I am in heaven eating the best duck I've ever tasted.

How many other entrepreneurial groups are doing something similar to what Chen is doing? His is one of the first such transactions, but in different ways and in different forms, several hundred SOEs have been effectively bought out through some combination of private equity investment and assumption of debt. This is in addition to several thousand that have been merged or acquired by other companies. The latter may still nominally be SOEs, but they are being run by entrepreneurial minded executives. Many of the new management teams are also introducing radically minded new management techniques to spur innovation and productivity, ranging from equity ownership for workers to respect for the ideas and human capital of the workforce.

## A long hill to climb

Not all of China's troubled SOEs can be cleaned up and restored to profitability through these means. For one thing, there aren't enough Chen Pings to go around: not enough entrepreneurs with vision, courage and a zest for risk-taking, who also possess capital, connections, and management skills.

Entrepreneurs have always been looked down on in Chinese history. Back in the days of Confucius, 2,500 years before Mao arrived on the scene, it was far more glorious to be a minor state official in China than to be a businessman. Even today, as China wrestles with the twin burdens of the debt-laden SOEs and the choking of growth, induced in part by the Asia crisis, entrepreneurs are tolerated rather than encouraged. This is all the more unfortunate as people like Chen could play such a powerful role in restructuring the nation's economy.

It is still difficult for them to get access to capital. More often than not, businessmen look to Hong Kong, or to foreign sources, for money. The banks keep pumping money into the failing, bureaucratically run enterprises, but give the cold shoulder to most of those who could provide the catalysts for change.

I have eaten the last morsel of duck I can possibly eat. Chen Ping has one more important point to make as a non-duck dessert arrives. Americans, he says, talk a lot about promoting the private sector in China. But when it comes time to choose their business partners, they inevitably gravitate toward the SOEs. This leads Chen to ask the blunt question 'Why do Americans prefer to do business with the communist SOEs, rather than with the capitalists like me?'

The answer, of course, is that for the time being (and notwithstanding all their problems) the SOEs still have more legitimacy and credibility in the eyes of foreigners. The legal and institutional status of private-sector entrepreneurs remains shrouded in what the Chinese poetically call the debate over the 'question of ownership'. Although China's National People's Congress moved in 1999 to adopt a few basic guarantees of private ownership and property rights, the legal and business infrastructure for truly privately owned companies remains murky.

I say goodnight to Chen and return to my hotel room to think over the deeper meaning of what he is trying to do. Which is that he – and thousands of entrepreneurs like him – are trying to build a true private sector. Not private in the way the word is used in Chinese economic parlance (where all it refers to are companies that are not directly state-owned), but private in the US sense of an enterprise being owned and operated by private individuals.

Chinese economic reform has been very reluctant to acknowledge an important role for private entrepreneurs. Most of the companies listed on the Shanghai or Shenzhen stock exchanges are not privately owned in the way this would be understood in the United States. Instead, they have a state, provincial or municipal government entity heavily involved in their ownership structure. What Chen Ping and many others are trying to do is to develop a true private sector and a true private equity market.

## Prospects

Given the need to continue moving what was once the world's biggest and most zealously socialistic economy toward the market, and given that much of the 'easy' part of this economic reform process has already been accomplished over the last 20 years, China is entering an incredibly challenging phase of its development. The boom years for foreign investment are over. China will have to offer more than the chimerical dream of accessing the huge market its 1.3 billion people represents. It will have to offer foreigners ease of investment and a variety of forms for that investment, ease of doing business in China, the reality of profits rather than endless promise, and ease of profit repatriation and exit strategy.

That's a tall order, especially for a country that believes that it has been insulated from the effects of the Asian crisis felt by its neighbours precisely because it maintained state political control over its equity and currency markets and allowed foreigners so few opportunities to exercise influence in these spheres.

One conclusion is that there is likely to be less appetite for foreign investment in China over the next five years than there has been in the past five. This reality is one reason that Premier Zhu Rongji has called for a period of domestically led investment and internally generated growth. That prescription, while logical, is also flawed. Currently, domestically led investment still means that the government and various state and quasi-state agencies and banks are doing most of the investing. These governmental bodies may be capable, in a Keynesian sense, of keeping the pump sufficiently primed to soak up some of China's ballooning unemployment and to maintain the growth of GDP at levels high enough to assure general political and economic stability. They are not, though, efficient users of capital.

And that's where a genuine private sector comes in. If a genuine private sector can develop in China, even if it remains a comparatively small slice of the overall pie, it can begin to bring the force and discipline of the market to bear on the rest of the economy. What is more, the relative vibrancy of Chinese domestic private equity will improve the overall climate and conditions for the efficient use of foreign equity investment as well. In other words, when foreigners can back genuine entrepreneurs like Chen Ping, they will be much more willing than they are now to participate in LBOs, mergers and acquisitions, and the restructuring of Chinese SOEs.

It falls to domestic private equity entrepreneurs like Chen to fight the long uphill battle. They have to prove that private ownership can motivate greater productivity and solve more problems more efficiently than the various forms of public and quasi-public ownership that dominates the Chinese economy. Even now statistics show that less than half of GDP comes from the directly owned state sector.

Domestic entrepreneurs will also provide the necessary pressure to make:

- domestic bank lending become more accessible and market-oriented;
- reductions in workforces acceptable to others throughout the economy;

- asset prices more rational; and
- enterprises (and their assets) more readily and efficiently tradable.

This will not be easy. But everything I have seen of China's fledgling entrepreneurs suggests to me that they will ultimately succeed. And in doing so, they will turn China into enough of a market economy that foreign financial investors will be able to succeed as well.

The coming transformation of 100,000 or more state enterprises will be a golden age for LBOs, mergers and acquisitions, and private equity of all types in China. However, it is still a long way off.

First, the fledgling experiments with private equity on the part of Chen Ping and his colleagues have to be successful. Not just profitable for the entrepreneurs which they will be, but also socially and economically successful. This experience and historical transition is needed, so that the Chinese political leadership begins to become convinced (as they are not convinced today) that a market economy in the fullest sense – including the ability for private individuals to own very large amounts of equity and to grow rich – is critical to the overall growth, development, prosperity and continued modernisation of China.

Chapter 5

# Private equity in Russia

Shiv Vikram Khemka
*SUN Group*

*'When he came to center stage, [the country's] crisis of self-confidence was in extremis. In terms of chaos, the entire system was mired in a stultifying paralysis. His role was to reawaken democracy and recreate an entrepreneurial economy out of these unpromising ruins. Ironically, his method of re-imposing order on the debilitated structure was to ask and be given emergency powers by Congress, and to rule for the next two years as a benign autocrat, attempting to rebuild the nation ...'*

Bernice Cohen in 'The Edge of Chaos', describing F.D. Roosevelt's first term in office as US President in 1933, following the Great Crash of 1929.

Since 1991, Russia has undergone massive economic and political change. President Yeltsin and his team of reformers, led by Anatoly Chubais, set out to dismantle the old centrally planned command system and to build a free market economy. Although their vision and intentions were admirable, they inadvertently unleashed in Russia a period of chaotic capitalism and economic volatility, including currency instability, growing fiscal deficits, and periods of hyperinflation. They did initiate, however:

- a legal and institutional framework for the ownership of private property;
- the creation of a rudimentary capital markets infrastructure and banking system; and
- the mass privatisation of over 250,000 state-owned enterprises.

## The private equity context

It would be hard to argue that the majority of the population is economically better off today than it was 10 years ago, given the effect of real price inflation and the breakdown of social support systems. It is clear now that the transition to a fully functioning and democratic free market economy will require tremendous capital resources, political will and time. Private equity investors will find many opportunities in this environment, but will also face significant risk.

### Privatisation and reform

Russia's mass privatisation programme had an immediate and generally negative impact upon the Russian economy. First, trade was liberalised and significant imports of food, spirits, tobacco and consumer goods flooded into the markets, draining valuable foreign exchange reserves. Simultaneously, export procedures were liberalised and the state lost its control over foreign exchange earnings.

Exhibit 1

**Phases of Russian economic transition**

| | |
|---|---|
| 1985–90 | • 'Glasnost' (openness) and 'Perestroika' (restructuring) introduced under Gorbachev. |
| 1991 | • Yeltsin comes to power and surrounds himself with a group of young economic reformers. |
| 1992 | • Gaidar's liberalisation policies. Inflation increases dramatically and output declines sharply. |
| 1992 | • Mass privatisation programme launched under the supervision of Anatoly Chubais. |
| 1993 | • Russia launches its own currency. |
| 1993 | • Parliament rebels against Yeltsin. Yeltsin attacks parliament building to end the uprising. |
| 1994 | • Monetary and fiscal policy tightened by the Russian central bank. IMF agrees to provide financial backing to the government budget. |
| 1995 | • Shares-for-loans programme adopted, whereby Russian banks provide one-year loans to the government, in return for which they acquire prized Russian companies. |
| 1995 | • Exchange rate corridor developed to gradually depreciate the rouble against the US dollar. |
| 1996 | • IMF agrees to provide a US$10.2 billion loan contingent upon a three-year programme of economic reforms. |
| 1997 | • Stock market boom. Stocks reach all-time high. |
| 1998 | • Stock market bust. Devaluation. Debt default. |
| 1999 | • Yeltsin resigns in favour of Putin. |

The result of this on Russian industrial enterprises during the first phase of privatisation (1992–94) was, in general, devastating. Plants that produced products for the domestic market suddenly faced severe competition, and many of them collapsed, unable to access adequate capital or management know-how needed to compete effectively. Plants that produced goods for export became cash cows for self-made traders eager to capture short-term gains and without adequate reinvestment soon started to fall into disrepair. Meanwhile, some businesses that had not existed previously, such as distribution and advertising, started to prosper. Access to capital in the first phase was limited to government budget resources, and trading profits. 'Voucher funds' set up during this early period made tremendous returns by buying companies at a fraction of their value and then selling them shortly thereafter to strategic or speculative financial investors.

The second phase of privatisation (1995–98) was characterised by the big 'loans-for-shares' schemes (Yukos and Norilsk Nickel) and other high-profile privatisations (Svyazinvest and Tyumen Oil). During this phase, most of the investment inflows into the Russian capital markets were speculative flows, led by hedge funds and other investors seeking high returns in new Russian equity and debt instruments. This led to a boom in the Russian capital markets (see Exhibit 2) and significant secondary market trading activity in a handful of Russian 'blue-chips'. The value of some of these stocks rose more than tenfold in a period of approximately 18 months.

Only a small amount of capital actually found its way into real investments in Russian companies. Many private equity funds were, however, set up during this period, a number of them investing in minority positions in relatively illiquid second- and third-tier stocks. Sometimes the investment included a board seat, but rarely gave the investor control of the company. After some repackaging, these companies could be touted by brokers as the blue-chips of tomorrow. By 'flipping' these holdings to portfolio investors eager to follow the profits made by other early investors in the Russian public markets, some of these private

Exhibit 2

**The Russian Trading System Index, 1995–99**

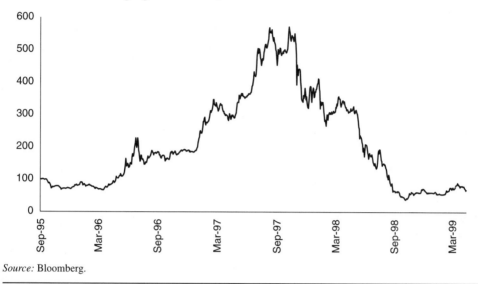

*Source:* Bloomberg.

Exhibit 3

**The rouble/US dollar exchange rate, 1995-1999**

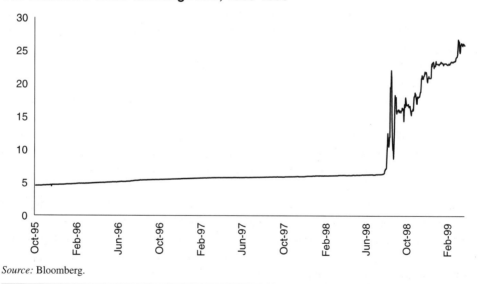

*Source:* Bloomberg.

equity funds made considerable profits. Only a few of these funds targeted traditional buy-outs, acquisitions or restructurings.

In August 1998, with the sharp devaluation of the rouble and the collapse of the Russian capital markets, over 90 per cent of the value of the public market was wiped out during a few days. The collapse of the banking system and the unprecedented government debt defaults only compounded these losses. Gains made during the previous five years were substantially eroded. Many private equity investors that had bought minority stakes in small companies realised that much of the value of their investments had disappeared, as had the possibility of any near-term exit. Several public markets funds and hedge funds were closed down.

The reforms of the 1990s took place without adequate controls and without the necessary rules, regulations and institutions that support a modern free market economy. This led to the concentration of wealth in the hands of a few, and to the impoverishment of the rest of the population. With low export prices for most commodities, including oil, an inadequate tax collection system, low foreign exchange reserves and substantial debt servicing commitments, the economy continues to look weak and is unlikely to recover in the short term. For private equity investors willing to take a medium to long-term view, however, although there are many risks, there still exist promising investment opportunities.

## Opportunities and risks

*'The best values are available in those nations where economic problems are most obvious'.*
Mark Mobius, 'On Emerging Markets'.

As a result of privatisation, it has become possible for private equity investors to buy stakes in a large number of Russian enterprises. Under the Communist regime all these enterprises functioned as production units, working to an annual government production plan. They did not have to worry about production costs, sales or marketing. Distribution logistics were also centrally controlled. GosPlan, the Soviet state planning agency, tried to coordinate supply and demand across all sectors of the economy. The Ministry of Foreign Trade controlled all import and export activity. There was no advertising and the domestic consumer had little product choice.

Since 1991, all this has changed, and companies cut loose as a result of privatisation need both capital and management expertise to survive. This has created the opportunity for a variety of different, often complementary, private equity investment strategies as detailed below.

- First, 'deeply discounted' asset-based investments. Investors can buy companies and their assets for a fraction of their replacement value, with the hope of either building a business around these assets, or of selling these assets to a strategic investor for a considerable profit.
- Second, export-oriented investments. These are applicable in industry sectors where Russian production is globally competitive (metals, oil and chemicals, for instance).
- Third, import substitution strategies. Upgraded domestic production can supply local demand for products that are currently imported or that are not available or affordable in the local market (such as food, beverages and pharmaceuticals).
- Fourth, investments that target the local consumer market. These may include investments in producers of cosmetics and personal care products, and service providers.
- Fifth, strategic and restructuring investments. These are applicable where it is possible to consolidate or restructure an industry and to build critical mass in a particular business (with producers of beer, cement, oil and gas, for example).
- Finally, investments that target growth sectors of the economy and businesses where it is possible to add value.

Although many ideas seem attractive, they must be assessed in the context of various Russian risks.

- First, and most importantly, is political risk. Apart from the risk of political instability at the national level, politics at the regional level can determine the success or failure of an investment.
- Second, macroeconomic issues such as currency stability and inflation make business planning and financing extremely difficult. They can influence global investor sentiment towards Russia and can unexpectedly change valuation expectations and exit possibilities.
- Third, microeconomic issues, such as the tax environment, the clarity of privatisation documentation and legal title, security arrangements, and the reliability of the management and shareholders, must be analysed carefully to avoid pitfalls.

The limited supply of domestic capital and the large number of potential opportunities offer the possibility of significant returns for foreign private equity investors able to identify and manage these risks. For example, SUN Group has been investing in Russia since 1992 and has made over 20 private equity investments during that period.

## SUN Group

Starting in 1958, the shareholders of SUN Group became one of the largest intermediaries of Soviet capital goods, infrastructure and services to India, working with a large number of companies in the power, mining, transportation, oil and gas and metallurgical sectors. This business was based upon the 'rupee–rouble' trade agreements that were signed between the two countries. Trade under this regime had reached, each way, over US$5 billion annually by 1990. The break-up of the former Soviet Union and the massive political and economic changes that resulted led to the collapse of the 'rupee–rouble' trade agreements and threatened SUN's underlying export business to India.

In 1991, SUN started to explore other opportunities in the new Russia and decided that direct investment into basic enterprises could yield significant returns. After looking at several industries with export potential such as oil and gas and timber, and after being advised by contacts in the government that these industries involved considerable political risk, SUN decided to analyse five basic industries, namely, cement, edible oils, beer, milk, and confectionery. Available information from secondary sources was not reliable, and SUN decided to pursue a 'hands-on' approach by researching both the industry as a whole, and its individual businesses. For example, to study the brewing industry, the SUN team, including two beer industry specialists from Canada, visited over 140 breweries throughout the former Soviet Union during an 18-month period.

Starting with its first investment in Russia in 1992, SUN has built up SUN Brewing, one of the region's largest brewing companies with 1998 sales of over US$280 million, by acquiring controlling stakes in regional breweries and consolidating them into a unified and restructured business. Today, SUN Brewing is listed on the Luxembourg Stock Exchange and has recently signed an agreement with Interbrew, one of the world's largest brewing companies, to continue building the business. SUN has made several other investments in Russia, in industries such as food processing, and oil and gas, through SUN Capital Partners, its regional private equity fund.

Exhibit 4

**SUN Group investments**

*Source:* SUN Group.

Private equity investors have taken different routes to investing in this market. SUN's approach has been 'hands-on', and people intensive. The experience that has been gained from this approach is summarised below.

## The investment process

### Deal flow

In Russia, as in many emerging markets, the main sources of deal flow remain the networks and relationships that one is able to build and maintain. In Russia, these networks are very diverse. Firstly, many former Communist Party members are today leaders of business enterprises, political factions and regional governments. Secondly, a number of young, dynamic entrepreneurs have emerged from the rough-and-tumble capitalism of the 1990s. Thirdly, liberal pro-reform politicians, working under President Yeltsin, continue to wield considerable power. Finally, various other organisations including political parties, former industry associations, scientific institutes and regional governments have all emerged as potential sources of 'deal flow'. What is essential, therefore, is the ability to determine the quality of investment proposals generated by a particular network of relationships. This requires local experience and careful judgement.

In a market where many people are looking for a quick way to wealth, proposals are often poorly supported, sometimes fraudulent and often full of hidden risk. It is, therefore, essential to determine the reliability of the people that bring you deal flow by using both in-house experience and other reference networks. The regions are becoming increasingly important as a source of deal flow and a strong regional contact base can help one evaluate and sort through local investment proposals.

Although banks and research groups are also sources, many have been built up to focus on speculative public market investment. There are very few people who can provide real value added insight into private equity situations. Superficial documentation and optimistic projections often hide the real business situation.

It is also important to take both a top-down and a bottom-up approach to sourcing deals. Ideas developed by members of the team from a theoretical perspective (strategies that have worked in other parts of eastern Europe, for example) should be studied. Meanwhile, ideas that appear through the network should also be taken seriously as many seemingly uninteresting proposals contain valuable leads. Finally, in order to attract good deal flow, it is imperative to develop a reputation as a serious, long-term investor.

## Due diligence

As in any private equity investment process, thorough due diligence is essential. However, Russia lacks much of the service infrastructure that exists in other countries to facilitate this due diligence process. Further, where this infrastructure exists, the cost of this due diligence is extremely high, its quality is marginal, and the teams often relatively inexperienced. An experienced in-house team must supplement any outside consultants in order to evaluate the potential risks of any investment.

Financial due diligence is an important initial step, as most Russian businesses are not financially transparent. The Russian accounting system was designed primarily for the tax authorities and not as a means of financial reporting to shareholders. Although one is able to get a sense of the numbers by converting these accounts into an International Accounting Standards (IAS) format, this information still has limited value. Companies often keep more than one set of books and it is difficult to access the real numbers.

Many transactions in Russia are also 'barter transactions' whether out of necessity, or to reduce taxes and financial scrutiny. It is critical therefore, to broaden one's financial due diligence to meet with suppliers and buyers of the company's products, and to cross compare information from one source with information from the local and federal tax departments and from other sources, such as competitors and employees. Only then can one get a sense of the real financial position of the enterprise where lax financial controls often result in poor record-keeping and occasionally improper financial conduct, benefiting a few managers at the expense of most shareholders, or benefiting one shareholder at the expense of everyone else.

Legal due diligence is time-consuming and fairly complicated, and it is essential to reconstruct the legal history of the enterprise. Old Soviet laws, new Russian laws and various amendments make legal analysis a minefield of risk, where there are few precedents and interpretation can be very diverse. Language difficulties can also be a barrier and can exacerbate some of these problems of comprehension and interpretation. It is essential to use local as well as western law firms to help form an opinion regarding the potential legal risks surrounding in an investment. Most legal due diligence yields a broad range of problems. It is essential to build the experience to analyse whether these problems are resolvable, not material, risky or completely unacceptable. This can be a difficult process in a country where there are few if any precedents and the judicial system is still in its infancy.

Commercial due diligence should be as broad-based as possible, encompassing issues such as: industry regulation, local politics, logistics, competition, raw materials availability, access to distribution channels, and environmental and security issues. This can help avoid surprises in the future. For example, just before closing one potential transaction, our financial due diligence revealed an asset on the balance sheet that was valued at zero. Although this was explained away by the local management as unimportant, further indirect investigation revealed the existence of a subterranean government facility located under this particular factory!

It is essential to understand the history and culture of the region where the investment opportunity exists because local politics and business practices vary widely throughout Russia. Some regions are also much more investor-friendly than others. Politics is a critical component of the due diligence process and political awareness and support by political players of one's investment is essential if one hopes to succeed. It is important to convince the local authorities of the benefits, in terms of future employment, taxes and regional development that an investment may bring.

Finally, the quality and the ethics of the current management team must be analysed. Once again, most managers have a short track record and have often had to cut corners because of a lack of proper guidance, training, volatile market conditions, lack of access to capital, or criminal interference. It is crucial to understand the real short and long-term motivations of the senior managers. If it is felt that the management team is inadequate, finding and replacing a management team, especially in the regions, can be a very difficult task.

## Structuring and closing the transaction

Most transactions do not withstand the process of thorough due diligence. Some do, and it then becomes important to negotiate and agree on a valuation and a capital structure. This step can only follow the due diligence process because so much depends upon what is discovered during the process.

Determining a valuation poses considerable challenges because:

- there are very few precedents;
- public markets are volatile and illiquid;
- there is general macroeconomic unpredictability; and
- the currency is unstable.

Typically, the seller will talk about 'asset value' and 'asset replacement value'. Since financial information is poor, earnings multiples are usually meaningless or misleading. Doing a discounted cashflow analysis based on poor financial information in an unstable economy with wildly fluctuating sovereign debt rates is no more useful. Further, since there are few relevant comparables the valuation process requires considerable experience and judgement.

To settle on a valuation, it is important to be conservative when estimating the amount of financial and other resources that will be required in the short and medium term. The adage that 'it always takes twice as long and costs twice as much' is worth remembering. In addition, the entry valuation must take into account various possible exit valuation scenarios.

Domestic and foreign debt is largely unavailable (except for established export-oriented projects), or is prohibitively expensive. Further, hard currency debt increases the risk for any company with domestic earnings in an environment of currency instability. Most investments are therefore substantially equity financed.

It is possible to structure an investment as a convertible or similar instrument to increase the security of the investment, but this capital must, at the end of the investment's life, provide an equity rate of return. Over time, as the banking system matures, the federal government credit rating improves and businesses develop a track record of servicing commercial loans, it is likely that debt financing will become more available. However, this is unlikely to happen in the near future.

The legal and financial structuring of the deal again needs considerable care. It must take account of the large number of regulatory approvals required, both at the local and at the federal levels. The full process opens up issues of confidentiality and poses bureaucratic hurdles, but can prevent problems in the future. A broad lobbying effort is an essential part of closing a transaction, and should include meetings with workers' unions, management, and regional and federal authorities.

In terms of the acquisition documentation (namely the investment agreement and the shareholders' agreement), it is important to understand that representations and warranties clauses have little meaning in most investment documentation in Russia. This makes detailed due diligence all the more important.

The method by which the acquisition is taking place (ie, whether through the purchase of secondary market shares or through a primary share issuance) will determine which other issues need to be addressed. These may include:

- assessment of counterparty risk;
- regulatory and shareholder approvals;
- payment terms;
- control over use of proceeds;
- tax structuring;
- currency risk; and
- minority protection issues.

Each issue needs careful and detailed analysis in order to protect against future problems. This can take considerable time and energy.

Once the intention to acquire becomes apparent, it is not uncommon to find large blocks of stock in the company being bought or consolidated by insiders looking to make a quick profit. They may:

- try to renegotiate a higher price for a consolidated stake;
- attempt to stop the transaction unless they are bought out ('greenmail'); or
- threaten to sell to a Russian or foreign competitor.

Insider trading is commonplace, and it is difficult to maintain adequate confidentiality.

Finally, in order to close a transaction, it is important to ensure the alignment of the major shareholders, the management team and other stakeholders through careful structuring. Without this alignment, the transaction may not close and may unravel in the future, as evidenced by the experience of many western investors investing in Russia for the first time.

## Managing the investment

The real challenge of building or restructuring a business in Russia begins once the investment has been made. Some private equity fund managers take a seat on the board of the company and allow the existing management team to continue to run the business. This can work if the management team is exceptional. Another approach which sometimes yields better results, is to be much more 'hands-on' and proactive in terms of the management of the business. A typical restructuring can include some of the issues described below.

## Corporate structure, business focus and corporate governance

A Russian company may, as part of its activities, be responsible for social infrastructure such as the running of schools, hospitals and housing estates. This legacy of the Soviet system has made it much more difficult for many enterprises to restructure. Although it is preferable to avoid investments that involve responsibility for this kind of social infrastructure, this is not always possible. In such situations, it is essential to try to refocus the business and to reduce the social burden that it carries.

Furthermore, it is important to establish a clear set of corporate governance principles and to make sure that these are understood. It is usually necessary to:

* clarify board and management responsibilities; and
* establish financial transparency, ethical standards and corporate values.
* Maintaining and enforcing these parameters is crucial in establishing credibility.

## Operational improvements

Usually, factory plant and equipment is inefficient, outdated and poorly maintained. As a first step, it is essential to focus on improving:

* the work environment;
* plant maintenance; and
* the efficiency and quality of production.

It is important to develop a quality-control system and to encourage the management and workers to take pride in their work. This is a time-consuming but critical first step.

Even when the equipment is relatively new, management attention is usually exclusively directed to output rather than to quality, cost or efficiency. This attitude dates back to the old Soviet planning system where production plans and output targets had to be met, regardless of other criteria. Most enterprises are not customer-oriented and there is usually inadequate emphasis on sales and marketing. This focus on production rather than marketing, distribution or service, means that investment in these enterprises is directed towards new equipment rather than towards building a better and more profitable business model. Only investment in assets is valued whereas investment in training and marketing is usually considered to be much less important.

However, this attitude can change quickly once the management team is exposed to the results of an integrated strategy. Many Russians workers are also well educated, have strong technical skills and are willing to learn and adapt to new ideas. Training and exposure to western business practices are nevertheless critical in encouraging management and workers to change their attitudes from an exclusive focus on production to an appreciation of the business as an integrated system. Younger professionals are usually more flexible and adapt more quickly, although the experience of older engineers and managers can be extremely valuable.

## Financial management

In general, financial control in most Russian enterprises is poor and real management accounting information inadequate. Profit margin erosion through over-invoiced purchases and under-invoiced sales is common. It is essential to ensure that this 'financial leakage' is controlled, either immediately or within a defined period. This may involve changing the management of the company or just tightening the control systems. Furthermore, there is often considerable waste. Savings can usually be made in:

- energy consumption;
- labour;
- raw material storage and use; and
- inventory management.

These, together with tighter cashflow management, can strengthen and improve the business. SUN Brewing, for example, has managed to reduce its consumption of energy and water by over 30 per cent during the last four years, and is able to manage its cashflow from plants across Russia on a daily basis. Some of these changes can be achieved easily, especially when the local management team is convinced of the benefits. Others take great effort and considerable patience.

Russian accounting practice, which is very focused on the revenue line, is an inappropriate and inadequate management tool. Russian accounting profits almost always overstate the profitability of an enterprise and thereby allow the tax authorities to collect more taxes. It is therefore essential to:

- establish a western standard of accounting, such as IAS, or United States Generally Accepted Accounting Principles (US GAAP); and
- put in place a computerised system that can provide pertinent information immediately.

Long delays in receiving information can be very damaging to a business where the environment is changing rapidly, and speed of reaction is essential. Again as an example, SUN Brewing moved first from Russian accounting standards to IAS and then to US GAAP, a process that took over two years.

Tax planning is also very important. The tax system is often arbitrary and very complex. The tax authorities assume that everyone is delinquent in paying their taxes. When paying taxes, it is imperative that everything is very carefully documented and fully explained. Foreign investors make an easy target for unscrupulous tax collectors and one is assumed to be guilty until proven innocent. It is also easy for tax authorities, in regions where tax collection is sparse and local government budgets are underfunded, to target successful companies and foreign investors in order to 'deepen' their tax collection efforts. It is easier for them to try to obtain more tax payments from a few companies than to build a broader tax base. It is, therefore, essential to maintain a very proactive and transparent approach to paying taxes.

Finally, the absence of an adequate commercial banking infrastructure and the prevalence of cash and barter transactions can make the logistical side of cash management a considerable challenge.

## Marketing, sales and distribution

Marketing in Russia is a concept that is only eight years old. Until 1991, advertising was scarce, and apart from Levi's jeans, Marlboro cigarettes and Pepsi, few other western brands were known. There were some well known local brands, but even these had become famous through their history and reputation rather than through a proactive marketing campaign. The entry of many western multinationals such as Coca Cola, Nestlé, Mars, Unilever, Procter & Gamble, and others, has changed all that. In the last few years, marketing campaigns have flooded all the major media channels and today marketing is considered to be an important part of any business strategy.

Significant opportunities exist to build brands, often at relatively low cost, and to win a place for them in the hearts and minds of local consumers. Maintaining the integrity and affordability of the brand is, however, a challenge in a country that is subject to volatile economic shifts. Furthermore, the initial infatuation with western brands seems to be fading. In that context, it has been interesting to note the emergence of strong Russian brands, both as a reaction to western brands and as a symbol of national sentiment and pride. Many multinationals have, therefore, also started building strong local brands in order to maintain sustainable positions in the local market. Market research, although still in its infancy, is developing quickly and will continue to provide guidance to companies wishing to grow their businesses in Russia. Russian managers have also learned a great deal about marketing during the last few years, and continue to benefit from exposure to western marketing experience.

In terms of sales and distribution, under the old Soviet system factories were simply production units, and the entire sales and distribution function (including exports) was managed through a number of large centrally controlled organisations. These companies had their own warehousing, transport and logistics operations, and prices and margins were all set by GosPlan. After 1991, this sales and distribution mechanism collapsed.

Plants suddenly found that they had to distribute and sell products themselves. Entrepreneurs and agents emerged to help them do this, and many criminal organisations that had previously established a grey market for goods found this to be an ideal opportunity to expand their own wealth and influence. Many buyers decided to integrate backwards into production and many producers to integrate forward into distribution and sales. The decision either to take on these roles internally or to contract them out depends on various factors, such as cost, existing infrastructure, competition and the threat of criminal interference. Dealing with the border authorities and with customs procedures can also be problematic in terms of bureaucratic hurdles, licences and lack of adequate infrastructure.

## Personnel and training

Finding and training the right management team is one of the most critical and difficult tasks in the Russian environment. A balance between expatriates and Russians and the right cultural mix can make all the difference between success and failure. It is essential to build a team that is adaptable, culturally sensitive, has enough local and international experience, and is able to remain positive in the face of a continual stream of challenges and problems. Leadership and motivation skills are greatly valued. In order to ensure that the team is working well, benchmarking and exposure to global industry norms are essential. Many people still have inaccurate perceptions about the relative efficiency or success of their enterprises in a global context. It is, therefore, important to expose them to global trends in their business, in order to show them the possibilities that lie ahead while alerting them to the dangers of complacency. Finding expatriates with necessary and relevant Russian experience is still difficult, and it is even harder to find expatriates willing to live outside Moscow and St. Petersburg.

## Growth and restructuring

To succeed in restructuring a company in Russia requires knowledge of the country, an understanding of the business and a long-term commitment to making the business work. More importantly, it requires a team that is experienced, capable and flexible.

## Execution

Merely sitting on the board of a company that one has invested in is not usually enough to ensure success. It is essential to have considerable input into the daily management of the company, ensuring the creation and implementation of:

- strong internal management systems;
- controls on the cashflows of the company; and
- a sound business strategy.

It is essential to be able to influence the people who are involved in running the business at all levels of the organisation. The consistent implementation and execution of a business strategy in a fast changing and difficult environment is the greatest challenge.

## Financing

Financing a business in Russia takes considerable effort, flexibility and management attention. The high cost of debt, the lack of a broad public markets infrastructure, the lack of real commercial banking activity, and the relatively few sources of equity capital all make it difficult for Russian enterprises to access adequate capital for restructuring and growth.

First, it is essential to improve the internal management of the company's cashflow, in order to generate capital for reinvestment in the business. To accomplish this:

- financial leakage must be stopped;
- the inefficiencies of barter must be eliminated;
- social overheads must be reduced;
- tax exposure must be controlled; and
- corporate governance and transparency must be improved.

All this is usually not enough, and is not achieved quickly. It is not unusual, therefore, for companies to need additional capital for growth and restructuring, beyond the initial investment. Although many investment banks are now beginning to work in Russia, it is still difficult to raise capital for most businesses. Private placements to Russian or regional funds, financing from organisations such as the International Finance Corporation (IFC) and the European Bank for Reconstruction and Development (EBRD), accessing the public markets through local listings on the public markets or through listings on a foreign exchange, depositorty receipt (American depositary receipt – ADR, and global depositary receipt – GDR) programmes, and financing from strategic investors are all avenues that must be explored. The variability of investor sentiment towards Russian projects means that timing is critical and can make all the difference between accessing reasonable finance or having to accept very unfavourable terms. Furthermore, the time required preparing for a financing and the ultimate cost of this process must not be underestimated.

Anyone who has worked in Russia for several years is familiar with the comment that 'the situation here is neither as bad as the western press makes out, nor as good'. Over the last few years there have been big swings in perception as to the on-the-ground reality for businesses in Russia. The media, by reflecting and influencing these swings in perception, plays a significant role in determining access to finance and the cost of that finance. Underlying these big swings in perception is the ever-changing political landscape in Russia. This immediately influences, perhaps excessively, the reaction of foreign financial investors to opportunities in Russia.

The clearest indicator of such overreaction is the market for public stocks, where liquidity and investor perception have taken little account of the underlying realities in many of the companies that have been promoted as investment opportunities by local brokers and investment banks. Many people have made and lost large fortunes by buying and selling these stocks over the last few years.

The risk/return profile for private equity investing is very different and requires a much longer investment horizon in order to achieve reasonable returns. In order to reduce short-term downside, investors must perform adequate due diligence and put appropriate control and oversight structures in place.

## Exiting the investment

The extreme instability of the Russian financial markets and the uncertain political climate make it very difficult to predetermine an exit strategy for an investment. It is therefore important to plan several exit strategies and to hope that at least one of them will offer attractive returns when one is ready to exit. It is also important to be flexible in terms of investment horizon, and to be willing to make quick decisions when a favourable opportunity arises. Possible exits include:

- listing on the Russian over-the-counter (OTC) market or through an international exchange;
- sale to a strategic investor; and
- sale to a large Russian financial institution or corporation.

### Listing

The volatility of the public markets makes it quite risky to plan an exit through this route alone. Furthermore, much of the value of the business may be associated with one's participation as a shareholder in the business, and it may be very difficult to exit completely or at a reasonable value. However, investors searching for good investment opportunities may be willing to pay a considerable premium for a well run, transparent Russian company with a good track record. A private placement to a group of investors willing to buy the company is also another feasible option as a pre-IPO investment.

## Sale to a strategic investor

Strategic investors, being long-term investors, are usually willing to pay for market entry, local brands and new opportunities. However, they are also very influenced by issues such as strategic fit, national politics, management challenges and the impact on their reputation. This can make them very bureaucratic and slow to reach a decision. Their due diligence process can also be exhaustive and can reveal sensitive information to a potential future competitor. The 'buy versus build decision' is one that is often not obvious, especially at this early stage in Russia's development, and many multinationals would rather build their own business from scratch than acquire one with potential risks and an unfamiliar management culture.

## Sale to a Russian institution

One possible private equity strategy involves an exit to a large Russian financial institution or corporation. Russian buyers, however, are still few and far between. They are probably the most conservative buyers in terms of price. They are also potential competitors, and care has to be taken in assessing counterparty risk and political alignment. Over time, however, this is likely to become an increasingly feasible exit option.

If Russia continues to develop into a more modern, free-market system, it is likely that the opportunities to exit through one or more of these routes will continue to increase.

## Conclusion

*'It's right to be an optimist, but be prepared for the worst!'*
Dean Mathey, 'Fifty Years of Wall Street' (Princeton, New Jersey, 1966).

It was highly unrealistic for anyone to have expected Russia to make a smooth and rapid transition to a functioning, free-market economy after 70 years of communism. As the last decade has demonstrated, the political and economic restructuring of the country has been fraught with difficulty.

Although the challenges that lie ahead are great, they are not insurmountable. Russia has enormous reserves of natural resources, a highly literate and educated population, a large industrial base and considerable infrastructure. However, the political will to create and support institutions that will establish a balance between adequate controls and necessary freedom is essential. It will be important to create the right conditions to attract significant foreign direct investment, including, for example tax reform, banking-sector regulation and effective bankruptcy procedures (see Exhibit 5).

Private equity investors will continue to have significant opportunities to generate returns and to build value in the Russian context. Nevertheless, this is not an easy market in which to operate and requires commitment, know-how and a dedicated local team in order to

Exhibit 5

**Conditions necessary to attract foreign direct investment**

- Political stability
- Tax reform and more effective tax compliance
- Currency stability
- Government debt restructuring
- Monetisation of the real economy
- Improved environment for corporate governance
- Functioning law enforcement
- A functioning banking system
- Bankruptcy legislation and procedures
- Effective measures to curtail capital flight
- Improved production-sharing agreement legislation

achieve success. Experience, good judgement, local knowledge and patience are essential factors in building a private equity business in this environment.

In the aftermath of the 1998 financial crisis, there were dire predictions of social unrest and political upheaval. Yet, the country managed to survive and stabilise, helped partly by buoyant oil prices. The fundamental question, of course, remains the political future of Russia and the likelihood and speed of its integration into the global economy. The faster this happens, the greater the opportunity for all investors. The risk, of course, is that Russia will pull back from integration, disillusioned with the experience of the last decade.

The peaceful transition to a newly elected Duma is, however, a sign of a maturing political system. Furthermore, the resignation of President Yeltsin offers the Russian people a unique chance to elect a president who can help build a new Russia, one with strong, stable institutions and an important role in global affairs.

## Case study: SUN Brewing

SUN Brewing provides many examples of the opportunities and pitfalls of investing in Russian companies. SUN Group began buying controlling stakes in Russian breweries in 1992, and by 1993 had acquired majority stakes in five breweries and significant minority stakes in several others. The consolidated company was named SUN Brewing. The breweries were operating at low capacity-utilisation levels, had sanitation and quality problems, had no strong brands, no distribution system and they were being run by management teams that generally lacked adequate business experience.

As a first step at the end of 1993, SUN Brewing raised money through a private placement to various private equity investors, in order to invest in the business. Although a number of international brewing companies were approached initially as potential partners, it soon became clear that these companies were too concerned about Russian political and business risk to inject significant management resources or capital into SUN Brewing.

SUN used this initial capital to bring in an international management team, upgrade the production facilities, introduce financial controls, and initiate the sales and marketing functions. Within a year, by the end of 1994, SUN had made considerable progress. SUN Brewing decided to approach western public investors with Russia's first GDR offering, which it managed to place at a 100 per cent premium to the previous financing. Within a week of raising this capital, the Mexican peso was devalued, triggering a collapse of emerging market stocks. Opportunities to raise money for most Russian companies disappeared. However, for the next 18 months, although SUN Brewing GDRs traded at a discount to the issue price, the company was able to grow using the capital it had raised. A year later the company also managed to list its shares on the Luxembourg Stock Exchange.

The tightening of financial controls at all the breweries caused local resentment. In one case, this led to a serious dispute with the management of a particular brewery over its ownership. As a result of SUN Brewing's inability to assert management control at this facility, the company deconsolidated this brewery's results from its financial statements. The somewhat irrational fear that this trouble would spread to other SUN breweries made external capital raising difficult, even when the market began to improve. In response, the company raised expansion capital in mid-1997 through a complex derivative structure with hedge fund investors, which provided them with equity returns on the upside and debt-quality security on the downside.

By the end of 1997, the steps taken by SUN Group to improve operations had yielded significant results. Revenues, which had been around US$40 million in 1994, were US$294 million in 1997 (see Exhibit 6). Losses of US$7 million became net profits of US$16 million. SUN Brewing had become the largest brewer in Russia.

The company had also become one of the larger taxpayers in the country, contributing close to US$100 million in value-added tax, excise and profits taxes combined for the 1997 financial year. Product quality had improved considerably, as evidenced by the many awards for its beers. Barter transactions had been completely eliminated and the finished goods inventory was rapidly moving to a just-in-time system. From an investor standpoint, the share price was at a 60 per cent premium to the December 1994 GDR price, and the trend was positive.

Exhibit 6

**SUN Brewing: net earnings and sales, 1994–97 (US$ million)**

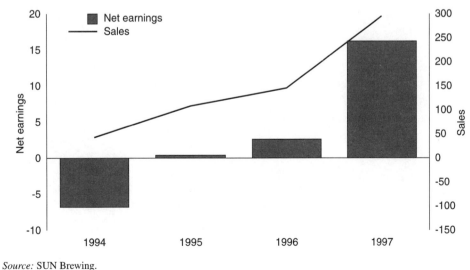

*Source:* SUN Brewing.

59

SUN Group therefore decided that the appropriate strategy for SUN Brewing would be to raise US$100 million in debt and US$100 million in equity (both to be traded on a US exchange), to continue to build the company for two to three years, and then to bring in a strategic partner. The company hired investment bankers and legal and accounting advisers, approached the credit rating agencies and prepared a prospectus in order to implement these capital-raising plans. One week before the company was to start the financing roadshow, Russia devalued its currency on 17 August 1998, and the SUN Brewing share price fell dramatically, wiping away 90 per cent of the company's value! The company was now left facing a debt obligation as a result of the 1997 financing and with inadequate reserves of capital for its continued growth. On 7 October the board of SUN Brewing resolved that the only likely route to capital was to find a strategic partner. After an intense period of negotiation with several potential partners, SUN Brewing finally agreed to enter into a partnership with one of the world's leading western brewers on the morning of 25 March 1999. The early morning news informed us that NATO had started bombing Yugoslavia, and the Russian government was fiercely opposed to this action.

Where does this leave SUN Brewing? The transaction with the strategic partner was struck at a price above the 1993, private placement share price, at a discount to the 1994 GDR price, and at a premium of over three times to the current market price. However, taking into consideration the strategic partner's commitment of capital, brewing assets, brands and management expertise, as well as SUN Group's Russian expertise, SUN Brewing, now renamed SUN Interbrew, should be able to continue to build a sustainable, long-term position as Russia's leading brewer. While the holding period for this investment has undoubtedly increased, the absolute return potential should not be materially lower than it was before the August 1998 Russian crisis.

Chapter 6

# Asian private equity – the Quantum Paradigm[1]

John-Paul Ho
*Crimson Capital Management*


In recent years, international investors have shown an increasing interest in Asian private equity. The performance of the Asian private equity industry, however, has fallen short of expectations. Hard data is not easy to obtain, but the consensus among the investors and fund managers we spoke with is that, with few exceptions, the returns of funds during this period have been disappointing in both relative and absolute terms.

In early 1999, interviews by the *Asia Pacific Private Equity Bulletin* confirmed this view:

> Our US private equity returns have been strong. But our experience in Asian private equity has been disappointing. There was little performance history and early returns look weak. To be competitive with US returns, we want Asian private equity to return at least 2.5–3.0x our investment over three to five years, and generate 25–30 per cent IRRs net of all expenses and carried interest.[2]
>
> The Asian private equity model generally has not generated a sufficient risk-adjusted return relative to other private equity opportunities around the globe. Much of this poor cash-on-cash performance is the result of the investment management side of the business. In the good years when allocations were targeting a hot Asia, many firms took investor capital yet did not invest properly in the underlying management company franchise to weather the lean years. The supply side of capital is equally to blame. Chasing geographic diversification and hot areas, investors did not properly identify enduring franchise players. We believe private equity management in Asia requires restructuring if it is to continue to attract institutional capital.[3]

During 1995–99, the MSCI All Country Regional Indices - Far East Free[4] (excluding Japan) registered an annualised return of -1.3 per cent in US dollar terms, largely due to the Asian financial crisis that commenced in mid-1997. Many industry watchers believe that the performance of Asian private equity funds has fallen significantly short of the poor Asian public market returns. Some have the opinion that a 0 per cent return would have been a top quartile performance.

## The Traditional Paradigm

In general, most Asian private equity fund managers followed what we call the Traditional Paradigm: investing broadly in a large number of passive minority interests in companies in established industries. This approach has generally failed to deliver attractive risk-adjusted returns, because it has had the odds stacked against it in each of the three major areas that drive returns: (1) long-term EBITDA (earnings before interest, tax, depreciation and amortisation, or cash flow) growth, (2) financial leverage and (3) multiple expansion.

## EBITDA growth

There are many reasons why few Asian companies have been able to deliver impressive EBITDA growth in recent years. Most industries in Asia are commodity businesses, with access to low-cost labour and capital as their main competitive advantages. Undisciplined management and an environment that was awash with bank and stock market capital fuelled excessive investment in manufacturing capacity, resulting in industry overcapacity, thin margins and poor return on equity (ROE).

When globalisation led to the dismantling of trade protection, many regional companies found it difficult to deal with the increased competition not just from their neighbours, but also from increasingly aggressive multinationals. The disappearance of easy money and local consumer confidence from 1997 onwards, caused by the financial crisis in Asia, and the devaluation of local currencies, only served to make matters worse.

Since private equity managers were typically limited to investments in private companies that could not qualify for a stock market listing or bank funding, they were naturally left with the smaller and lower-quality companies in each sector. Often these private companies had weaker market positions, under-developed finance and MIS systems, and less seasoned management teams. Consequently, many Asian private equity funds found that their portfolio companies were among the ones hardest hit by the Asian crisis.

## Financial leverage

Ironically, despite the abundance of bank loans available to those with the right political connections, real estate that could be mortgaged, or listed shares that could be margined, very little financing has been available in Asia for leveraged acquisitions. Although a few leveraged deals have been completed, cash flow-based non-recourse loans have been, and continue to be, a rarity in Asia. The local banks are not comfortable with this type of lending, and the foreign houses have generally not found it worth their time to develop either the senior or mezzanine markets because of the small sizes and number of transactions in the region.

## Multiple expansion

Thus, private equity funds were left with a strategy of buying at a low multiple and selling at a higher multiple by investing in pre-IPO minority stakes of companies at a discount to public market valuations. The abundance of capital prior to the Asian crisis made buying at low multiples difficult, resulting in fairly narrow discounts to potential public market multiples. So long as Asian stock markets were hot, however, the strategy had some success, as private equity investors were able to sell their stakes through highly priced IPOs.

After the onset of the Asian crisis in 1997, multiples declined for a while but not as much as financial investors had hoped for, and not for long. Bottom-fishing private equity funds have had a challenging environment due to increased competition from aggressive multinationals, the overhang of demand from large new private equity funds raised by both existing players and new entrants, and the recovery of most stock markets.

## The Control Paradigm

After the Asian financial crisis, the Asian private equity industry is trying to reinvent itself by gaining control of over-leveraged assets and restructuring both the balance sheet and operations of these companies – what we call the Control Paradigm. The thesis is that Asia is in the midst of a massive restructuring and there will be numerous opportunities of this type.

This approach certainly has the potential to be more appealing than the Traditional Paradigm, but it also faces numerous challenges. For example, it is not clear that there will be many opportunities to gain control of attractive businesses at a reasonable price. First, asset values have already rebounded. Also, relative to the United States, few countries in the region have legal systems that give the banks the power to foreclose, hence the clearing mechanisms for assets in these countries are poor. Furthermore, Asian families remain reluctant to give up control of businesses, except of their less attractive assets. And the competition from strategic investors is keener for control stakes than it is for minority stakes. In addition, there is a large supply of new capital entering Asia targeted at restructuring opportunities.

Finally, most takeover targets in Asia are in old industries, where the risk–reward equation for the overhaul of an enterprise may be unattractive. If one is taking over an Asian company that has been established for many years, then one is likely to pay a substantial premium over book value for the privilege of cleaning up the former owner's mistakes, with the need to transform a well-entrenched corporate culture and replace the old infrastructure. Without injecting new technology or applying a new business model, it is not clear whether the Control Paradigm investment will deliver the upside commensurate with the effort and risks involved in restructuring an Asian company.[5]

Going forward, whether taking controlling stakes is the most convincing investment strategy, it is perhaps too early to say. While I think that there will be some good opportunities, I am doubtful that a generalised buyout market in Asia could reap the kind of returns it has in Europe and the United States. Unlike those markets, Asia has yet to develop its debt infrastructure to support this kind of activity. What I would advocate is focusing on quality companies rather than control. By this I mean companies that are absolutely transparent with investors as well as being attractive businesses with a proven track of success before and during the Asian financial crisis and, we believe, will show even higher performance returns as Asia restructures its economies.'[6]

## The Quantum Paradigm

There is a third approach that has a proven track record of success prior to and during the Asian financial crisis, and we believe will demonstrate even better returns as Asia restructures its economies. We call this approach the Quantum Paradigm because it requires entrepreneurs and investors to make 'quantum' leaps in strategic thinking and analysis, and not to rely on just historical financial analysis, existing and accepted trends, or conventional wisdom. It focuses on investments that create and build companies with new products, services, technologies or business models in industries undergoing rapid change.

The Quantum Paradigm usually involves one of two major approaches:

1. Transferring new technologies, products/services or business models from the United States and Europe into emerging, high growth Asian markets; or
2. Applying Asia's strengths to develop competitive companies in the global value chain: understanding how technology and other forces are transforming a global industry's structure, and discerning where Asian companies can use their competitive advantages to exploit the resultant changes.

## Transferring new technologies, products/services and business models to Asian markets

There are many opportunities to transfer successful products and ideas from the United States or Europe to Asia. For example, industries that are mature in the West have the potential to experience high growth rates in Asia, for example the telephone equipment switching market in China over the past several years. The challenge is to judge what products, technologies, and business models will be suitable for each country's particular stage of economic development and what adaptations will be necessary given local market, cultural, and regulatory differences.

### Chain stores

Applying a US style chain-store strategy to Asian markets that were traditionally fragmented has proved to be successful for several Asian entrepreneurs with 'out of the box' foresight.

For example, Holiday KTV, a privately held company, has become the largest karaoke chain operator in Taiwan, with 58 stores island-wide and over 1 million customers per month, in an industry consisting of mostly 'mom and pop' karaoke stores. Karaoke stores offer consumers the opportunity to sing along to the accompaniment of pre-recorded music in individual rooms.

Holiday has differentiated itself from its local competitors with its chain-store approach by employing professional management, strictly standardising its service offerings, and achieving economies of scale in information systems, construction, and purchasing.

Holiday's success has been based not only on US chain-store concepts, but also on management's ability to adapt its strategies to the local market. In rolling out its stores in Taiwan, Holiday targeted students and the young working class, and aimed to provide up-to-date song selections in a comfortable environment with low charges. As it contemplates entering the Hong Kong market, it is considering a modification in its value proposition; it will likely go upscale as a result of its market research.

In the casual wear retailing industry, entrepreneur Jimmy Lai successfully modified the Gap store concept and built Hong Kong-based Giordano from scratch into a regional chain which today has revenues of over US$330 million, and more than 680 outlets in 11 countries. Lai recognised that the combination of a good value-for-money concept, a much higher level of customer service, and a simple, relaxed fashion style would be very appealing to young Asian consumers. When he first introduced Giordano in Hong Kong in the early 1980s, the concept of a chain of clean, modern stores with cheerful and helpful sales staff selling a range of inexpensive but consistently good-quality clothing was a novel one.

Lai adapted the Gap's business model to Asia by using much smaller stores and emphasising high turnover per square foot in order to offset Hong Kong's very high rents. He also built an in-house production capability in China to take advantage of Hong Kong's proximity and production management capabilities, and tailored his products to the tastes of Hong Kong's large urban middle class.

The fast food chain Jollibee in the Philippines is another good example of how flexibly adapting a Western model to Asian tastes can reap outstanding success. Jollibee's founders copied the McDonald's format religiously, but modified the menu to take into account the local penchant for sweeter and spicier hamburgers, and offered non-burger choices such as chicken and Filipino dishes. Jollibee has beaten McDonald's at its own game, and is now the country's largest fast food chain, with sales of more than US$300 million and over 550 outlets.

## Transferring business-to-consumer Internet models to Asia

Looking forward, the Internet is likely to be the US transplant that will have the greatest impact on Asia. Asia has one of the world's largest and least-tapped Internet markets, while Asia comprises close to 50 per cent of the world's population and 40 per cent of global GDP. Asia's New Economy is two to three years behind the United States as shown by its low absolute and relative number of Internet users compared to the United States, but the gap continues to narrow at a rapid pace.

Goldman Sachs predicts that the number of people accessing the Internet in Asia (excluding Japan) will grow from approximately 15 million users in 1998 to over 200 million by 2003, with China and India accounting for 75 per cent of users and Taiwan, Korea, and Australia accounting for another 20 per cent.[7] And with the deal in November 1999 between Washington and Beijing on China's entry into the World Trade Organisation, the pace is bound to increase as the Chinese phase out restrictions on foreign ownership of local Internet companies. At end-1998, the United States had 62 million Internet users, and this is expected to grow to nearly 150 million users by 2003, or at about half the growth rate of Asia.

Given the accelerating use of the Internet by Asia's population, we believe that transferring successful Internet business models from the United States to Asia will prove to be highly lucrative. Tailoring offerings to Asian consumers' needs is likely to be among the keys to success. For example, although Yahoo! has a well-known brand name, it has been unable to leverage this into a market leadership position in Greater China, Taiwan and Hong Kong. In fact, Yahoo! is overhauling its Chinese site and forming a new partnership with Chinese software maker Founder, a powerful 'red chip' or state-owned company traded in Hong Kong. Home-grown portals such as Sina and Dreamer, however, have developed leading positions by offering a wide range of localised content, as well as identifying unique niches that appeal to Asian customers.

Dreamer, for example, has grown to be one of the top five portals in both Taiwan and southern China, despite having been established only in October 1998. Its success is in large part due to its ability to develop offerings that are a success with local customers such as a portal dedicated to Chinese women's interests, the world's first search engine and directory for MP3 files of Chinese language songs, and very popular local auction sites.

While we believe that Asia's Internet space will likely evolve in many ways similarly to the United States from access to advertising to e-commerce, it will still find its own, unique evolutionary path. And Asia's New Economy will differ from that of the United States by more than just the requirement of local content. Some of the differences will include (1) a greater role for alternative Internet access mediums besides the PC, (2) Asia being a collection of non-homogenous consumer markets, (3) fulfilment and settlement obstacles, and (4) regulatory and legal issues.

### Multi-platform access in addition to the PC

PCs are the most common medium used to access the Internet in the United States. However, in Asia alternative platforms may play a role in addition to PCs, given the low number of PCs across Asia. Lower per capita incomes make PCs an expensive device for most Asian consumer. However, many consumers receive television through satellite and cable (110 million cable TV subscribers across Asia), and so the lower-cost set-top box might become a major Internet access platform in Asia through cable and satellite. In addition, Asia has significant penetration of wireless and in many countries the cellular phone is a consumer's primary telephone. Wireless Internet access through smart phones or other portable Internet access devices may become the primary Internet access device for many Asian consumers (see the section on Japan).

### Asia is not one market

Asia consists of several non-homogenous markets with yet to be proven advantages for global or regional players. Countries differ by language, culture, lifestyle, stage of economic development, consumer behaviour, regulatory and legal environments, population size, telecommunications infrastructure, and development of the Internet. Thus, there is a real need to adapt New Economy business models to the local environment. Local providers have a better understanding of their home markets than foreign competitors, but they also need to have an in-depth knowledge of the newest trends and technologies affecting the New Economy. In addition, they may lack the scale, especially in terms of financial resources, as they compete with regional and global Internet players.

A regional player (Asian operations of a global player or Asian regional player) may have certain advantages, such as economies of scale in signing international advertising and content deals. However, the jury is still out as to whether a regional business model will see significant operational synergies or simply become a regional investment holding company. To date, Asian users have favoured localised offerings and have not been swayed by US players that simply translate their existing content into local Asian languages. Not surprisingly, international players including Yahoo!, Excite, Lycos, AOL, and CMGI have all become partners of local players.

### Fulfilment and settlement obstacles

Fulfilment (or distribution of goods purchased on the Internet) is an important element of the success or failure of e-commerce companies. Fulfilment is a much more complicated challenge in Asia than in the United States because of physical distances, customs regulations, currency volatility, and more fragmented and disparate supply chains and distribution channels. Also, Asia's less sophisticated payment systems and the lower penetration of credit cards will act as a hurdle for the business-to-consumer commerce (B2C) market.

### Regulatory and legal issues

Asia's regulatory and legal environment regarding the Internet lags behind that of the United States, and entrepreneurs need to be in touch with the policies and directions of local authorities in this regard and respond appropriately.

## Applying Asia's strengths to develop competitive companies in the global value chain

The second approach involves understanding how new technologies, products/services or business models are affecting industries globally, determining Asia's role in the global industry structure, and discerning how an Asia-based company can create competitive advantages to exploit these trends. Industries in which this approach has had notable successes include the semiconductor, personal computer, and telecommunications industries (see Exhibit 1).

## Semiconductors

Consider the Taiwan Semiconductor Manufacturing Co. (TSMC), the number one semiconductor manufacturer in the world based on return on investment (ROI). TSMC was founded by Morris Chang, a former senior executive of Texas Instruments' semiconductor operations, who returned to Taiwan to help the country develop its semiconductor industry. In 1986, Morris spun off TSMC from a government entity, setting up an independent wafer fabrication foundry and creating an important new business model (see Exhibit 2).

Traditionally, design, manufacturing (wafer fabrication, packaging, and testing) and marketing of semiconductors were all performed in one company: large integrated design and manufacturing (IDMs) companies such as Intel, National Semiconductor, Motorola, and Texas Instruments. Thus, in order to start a new semiconductor company, one had to fund not only the design and development of a semiconductor chip, but also the building of a complete manufacturing plant. As the scale and required capital expenditures of such

Exhibit 1

### Successful Quantum Paradigm industries

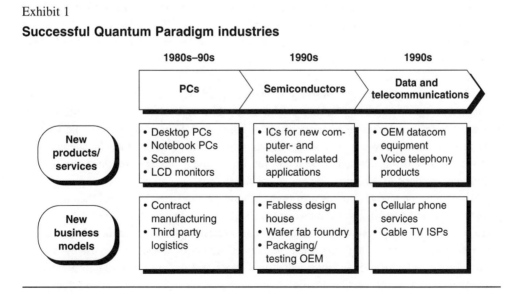

|  | 1980s–90s | 1990s | 1990s |
|---|---|---|---|
|  | PCs | Semiconductors | Data and telecommunications |
| New products/ services | • Desktop PCs<br>• Notebook PCs<br>• Scanners<br>• LCD monitors | • ICs for new computer- and telecom-related applications | • OEM datacom equipment<br>• Voice telephony products |
| New business models | • Contract manufacturing<br>• Third party logistics | • Fabless design house<br>• Wafer fab foundry<br>• Packaging/ testing OEM | • Cellular phone services<br>• Cable TV ISPs |

Exhibit 2

## Taiwan Semiconductor Manufacturing Corp.

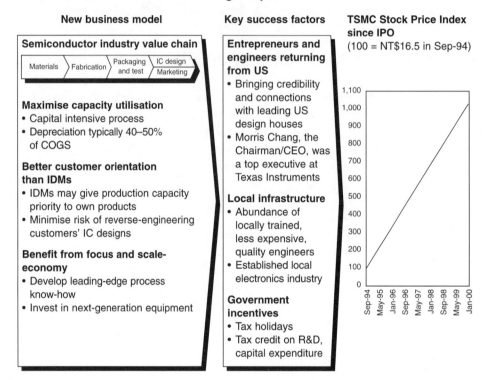

**New business model**

Semiconductor industry value chain

| Materials | Fabrication | Packaging and test | IC design / Marketing |

**Maximise capacity utilisation**
- Capital intensive process
- Depreciation typically 40–50% of COGS

**Better customer orientation than IDMs**
- IDMs may give production capacity priority to own products
- Minimise risk of reverse-engineering customers' IC designs

**Benefit from focus and scale-economy**
- Develop leading-edge process know-how
- Invest in next-generation equipment

**Key success factors**

**Entrepreneurs and engineers returning from US**
- Bringing credibility and connections with leading US design houses
- Morris Chang, the Chairman/CEO, was a top executive at Texas Instruments

**Local infrastructure**
- Abundance of locally trained, less expensive, quality engineers
- Established local electronics industry

**Government incentives**
- Tax holidays
- Tax credit on R&D, capital expenditure

**TSMC Stock Price Index since IPO**
(100 = NT$16.5 in Sep-94)

* Including wafers, masks, and BGA substrates.

wafer 'fabs' grew exponentially with the introduction of more and more advanced technologies, it became prohibitively expensive to start a semiconductor company. Venture capitalists began to back 'fabless' semiconductor companies which focused on design and marketing of chips and outsourced manufacturing to the large IDMs. However, this model resulted in the fabless companies competing for capacity with in-house efforts of these IDMs as well as the risk of leaking intellectual property to potentially competitive internal products of the IDMs.

To address these problems, Morris Chang created TSMC as the first pure, independent foundry that only focused on wafer fabrication for third-party design houses without any internal design and marketing of semiconductor chips. TSMC grew to become the world's leading semiconductor wafer foundry by leveraging Asia's (1) abundance of talented, but lower-cost engineering talent, (2) personal and professional linkages between the Silicon Valley talent pool of Asian-American engineers and their Asian counterparts, (3) government incentives to encourage development of high-technology industries, (4) excellence in manufacturing, including quality, yield management, and process technologies, and (5) development of world-class systems companies that created additional demand for these semiconductors in the PC and consumer electronics industries. TSMC's success eventually spawned the development of an entire industry of successful Asian semiconductor foundries, packaging and test companies, and design houses.

## Personal computers

Similarly, Taiwanese entrepreneurs have changed the face of the PC industry by separating the design, manufacturing, sourcing and logistics processes from marketing and sales. US companies such as Dell and Compaq focused on marketing, sales and distribution, while their Asian partners focused on original design manufacturing (ODM), original equipment manufacturing (OEM), sourcing and global logistics.

Today, Taiwan is the place where US corporations turn to for producing most high-technology goods. The PC price wars of the past few years, which established enduring demand for more economical models, have helped make the Taiwan connection indispensable for computer makers. Taiwan is the world's largest producer of monitors, desktop scanners, modems, and seven other categories of information-technology (IT) equipment. Taiwanese companies make a quarter of Compaq Computer Corp's desktop computers, 40 per cent of IBM's and 60 per cent of Dell Computer's. Taiwan accounts for the production of 49 per cent of the world's notebook computers, making it the world's largest producer, ahead of Japan.

Why do Taiwanese companies epitomise the successful implementation of the Quantum Paradigm? In Taiwan, business moves at a lightning-fast pace. Time-to-market counts in the fast-changing high-technology industry. The best Taiwanese companies are the epitome of efficiency, moving a concept from the drawing board to the production line in 90 days, less time than Japanese or Korean giants need just to make a decision. Taiwanese companies have also developed best-of-breed IT systems to maximise the efficiency of their supply and distribution chains to service demanding customers such as Dell and Cisco and the rest of the global high-technology industries. More importantly, not only have they linked these IT systems to emerging technologies such as the Internet, but they also have developed their corporate cultures to compete on 'Internet' time throughout their entire organisations.

Having a sense of where a company fits into the international value chain is also critical. Taiwanese manufacturers have figured out precisely where they can prosper in the value chain of the global high-technology industries. The island is among the richest Asian economies and does not have cheap factory labour. Instead, Taiwan thrives on a relatively inexpensive skilled workforce compared to that of the United States. Taiwan's workforce enables it to claim the middle ground between low-end, labour-intensive economies and the advanced technology domains of the United States and Japan.

Specialisation reduces costs and increases ROI. Most of the Taiwanese companies are small firms devoted to making a few components on which their very survival depends. They have elevated to a fine art such seemingly mundane tasks as controlling inventory and overhead expenses. For example, one cost-saving technique used by Taiwanese companies is called 'modular manufacturing', in which price-sensitive parts are left out of PCs and then shipped to distributors for installation at the last possible moment before the machines are sold.

Taiwan also has the good fortune to be intimately linked with Silicon Valley through personal and professional networks. During the 1960s, while the island's entrepreneurs were furnishing the developed world with plastic and polyester, its universities were graduating mathematicians and scientists who went on to earn advanced degrees in the United States They found jobs at leading US corporations and its best and brightest students became some of the leading Silicon Valley technologists in the 1970s and early 1980s. Many of these technology leaders returned to Taiwan to jump-start the development of Asian technology companies.

The society also values entrepreneurs and rewards risk-taking. Taiwan starts more than 100,000 companies annually, and is an intensely competitive environment. As a result,

Taiwanese companies act very similarly to Silicon Valley companies in terms of entrepreneurship, business culture, and growth potential.

## Telecommunications equipment and multimedia devices

Despite Asia's relatively slower development in the Internet revolution, Taiwanese companies have already utilised their strengths in speed, manufacturing, and yield management to exploit the Internet-driven global growth of demand for data and telecommunications equipment and multimedia devices. For example, Accton and D-Link have become leading OEM suppliers of datacom equipment including network cards, hubs, and routers for first-tier customers such as Cisco, 3Com, Bay Networks, IBM, and Cabletron.

Princo is an example of a company that is exploiting the global growth of multimedia applications driven by the Internet. Princo is the largest non-listed CD-R disk manufacturer in Taiwan. CD-Rs are blank CDs that can store data, audio, graphic, video, and multimedia files. As Exhibit 3 shows, global shipment of CD-R is projected to grow at a phenomenal CAGR of 121 per cent between 1998 and 2001, and reach 7.5 billion disks in 2001. The principal driver for this exceptional growth is the Internet-driven proliferation of audio, graphic, video, games, and multimedia files and the need to store them.

Taiwan and Japan are today the world's largest producers of CD-R disks. Leveraging on their traditional manufacturing process, Taiwanese companies have achieved comparable quality at lower costs than their Japanese counterparts. During 1999, Taiwanese companies increased capacity by 10–20 per cent per month, equivalent to a tripling to an eightfold increase in capacity over 12 months. As a result, Taiwan's share of world production reached around 76 per cent at the end of 1999 and is expected to continue to rise. Companies like Princo have created proprietary manufacturing processes that allow them to achieve exceptional margins and are continually improving these processes with each new product generation.

---

Exhibit 3

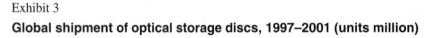

**Global shipment of optical storage discs, 1997–2001 (units million)**

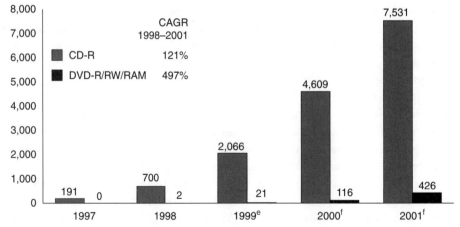

[e] Estimate.
[f] Forecast.

*Sources:* Dataquest, Disk/Trend Reports, Fujiwara, IDC, Japan Storage Media, Industry Association, Jardine Fleming.

Princo is prepared for the increased demand for storage and bandwidth as a result of multimedia applications (e.g. video). The company has already developed the production capabilities to compete in next generation markets such as DVD.

## Business-to-business e-commerce

Looking forward, we believe that there is also an exciting opportunity for Asian exporters in the area of business-to-business (B2B) e-commerce. In 1998, out of the US$914 billion in goods imported into the United States, Asia accounted for 38 per cent of the total. During the same period, intra-Asia trade was worth approximately US$1 trillion. E-commerce will alter the dynamic of how this flow of goods occurs and promises to disrupt and reshape the structure of industries and companies throughout the Pacific Rim. IDC forecasted that B2B e-commerce in Asia-Pacific is expected to grow from US$3.3 billion in 1998 to more than US$100 billion in 2003, implying an annual growth of nearly 100 per cent.

Trading of goods involves basically three major functions: (1) procurement, (2) finance, and (3) logistics. Procurement involves buyers identifying and qualifying vendors, specifying the products and features, and the ordering process. To finance the trade, buyers and sellers must pay and insure the products, obtain letters of credit and assess credit worthiness. And finally, buyers and sellers must arrange for the physical logistics of transporting the products, inspecting quality, clearing customs and handling returns (see Exhibit 4).

In the US market, trading activities are relatively straightforward and are usually arranged by buyers and sellers themselves. However, in Asia physical distances, multiple

Exhibit 4

**Opportunities to leverage the Internet**

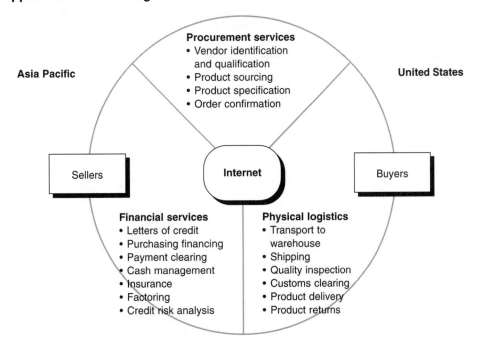

Exhibit 5

**Current complex manufactured products supply chain**

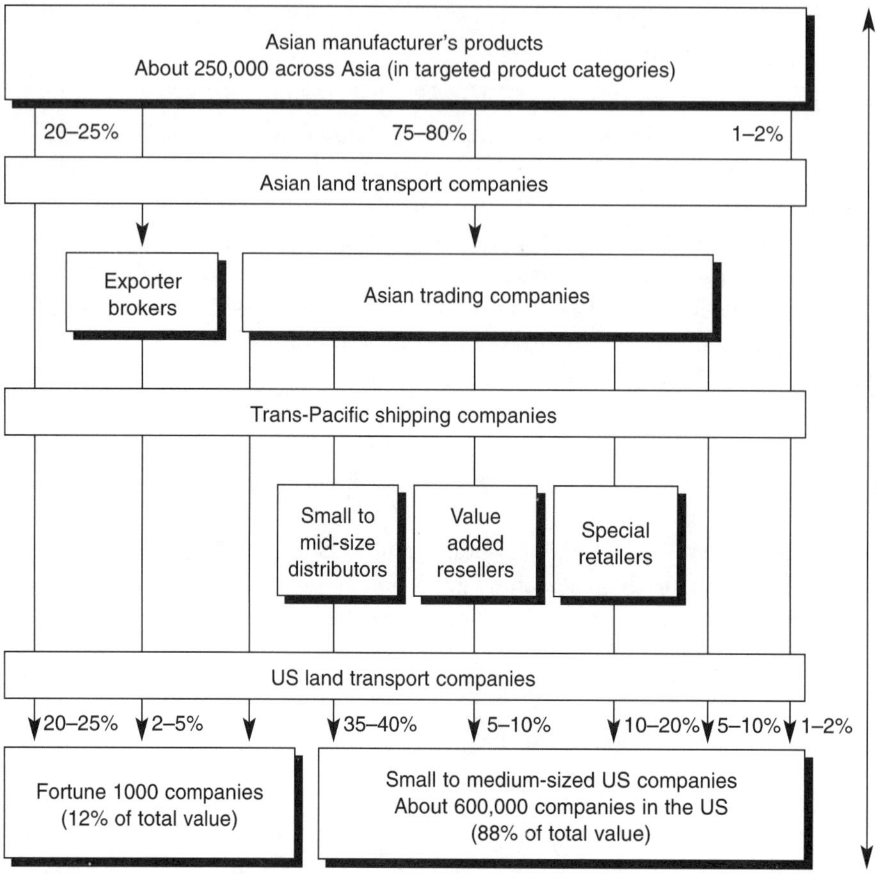

Note: Percentages in the diagram represent typical volume breakdown.

time zones, differences in cultures and business practices, lack of transparency in financial accountings, legal and regulatory issues, customs regulations, currency volatility and political risks all contribute to make cross-border trade a much more complicated and challenging task. Across the Pacific Rim, these barriers have resulted in the development of complicated and inefficient supply/distribution chains of intermediaries (see Exhibit 5).

Currently most B2B transactions in Asia are conducted by phone and fax and personal interaction. There is limited information flow during the process of procuring and distributing products. Furthermore, most vendors in Asia do not have sophisticated information systems capable of collecting, accessing, analysing, and exchanging inventory and logistics tracking information that can streamline and optimise efficiency and effectively manage these global trading networks. In fact, this complex, multi-layered and IT-poor supply chain results in trade-related costs for many manufactured products that may comprise up to 50 per cent of the value added for many imported products (see Exhibit 6).

The Internet is poised to change the face of B2B commerce by significantly reducing the barriers and inefficiencies in international trade. The success of the Internet in streamlining

Exhibit 6

**Estimated costs of Asian manufactured products imported into the United States (%)**

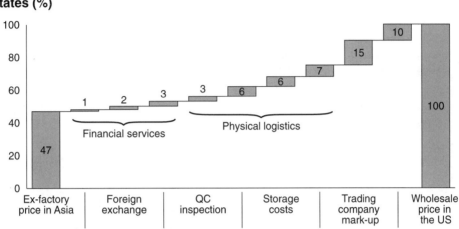

*Sources:* Interviews.

B2C commerce is encouraging companies to seek similar efficiencies in their transactions with other businesses. The Internet can reduce the number of middlemen and lower costs through increased efficiency and economies of scale. And, perhaps most significantly, it can increase the efficiency and speed of the flow of goods such that the inventory levels and cycle times of the entire supply/distribution chain are optimised.

Some companies have started to automate their purchasing and trading activities using Electronic Data Interchange (EDI), but EDI can only handle a one-to-one or one-to-many relationship. Companies like Dell and Cisco, due to their 'gorilla' position in their respective industries, have achieved enormous efficiencies and cost savings through working with their suppliers utilising EDI. However, recently they have leveraged Internet and e-commerce technologies to create another quantum leap in cost savings and industry-wide improvements in productivity.

Other companies have emerged in the United States, including Ariba, Commerce One, FreeMarkets and Chemdex, that offer a marketplace for connecting buyers and suppliers in trading communities over the Internet. Ariba focuses on automating the procurement process for large multinational companies by creating a marketplace for indirect resources including professional services, information technology, MRO (maintenance, repair and operations) supplies, travel and entertainment expenses and office equipment. Commerce One also focuses on indirect resources, but its target customer base is broader and includes organisations of all sizes. FreeMarkets focuses on on-line auctions for buyers of direct resources including industrial parts, raw materials and commodities. Chemdex focuses on creating a marketplace within a vertical market of chemical materials and equipment used by life-sciences companies.

Creating new marketplaces on-line is only the first step in fully realising the potential of the Internet in optimising trading activities. The challenge across the Pacific Rim is to go beyond the successes discussed in the United States and leverage the Internet to automate, streamline and integrate all of the major processes involved in procurement, financing, and logistics.

For example, MedChannel is a new company developing an Internet-based solution for the global medical supplies industry, using the tools of B2B e-commerce to reshape outmoded and inefficient supply chains and distribution channels, as well as exploit Asian production sources.

The commodity medical supply market is worth about US$35 billion in the United States and about US$90 billion worldwide. Most of the world's commodity medical products are manufactured in Asia, in countries such as China and Malaysia where nearly all of the world's latex medical gloves are produced. Most of these supplies coming out of Asia into the United States are branded by one of the large US suppliers, such as Johnson & Johnson, Becton-Dickinson, and Tyco. While some of the medical supply manufacturers in Asia are owned and/or directly controlled by these US providers, most are independent and are free to supply products to more than one customer.

There are many intermediaries and product handoffs on both sides of the Pacific in today's medical supply chains. There is very little use of technology in supply chain communications: transactions are made via phone and fax, and there is little information shared beyond the most immediate trading partner along the chain. This results in unclear demand signals coming back to the manufacturers and logistics companies in Asia, and difficulties for these Asian suppliers in planning production in order to achieve the best utilisation of fixed assets and the lowest cost. In addition, the poor access to information necessitates the holding of excessive stock inventory at each step along the supply chain.

MedChannel is building an Internet-based B2B information platform for the medical supply industry. Because a vast majority of the manufacturers, logistics companies and purchasers in this industry are too small to justify investment in EDI-based systems, and because few are tied to a single upstream supplier or downstream customer, the Internet is an ideal medium for providing access to critical data all along the supply chain. MedChannel is establishing partnerships with Asian manufacturers, logistics providers, and financial institutions in order to integrate all of the major trading activities involved in the distribution of medical supplies. Because MedChannel's solutions are Internet-based, there are no expensive systems for partners and customers to purchase or install.

The MedChannel solution provides benefits at every stage of the medical supply chain, creating long-term partner relationships. Manufacturers, logistics companies and distributors receive clear and timely information on customer demand, product/order status and capacity, all of which can be used to streamline and optimise operations, and reduce inventories, handling costs and cycle times. MedChannel also intends to use the Internet to aggregate demand in fragmented customers markets such as the physician office and home care markets. Purchasers of medical supplies will benefit from efficient purchasing processes, reduced costs, inventory tracking, paperless data storage and secure payment.

MedChannel believes that the cost of supplying medical commodities to US customers can be reduced by 15 per cent almost immediately, with savings of up to 40 per cent possible over time. Inventories in the hospital supply chain can be reduced by about 30 per cent, and inventories in the less efficient US physician supply market can be cut nearly in half with better and more timely information.

## Outsourcing and e-commerce support services

Another area where driving global changes in technology are creating new opportunities for

Asian companies is the outsourcing of back office support functions. As telecommunication costs plummet, it makes increasing sense for Western companies to outsource their call centre activities offshore to countries such as the Philippines where there is a large pool of inexpensive, college-educated and computer-literate talent costing under US$1.50 per hour compared to over US$10 per hour in the United States

Call centres in the Philippines will handle 1–800 inquiries for US clients using local customer service representatives. The Philippines is an ideal location for call centres because of its Americanised English, service culture and competitive deregulated telecommunications environment.

US companies have indicated that they are enthusiastic about using offshore resources, not only because of the cost savings, but also because of the improved quality. Philippine call centres will be able to field college graduates with low turnover rates, whereas US call centres operate in a very tight labour market and must employ high school graduates who often stay in their jobs for only 6–12 months.

The trend in the West of moving away from bricks and mortar favours countries like the Philippines. As companies increasingly sell their products on-line, they will need fewer stores, but will continue to need sales clerks to provide customer service. Instead of being behind counters, clerks will now sit behind PCs and assist customers by phone and e-mail. With the advent of steep drops in telecommunication costs, it no longer makes a difference where the store clerk is located; he could be in Dayton, Ohio, or in Manila.

The opportunities are not limited to voice call centres. Companies such as America Online are already using the Philippines as a base to answer e-mail inquiries, and eventually inquiries will be handled via Web-chat and Voice over the Internet as well. Other back office functions, such as financial transactions and processing of insurance claims, bookkeeping and software maintenance can also be outsourced to far-away locations.

## Japan joins the Quantum Paradigm

The opportunity in Japan epitomises both elements of the Quantum Paradigm. Not only do we expect to see Internet business models from overseas flourish in Japan, but new and interesting twists – such as innovations in hand-held devices for accessing the Internet – will create opportunities for exporting business models to more 'mature' Internet markets.

Only recently has private equity investment as we know it in the United States begun to be practised widely in Japan. Few of the more than 150 venture capital firms in Japan are independent companies. Most are affiliated with and staffed by managers of larger, more traditional financial institutions. These managers rarely have either entrepreneurial experience or the authority to do deals on their own. They follow the parent institutions' inclination to collateralise assets as early as possible. This pattern is reinforced by strict listing requirements limiting exit options for private equity. For OTC listings in 1998, the average time elapsed since company establishment was over 20 years. As a result, even for JAFCO, the largest venture capital firm in Japan and the pioneer of the limited partnership fund, loans constituted a large proportion of assets until just a few years ago.

However, the stage is set for change. Several start-up companies have listed directly on Nasdaq. Two new Japanese exchanges have announced listing requirements more favourable to start-ups. These events are the result of the change in the underlying trends that started in the early 1990s when the bubble economy collapsed.

First, the Japanese economy has truly started to open up to international investment. The government has recognised that the Ministry of Finance convoy system of finance ultimately reduced the competitiveness of Japanese corporations in international markets. Recently, not only the financial sector but also the telecommunications, retailing, and farming sectors have been deregulated to varying degrees. The acquisitions of Yamaichi Securities by Merrill Lynch, and the Long Term Credit Bank of Japan by Ripplewood, would have been unthinkable just a few years ago.

Second, corporate decision making is becoming less dependent on consensus and more on speed. With increasing uncertainty about sources of future profit, firms have learned that they must respond to opportunities more nimbly if they are to compete in the global environment.

Finally, Japan is becoming a more diverse place. Obtaining a place at Tokyo University and working in a large corporation for life is no longer the goal of every high school student. For one thing, few corporations can guarantee such a career any more. Corporate layoffs and a shortage of jobs for new university graduates have led to a recognition that individual abilities must be developed as a matter of career survival. At the same time, the accumulated affluence and long-term influence of Western values have led to a shift in social priorities. Quality of life and individuality have gained increasing importance.

These shifts are reflected in and supported by the emergence of the new stock exchanges mentioned earlier. They will also support the growth of Internet businesses. At the end of 1999 Internet access was estimated to be available in 14 per cent of Japanese homes, representing approximately 20 million users. Eventually, the Japanese Internet market is expected to grow to 30–40 per cent the size of the US market, according to Merrill Lynch estimates. In the immediate future, three factors are accelerating Internet penetration in Japan.

First, access is getting cheaper. The deregulation of telecommunications has broken the monopoly NTT had on the market. A joint venture formed by Softbank, Microsoft, and Tepco is planning to undercut NTT by offering lower-priced access via Tepco's private fibre network. Sony is planning a similar network solution using wireless local loops. Price competition is expected to drive down access costs. Competition among PC manufacturers will further drive penetration into the home.

Second, alternative Internet access devices are wildly popular in Japan. For example, more than three million NTT DoCoMo i-mode cellular phones, which allow continuous access to the Internet, have been sold since its release in February 1999. Within its display (six lines of 15 characters each) a user can send and receive mail, transfer money from a bank account, buy tickets, trade stocks, and get information about restaurants, movies, etc. Separately, game machines are going to be equipped with modems. Over 25 million units of these devices are expected to be sold in Japan within the next few years. Japan's substantial headstart in developing a critical mass and agreeing a technical standard gives it a big advantage in the critical wireless Net access services.

Finally, a proliferation of Japanese language content is attracting more users to the Web. Early users in Japan sought out business or academic content, often in English. Now there is a variety of content serving various interests, all in Japanese. This has attracted advertising spending, leading to more content generation, and so on.

What are the investment opportunities? Initially, expect rapid growth in areas related to access and portals in particular. After access the next wave will be in content. Special attention should be given to services developed for i-mode and other alternative Internet access devices.

As in the United States, the value of brand names cannot be underestimated. Many successful Japanese sites are click-and-mortar initiatives by existing brands. However, as with Amazon in the United States, new brands can be created with new value propositions. Rakuten is just such a case, becoming the number one shopping mall site in Japan by providing high-quality services for both users and tenants.

Ultimately, as in the United States, the largest potential for Internet growth is in B2B. Continued deregulation and competition, accompanied by corporate restructuring and divestitures, will create numerous opportunities for disintermediation and new business models taking advantage of the unique efficiencies afforded by the Internet. Investing in players with the right models could yield extraordinary returns.

## What does it take to win?

Today, organisations that intend to compete using the Quantum Paradigm require access to the very best talent, technologies, partners, and customers on a global basis, and they need it now, in fast-moving markets in which time has become the scarcest resource. In this environment, the best entrepreneurs will be looking to team up with venture capital firms which can not only provide capital, but can also help them achieve their vision and build their com-

Exhibit 7

**Capabilities required to fund successful companies with new products/technologies or new business models**

**Strategic vision**
- Anticipate and understand new business models
- Envisage Asia's role
- Quantify market/opportunities

**Technology/industry expertise**
- Assess technology feasibility/maturity
- Building technology teams
- Assist in cost-down manufacturing logistics sourcing

**Despite oversupply of private equity funds, investors with these skills can still generate high returns**
- Few competitors with required skill sets
- New economy driving exponential growth and opportunities

**Entrepreneurial experience**
- CEO skills in start-up environment
- Flexibility to effect changes in strategic direction
- Manage both business and technology objectives

**Pan-Pacific presence to access key success factors**

| • US | • Japan | • Rest of Asia |
|------|---------|----------------|
| Market access | Consumer electronics | Market access |
| Asian-American engineers/ entrepreneurs | Market access | Manufacturing know-how |
| Internet models | Broadband wireless | Logistics, sourcing, supply chain management |
| Strategic partners | Strategic partners | Strategic partners |

panies in high-speed, fast-changing environments. Private equity/venture capital firms who intend to invest based on the Quantum Paradigm need to have: (1) strategic vision, (2) technology/industry expertise and relationships, (3) entrepreneurial experience, and (4) a pan-Pacific presence (see Exhibit 7).

## Strategic vision

The leadership of the firm must have an in-depth understanding of new business models, trends, and competitive dynamics in the New Economy, and the ability to think 'out of the box' to envision and assess their impact on industry structures and value chains on a global basis. The partners' knowledge should be not just intellectual, but developed from actual experience, having worked in or with high-technology and New Economy companies, and ideally in various geographical locations and cultures as well as during the start-up, growth and mature stages of company development.

## Technology/industry expertise and relationships

It is important that the firm has within its partnership individuals with backgrounds in technology who can help assess the impact and risk presented by a continual flow of new and disruptive technologies, as well as possess the intuition necessary to maximise technology for effective change. In addition, the firm needs to have a proven relationship network of strategic partners, managers, engineering talent, and market access channels to help its portfolio companies access the 'best-of-breed' resources wherever they are located, especially in the sectors listed in Exhibit 8, due to their importance in the New Economy across the Pacific Rim.

## Entrepreneurial experience

Given that most Quantum Paradigm companies will be start-up or early-stage companies, venture firms must bring entrepreneurial and company-building experience to the table. We believe that the team at the venture firm must be entrepreneurs themselves, individuals who share the curiosity, energy, drive and passion of the entrepreneurs as well as their visions of building great companies that will change and add value to their industries and society.

In addition, the venture team must earn the right on a daily basis to be partners with these entrepreneurs. They must bring the best ideas and strategic thinking to the boards of the portfolio companies and have the flexibility and commitment to support their companies as these start-ups adapt to inevitable changes in their plans. They must have the industry contacts, reputation, and judgement to help entrepreneurs rapidly assemble the people, technology, partnerships and financing to reach critical mass. Finally, they must coach the founding team to evolve and develop the necessary managerial skills to steer their companies through the different phases of their life cycles.

## A pan-Pacific presence

A pan-Pacific presence enables private equity firms to extract the best from each country and bring these insights, technologies, and capabilities to assist their portfolio companies in competing in the global marketplace.

Exhibit 8

## New economy sectors for the Pacific Rim in the year 2000 and beyond

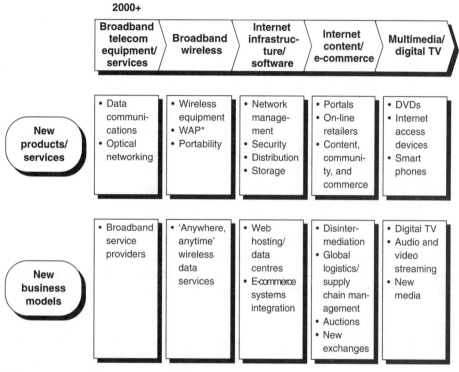

*Wireless access protocol.

## Silicon Valley

Silicon Valley is a fountainhead of new technologies and innovative business models that are creating the New Economy. A presence in Silicon Valley is essential for firms to access leading-edge ideas, technologies, and companies.

The Silicon Valley offers an Asian talent pool rich in technological experience. Over the past two decades Asian immigrants have enrolled in the best universities in the United States On graduation, they have joined the Valley's most innovative companies, helping to make companies like Yahoo!, Sun, Oracle, Cisco, and Netscape, to name a few, household names. These immigrants have been, and continue to be, a driving force in transforming the Valley into the world's leading technology centre. Some may work for the best companies, but others are among the Silicon Valley's most active entrepreneurs. In fact, to date Chinese and Indian immigrants have founded approximately 29 per cent of the companies founded in Silicon Valley between 1995 and 1998.

Venture firms can find an enormous number of investment opportunities funding these entrepreneurs either in the United States, or as they return to their home countries to put their knowledge to work in a venture of their own or as partner with companies in their native lands. Interlinked by family, school ties, cultural bonds and professional relationships throughout the Pacific Rim, this Silicon Valley-based network of Asian technologists and entrepreneurs will be one of the most powerful driving forces of Asia's growth in the new millennium. Access to its knowledge, resources, and talent will be key to the success of any venture firm that aspires to be a leader in the Quantum Paradigm in Asia. Venture firms that can effectively access Silicon Valley's Asian community will have many opportunities to fund growth opportunities, both in the United States and in Asia.

### Japan

Japan is another key linchpin in the Quantum Paradigm. Because of the leadership roles that it will play in the broadband multimedia and 'anywhere, anytime' wireless connectivity sectors of the New Economy, a strong presence in Japan is critical to a pan-Pacific venture capital firm's success with the Quantum Paradigm.

Japan dominates the global consumer electronics industry with world-class competitors such as Sony, Panasonic, Toshiba, Nintendo and SEGA, and is making billions of dollars of investments in new multimedia technologies for home entertainment (digital TV and cameras, set-top boxes, displays, gaming and animation software), and portable Internet access devices. Leveraging this position, Japan is poised for a leadership role in the next generation as the Internet evolves to broadband delivery, content, media and interactivity.

In addition, Japan already leads the world in broadband, 'anywhere, anytime' wireless connectivity. More than 3 million units of the DoCoMo i-mode cellular phone will be sold in its first year of launch. Finally Japan will be one of the first countries to build out broadband wireless networks. Japan will clearly be a key country in developing leading-edge ideas, products, content and services for the New Economy.

### Greater China and the rest of Asia

Other parts of Asia offer other essential resources. Greater China contributes the strengths of three countries: (1) China with its huge potential markets and a vast pool of skilled and low cost technicians, software specialists and engineers, (2) Taiwan with its proven world-class engineering, manufacturing, logistics, and sourcing skills for global high-technology industries, and (3) Hong Kong with its well-developed service industries and trading expertise. Australia, Korea and Singapore are also players in the New Economy with their highly educated and technologically skilled work forces. The Philippines with its educated, English-speaking, yet relatively low-cost workforce, makes it an ideal outsourcing support centre for the global New Economy. India completes the picture as the source of some of the world's most talented leaders in technology and engineers, along with its enormous potential market and deep pool of talent for creating software.

## Conclusion

The Traditional Paradigm of investing in a broad portfolio of passive minority stakes in long-established companies has proved to be disappointing for the Asian private equity industry. The more recent Control Paradigm of taking over Asian companies and restructuring them has more promise, but it is still not clear whether there will be enough attractive opportunities of this type, and if the upside will commensurate the risks and efforts involved in turning around companies in old industries.

We believe that a new approach, the Quantum Paradigm, may have the best risk–reward profile for investing in Asia. Entrepreneurs and investors who can make 'quantum' leaps by challenging the status quo and conventional thinking have the opportunity today to generate excellent returns as Asian industries undergo the sweeping changes wrought by both the Asian crisis and the global Internet revolution. There will be many opportunities to transplant Western technologies and business models to Asian markets, as well as to carve out new export niches for Asia in the rapidly changing global supply chain.

Successfully executing this new approach will be challenging, as it requires a thorough grasp of where the New Economy is headed, the network to assemble the best resources possible, and the experience to convert ideas, business plans and teams into bona fide enterprises. For those that can deliver each of these requirements, however, the next decade in Asia will present extraordinary opportunities.

---

[1] This chapter was written by John-Paul Ho and his partners and colleagues at Crimson Capital Management.

[2] Senior investment officer of a major US corporate pension fund, *Asia Pacific Private Equity Bulletin*, January 1999.

[3] Managing director of a leading global fund of funds, *Asia Pacific Private Equity Bulletin*, January 1999.

[4] MSCI Free indices reflect actual buyable opportunities for global investors.

[5] Japan and Korea, with their highly educated workforce, sizeable domestic market, deep technological base, and global distribution channels and brands may be exceptions to this view.

[6] Investment director of a leading European fund of funds investing in Asia, *Asia Pacific Private Equity Bulletin*, January 1999.

[7] Goldman Sachs Investment Research – *Asia Internet,* 14 October 1999.

Part III

# Buyouts, mezzanine and specialised forms of finance

Chapter 7

# Management shrugged: the case for leveraged buyouts

Donald J. Gogel
*Chief Executive Officer, Clayton, Dubilier & Rice, Inc.*

More than a decade has passed since corporate raiders, junk bonds and the power of Drexel Burnham dominated the pages of the financial press and the agendas of major corporate boards of directors across the US. Yet, the impulse to improve financial performance through 'reengineering' operations, 'restructuring' portfolios and balance sheets or 'rethinking' strategy and organisation is still the dominate theme of corporate life.

In the rough and tumble world of competitive business, change and adaptation are critical to sustaining success longer than a brief moment in time. Shifts in technology, demographics, culture, fashion and customer needs demand a responsiveness that is difficult to manage for large corporate enterprises built primarily on the logic of economies of scale and functional prowess in engineering, manufacturing, marketing and sales.

Many chief executives today would describe their primary challenge as 'managing change', by which they mean both the need to build new skills and the effort to overcome the obstacles imposed by current and past practices. By their nature, corporations organise activities around products, customers, markets and functional activities. But the very act of organisation is a compromise with the future. As organisations try to achieve maximum performance on currently defined tasks they ensure a level of inflexibility that makes it difficult to anticipate and make changes to meet new market needs and match new competitive challenges. As they build new skills, they find those skills increasingly inappropriate for performing the tasks of the past.

More than anything else, LBOs are an opportunistic response to the difficulties encountered by current owners and managers to sustain or improve performance of their 'old' or 'non-core businesses' while they are building new capabilities for the future. Buyout groups ('private equity sponsors' in the more polished vernacular of the late 1990s) seek investments where current owners find themselves unwilling to undertake the next generation of changes required to fix businesses and make them more profitable. Often, and with good reason, these businesses are 'orphans' that have been unable to attract or warrant the management talent or capital needed to continue their growth.

This is no failure on the part of the current corporate owner. On the contrary, it is usually an extremely studied and appropriate response to changed conditions. The decision by the IBM Corporation to sell its Office Products Division in 1991 to Clayton, Dubilier & Rice (CD&R) reflected an assessment that IBM had more attractive opportunities than those presented by the low price/low margin typewriter and printer business which was increasingly coming to resemble the consumer electronics market. The decision by Westinghouse in 1994 to sell its Wesco distribution business reflected a strategic assessment that captive distributors were an ineffective channel to customers. The decision by the Gillette Corporation to sell its direct sales cosmetics business, Jafra, in 1998, reflected a judgement that a direct sales channel was never going to be compatible with Gillette's massive investment and franchise in the retail channel. All of these decisions rested on the calculus that concluded that the target business would not contribute to shareholder value.

Why then, if corporate strategists and boards of directors, armed with investment banker opinions, conclude that a business is not worth keeping, should an LBO firm be able to create value?

Of course, buyout firms do not always create value through the acquisition of unwanted corporate divisions. But the fact that they have succeeded often enough to attract more than US$100 billion from investors who believe in the magic of buyouts suggests that they may hold some structural or behavioural advantages that the buyout firms bring to bear in making their investments.

I believe that is exactly the case. Buyout firms have at least five relatively simple, key advantages that account for a great deal of their success:

1. The Hawthorne effect;
2. The 'vision thing';
3. A dream team of management all-stars;
4. Stock ownership and cash incentives; and
5. A sense of urgency.

## The Hawthorne effect

In a famous 1930s study of industrial organisation at the Western Electric's Hawthorne plant in Illinois, researchers found that productivity at the factory increased when changes were made in working conditions. A well-known, if obvious, conclusion of the study was that workers like to have people pay attention to them. The Hawthorne effect has since been used to describe changes in behaviour that are induced by management's 'paying attention'.

In many ways, buyout firms and management teams have the benefit of the Hawthorne effect as they negotiate, finance and close a leveraged transaction. First and foremost, a management buyout involves a change of control, an event that is by definition a transformation. The buyout unleashes a number of powerful forces that enable firms like CD&R to initiate a broad range of changes. The buyout process subjects management plans in every geographic, product and functional area to critical review, not only by the buyer, but also by the buyer's banks, and often by broader capital markets. Such a review typically challenges old ways of conducting business and forces the consideration (and sometimes adoption) of new business practices.

Although not necessarily part of the buyout process, buyouts are also associated with a host of attention-getting changes: a change in corporate name and logo, articles in the local newspapers, a new boss. Everyone is paying attention and, in such a setting, management teams are typically more successful in bringing about change.

When CD&R acquired the Allison Engine Company from General Motors Corporation in 1993, many of these factors came into play. Allison, a leading designer and manufacturer of aircraft engines, primarily under military contracts, was facing an uncertain future in face of major budgetary cutbacks. With a large unionised workforce that was assembled to meet the peak demands of production during the Reagan years, and new series of engines still in development, Allison had lost several hundred million dollars in the early 1990s.

The buyout of Allison was a very public event. National and local union leadership, the mayor of Indianapolis, bank lenders, lawyers, accountants and many others focused on the divestiture. Everyone expected change. Some feared a sale to another aircraft engine manufacturer that would, perhaps, close the factory and reduce employment.

When the acquisition of Allison by a fund organised by CD&R was finally completed, more than a year after the earliest announcements, the management team was ready to implement a series of changes to transform the military contractor into a leading manufacturer in key segments of both the military and commercial aviation markets.

## The vision thing

Buyouts also typically provide an occasion for thinking about business strategy, and an opportunity to reconsider assumptions about how a business tries to sustain (or regain) its competitive advantage. Elements of strategic thinking that help shape the investment rationale put forth by the buyout sponsor include consideration of the company in terms of:

- its low-cost position;
- its product positioning along price/performance parameters;
- its technology assets;
- its target markets and customers; and
- the breadth of its distribution channel.

The impetus for rethinking strategy starts with resource allocation. The very act of financing a buyout requires a host of assumptions as to how capital will be allocated, as well as the timing and level of return on investment.

At the same time, a buyout provides an effective platform to address external challenges, such as competitively disruptive technologies. The brand of dynamic business planning that has often been associated with successful buyouts is well suited to meet the demands of today's digital economy. Dealing with the impact of technology and the Internet requires the capacity to constantly rethink old business paradigms and to do so using time-frames measured in months rather than years. The management of Lexmark International demonstrated this ability when they realised the potential of their obsolescent assets while simultaneously investing in innovative new technology to make a different business for a different future.

## A vision for Lexmark International

When the IBM Office Products Division emerged as Lexmark International in 1991, CD&R and the new management faced a major challenge. They had to chart a new course to take the typewriter and impact printer business into the growing laser printer market dominated by Hewlett Packard. With unit volume and revenue from the 'old' product line in decline, a new strategy was urgently needed.

The vision of a new Lexmark did not emerge, phoenix-like, at the closing. Rather, it started with the insights developed by a few CD&R partners (notably Martin Dubilier and Chuck Ames) and the new management team, led by the chief executive officer, Marvin Mann, and chief technologist, Paul Curlander.

Curlander led a revitalised product development effort to develop faster and less costly laser printers and to reduce the product development cycle from 30 months to under 16 months. He also started on a path to increase the software capabilities of the company (as a result of which Lexmark subsequently became the leading provider in several parts of the market for networked laser printers). The company also started on the development of a proprietary inkjet technology that today supports the sale of more than two million inkjet printers a year. Mann and Ames helped to shape a new distribution strategy by establishing a dedicated sales force organised by industry segments. They subsequently expanded distribution even further, establishing retail distribution in more than 20,000 locations. The team also began developing a manufacturing strategy to shift new production of ink cartridges to Mexico, eastern Europe and Scotland.

Piece by piece, function by function, a new Lexmark began to take shape. Of course, such strategic repositioning could have taken place outside of a buyout setting. But the confluence of timing, people, capital, motivation and incentives that come together in a buyout made it more likely to succeed.

Lexmark today is a global leader in the printer market with over US$3 billion in sales and a market capitalisation of more than US$4 billion.

## A dream team of management all-stars

Many, if not most, management buyouts include the existing management team. Typically, with the help of the buyout firm professionals, a few new managers are recruited to the team. This usually occurs as a part of a systematic process to a assess the quality of managers in key jobs. At a minimum, this discipline forces an evaluation of management capabilities that is extremely difficult in most steady-state organisations where weaknesses are much more readily tolerated.

Since professionals in most buyout firms, particularly ones like CD&R that include seasoned corporate leaders from major industrial enterprises, have the experience to offer insightful and independent assessments of management talent. As a result, most buyouts lead to the addition of new managers in several 'skill positions', such as purchasing, finance and information technology. Occasionally, there are circumstances where an almost all-new management team must be recruited. This can occur when division managers are expected to return to the parent company at the close of the transaction, or in certain special circumstances. Kinko's was one of these special cases.

CD&R has been successful in attracting many extraordinary people to the ranks of its professional staff as well as to the management teams and boards of directors of its portfolio company. For example, in recent years the firm has attracted top executives from General Electric Company and IBM as full-time principals of the firm. It has recruited senior executives to leadership roles in its portfolio companies from Avon, Compaq, PepsiCo, Rockwell and Wal-mart. It has constituted boards with outstanding individuals, who have experience at Bechtel, Brascan, Eaton, ITT, McKinsey. McDonald's and Tyco international.

Although the opportunity to build a new or stronger management team is always available to a company, the dynamics of timing and expectations make it the rule in buyouts and the exception for most corporations.

## Stock ownership and cash incentives

The enormous run of the bull market during the past decade has focused a great deal of attention on the wealth created by stock options. But managers riding stock options are altogether different from managers investing their own capital and incurring recourse debt to invest in an LBO.

In a typical LBO, the senior management team of five or ten executives will purchase common stock representing a significant portion of the executives' net worth. The investment decision provides additional comfort to the buyout sponsors, who like to know that their executives are fully committed to the buyout.

Wesco Distribution, formerly the Westinghouse electrical supply distribution business, provides an instructive illustration of the power of stock ownership and how it focuses management on specific performance-enhancing mechanisms.

## Stock incentives at Wesco

CD&R acquired Wesco in 1994 for US$340 million. At the time, Westinghouse oversaw an array of organisations that ranged from manufacturing nuclear power plants to managing a chain of television and radio stations to making light bulbs. For the sprawling Pittsburgh conglomerate, its electrical products distribution division was not only a neglected unit, but a money losing one at that. Revenues of the conglomerate had fallen to less than US$1.6 billion in 1993 from US$1.8 billion in 1990, and employees were jumping ship at an annual rate of 25 per cent.

After the acquisition, CD&R introduced a new incentive plan to motivate and reinforce new behaviour. In addition to direct stock ownership, top managers of every CD&R portfolio company (and, often, mid-level managers and other employees as well) receive stock options, which vest with both length of service and attainment of performance goals. Bonus plans also are typically altered to link them more closely to specific targets. For example, Wesco's sales bonuses historically had been paid on return on investment targets, which allowed generous pay-offs on lower sales volume. Since the priority was to increase sales, the reward system was changed immediately to pay on gross margin dollars.

With the new emphasis on sales growth, the company also developed a new value system – one that began and ended with the customer. Wesco redefined its business strategy to include a sharper, market-segment oriented focus with a dedication to customer, employee and supplier satisfaction. Management started to anticipate and satisfy the needs of its customers rather than simply pushing specific products. It also began leveraging its sales force to build a highly effective national account strategy.

Wesco soon rebounded and achieved double-digit sales growth in 1995. Consumed with the need to bring about operational improvements and profitable change, Wesco increased sales and profits every year under new management, achieving operating income of US$80 million in 1997 compared to a loss of US$11 million in 1993. Wesco was sold to a financial buyer in 1998 for approximately US$1.1 billion, and its managers, who owned 17 per cent of the equity, were able to realise more than US$100 million on their original investment.

## A sense of urgency

Time is perhaps the greatest lever of all in an LBO. Although a long-term perspective is required in developing strategy, it is often an obstacle and can be used as an excuse for not moving quickly to implement required changes in a business.

At some level, a leveraged buyout creates a sense of urgency to get things done. The need to pay off a significant amount of debt certainly plays a role in creating that urgency. Monthly interest payments that often chew up 50 per cent or more of a company's cashflow tend to get the attention of every executive and, sometimes, all employees. The burden of annual amortisation payments is a major spur to action.

In a non-leveraged company, an increase in inventory levels is likely to engender a response measured in months. The inventory builds up during the last month of a quarter, but, since it is only a month, the increase will not draw attention. It is discussed in a quarterly operating review at the end of the next quarter. The responsible executive promises to address the problem and report on progress at the next quarterly review.

In a buyout, a good chief financial officer and line executive will have identified the build-up in the first month, and by the end of that month, in the first quarterly review, will report on actions being taken to address the issue. Follow-up will be weekly. This example may be overdrawn, but the sense of time moving at a different speed is not. And speed is a competitive weapon.

At Lexmark, development teams were able to reduce product development cycles from three years to 16 months. At Kinko's, the roll-out of a new self-service copier programme to all 900 stores took three months, compared with the year-long introductions that characterised the past. At Wesco, pricing changes are now implemented in real time. At Jafra Cosmetics, new markets have been established in Poland and Brazil in a matter of months, whereas past efforts were subject to long delays.

## Global change

It has been said that there is no resting place for an enterprise in a competitive economy. More than anything else, buyouts embody the principle that to build long-term value, incremental change won't work. What is required to reinvigorate a moribund organisation usually is exponential change; a relentless focus on bringing about operational improvements; the capacity and willingness to cut the Gordian knot. As a form of corporate ownership, buyouts produce a sense of urgency for change. There is the flexibility and capability to intervene quickly and decisively to reverse poor performance. No staggered boards. No poison pills. No need for proxy fights. The buyout sponsor has control and can intervene as needed. This capability is essential for taking businesses to places they would not formerly have even aspired to go.

The Hawthorne experiment illustrates that change can generate positive and even complex results. But change alone is not good or its positive effects always long lasting. Change must be coupled with a clear vision of what needs to be done to help a business improve its competitive advantage. It's not as simple as changing a light bulb. Something more is required than a management team that possesses the obvious skills to carry out the plan efficiently. Buyouts also create a uniquely self-critical environment to improve effectiveness, not just efficiency. They encourage management to turn the cube on its edge and do the right things for a business; not simply to do things right. As Peter Drucker, the well-known management expert, noted: 'There is surely nothing quite so useless as doing with great efficiency what should not be done at all.'

Likewise, there is clearly no shortage of change in an ever-shrinking global financial village. The changes taking place in Europe today are reminiscent of those in the United States in the late 1970s. With deregulation and economic integration, not to mention a growing appreciation of equity, Europe-based corporations are changing to deal with the inevitable competitive pressures of economic integration. Increasingly, they are divesting non-core divisions, pursuing wide-scale restructurings, or simply looking for long-term sources of capital for promising product development programmes, such as Fairchild Aerospace sought from CD&R and Allianz Capital Partners to fund its new generation of airline and business jets.

When the private equity industry was just forming some 20 years ago, corporate America considered many of the value-building initiatives radical. When management or corporate orphans shrugged back then, LBO teams shouldered what conventional wisdom saw as irretrievably troubled businesses. But that, too, has seen change and those same principles employed by buyout sponsors today are widely embraced. As companies around the world aggressively position themselves for what promises to be an even more competitive future, it is likely that they will look to private equity firms to provide the next generation of changes required to fix unwanted divisions -- the very same role buyout specialists have performed in restructuring US businesses.

Chapter 8

# Leveraged management buyouts at KKR: Historical perspectives on patient equity, debt discipline, and LBO governance[1]

George P. Baker
*Harvard Business School*

George David Smith
*Stern School of Business*

As with all forms of private equity investing, leveraged buyouts require close evaluation, sophisticated financing, diligent oversight and patience. What makes the LBO distinctive is that it employs high leverage in the initial financing, and that it is normally a rehabilitative acquisition strategy undertaken in mature sectors of industry where an underperforming (really undermanaged) companies are ripe for rejuvenation. It was in its formative stages, and remains, a highly specialised technique for acquiring assets and improving their value. What makes it historically important is that its impact – the lessons it has to teach about incentives for management and corporate governance – have spread to the wider corporate world.

Antecedents to the modern LBO can be traced back to the 19th century, if not before, but the modern LBO was developed gradually after World War II in arcane corners of small business finance. More often than not, the LBO was intended as a 'friendly' takeover strategy, in which a target company's key executives stayed on to run the companies that had been acquired and financially restructured. Kohlberg Kravis Roberts & Co. (KKR), whose founders helped pioneer the LBO at Bear, Stearns & Co. as early as 1968, was the first to apply the technique both systematically and successfully over a series of transactions. From 1976 to 1989, after which the long-sustained activity in M&A during the 1980s subsided, KKR completed 38 transactions, or 'deals', for their limited equity partners in five different LBO funds – pools of equity capital that KKR as general partner had discretion to invest in limited partnerships organised for discrete acquisitions.

In the early years, KKR's target companies were neither sick companies nor turnaround candidates – they were reasonably healthy concerns that could be improved through more aggressive management and better operating disciplines. From the beginning, Messrs. Kohlberg, Kravis and Roberts understood that the feasibility of any LBO had to be measured not by conventional measures of profitability, but rather by its cash flows,[2] which would have to be sufficient to pay down debt without debilitating operations.

Such deals were radical and daring by then conservative M&A financing standards; it was no easy business to find backers. High leverage offered prospects for high upside gains for lenders and equity investors alike, but left little margin for error. Bankers demanded their interest and principal on strict time schedules, and had to have faith in that they would get their due. On the other hand, it would normally take years to improve performance to the point where the market value of the equity would yield a high enough return to compensate equity investors for the risk of their investment. Hence, equity holders had to be patient, just as lenders had to have faith. The LBO was not some sort of get-rich-quick scheme. Over time, KKR would hold equity interests in the majority of its companies for an average of more than six years.

The combination of high risk and the need for patience was familiar in the small world of small company venturing, where KKR found some of its first allies. The firm's first equity fund was formed with less than US$35 million contributed by a few individuals along with a handful of banks where venture specialists could be persuaded to participate, and a few insurance companies.

Of course LBOs were quite different from cash-poor new ventures that could ill afford debt. Although modest in scale, the early LBOs were limited to closely held or small, cash-rich manufacturing companies in mature markets. Scepticism was hard to overcome, despite the success that Kohlberg Kravis and Roberts had with several small transactions at Bear, Stearns. KKR's first deal as a firm, in early 1977, was the buyout of A.J. Industries, a small conglomerate manufacturing company. It was impossible to persuade anyone to provide subordinated debt for the US$94 million transaction, and so the deal's 66 per cent leverage rested entirely on senior bank debt. In 1979, the US$380 buyout of the publicly traded stock of Houdaille Industries with 86 per cent leverage financed by a multi-layered array of senior and subordinated securities sent shock waves through Wall Street and the Securities and Exchange Commission. Prior to the deal being closed, the Houdaille stock had never been traded as high as KKR's offering price. That would never happen again. Post-Houdaille, KKR was able to attract a widening circle of institutional lenders, as well as equity investors. Five more funds with ever-increasing pools of equity capital were formed in the 1980s; the 1987 Fund invested more than US$6 billion in equity before it was finished.

By the mid-1980s, KKR was acquiring ever-larger companies across a wide spectrum of US industry: perishable consumer products, broadcast and cable television, food and speciality retailing, packaging, printing, real estate and natural resources. It was acquiring sick as well as healthy companies; the horribly mismanaged Beatrice Companies, acquired for more than US$8 billion, was one of KKR's more notable successes. After 1984, when the burgeoning market for high-yield securities suddenly made highly leveraged transactions feasible for multibillion dollar companies, KKR deftly exploited 'junk bond' financing and moved to the centre of the 1980s market for corporate control. In 1989, after its memorable acquisition of RJR Nabisco, had KKR been an industrial holding company, it would have ranked in sales fifth in the United States behind General Motors, Ford, Exxon and IBM.

Ranging in transaction value (equity investment plus financing costs) from the US$12.7 million Eagle/FB Truck Line deal in 1979 to the US$31.4 billion RJR Nabisco buyout in 1989, KKR applied the same basic, tripartite principle to virtually all 38 buyouts we studied in detail between 1977 and 1989. The principle was elegantly simple: (1) acquire undermanaged companies with high levels of debt financing; (2) make their managers owners; (3) monitor post-deal managerial performance rigorously – all for the sake of improving the long-term value of the assets. Virtually all the buyouts we studied have either been completely sold off or have had at least ample time to demonstrate how the initial investments actually turned out in the long run. What we found were some common patterns of success, even as we discovered a high degree of variation among acquired companies, potential sources of value creation and post-deal strategies for realising value.

## Financing leveraged acquisitions

Acquiring a company with high levels of debt – KKR's leverage (total debt-to-asset) ratios ranged from 58 to 93 per cent in our sample – had three key advantages for making LBOs work. In the first place, high levels of debt financing enabled equity investors with limited capital to realise huge gains as the debt was paid down. From management's standpoint, the high debt ratio shrank the equity portion of the financing of the deal to levels at which top executives could afford to buy into the deal with a significant portion of the equity, 10 to 20 per cent of it in many cases. From KKR's standpoint, the debt also served as a useful tool, as the need to make timely debt repayments compelled managers to improve performance. Indeed, the leverage in LBO financing served a paradoxical function. On the one hand it liberated managers, enabling them to become entrepreneurial owners of their businesses; on the other it shackled them to strict operating budgets, locked in, as they were, by external debt covenants.

There was no formula, strictly speaking, in the financing of a KKR buyout. Each company KKR decided to pursue (out of scores that were screened by its growing staff of professionals) presented a different set of opportunities and problems. Each financing was crafted to fit the perceived situation. Each took into account the preferences of lenders as well as the needs and capabilities of the companies involved. Each was designed to maximise operating cash flows through creative approaches to layered debt structuring and the minimisation of tax liabilities.[3] Each was unique in its combination of senior and subordinated debt and in the kinds of securities employed. Such flexibility was key to assuring success. It was never enough to ascertain that the company's stock was undervalued; it was important to form a clear picture of where and how value could be unlocked. James Greene, who joined the firm in 1986, learned just how specific each buyout transaction was, and just how much had to be settled in the minds of everyone concerned before the financing took place:

'It was a matter of understanding at the outset, before we bought anything, what the company's objectives were, how its management thought it was going to attain those objectives, what kind of capital they needed to spend, what kind of investment in R&D, people, equipment, software, and so on. Then we structured the balance sheet and leveraged the company appropriately.'

Nevertheless, some rules of thumb were worked out in the early years. There was an overarching financial framework within which the large majority of KKR's deals fit. In its pro forma plans, KKR would propose to acquire companies with about 10–20 per cent equity and 80–90 per cent debt. Of that, senior bank debt was to have fairly short (five-year) repayment requirements, while subordinated debt typically had somewhat longer terms. A typical plan for a KKR buyout would show an acquired company repaying the debt within five to seven years. By then significant gains in the operating performance of the assets would, one hoped, yield high enough returns to compensate for both the perceived risks of highly leveraged transactions and the premium over prevailing market values that had to be paid to buy out the departing equity holders.

KKR and other early LBO practitioners recognised that the key to 'super-normal' equity returns was the then rather unconventional idea that asset growth was not necessarily the path to value creation. The leverage in the deal was there to force changes in performance – in some cases radical downsizing and cost cutting; in others just incremental operating improvements; in still others aggressive expansion – that could be converted into long-term capital gains.[4] The role that debt played as a tool is worth emphasising, if only because it shows just how wrong prevailing abstract economic theories regarding capital structure could be in the real world. The way a company is financed not only affects its cash flows but also the way it is managed. Debt was not only a financing technique, but also a tool to force change in behaviour.

A good example is Fred Meyer, Inc., a West Coast retailing chain that KKR acquired in 1981. Realising that Fred Meyer's real estate holdings were seriously undervalued, KKR acquired them through a limited partnership separate from the one it set up to buy out the stores. This enabled KKR to borrow more for the deal, of course, but more important, by renegotiating the real estate leases with the operating company to reflect prevailing market rates, Fred Meyer managers were forced to change their priorities. They curtailed store expansion, which had been their wont, and focused instead on improving the profitability of existing properties.

## Governance and the LBO association

In its communications to its limited partners KKR always described the leverage in its buy-outs simply as a 'financial technique'. It was more than that. The leverage was inextricably linked to management performance in the post-buyout environment. If the price paid for a company were too high, the demands for debt repayment could undermine the best efforts of management to achieve long-term strategic and operating efficiencies. At the same time, the debt imposed an ironclad discipline on budgets, compelling management to take the actions necessary to fix short-term problems. The ability of managers to operate under the discipline of debt demanded competencies that were often untested in normal corporate environments.

To ensure that everything was working in timely fashion, the buyout firm exercised continuous oversight of the board. Indeed, as KKR's explained to its fund investors, 'the ongoing monitoring role [was] equally as important as the initial structuring and consummation of the transaction.' When the LBO deal closed, everyone – KKR and its equity partners, senior and subordinated lenders, and corporate management alike – 'bought in' to a strategy and operating objectives that would be constrained by high debt service for at least two to three years. Debt covenants and projections for meeting them became imperatives for improvements in economic efficiency. Nonetheless, the results were never predetermined. The ultimate success of a buyout was contingent on human factors, chief among them the relationship between the KKR-led board of directors and the company's top management.

In monitoring bought-out companies, KKR and other LBO firms developed a distinctively new form of business organisation, which in the jargon of institutional economics is called the 'LBO association'. Although it looks a bit like a conglomerate in that it is diversified and acquisitive, the LBO association is not a corporation and does not function like a holding company; it is a set of limited partnerships organised as discrete equity funds the LBO association allows its constituent companies to float on their own bottoms. There is no consolidation of accounts, intercompany transfers of cash, or cross-subsidisation. There are no forced interfirm sales, commonly imposed information systems, or any other attempts to achieve either uniformity in practice or operating, financial and technical synergies. There is 'no black book', KKR's Henry Kravis explained. 'We try to work with whatever structures and systems a company has used historically and go from there.'

Nor is the LBO association a mere portfolio of investments, since each company is actively overseen and influenced by the general equity partners. As it evolved, the LBO association became a means for imposing a common oversight regime through a commonly experienced group of LBO-seasoned board directors. Through its long-standing relationship with law firms, accountants and consultants, KKR could bring legal, financial and management expertise to meet specific organisational needs and could apply its experience in high-level financings, including public offerings and balance sheet restructurings. Most of all, KKR, whose professionals dominated each constituent company's board, could watch its investments closely and knowledgeably to a degree uncommon in the world of corporate governance.

The mission of the buyout board, from the first day of its control over a company to the last, was to ensure the creation of long-term value. This objective had to be managed carefully, as KKR often found itself acting as a buffer between managers with visionary goals and somewhat impatient institutional fund investors. Managers had to watch their costs, but they also needed support for their business-building strategies: funds for capital investment, for research and development, for marketing. 'We are long-term players,' KKR partner Perry Golkin explained:

'We can't manage quarter to quarter with respect to our fund investors. We often get pressured to issue monthly reports when we don't even want to do quarterly reports, because it misses the point philosophically. We still won't value the privately held companies more than annually. If the plan is to build value over time you think about things differently; you have to be patient.'

Patience was evidenced by the holding periods for most KKR investments. The mean number of years KKR held equity in (and hence influence over) its companies was 7.6 years; the median was 6.2 years. In only four cases was KKR able to sell off a company's equity for a satisfactory gain in less than four years. Such quick turnarounds occurred only when the market for a certain class of assets, such as cable television in the mid-1980s, was so robust that KKR seized the opportunity to realise the windfall for itself and its equity partners. Usually, value had to be created by long and sustained hard work, not by fortuitous circumstances.

Board governance at KKR was characterised by frequent contact between corporate executives and leading directors, who were most heavily engaged during the first three years or so after a buyout. Detailed written monthly reports sent to KKR formed the basis for ongoing discussions between CEOs and chief financial officers on the one hand, and KKR on the other. Formal board meetings were less important. Monthly and quarterly meetings were less important than the frequent conversations, sometimes daily, between director and manager.

Management decisions were to be listened to, questioned, and even debated, but rarely overruled. KKR exercised a board's authority to review and help implement strategic financial decisions. It provided advice on accounting and control systems. It insisted on continuous and interactive discussions with management. It did, in short, what corporate board directors are supposed to do, but it did not dictate corporate strategic or operating decisions or meddle with their implementation. And, as we show in more detail below, KKR boards proved to be willing investors in management strategies. Capital expenditures, investments in research and development, and employment were generally sustained or increased over pre-buyout levels in KKR companies. Charitable contributions and community involvement were encouraged.

Continuous communication – candid, informal and fluid – enabled KKR to better grasp the changing realities of its holdings while providing managers opportunities to get their ideas heard, their plans reviewed, and ultimately their strategies represented and defended to KKR's limited partners. As one manager put it, the KKR board process served not only as a monitoring device but also as a useful consultancy. 'I like to bounce ideas off of smart people,' he said, and 'KKR has an extremely dense population of smart people. It doesn't matter who you talk to, you get ... well-thought out answers, almost on any subject, but most certainly on those subjects where their strengths lie.' Those strengths, he noted, were precisely in those financial areas that KKR reserved to itself – in the buying and selling of businesses, in the arranging of financial market transactions.

Therefore, serious tensions in the boardroom were rare. Our interviews with KKR partners and company CEOs alike revealed little conflict. Chief executive Donald Boyce of Idex, for example, said that while it was natural enough for financiers and managers to see the world differently, KKR never interfered with his management of Idex. And although Charles Perrin, the CEO of Duracell, recalled a couple of boardroom conflicts, one over a stock buy-back proposal (management favoured it, KKR did not) and a plan to construct a new headquarters (KKR acceded after finding a less expensive way to finance it), such conflicts rarely arose. KKR partner Scott Stuart noted that directors tended to be more conservative than managers in post-buyout M&A activity, and that disagreements might surface over changes in capital structure that could alter management's stockholdings, but he could recall no systematic biases that divided managerial from investor interests in KKR firms. 'The fact that managers are so heavily invested financially in their businesses takes care of more than 90 per cent of the problems,' he noted. 'The rest, we simply work through.'

## No 'cookie-cutter' strategies

KKR saw its role as one of ensuring that managers were working day-in, day-out to make the major changes, the incremental improvements and the investments necessary to maximise longer-term shareholder value. How managers accomplished these tasks was left to them to decide; KKR was loath to impose its views on strategy or operating philosophy. Some companies aimed at creating value by streamlining bloated and inefficient operations through staff reductions, divestitures or through simple 'blocking and tackling', improving the efficiency of day-to-day operations and accounting controls. Others were charged with unleashing the entrepreneurial energies of former corporate subsidiaries. Still others found value in financial restructuring. All were aimed toward improving shareholder value and diminishing management's tendencies toward investments – pet projects, perquisites, acquisitions and employment growth – that had little prospect of flowing to the bottom line.

Former SEC commissioner Joseph Grundfest observed that 'the perception that many contemporaries had that the leveraged buyouts were mere "cookie-cutter" transactions was more fiction than reality.' This was especially true about what happened after the buyout financing was closed. Consider, as examples, two very different cases of post-buyout value creation.

## Safeway

Safeway Corporation, which KKR acquired in 1986 at a cost of US$4.8 billion, with 86 per cent leverage, was suffering from a severely non-competitive cost structure. It had too many workers earning wages that were far higher than industry average, too many money-losing stores and inefficient operations. Drastic measures, including store closings, renegotiated union contracts, layoffs and changes in work regimes, engendered a great deal of pain for employees and managers alike. One of the most important reforms was to evaluate the company's divisional managers not on sales, but on how well their operations earned a return on market value (ROMV).[5] This change encouraged division managers to work harder to keep costs in line and to become more alert to opportunities to sell off underperforming assets. Managers responded by paying closer attention to local store operations, labour efficiencies and inventory controls, and to sell off stores whose cash flows from operations did not justify their high-priced location. Since targets unmet were bonuses unearned, profitability and efficient asset utilisation replaced growth as the key measure of a division manager's success. It worked. By 1990, Safeway was once again poised for growth in employment and revenues. By 1997, when we completed our study, Safeway, despite many fits and starts, had long since resumed growth in revenues and employment, and KKR had earned on its 1986 equity investment an annualised return of 42.7 per cent.

## Duracell

Duracell Corporation presents an interesting contrast. As a division of Kraft, the processed food giant, the battery manufacturer was a classic 'orphan', – too small and too different from its parent company's other businesses to get the kind of senior management attention it required. The buyout was initiated by Duracell's managers, who felt hamstrung by what they regarded as laborious bureaucratic procedures, incessant meetings and corporate presentations, which they felt impeded their ability to implement their own company-specific marketing and investment strategies. In short, the problem confronting Duracell at the time of its buyout was not one of creating value through a restructuring of its business, but rather one of unlocking unrealised value in a basically healthy enterprise.

The plan KKR developed at the time of the buyout was simply for management to find the best way to increase business. There was no thought of divesting any assets after the buyout. Operating efficiencies were to be reaped by reorganising some underperforming operations, in particular by eliminating small plants and consolidating production. KKR encouraged Duracell to continue to increase its sales, to continue its international expansion, to promote its products through aggressive marketing and advertising, and to invest in the research and development necessary to make its batteries longer-lived and more environmentally friendly. In other words, KKR, would simply unshackle Duracell's management to grow their business in accordance with what CEO Robert Kidder and his staff had projected in a very aggressive five-year plan, a plan that promised annual sales growth at more than 15 per cent. What Duracell's management had to learn was how to focus on cash flows and efficient asset utilisation, taking into account the opportunity cost of the capital employed in any given operation. They began forecasting the performance of their investments on the basis of 'economic value added' measurements that were designed to assess projects and performance in ways that reflected valuations in the capital market. It was these types of measures that helped align the thinking of management with that of investors.

From the outset, KKR supported Duracell's strategies for growth and innovation. Developing new products was a priority for Duracell's management. 'Not once in the seven or eight years that I was there working with them', said Robert Kidder, 'did Henry Kravis or George Roberts, or any one of the board members, ever ask, "How can we cut R&D?" In fact, they asked just the opposite, "Should we be investing more in R&D in order to insure that we have a technological edge for the long haul?"' By the same token, as owner-managers Duracell's executives sensed the limits of their ambitions, and exercised appropriate restraint. 'Did we all of a sudden go crazy spending capital,' Kidder asked rhetorically? 'No. Did we all of a sudden give crazy increases in compensation? Absolutely not. After all, we also owned the company.'

Duracell's new products – environmentally friendly and longer-lived batteries made from new materials along with novel marketing and packaging innovations – breathed new life into a sleepy industry, earning extraordinary returns. Cash from operations increased by an annual compounded rate of 17 per cent between 1989 and 1995. Higher gross margins were achieved through improved manufacturing efficiencies – the results, largely, of new capital investment, as well as of rigorous cost control systems that had been put in place soon after the buyout. On the sale to the Gillette Corporation of their remaining holdings in Duracell, KKR, after nearly eight-and-a-half years, had reaped a 40 per cent annually compounded total return on its original equity investment.

## Distressed deals and reputation

Leverage is especially unforgiving to weak financial structure, poor business judgement or bad management. It is also possible for good decisions and sound stewardship to be overwhelmed by such uncontrollable factors as market dislocations and threats from the larger social and political environment. Accordingly, not all of KKR's deals we studied succeeded. KKR experienced problems in many of its investments made during the years 1977–89, but the vast majority of those problems were remediable. During that period, four of KKR's fund buyouts defaulted (through either technical default or actual missed payments.) Three, Eaton Leonard, Seaman Furniture and Walter Industries, filed for bankruptcy. Eagle/FB Truck Line (EFB), a US$12.7 million deal, did not file for bankruptcy, but was liquidated after a strenuous attempt over a three-year period to make good on its debt. Of course, KKR's shortcomings are most often associated with its largest investment, RJR Nabisco, which actually never went into default, but failed to generate meaningful returns to its equity investors.[6]

There is not enough space in this chapter for detailed explanations, but briefly the reasons for failure were controllable as well as uncontrollable situations. EFB was a poor candidate for leverage; it was operating in a regulated industry dependent on highly cyclical revenues, and the quality of its management was uncertain at best at the time of the buyout. When deregulation of the trucking sector occurred, soon after the buyout, EFB was swept away by the competition. Eaton Leonard, a high-growth speciality machine tool manufacturer, was more like a new venture in its economic characteristics, hence unsuited for leverage. Its demise was hastened by poor management and weak monitoring. Seaman Furniture was a regional company caught in a regional recession. Compounding the problem, according to KKR's own analysis of that company's bankruptcy, was that its CEO had not been required to invest enough of his own net worth in the business after the buyout, and he soon lost interest. There was no one to replace him from within the ranks, and good talent outside was hard to find. By contrast, Walter Industries, a diversified construction business bought out in 1987, would have been a successful deal had it not been laid low by litigation involving a former subsidiary that had once manufactured asbestos-related products. Walter's operations grew steadily more efficient following the buyout, but its cash flows became hostage to the claims of plaintiffs.

Our finding on RJR Nabisco is that its post-buyout problems had no single cause. To say that KKR overpaid for the company (the common assumption as to what happened) is too simplistic. That company's first big problem, a looming threat of default, occurred because KKR overleveraged the buyout with variable rate securities. RJR Nabisco's balance sheet was insufficiently robust to cope with the temporary collapse of the junk bond market in 1990. The flexibility that had been a hallmark of most KKR deals was missing here. A reset provision on the junk bonds employed in the original financing posed a more severe limitation on the company's ability to meet its debt service than had been anticipated in KKR's worst-case projections. To deal with this crisis, KKR restructured the RJR Nabisco debt, doubling its equity investment in the company.

After that, RJR Nabisco looked as if it could still be highly profitable over the longer term. In its initial public offering in 1991, the company issued 115 million shares of common stock, which was snapped up at US$11.25 per share, representing a doubling in value of the US$5.61 blended cost of KKR's equity investments. But by May 1993, RJR Nabisco's stock had plunged to around US$5.50 per share, and it has languished at low levels ever since. A combination of cut-throat competition in the tobacco industry and increasing social and legal pressures on tobacco products undercut RJR Nabisco's remarkably successful efforts to shed underperforming assets, improve management discipline and increase operating efficiency.

The fate of those buyouts is revealing not only what could go wrong, but how the LBO firm had to function in adversity. Managing buyouts meant managing the relationships with everyone who had a stake in them. At the moment a buyout is concluded, its leveraged capital structure bound managers, owners and lenders alike into a community of interests to which the buyout firm was responsible. Financial distress would inevitably cause friction among these constituencies. Bankers would weigh in with their covenants, bondholders with their claims, and equity owners with their pleas for patience. It was in KKR's interest not simply to seek to honour its debt obligations, but to work hard to resolve the tensions between different classes of lenders, and also between lenders and owners. In some of its faltering buyouts, as with EFB and Walter, KKR made extraordinary efforts over several years to work through problems in order to repay lenders, even as the prospects for equity returns grew dim. In the case of RJR Nabisco, KKR finally got out by swapping that company's shares for those of Borden, Inc. The equity holders to this date have earned little or nothing on their investment in that deal, but the lenders could not complain.

Such sustained commitment to resolving financial problems, even when the game was up for the equity investors, was built into the incentive structure of the buyout business. Why did KKR not simply walk away from its small investment in EFB? Why did it not do the same with Walter Industries? Once it became clear that legal liabilities would impair its ability to generate returns to the partnership, it would seem to have been easy for KKR, with its huge pool of invested equity, to bail out from the US$143 million invested in Walter. KKR's concern for creditor interests was tied to longer-term motives; its success in raising money for future transactions depended on its reputation, not simply for making money, but for dealing fairly with all its investors. As George Roberts put it:

'We didn't have a perpetual capital source like General Motors .... We were accountable to all our investors – lenders, fund partners, managers – all. It was their money. I didn't like losing my own money, but I hated losing someone else's worse than I did my own. We had to take all those relationships seriously.'

## Legacies

Markets mature, profits attract competition and innovations become commonplace. By the mid-1980s, buyout techniques had become more widely appreciated by both worthy and less competent new practitioners of the art. As competition increased, the market for corporate control overheated. The prices of all corporate assets rose to levels that made leveraged deals more risky. Then, in 1990, the wave of mergers on which the expanding LBO market had been riding came to an abrupt end. The collapse of the junk bond market and new political and regulatory pressures made highly leveraged transactions more difficult to finance. Squeezed on all sides by growing competition, poor market conditions, political pressures and public hostility, the buyout seemed permanently crippled if not doomed. Yet, contrary to predictions, the management buyout was revived as the 1990s progressed. A corporate restructuring wave began to swell in 1992, and US M&A deals grew to a staggering US$1 trillion in aggregate annual value in 1997. Equity and cash were the preferred currency in the 1990s for corporate-financed acquisitions, but opportunities for leveraged transactions soon resurfaced, even if not at the levels they had reached in the mid-1980s. Equity became more advantageous for corporations to issue, banks were more likely to demand higher coverage of senior debt with cash flow, and LBOs employing very high levels of leverage became far less common. Leverage ratios were closer to 60–75 per cent, rather than 80–95 per cent, even for smaller deals. While these lower levels of leverage might dampen equity returns somewhat, 60 per cent was usually high enough to keep managers on point during the critical, early stages of post-buyout operations.

LBOs, meanwhile, had become standard components of institutional equity portfolios. This once exotic financing technique moved from the peripheries of corporate finance into the mainstream – so much so that the most formidable competition to buyout firms came from the so-called 'strategic' or corporate buyers of undervalued assets. Speciality houses proliferated as well. In 1997, there were estimated some 800 'LBO equity' partnerships. Most were small boutiques, but the high end of the market had also become crowded with more than able practitioners – firms like Hicks, Muse, Blackstone Group, and Donaldson, Lufkin & Jenrette.

While some observers worried that too much money might be chasing too few deals, the LBO began to spread to Europe, and was arousing interest even in the more closed corporate environments of Asia. Even in the United States, companies would continue to fall into disrepair. The more creative LBO houses found niches in which they could more easily exploit their firm-specific strengths. Those with turnaround management skills, such as Clayton & Dubilier, looked for opportunities among troubled divisions of large corporations. Others focused on particular industries to which they could bring concentrated managerial and financing expertise. Some chose to remain small and concentrate on a few select transactions. Still others – like Blackstone and the Carlyle Group – teamed up with strategic buyers in joint acquisitions, adding equity capital and sophisticated financial expertise to the corporation's managerial acumen and industry-specific knowledge. Welsh, Carson, Anderson & Stowe, a specialist in the health care and information industries, provided most of the subordinate debt financing in addition to the equity for its deals, which enabled it to compete more directly with strategic buyers. KKR could capitalise on its long-standing reputation for meeting its obligations and its accumulated experience in financing buyouts across a wide range of industries under a variety of investing conditions. Perhaps more important, the firm had shown an uncommon ability to attract, train, acculturate and keep talented practitioners. Turnover of professionals at KKR was very low.

Under more competitive condition, buyout firms came under pressure to reduce their fees, even as they had to be wary of overpaying for deals. When KKR launched its campaign for the 1996 Fund, it was met with demands for 'pooling' – that is, the aggregation of profits and losses across the deals – in order to achieve what institutional investors were calling for: a better 'alignment of interests' between general and limited partners. Henceforth, KKR would derive its carry – its profits on deals – from the net of total Fund profits and losses. Under the terms of its 1996 Fund agreement, KKR also adjusted its traditional transactions and management fees so that they would come down in percentage as investments grew larger.

As the buyout became more common, its influence on corporate strategy and governance took wider root. Its basic principles – aligning management and ownership interests, insisting on more accountability to investors, imposing more rigorous board oversight – had penetrated the executive suites and boardrooms of the nation's leading corporations. KKR's last deal of the 1980s was but one example for corporate executives to follow. The organisation of K-III (now Primedia, Inc.) was an acquisitions partnership between KKR and a group of managers with no initial assets. The partnership's mission was to seek out and acquire companies in specialised information media. In setting up K-III, KKR was effectively outsourcing LBO functions to trusted experts in a defined set of related businesses. This 'leveraged build-up' demonstrated how the buyout principle could be extended to the strategies and structures of corporations themselves.

Large investors have also gained much from the experience of buyout activity. While anti-takeover legislation in many key states and more sophisticated poison pill defences have given incumbent managers breathing room, institutional investors have become more assertive than ever before, pressing board directors for timely information and justification of corporate policies. Institutional investors learned that they had the ability, as well as the right, to use the power of equity to reform underperforming corporations. Although institutional investors are not represented on corporate boards, they can always get a hearing. They have become more vocal in their reactions to managerial problems and have been increasingly influential in pressuring board directors to link executive pay to performance as reflected in equity values. Within the boardrooms, non-executive directors have increasingly acquired significant equity holdings in the companies they oversee. While there can be little doubt that most boards remain creatures of their corporations' CEOs and are not very effective in their monitoring, they are less supine and more likely to move against poorly performing managers when problems begin to surface.

An even more significant impact has been made on corporate executives. Today, managers are generally more concerned with maintaining 'core competencies' rather than expanding lines of business, with maximising economic values than with building corporate empires, with promoting entrepreneurial behaviour in the ranks rather than reinforcing bureaucratic compliance with the status quo. Corporate budgeting has become more rigorous, organisations less fat, and restructuring more routine throughout the corporate economy. All this has occurred as managers have relearned the virtue of hitching their personal fortunes to those of their shareholders. In 1997, the Business Roundtable's new 'Statement on Corporate Governance' reflected a profound change in the collective thinking of the nation's more prominent senior executives. '[T]he principal objective of a business enterprise is to generate economic returns to its owners,' it states. 'If the CEO and the directors are not focused on shareholder value, it may be less likely the corporation will realise that value.' The statement goes on to emphasise the utility of aligning shareholder and managers' interests with compensation systems that link both managers' performance and board monitoring more closely to stock values. That corporate profits and productivity have been rising substantially for the first time in decades is due in part to the results of these changing attitudes and behaviour among owners and managers alike.

As for the financial community, an important lesson from KKR's experience is that there is no easy path to long-term success through financial engineering. The mere use of leverage to acquire the 'undervalued' equity of companies was never a formula for getting rich quick. LBO equity investments had to be as patient as the debt was impatient. It was only through a carefully nurtured combination of flexible financing, strong management talent, well-structured incentives, active board monitoring and constant attention to the details of problems that KKR could earn consistently good returns on its investments. Overall, KKR's investments yielded the extraordinary returns to justify their risks. The full economic return on all its investments was 28.2 per cent per annum from 1976 to 1977, or double that of the S&P500.[7]

In a more fundamental historical sense, KKR's legacy is this: its management buyouts helped to breathe new life into the moribund state of American capitalism, which in turn stimulated a new era of sustained economic growth, vibrant securities markets and, at the time of writing, nearly full levels of employment. Many macro- and microeconomic factors have contributed to these happy circumstances, yet the catalytic role of the management buyout cannot be denied. Once scorned as a dangerous form of paper capitalism, it demonstrated the beneficial effects of linking the interests of managers and owners in the common pursuit of value. It showed how creative financial strategies could impel and assist corporate reform and how varied the paths to value creation were. It showed how rigorous board oversight mattered to the health of an enterprise. As both a prod to action and as an example, the management buyout has helped to restore American business to its vital promise.

---

[1] This chapter is adapted from *The New Financial Capitalists: Kohlberg Kravis Roberts and the Creation of Corporate Value* (Cambridge University Press, 1998), from which all quoted materials are drawn. The book contains more detailed analyses of the events referred to in this chapter, along with complete data on transaction costs, leverage ratios and returns for all KKR transactions up to 1997.

[2] The cash flow of a company is typically measured as earnings before interest and taxes (EBIT). This principle can be refined to include the adding back of non-cash expenses, such as depreciation and amortisation, in a measure often presented in accounting reports as EBITD, EBITDA, EBDIT, EBDITA, or simply 'cash flow from operations'.

[3] Much has been made of the role of tax strategies in KKR deals, which employed schemes, now disallowed by the IRS, such as 'step-ups' in depreciation schedules, acquisitions through 'mirror subsidiaries', and the like. It is important to understand that tax strategies were not in themselves major sources of value creation so much as a strategic imperative to enable KKR to outbid other potential buyers.

[4] To see how this works in general terms, imagine an all-equity company that is bought for US$100 million. Before the acquisition, this company generates US$10 million in cash flows, just enough to give shareholders a 10 per cent return. The acquisition is financed with US$90 million in debt and US$10 million in equity. The company is then able,

though improved operations, superior asset utilisation and careful capital investment, to increase cash flows from US$10 million to US$20 million per year, without either increasing or decreasing the value of the assets. By paying no dividends, and by using this US$20 million in cash flow strictly for debt service, this company can pay down the US$90 million of debt (at an interest rate of 10 per cent) in about six years. At the end of that period the company would still be worth US$100 million, but it would now be all equity. In other words, the original US$10 million equity investment has been transformed into one worth US$100 million for a 47 per cent compound annual rate of return!

[5] ROMV was calculated as cash flows from each store divided by the appraised (expected market) value of its assets; this required an analysis of thousands of leases and contracts. Diverse accounting procedures were translated into standard GAAP formats in order to get a distinct and comparative picture of each division.

[6] The industry-wide data are imprecise, but Kaplan and Stein, using a sample of 124 of the largest leveraged buyouts in the 1980s, find a default rate on LBO debt of about 2 per cent on buyouts organised before 1985 and a default rate of about 27 per cent on buyouts organised between 1985 and 1989. Of these later defaults, slightly more than a third went formally bankrupt. Steven Kaplan and Jeremy Stein, 'The Evolution of Buyout Pricing and Financial Structure in the 1980s', *Quarterly Journal of Economics* (1993), pp. 313–57.

[7] After KKR's management fees and 'carry,' or its percentage of the profits, the full economic returns on KKR's first seven funds as of year end 1977 are as follows: 1976 (seven deals), 39.9 per cent; 1980 (eight deals), 29 per cent; 1982 (five deals), 47.6 per cent; 1984 (eight deals), 33.4 per cent; 1986 (four deals), 36.1 per cent; 1987 (13 deals), 16.1 per cent. The 1987 Fund's return has been depressed by the low 2.8 per cent return from KKR's over-sized investment in RJR Nabisco/Borden Inc. The stated returns for KKR's investments from its 1993 Fund are obviously immature, but as of year 1997, the total return for that fund was posted by KKR as 27.7 per cent. For fuller details on fund investments and individual company returns, see the appendix of *The New Financial Capitalists* (Cambridge University Press, 1998).

Chapter 9

# The evolution of US corporate governance: we are all Henry Kravis now

Steven N. Kaplan
*Leon Carroll Marshall professor of finance,*
*Graduate School of Business, University of Chicago*

The 1980s brought a phenomenal dollar volume of corporate takeovers and restructuring activity. The annual value of acquisitions exceeded 6 per cent of the (year-end) market value of US equities in only nine years between 1968 and 1996. Seven of those years were in the 1980s (see Exhibit 1). The annual measures understate the true extent of takeovers and restructurings in the 1980s because many firms substantially restructured without being taken over. According to Mitchell and Mulherin[1], 57 per cent of large US firms were either takeover targets or restructured on their own between 1982 and 1989.

In addition to the unusual volume of activity, takeovers and restructurings in the 1980s were distinguished by their use of leverage and their hostility. The takeovers and restructurings of the 1980s coincided with and helped to cause an increase in corporate leverage in the United States. With the increase, leveraged buyouts (LBOs), Kohlberg, Kravis & Roberts (KKR) and Michael Milken became household names. The extent of this activity was so great that from 1984 to 1990, net new issues of equity were negative. While acquisition activity has rebounded since 1992, the volume of highly leveraged transactions has not (see Exhibit 2).[2]

The 1980s also saw the emergence of the hostile takeover and the corporate raider. Raiders like Carl Icahn and Boone Pickens became household names. Mitchell and Mulherin [1996] found that more than 30 per cent of a given sample of firms:

- had received explicit hostile takeover bids (bids pursued without the acquiescence of target management); or
- were restructured in response to hostile pressure (particularly purchases of blocks by corporate raiders).

However, despite the recent upsurge in acquisition activity, raiders have not reappeared and hostile takeovers have become less frequent. Exhibit 1 shows all acquisition volume as a percentage of total year-end stock market value for the years 1964 to 1996.

While acquisition activity has dropped since 1992, the volume of highly leveraged transactions has not. This is demonstrated in Exhibit 2.

This chapter considers why LBOs and raiders were prominent in the 1980s, and, to a lesser extent, what drove takeover activity during that decade. It then examines US corporate governance today and offers explanations as to why LBOs and raiders have not reappeared to

Exhibit 1

**All acquisition volume as a percentage of total year-end stock market value, 1964–96 (%)**

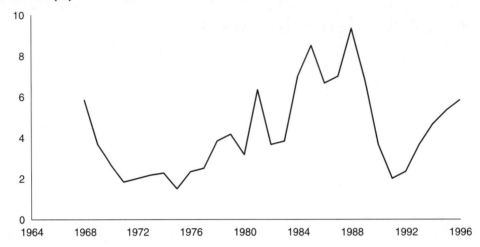

*Sources:* Mergerstat, author's calculations.

Exhibit 2

**Going-private volume as a fraction of total stock market value, 1976–96 (%)**

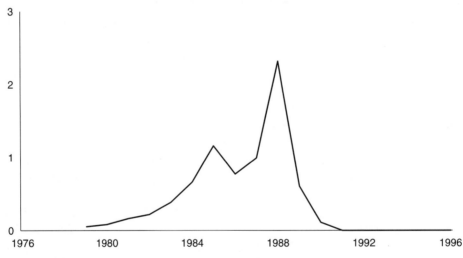

*Sources:* Mergerstat, author's calculations.

the same extent despite the recent resurgence of takeovers. One important reason, as will be argued here, is that today's shareholders, boards, and managers have learned the lessons of the 1980s. In that sense, we are all Henry Kravis now. Reference is made to a number of publications that have been used in the preparation of this chapter. Readers wishing to look at the issues discussed here in more detail will find footnotes and the bibliography at the end of the chapter useful.

## The takeover and restructuring wave of the 1980s

### The insights of LBOs

The LBOs of the early 1980s were based on four insights.

- Firstly, the high amount of debt incurred in LBO transactions imposed a strong discipline on the managers of the buy-out company. It was no longer possible for managers to treat capital, particularly equity capital, as being without cost. On the contrary, failure to generate a sufficient return on capital meant default.
- Secondly, LBOs provided managers with substantial equity stakes in the buy-out company. These stakes gave managers the incentives to undertake the buy-out, to work hard to pay off the debt and to increase shareholder value. If successful, the company managers could expect to make a great deal of money. One estimate[3] reports that chief executive officers in LBOs increased their ownership stake from 1.4 per cent pre-LBO to 6.4 per cent post-LBO. Management teams, overall, experienced similar increases. In 1980, this approach to executive compensation differed fundamentally from common practice. At this point, management ownership of stock and options was modest. Management was loyal to the corporation, not to the shareholder.[4] Managers wanted continuity and growth because that was good for employees.
- Thirdly, LBO sponsors and associations monitored the leveraged companies closely. Unlike public company boards that were large and dominated by distant outsiders with small ownership stakes, LBO company boards were small and dominated by LBO sponsors with substantial equity stakes (and a vested interest in the success of the company).
- Finally, the LBOs of the early 1980s also benefited to some extent from favourable tax rules.[5] These rules were eliminated by the Tax Reform Act of 1986.

What did these insights lead to? In the first half or the 1980s, the LBO insights led to great success. As documented in Kaplan and Kaplan and Stein[6], buy-out companies experienced improved operating profits and few defaults. Adjusting for the overall stock market or industry, these early buy-outs generated abnormally positive returns. Because the overall stock market increased over this period, buy-out sponsors earned substantial nominal returns. These results led some Jensen[7] to argue that the advantages that LBOs offered were so great that public corporations would soon disappear.

The LBO experience was substantially different in the latter half of the 1980s. Many LBOs defaulted, some spectacularly. As Kaplan and Stein[8] document, roughly one-third of the LBOs completed after 1985 subsequently defaulted on their debt. This led to much criticism of LBOs and, in fact, of the philosophy of the early 1980s as a whole. But did this default experience mean that LBOs insights were wrong?

The evidence[9] indicates that it was not, even in the late 1980s. Overall, the larger LBOs of the later 1980s also generated improvements in operating profits, notwithstanding the relatively large number of defaults.

Even for deals that defaulted, research[10] shows that the LBO companies retained approximately the same value they had attained before the LBO. In other words, the net effect of the LBO and default on capital value was slightly positive. The case of Federated Department Stores described by Kaplan[11] illustrates this effect.

Campeau's 1988 acquisition of Federated is still widely considered the nadir of LBOs and the 1980s (see Loomis and Rothchild)[12]. Yet the facts say otherwise. On 1 January 1988,

Federated's debt and equity traded at US$4.25 billion. From that point until the company emerged from bankruptcy in February 1992, Federated returned roughly US$5.85 billion in value (adjusted for changes in the S&P 500). In other words, Federated was worth US$1.6 billion more because of Campeau than it would have been if it had matched the S&P 500. Unfortunately for Campeau, he paid US$7.67 billion (again, adjusted for the S&P 500).

Combining the marginally positive results for LBOs that defaulted with the largely positive results for LBOs that did not default, leads to the conclusion that, on average, LBOs, even in the late 1980s, increased value substantially.

The logical question is, if LBOs increased value, why did so many default? The answer is simple. The success of the LBOs of the early 1980s attracted entrants and capital to the LBO market. Those entrants understood the basic LBO insights. Because so many understood the insights, the purchase prices for LBOs began to reflect the insights. As a result, much of the value of the improved discipline, incentives and governance accrued to the selling shareholders, rather than to the post-buy-out LBO investors. The key point is that the combination of gains, to pre-and post-buy-out investors was positive overall. The LBO insights and benefits were real.

## Why the takeover and restructuring wave of the 1980s?

More generally the takeover wave of the 1980s appears to have been a capital market response to corporate governance deficiencies. This is the only explanation that satisfactorily explains the takeover wave.

Jensen argues[13] that changes in technology, regulation, competition and capital markets led to a large amount of excess capacity in US corporations. According to Jensen, the capital markets in the 1980s provided the necessary catalyst to eliminate that excess capacity because internal control systems (incumbent management and boards of directors) largely failed to bring about a timely exit. Leveraged acquisitions, LBOs, hostile takeovers and stock buy-backs were particularly successful in eliminating excess capacity. This was because the debt service requirements that usually accompanied them prodded managers into finding ways to generate cash (and prevented them from wasting it). Jensen also places emphasises on the improved management incentives associated with LBOs and raiders who pursue hostile takeovers.

A second major explanation is articulated by Shleifer and Vishny,[14] who argue that 'the takeover wave of the 1980s was to a large extent a response to disappointment with conglomerates' that had been assembled in the conglomerate acquisitions of the 1960s. Corporate America 'returned to specialisation.' Companies sold unrelated businesses and expanded into related businesses. 'To a significant extent the 1980s reflect the deconglomeration of American business. Hostile takeovers and leveraged buy-outs … facilitated this process.'[15]

While there is undoubtedly some truth to both the excess capacity and specialisation explanations, neither fully explains the 1980s. Jensen's notion of excess capacity makes some strong assumptions about investment. He argues that firms involved in takeovers and buy-outs were spending too much money on capital expenditures. If Jensen is right, after the corporate control transaction, these companies should have been spending less. The evidence for this, unfortunately, is mixed.

Kaplan and Stein find strong evidence[16] that management buy-out firms make large cuts in capital expenditures. Servaes[17] however finds no evidence to suggest that targets of all takeovers, of hostile takeovers and of going private transactions over-invest in capital expenditures before the takeover. Furthermore, Healy, Palepu and Ruback[18] find no evidence of significant changes in capital expenditures to sales for a sample of large takeovers in the early 1980s. Using qualitative data, Bhagat, Shleifer, and Vishny[19] find no evidence of this either.

Shleifer and Vishny[20] make the strong prediction that US business became less diversified during the 1980s and that the deconglomeration value was increased. Again, the evidence in support of these arguments is less strong than is commonly believed. While US business did become less diversified during the 1980s, the decrease was not large.

For example, Montgomery[21] finds that the typical S&P 500 firm in 1991 had the same number of industry segments as the typical S&P 500 firm in 1981. Similarly, Liebeskind and Opler, and Comment and Jarrell[22] find only modest declines in diversification during the 1980s. Finally, Mitchell and Mulherin[23] find that takeover activity in the 1980s clustered in particular industries at particular points in time. In contrast, takeover activity in the 1960s and 1970s exhibited no such clustering. These results seem less about breaking up conglomerates than about restructuring industries.

The most convincing explanation for the 1980s, articulated by Donaldson,[24] argues that the rise of institutional shareholders and the greater availability of information to the capital markets placed more pressure on corporate management to maximise shareholder value. He calls the 1980s the 'decade of confrontation'.[25] The governance and ownership structures of the 1960s and early 1970s were not sufficiently efficient for the financial markets of the 1980s. As of 1980, management was loyal to the corporation, not to the shareholder. This loyalty led to under-utilised resources – organisational slack, operational slack, and mismatched product lines.

The 1980s introduced shareholders to the possibility of rebellion. Mechanisms that had not existed before were open to them. The results shown in some studies[26] that takeovers are more likely for firms with relatively low valuations is consistent with this explanation.

In sum, the takeover and restructuring wave of the 1980s is best explained by an ascendancy of the capital markets over corporate managers. This is shown in a variety of ways:

- in some cases, the capital markets reversed ill-advised diversification;
- in others the capital markets helped to eliminate excess capacity; and
- in others still, the capital markets disciplined managers who had ignored shareholders to benefit other stakeholders.

LBOs and the insights behind them are particularly representative of the changes that the capital markets imposed.

## Corporate governance in the 1990s

At the end of the 1980s, the takeover wave ended. As Exhibits 1 and 2 show, both takeover and LBO volume declined substantially in 1990. At the time, anti-takeover legislation and jurisprudence, overt political pressure against leverage and a credit crunch were among the explanations proffered for the decline.[27]

Since then, the political pressure against leverage and the credit crunch have both abated, yet LBO volume and raiders have not reappeared. Furthermore, the resurgence of takeover activity in general suggests that anti-takeover laws and amendments are not terribly effective. The most compelling explanation for the rise and fall of LBOs and raiders is that shareholders and corporations increasingly obtain the benefits of LBOs and raiders on their own. In other words, we are all Henry Kravis now (or at least, like Henry Kravis was in the early 1980s).

## The application of LBO insights

Corporations have achieved the three primary LBO insights without actually doing LBOs. Recall that the LBO insight is to impose a cost of capital on management, so that management does not view (equity) capital as costless. Corporations (and consulting firms) now implement this insight through innovative performance measurement and compensation programmes. The best-known of these programmes are marketed by consulting firms. For example Stern Stewart markets economic value added (EVA), and The Boston Consulting Group (and its Holt Value Associates subsidiary) markets cashflow return on investment (CFROI). EVA, CFROI and their analogues compare the after-tax profit earned by a company or division to the after-tax profit required by the capital invested (the product of capital employed and the weighted-average cost of capital).[28]

While it is reasonable to argue that these programmes do not impose as much discipline as the debt in an LBO would, it is unreasonable to argue that these programmes do not impose any discipline at all. (These programmes also avoid financial distress costs that are sometimes associated with LBO debt.)

There is also anecdotal evidence that companies increasingly approach decisions with the goal of maximising shareholder value. For example, consulting firms such as McKinsey & Co. routinely measure the effects of their consulting assignments on shareholder value.[29]

Compensation committees and consultants increasingly apply the second LBO insight – providing more high-powered incentives to top executives. In a widely cited article Jensen and Murphy,[30] find that the compensation of top executives in the United States is relatively insensitive to the performance of their companies' stock. This appears to be changing. The use of stock options, restricted stock grants and other forms of equity-based compensation has increased substantially over the last few years. A recent paper by Hall and Leibman[31] finds a remarkable increase in equity-based compensation for chief executive officers in the United States. From 1980 to 1994, the average annual CEO option grant (valued at issuance) increased more than sevenfold from US$145,000 to just under US$1.2 million. As a result, equity-based compensation made up almost 50 per cent of total CEO compensation in 1994, compared with less than 20 per cent in 1980. This increase, combined with the strong performance of the stock market is partially responsible for the even larger realised increases in top executive compensation.

Again, the increased emphasis on equity-based compensation among corporations in general has as its direct antecedent the emphasis by LBO sponsors on such compensation. Indeed, it is arguably the case that the large pay-offs earned by LBO sponsors and, more importantly, by the top executives of LBO companies, made it more acceptable for top executives of public companies to become wealthy through equity-based compensation. Coca-Cola's US$100 million-plus restricted stock grant to Roberto Goizueta, and Scott Paper's compensation contract for Al Dunlap are two of the more prominent examples.

Finally, public companies appear to be increasingly applying the third LBO insight – closer and more active monitoring by boards and shareholders. There is increasing pressure on boards to become more active and more shareholder-oriented.

For example, the National Association of Corporate Directors[32] calls for a substantial increase in equity-based compensation for directors. Milstein[33] has called for boards to become more active, and has helped implement that recommendation in a number of institutions. In a survey of institutional investors, Felton et al.[34] find that many will pay a premium of approximately 10 per cent for companies with good corporate governance. Given these developments, I would confidently predict that boards will continue to evolve to be more like LBO boards – smaller boards with more equity ownership.[35]

Shareholders have also increased the pressure they place on corporate boards and corporate management. CALPERS (California Public Employees' Retirement System), USA, and the Council of Institutional Investors have mounted active and public campaigns against a selected group of underperforming and undergoverned public companies. Other investors (the most prominent of whom include LENS and Michael Price's Mutual Shares) appear to target underperforming, undergoverned companies one at a time and attempt to change governance (and performance at those companies. In other words, today's institutional shareholders are the raiders and LBO sponsors of the 1990s.

Although the academic literature indicates that these campaigns have met with mixed success,[36] it seems likely that the pressure – overt, covert and implied – from shareholders has increased. This is important because it means that companies and their boards are likely to initiate LBO-type responses without overt, or even covert, pressure. In other words, 'the hand writing is on the wall', and companies are responding to it.

## Why is all this happening now?

While it is clear that public companies are increasingly applying the insights emphasised by the LBOs of the early 1980s, it may be less clear whether this will continue. To answer that question, it is important to understand why all this is happening now. There are at least three interrelated reasons.

- Firstly, the shareholdings of professional, institutional investors continue to increase. For example, Poterba and Samwick[37] show that individual ownership of corporations in the United States declined from 70 per cent in 1970, to 60 per cent in 1980, and to 48 per cent in 1994. Those figures include the ownership of private companies. Individual ownership of public companies is even lower. This means that sophisticated shareholders, who like higher stock returns, own an increasingly large fraction of US corporations.
- Secondly, in 1992, the Securities and Exchange Commission (SEC) substantially reduced the costs to shareholders of coordinating challenges against underperforming management teams by relaxing the proxy rules regarding shareholder communications. Under the old rules, any time a shareholder wanted to talk to 10 other shareholders, that shareholder had to file a detailed proxy statement with the SEC before talking to others. Under the new rules shareholders can essentially communicate at any time in any way as long as they send a copy of the substance of the communication to the SEC afterward. The rule change has lowered the cost of coordinating shareholders and challenging management teams, because it has reduced the money and time that has to be spent obtaining SEC approval. It is telling that the Business Roundtable and other management organisations were extremely hostile to this rule change when it was proposed. Combined with the increased concentration of institutional holdings, means that it is now substantially less expensive for several large shareholders to confront managers and boards of underperforming companies.

Exhibit 3

**Capital income relative to tangible assets, 1959–96**

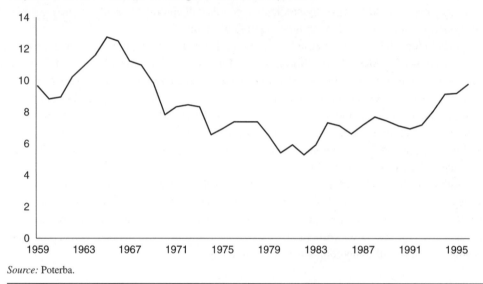

*Source:* Poterba.

- The third reason for the corporate governance changes we see today is the SEC's requirement, introduced in 1992, that public companies provide more detailed disclosure of top executive compensation and its relation to firm performance, particularly stock performance. This requirement had two effects. First, it focused boards of directors on stock performance. Companies now routinely report firm, industry and market stock performance in their proxy statements. This represents a substantial shift from the pre-1980s, when companies were more likely to focus on earnings-per-share, growth and other measures that might or might not affect company stock performance. The requirement also makes large equity-based compensation packages defensible, if not desirable. Boards of directors are unlikely to be criticised by shareholders or by the press if company executives are compensated based on stock performance. Executive compensation will be high only if the company has performed well.

## Is there any evidence that corporate performance has improved?

If corporate governance has improved since 1980, first through the wave of takeovers and restructurings, and then through pressure from institutional investors, corporate profitability should have improved as well. Of course, many other factors are involved, so this comparison can only be suggestive rather than definitive. Nevertheless, Poterba[38] finds that US corporate profitability has rebounded significantly since the early 1980s. Exhibit 3 shows Poterba's data, which measures the sum of corporate profits and interest relative to tangible assets. This series bottoms out in the early 1980s.

## How well does the US system work?

Both US capital markets and US corporate governance have been successful relative to those of other countries over the last 15 years. In the 1980s, some observers[39] compared the US systems unfavourably with the German and Japanese systems, which were seen to be superior, particularly in their ability to manage for the long term. Other commentators[40] assert that Japanese and German managers face many of the same 'incentives' as managers in the United States, including dismissal for poor earnings and stock performance.

The main difference is that the United States provides stronger incentives to maximise shareholder value when performance is not obviously poor (through greater management equity holdings, takeovers and an increased ability to pay cash out to shareholders). With the clear successes of the US capital markets over the last 15 years, the German and Japanese systems have begun to move closer to the US model.

Despite the recent US successes and the ascendancy of shareholder power, some observers still argue that the US system is badly flawed. Although it is impossible to test this definitively, the fact that there has been a resurgence in takeovers, but not in plain vanilla LBOs (particularly of public companies), suggests that US companies are obtaining, or being pushed to obtain, many of the benefits of LBOs and takeovers. As institutional investors and boards continue to become more sophisticated, I would expect them to become more proficient at securing these benefits.

This chapter is an amended and updated version of an article that originally appeared in, and is reprinted with permission from:
*The Journal of Private Equity* Volume 1, Number 1, Fall 1997.
© Euromoney Institutional Investor plc. All rights reserved.

## Bibliography

Jensen, M.: 'Takeovers: their causes and consequences', *Journal of Economic Perspectives*, 2 (1998).
Mitchell, M., and Lehn, K.: 'Do bad bidders become good targets?', *Journal of Political Economy*, 98 (1990).
Romano, R.: 'A guide to takeovers: theory, evidence, and regulation', *Yale Journal on Regulation* (1992).
Stewart, B.: *The Quest for Value*, Harper Collins (1991).

---

[1] See Mitchell, M., and Mulherin, H.: 'The impact of industry shocks on takeover and restructuring activity', *Journal of Financial Economics* (1996).

[2] Exhibit 2 presents Mergerstat's series of going private transaction volume. While such transactions technically include both leveraged buyouts and non-leveraged buyouts, as a practical matter, they consist almost entirely of LBOs.

[3] Kaplan, S.: 'The effects of management buyouts on operations and value', *Journal of Financial Economics*, 24 (1989a), pp. 611–632.

[4] As discussed in: Donaldson, G., and Lorsch, J.: *Decision Making at the Top*, New York Basic Books (1983); Donaldson, G.: *Corporate Restructuring*, Harvard Business School Press (1994); Jensen, M.: 'The modern industrial revolution', *Journal of Finance* (1993); and Jensen (1988).

[5] See Kaplan, S.: 'Management buyouts: evidence on taxes as a source of value', *Journal of Finance*, 44 (1989b).

[6] See Kaplan (1989a) and Kaplan, S., and Stein, J.: 'The evolution of buyout pricing and financial structure in the 1980s', *Quarterly Journal of Economics* (1993).

[7] See Jensen, M.: 'The eclipse of the public corporation', *Harvard Business Review*, 5 (1989).

[8] Kaplan and Stein (1993).

[9] Kaplan and Stein (1993).

[10] See Andrade, G., and Kaplan, S.: 'How costly is financial (not economic) distress? Evidence from highly leveraged transactions that became distressed', working paper, University of Chicago (1996).

[11] Kaplan, S.: 'Campeau's acquisition of Federated: post-bankruptcy results', *Journal of Financial Economics* (1994a).

[12] See Loomis, C.: 'The biggest, looniest deal ever', *Fortune* (18 June 1990); and Rothchild, J.: *Going for Broke*, Simon and Schuster (1991).

[13] Jensen, M.: 'Agency costs of free cash flow, corporate finance and takeovers', *American Economic Review*, 76 (1986); and Jensen (1988, 1989 and 1993).

[14] Shleifer, A., and Vishny, R.: 'The takeover wave of the 1980s', *Science*, 249 (17 August 1990).

[15] Shleifer and Vishny (1990).

[16] Kaplan (1989a) and Kaplan and Stein (1993).

[17] Servaes, H.: 'Do takeover targets overinvest?' *Review of Financial Studies*, 7 (1994).

[18] Healy, P., Palepu, K., and Ruback, R.: 'Do mergers improve corporate performance?', *Journal of Financial Economics* (1992).

[19] Bhagat, S., Shleifer, A., and Vishny, R.: 'Hostile takeovers in the 1980s: the return to corporate specialisation', *Brookings Papers on Economic Activity: Microeconomics* (1990).

[20] Shleifer and Vishny (1990).

[21] Montgomery, C.: 'Corporate diversification', *Journal of Economic Perspectives*, 8 (1994).

[22] Liebeskind, J., and Opler, T.: 'The causes of corporate refocusing: evidence from the 1980s', working paper (1994); and Comment, R., and Jarrell, G.: 'Corporate focus, stock returns and the market for corporate control', *Journal of Financial Economics*, 37 (1995).

[23] Mitchell and Mulherin (1996).

[24] Donaldson (1994).

[25] Donaldson (1994).

[26] Morck, R., Shleifer, A., and Vishny, R.: 'Alternative mechanisms for corporate control', *American Economic Review* (1989); and Berger, P., and Ofek, E.: 'Bust-up takeovers of value-destroying diversified firms', *Journal of Finance* (1996).

[27] For a discussion of these explanations see: Jensen, M.: 'Corporate control and the politics of finance', *Journal of Applied Corporate Finance* (1991); and Comment, R., and Schwert, G.W.: 'Poison or placebo?', *Journal of Financial Economics*, 39 (1995).

[28] The after-tax profit used in this calculation is not the company's actual net income, but a construction, referred to as NOPAT (net operating profit after-tax), which measures the after-tax profit that the company would have earned if it did not have any debt. For a more detailed description of one of these programs, EVA see Stewart [1990].

[29] For McKinsey's approach, see Copeland, T., Koller, T., and Murrin, J.: *Valuation: Measuring and Managing the Value of Companies*, John Wiley & Sons (1994).

[30] Jensen, M., and Murphy K.J.: 'Performance pay and top management incentives', *Journal of Political Economy*, 98 (1990).

[31] Hall, B., and Leibman, J.: 'Are CEOs really paid like bureaucrats?', working paper, University of Harvard (1997)

[32] National Association of Corporate Directors: 'Report of the NACD Blue Ribbon Commission on Director Compensation' (1995).

[33] Milstein, I.: 'The evolution of the certifying board', *Business Lawyer*, 48 (1993).

[34] Felton, B., Hudnut, A., and Von Heeckeren, J: 'The dollar value of board governance', *Mckinsey Quarterly* (1997).

[35] For a description of LBO boards see: Gertner, R., and Kaplan S.: 'The value-maximising board', working paper, University of Chicago (1996).

[36] For example, see: Gillian, S., and Starks, L.: 'Relationship investing and shareholder activism by institutional investors', working paper, University of Texas (1995); and Opler, T., and Sokobin, J.: 'Does coordinated institutional activism work?', working paper, Ohio State University (1996); and Smith (1995).

[37] Poterba, J., and Samwick, A.: *Brookings Papers on Economic Activity* (1996).

[38] Poterba, J.: 'Recent developments in corporate profitability', working paper, MIT (1997).

[39] Porter, M.: 'Capital disadvantage: America's failing capital investment system', *Harvard Business Review* (Sep–Oct 1992).

[40] Kaplan, S.: 'Top executive rewards and firm performance: a comparison of Japan and the US', *Journal of Political Economy*, 102 (1994b); and Kaplan, S.: 'Top executives, turnover, and firm performance in Germany', *Journal of Law, Economics, & Organisation*, 10 (1994c).

Chapter 10

# Chameleon of the 1990s: considering mezzanine finance and its place in the spectrum of private equity investments

Ron Kahn and Susan Wilson
*Duff & Phelps, LLC*

## 'Is it debt, or is it equity?'

For years, mezzanine investors have been asked the question. Categorising mezzanine securities as debt or equity has always been difficult because mezzanine securities are a hybrid of debt and equity. These securities are typically structured as an unsecured note, subordinated to all senior debt, and combined with a detachable warrant or equity position in the issuing company. Thus, mezzanine providers have a dual role as both lenders and investors. Providers of mezzanine capital are often described as 'schizophrenic' because they sometimes behave like lenders while at other times they act like equity investors. As lenders they are concerned about the stability of cashflow, high interest and fixed-charge coverage, and the amount, amortisation and collateral of senior debt with priority to them. But as equity investors, they are equally interested in 'upside', or the potential ability of a company to achieve superior results and create value for shareholders.

As a response to this moderately schizophrenic position, the mezzanine market has evolved into a bifurcated market marked by two different camps of providers who approach mezzanine finance quite differently. One camp, consisting primarily of insurance companies, takes a lending approach to mezzanine. These providers tend to focus, above all, on the preservation of capital in their transactions, emphasising such issues as consistent historical cashflows and the strength of the equity sponsor. The second camp of providers leans toward an equity approach to mezzanine groups. Comprised of mezzanine limited partnerships and several commercial bank mezzanine groups, these providers focus on capital appreciation in their investments.

This bifurcation is a result of the market becoming more efficient, offering different mezzanine solutions based on the specific risk/return parameters of an individual transaction. Market bifurcation is a positive trend and the two groups will likely continue to co-exist because they provide different capital alternatives for different issuer needs.

## Insurance companies as mezzanine providers

Historically, insurance companies have been the largest providers of mezzanine capital for acquisitions and growth capital of middle-market companies. Insurance companies exhibit a number of characteristics that make them well suited to providing longer-term mezzanine capital and also help explain their investment approach. Firstly, the composition of their liabilities (life insurance policies and annuities) is well matched to investments with longer average lives. This is in contrast to those commercial banks that are funded mainly by consumer deposits. Secondly, because of their long-term investment horizon, insurance companies are less concerned about the short-term earnings fluctuations often found in middle-market companies. Finally, insurance company providers are generally welcomed by both middle-market companies, which often find their growth stunted by lack of capital, and senior lenders, because mezzanine capital represents long-term, uncollateralised capital, junior to a senior lender.

Insurance companies typically bring a portfolio approach to mezzanine capital, which explains why their demand and pricing for mezzanine capital may fluctuate over time. Because they manage large investment portfolios, the investment officers responsible for mezzanine transactions are familiar with a wide variety of asset categories and are able to understand where mezzanine capital fits along the risk/return spectrum. Returns available on senior notes, junk bonds and public equities provide a benchmark for comparing returns on mezzanine capital and may affect the appetite an insurance company has for this type of security. As interest rates and securities' spreads fluctuate, insurance companies can, and do, adjust the returns demanded of new mezzanine transactions.

## Others enter the market

The rates of return realised by insurance companies on their mezzanine investments attracted the attention of traditional senior lenders such as banks, commercial finance companies, and savings and loan institutions that were eager to improve their return on assets. As a result, during the mid-1980s, senior lenders provided mezzanine capital by 'stretching' beyond their traditional cashflow lending parameters to finance a greater portion of a company's capital structure. In such situations, the distinction between true senior debt and subordinated or mezzanine debt was blurred. Often, all of the interest-bearing capital of a transaction was characterised as senior debt. No separate layer of the capital structure was carved out with rights subordinate to those of a senior debt holder because the senior debt and the subordinated debt were provided by the same party. However, the senior lender would require some form of equity interest or warrant to compensate for the additional risk assumed by lending beyond traditional formulae. The existence of a warrant for the senior lender indicated that mezzanine risk was being assumed for some portion of the senior debt financed.

For many traditional senior lenders, providing stretch senior debt with a warrant was their first experience of funding mezzanine capital. However, inevitably as some of these original stretch loans developed credit problems, the benefit of having stand-alone mezzanine capital became apparent. Especially in troubled situations, the distinction between mezzanine capital and senior debt regarding priority is critical. Separate note agreements and an inter-creditor agreement help define the rights of each party as far as distressed credits are concerned. These issues led several commercial banks to organise separate units responsible for originating, evaluating and monitoring the bank's mezzanine transactions. These groups grew and developed their own identities and philosophies, and continue to be active providers of mezzanine capital.

## The mezzanine credit crunch

The financing environment changed dramatically in late 1989 as purchase-price multiples peaked and portfolio problems began to emerge among those institutions most heavily involved in financing leveraged buy-outs and real estate. The lending practices of both banks and insurance companies came under increased scrutiny by federal regulators who were determined to avoid a repeat of the savings and loan debacle. Higher-risk transactions now required correspondingly higher capital reserves, in effect making the former more costly to provide. Portfolio concentrations of higher-risk credits could also lead to rating downgrades for financial institutions. These issues created a 'flight to quality' among stretch senior lenders and insurance companies during the period 1990–91. Many sharply curtailed their lending to middle-market companies, creating the opportunity for a new group of third-party mezzanine providers, distinct from insurance companies and traditional senior lenders, to enter the market.

## Development of mezzanine limited partnerships

Mirroring the fund-raising process followed by private equity limited partnerships, experienced mezzanine professionals, many of whom had worked as mezzanine providers at insurance companies or banks, organised special-purpose mezzanine limited partnerships (MLPs) to provide mezzanine capital to middle-market companies. MLPs are funded primarily by pension funds and endowments that are characterised by a portfolio mentality that allows them to view mezzanine as an alternative investment, well diversified within a much larger investment portfolio. Unlike insurance companies, pension funds and endowments lack the in-house infrastructure necessary to originate and monitor individual mezzanine transactions. Therefore, they entered this asset class as limited partners, relying on experienced mezzanine professionals (the general partners and fund managers) to make individual investment decisions.

The incentive compensation structure of MLPs is perhaps one of the most important characteristics affecting the investment decisions of these funds. Like the private equity partnerships on which they were modelled, the general partners of an MLP receive an annual management fee, generally determined as a percentage of the fund's size and designed to cover operating expenses. Also, more importantly, the general partner receives a 'carried interest' or percentage of the capital gains realised on investments, a perk designed to align the interests of both the fund manager and the limited partners by motivating the general partner to select attractive investments.

Therefore, while limited partners receive capital gains in proportion to the amount they contribute to an MLP, general partners usually receive a carried interest of 20 per cent of any fund profits to reward them for investing wisely. This provides a strong motive for investing in transactions that create significant capital appreciation. Many commercial bank mezzanine units have followed suit by allowing their mezzanine professionals to share in the capital appreciation of their investment portfolio. (This has become a key strategy in retaining mezzanine professionals who might otherwise be lured away by MLPs.)

## Interest rates and mezzanine availability

While portfolio quality and ratings issues instigated the flight to quality among insurance companies, the declining interest rate environment of the early 1990s contributed to their continued absence from the mezzanine market. As large investors in fixed-income securities, insurance companies benefited handsomely from declining interest rates, posting strong results, often risk-free, on their bond portfolios. This environment presented less incentive for insurance companies to pursue re-entry into the mezzanine market. As investors who manage large portfolios of diverse securities, insurance companies behave with a portfolio mentality. Events in related securities markets have a direct impact on their investment appetite in the mezzanine market.

Rising interest rates were important in motivating insurance companies to re-enter the mezzanine market during 1994. Just as the bull bond market kept these investors out of the market earlier, the fixed-income bear market of 1994 drove insurance companies in search of investment alternatives providing more attractive returns.

## The bifurcated mezzanine market

The divergent backgrounds and motivations of insurance companies, commercial bank mezzanine groups, and MLPs have created a bifurcated mezzanine market. The history and personal motivations of these different investors may explain how their investment philosophies differ and why the market has diverged.

From an historical standpoint, the development of mezzanine capital into a stand-alone layer of the capital structure highlights the pricing differences between senior debt and mezzanine capital. Throughout the mid-1980s to the early 1990s, a rather wide disparity existed between senior debt, typically price between prime and prime plus 200 basis points, and mezzanine capital, priced to yield roughly an annual compounded internal rate of return (IRR) of 20–25 per cent. This pricing disparity produced an opportunity to create a security designed to fit between these two products along the risk/return spectrum.

As previously discussed, the investment philosophy of insurance companies is driven by their portfolio approach and broad experience as investors in a variety of asset categories included fixed-income securities, public equities, and real estate. From this vantage point, insurance companies could readily identify the pricing disparity between senior debt and mezzanine capital. Also important to note, insurance companies do not have the staff required to provide heavy monitoring of individual investments and must allocate their scarce resource (personnel) as efficiently as possible. Consequently, upon their re-entry into the mezzanine market, insurance companies were well positioned to target mezzanine investments that fitted along the lower end of the risk/return spectrum. Such investments provide attractive returns relative to alternative investment opportunities (fixed-income, public equities) while requiring less intensive credit monitoring. As a reflection of this strategy, insurance companies may be more likely to invest in companies characterised by strong historical earnings, stable and predictable cashflows, diversification of both products and customers, an experienced sponsor (ideally, a large private-equity fund), and a well-capitalised balance sheet.

These motivations are more consistent with a lending approach to mezzanine investing. Insurance companies are likely to be the primary providers of this type of mezzanine capital, focusing more on higher-quality investments that emphasise the preservation of capital. Also, they may value a strong equity sponsor – one capable of providing portfolio monitoring and supplementary capital – more than potential capital appreciation. In exchange, these investors are willing to accept correspondingly lower risk/return parameters for their investments. Accordingly, the current all-in IRR on these type of investments will hover around the 16 per cent and 20 per cent range.

Alternatively, the incentives and compensation structures of the commercial bank mezzanine groups and MLPs motivate these investors to focus more on capital appreciation in their investment decisions. Because these individuals can gain personally from capital appreciation, they tend to have more of an equity approach to mezzanine investing, focusing on the potential upside of a transaction. Such mezzanine investors are often more willing to devote greater resources to transaction origination and portfolio management, again emphasising an interest in creating value through this process. Also, these investors may be more willing to pursue transactions that have weaker capital structures, partnering directly with management themselves. As a result, this capital tends to require IRR in the 21–25 per cent range.

The mezzanine market, comprising lenders and investors who have different funding sources and motivations, is very different from the senior debt and private equity markets. While the senior debt market includes a variety of different financing sources such as banks and commercial finance companies, the way in which individual lending officers across such institutions are compensated is fairly uniform. Likewise, private equity professionals generally tend to be compensated with base salaries supplemented by equity incentives in their portfolio companies. The mezzanine market is unique in that its professionals have varying personal and institutional motives that drive their investment philosophies. Among the most important groups of mezzanine providers – insurance companies, commercial bank mezzanine groups, and mezzanine limited partnerships – both institutional and personal motivations have diverged, creating a bifurcated mezzanine market.

## Capital flows to mezzanine

What determines the amount of capital allocated to the overall mezzanine market? Do capital allocation decisions affect market bifurcation? Understanding the factors that determine capital allocations helps explain why the mezzanine market has evolved to its current state.

### Pension funds and MLPs

Public and corporate pension funds are some of the most important institutional investors funding MLPs. These investors categorise mezzanine as an 'alternative investment' along with real estate, private equity and hedge fund investments. When making a decision about whether or not to invest in MLPs, pension funds generally compare and evaluate mezzanine returns against those achieved by the private equity market. However, the benchmarking of mezzanine against private equity leads to some interesting results.

With no clear way of 'risk adjusting' mezzanine returns, many pension funds avoid the mezzanine category altogether. If mezzanine is benchmarked against private equity without any adjustment for risk, its returns generally will appear lacklustre. A mezzanine group with a gross portfolio IRR of 25 per cent appears inferior to a private equity fund with an IRR of 35 per cent. While conceptually accepting that mezzanine may be less risky than private equity, the investment officer for alternative investments is evaluated on the overall return of the alternatives portfolio, and does not benefit from maximising the risk-adjusted return. Thus, benchmarking appears to be a critical factor in explaining the flow of pension fund money into the mezzanine category.

121

Those pension funds that do invest in mezzanine tend to back funds that are strongly equity-oriented in their investment approach. While more traditional, debt-oriented mezzanine may offer compelling returns *vis-à-vis* its risks, pension funds appear more interested in capital appreciation for their alternative asset portfolios. If they are going to invest in mezzanine, they will typically lean towards funds that seek transactions without sponsors, or take a meaningful preferred or common equity position along with their traditional mezzanine investment. They prefer to back mezzanine groups with a gross IRR of closer to 30 per cent and a strong equity orientation.

## Insurance companies

Who is backing more traditional, debt-oriented mezzanine? Institutions that benchmark mezzanine against the bond market, insurance companies being the best example. Insurance companies tend to have an excellent understanding of the risk-adjusted yield curve. When mezzanine, on a risk-adjusted basis, looks attractive compared to other fixed-income investment alternatives, insurance companies tend to increase their capital allocations to mezzanine. Coincidentally, we are aware of at least one insurance company that benchmarks mezzanine against a combination of high-yield debt (60 per cent) and the Russell 2000 index (40 per cent). The actual percentage weighting is a true indication of an investor's debt versus equity orientation.

## Commercial banks

In general, commercial banks tend to benchmark against the bond (or debt) market. For example, when the senior debt market becomes competitive and price sensitive, banks' interest in mezzanine tends to peak. Banks and bank mezzanine groups seem to perceive a better risk/return opportunity in mezzanine as opposed to commercial lending, and such benchmarking drives their capital allocation.

Although banks may benchmark against the bond market, they may be the most opportunistic of all mezzanine investors. That is, they can be either debt- or equity-oriented in their investment approach. The best bank mezzanine groups grow from institutions with experience in both private equity and senior lending. While their understanding of the bank lending market enables them to evaluate debt-oriented mezzanine investments, their private equity background provides them with the skills necessary to consider more equity-oriented mezzanine. This unique perspective allows them to invest in either type of mezzanine investment, and it is up to them to select those with the best risk/return dynamics.

How investors benchmark mezzanine investments determines how they allocate capital to the mezzanine market. Pension funds benchmark mezzanine against the private equity market, often without an adjustment for risk. Thus, they tend to back mezzanine funds with an equity-oriented investment approach. Insurance companies benchmark against the bond market, increasing their capital allocation to mezzanine when its risk/return parameters look attractive compared with junk bonds. Finally, banks also benchmark against the bond (or senior debt) market, increasing their allocations as mezzanine looks more attractive than traditional senior loans. Thus, capital allocations themselves influence and help drive the bifurcation in the mezzanine market.

## The mezzanine market today

Today, the equity-oriented mezzanine groups (especially MLPs) are competing directly with private equity sponsors and developing innovative deal structures in order to be competitive. MLPs bring a different perspective than private equity investors to some of the more critical issues of equity investing such as return requirements, control, and carried interests. We have seen mezzanine investors develop innovative structures that allow owners and managers to gain greater ownership and control up front and retain it as planned if performance goals are met. This perspective is in contrast to that of a private equity sponsor who is only willing to let management earn additional ownership *after* performance is proven. Such diverse tactics as current pay interest, payment-in-kind dividends, contingent warrants, claw-backs, trigger events, puts, priority distributions, and many more, have all been effectively deployed by mezzanine funds to win over management teams, yet justify their risk/return requirements.

Historically, mezzanine investors generally have not had majority control of their investments. In fact, mezzanine investors usually hold warrants for far less than 50 per cent of any one deal. The most seasoned mezzanine investors understand the risks involved in minority investing and have spent years learning how to influence without holding the reins. In contrast, control is often an important hallmark of private equity investing. Many equity funds are specifically charged with taking a control position in their investment. As a result we have seen management teams favour mezzanine investors that do not make control the threshold issue in investment decision. Management teams that are confident of their company's prospects are all too willing to provide mezzanine investors with more stringent covenants and other corporate governance rights in order to preserve control.

The equity ownership offered to management ('carried interest') is another area where private equity investors may be less flexible than their mezzanine counterparts. The carried interest of between 20 and 25 per cent that private equity firms offer their management teams, whether earned at close or performance based, has become a standard within the private equity world. Why? This may relate to the issue of control and a need to own 51 per cent of a company. Or perhaps it is because it parallels the carried interest that most fund general partners are able to negotiate from their limited partners. However, from a mezzanine investor's viewpoint, if the numbers work at a higher carried interest level, there is every reason to offer more, especially when tied to performance. This is particularly true in competitive situations. Today, winning the support of management is often a critical element in winning a deal. With the flexibility to take minority positions and offer more than a traditional 20 per cent carried interest, equity-oriented mezzanine funds can be the darling of management teams.

## Where the trends may lead

By re-evaluating traditional views about control and equity incentives, mezzanine groups seem to be carving out a niche for themselves in financing both traditional middle-market companies and management buy-outs. We expect this trend to continue with equity-oriented mezzanine groups continuing to evolve as direct competitors to private equity funds. The pressure to achieve portfolio returns in the mid-20 per cent range in order to successfully raise subsequent funds will drive MLPs, in particular, towards an ever-increasing equity approach in their investment decisions.

In contrast, the debt-oriented mezzanine providers can be expected to continue seeking transactions with lower risk/return profiles. Driven by an ongoing need to invest large dollar amounts efficiently, we expect mezzanine investors to pursue transactions with risk parameters closer to those of a high-yield bond and more debt-oriented in nature. Thus, market bifurcation should continue within the mezzanine industry for some time as different providers pursue transactions with divergent risk/return expectations.

This chapter is an amended and updated version of an article that originally appeared in, and is reprinted with permission from:
*The Journal of Private Equity* Volume 1, Number 4, Summer 1998.

Chapter 11

# Private financing of public companies

Gianluca Cicogna and Claudio Guazzoni
*Zanett Lombardier Fund*

There are numerous links between private and public equity. Among the many ways private and public markets may be linked, public companies may be a source of investment opportunities for private equity investors. Such investments may take the form of a buy-out, where a company or one of its divisions is taken private or in a private purchase on special terms of a portion of a public company's equity. In the latter case, the private equity investor purchases stock at a discount and the companies get timely and direct access to capital when they need it.

This chapter provides an overview of:

- the evolution of the market for private placements in the United States from the issuer's perspective;
- the growth of private placements as a viable investment strategy from the investor's standpoint; and
- the approach used by sophisticated investors, showing how it is possible to enhance returns and reduce volatility in private placement investment portfolios.

## The issuer's side of the private placement market

We define the modern private placement market as having commenced in the early 1990s and continuing through to the present. In the early 1990s, the issuer universe was small and there were a correspondingly small number of dedicated investors in private placements. Private placements were the financial instrument of choice for highly speculative companies that were otherwise unable to access the capital markets in a timely manner.

During much of the 1990s, as the market developed, private placements were increasingly used to supplement more traditional methods of financing such as secondary public offerings. At the same time, issue sizes increased. Along with an increase in the average issue size came a general upgrade in the credit quality of these new issues. This trend has continued to the present, as represented by a broad based participation by a growing number of companies. The growth of the market on the supply side is not that surprising, given the versatility, flexibility and relatively lower hard and soft costs associated with private placements.

These days private placements of securities, often at discounts to the publicly traded price of the stock, are increasingly being used by rapidly growing small-capitalisation public companies rather than public offerings for several reasons:

- where companies need to move quickly, private placements, which take several weeks, are much faster than public offerings, which often take several months;

- the Securities and Exchange Commission (SEC) disclosure rules are less burdensome for private placements compared with public offerings; and
- there are far lower expenses associated with private placement offerings compared with public offerings.

Offerings of discounted stock are typically structured as 'Regulation D' transactions, which are private placements exempt from registration under the US Securities Act of 1933, as amended. Under Regulation D, companies prepare a private offering memorandum that includes all material information about the offering such as the intended use of the proceeds of the offering, risk factors, fees and expenses and other pertinent disclosures.

Securities offered generally take the form of convertible securities, typically through the issue of preferred shares or debentures. Both of these can be converted into shares of common stock at some point in the future (typically after a holding period ranging from several weeks to several months).

Investors are attracted to these structures by current income in the form of a coupon (usually paid quarterly), and benefit from a more senior position in the company's capital structure compared with the holders of common shares. They then have the ability to convert the instrument into common shares at any time in the future they choose following the expiry of a pre-agreed holding period.

The company benefits from instant equity financing, while having the opportunity to ride its share price for a certain amount of time. If the stock price goes up, it will have optimised its dilution as it will have to issue fewer shares.

## The investor side of the private placement market

In the early 1990s, the universe of investors who participated in private placements in the United States was limited and mainly comprised individual investors. It was within this environment that a small group of professional investors, focusing on 'Regulation D' private placements, evolved.

Today, the private placement market is more efficient but still provides opportunities for superior risk-adjusted rates of return. Rather than the 'gunshot' approach typical of individual investors in the past, many of whom were very successful in early 1990s, sophisticated analytical and portfolio management techniques need to be employed in a disciplined manner in order to flourish in the current environment.

We estimate the total market for private placements in the United States was over US$60 billion during 1998, involving more than 600 participants in the market. Much of this issuance was in large transactions such as:

- Xerox Corporation's US$1,012,198,000 convertible subordinated debenture due in 2018 (yield to maturity 3.625 per cent); and
- Western Digital Corporation's US$460,129,812 zero coupon subordinated debenture due in 2018 (yield to maturity 5.25 per cent).

Most of these larger transactions were structured to provide investors with a guaranteed coupon equivalent to market-type interest rates, and the opportunity for additional upside if the issuer's stock price moves up over time.

The market for private placements at a discount to market, the focus of this chapter, is far smaller, although several large transactions have been concluded in this area of the market. These include America Online's US$350 million 4 per cent convertible subordinated notes due in 2002. These notes are convertible at any time into common stock (unless previously redeemed by the issuer) at a conversion price that was below market at the time of issuance.

We estimate the market for private placements at a discount is no more than 10-20 per cent of the overall private placement market or US$6-12 billion in 1998 and growing. In this area of the market, trading is dominated by a handful of sophisticated investors and dedicated boutiques.

There has been a significant growth in dedicated boutiques with expanded resources in research and computer systems, and many of the newer entrants into the market rely on a 'black box' formula-based approach. The use of such resources may be a weak and unreliable substitute for experience and acumen in managing a portfolio of private placements through rapidly changing market environments.

Fundamental research, a steady flow of investment opportunities and sound judgement are the critical requirements for a successful long-term investor in this strategy.

## A brief overview of private placements theory

The objective of the private placement is to:

- identify small-cap or micro-cap companies (typically companies with a market capitalisation of less than US$500 million) with immediate cash needs; and
- structure the purchase of a restricted equity security in a privately negotiated transaction with the company.

This purchase is typically at a discount to the current market price, or at a pre-agreed discount to the market price at some point in the future, when the investor is in a position to convert the instrument into ordinary shares and sell into the market.

The investor attempts to mitigate the risks of such investments and enhance the returns by negotiating the purchase of equity or equity-linked securities, which may be structured to include a security interest in the underlying assets of the company, as well as warrants to purchase additional shares at attractive values. Additionally, investors strive to reduce market risk by implementing a 'look-back' feature. This allows them to purchase shares at a discount to future market value determined over a period of several days. This feature is intended to enable the investment to approach market neutrality at all times.

There are several ways to hedge market risk, but most boil down to the company issuing additional shares to the investor if the stock price falls. The investor can take advantage of upside volatility through warrants and also by negotiating a ceiling price in the transaction so that if the stock moves above that price in the future the investor will never pay more than that price for the stock when it comes time to convert (this is clearly highlighted in the upcoming example).

The ever-increasing size of the convertible market in the United States and other countries indicates that issuers are willing to sell volatility on their stock. What investors offer issuers is ready access to new equity capital. Typically, public companies that raise capital in the private market offer this new equity at a discount to the current stock price; this discount is usually between 5 per cent and 20 per cent. The placement agent then structures a transaction that maximises its ability to place the securities with its clients, who typically benefit from a rise in the stock price.

To implement such a strategy, both the quantitative trading skill and the traditional private equity thought process are required to source, structure and manage the positions.

## How private placements work in practice

As an illustration, we provide a practical guide to private placement investing, looking at both a simplistic approach, and a more sophisticated approach which we could consider incorporates the critical elements of a disciplined approach to private placement investing.

### The simplistic approach

A simplistic but rather high-risk approach is to find companies that are badly in need of the cash to sustain a high burn rate (such as biotechnology companies) and then negotiate the purchase of equity or equity-linked securities at a significant discount to the current or future market price.

If the company needs the cash badly enough, it may be willing to give the investor both a high coupon (up to 2 per cent per month in some instances), and a very large discount to the present or future market price (we have seen discounts as high as 35 per cent), despite the dilution that this will entail for company's common shareholders.

The investor is attracted by the possibility of the huge returns he may receive, provided there is enough liquidity in the company's stock when it comes time to convert the instrument into ordinary shares and sell the stock into the market. The advantage of this approach is that it obviates the need for serious due diligence and credit analysis. The danger is that liquidity may dry up in the market and that the investor may then be unable to unwind the position before the company runs out of cash. We have witnessed many investors who practice this form of private placement investing and we salute them for their bravery. Their approach is not for the faint-hearted.

### The sophisticated approach

A more sophisticated approach involves capitalising on the inefficiencies of the micro-cap and small-cap sectors by identifying fundamentally strong micro-cap and small-cap companies that have immediate capital needs. Having done this, the next step is to privately negotiate, primarily through Regulation D, the purchase of equity or equity-linked securities in these companies directly from the company. The process and structures are essentially the same as for the simplistic approach (although the coupons and discounts may be far smaller); the key difference is in the quality of the target companies.

The investor should be looking for companies that are fundamentally undervalued. One of the primary reasons why a target company's stock may trade at a steep discount to its implicit value is the company's inefficient and inadequate access to sources of capital to fuel growth. The new equity, combined with the resulting additional debt capacity, should provide immediate growth creating a jump-start to earnings and cashflow that should result in an increased stock price.

One approach finds that the most profitable investments are those where the proceeds from the private placement are used to finance a specific near-term event, such as an acquisition, which can act as a catalyst for the stock to be revalued upwards. Ideally, a public company acquires a private company at a low multiple and then seeks to increase both revenues and profits by improving management, cutting costs, leveraging combined distribution channels, and consolidating expenditure on overheads, research and development, and advertising.

Historically, acquisition finance has provided low risk and sustainable capital gains for a private placement portfolio. Successful consolidations have been pursued through the acquisition of companies involved in a variety of industries, including: hearing-aid distribution, agricultural seed development and sales, domestic alarm services, car dealerships, information technology services, and physical rehabilitation products manufacturers and distributors.

Each investment should be approached with the mindset of an 'owner' with a medium-term perspective. Each investment decision should be based on a thorough analysis of:

- the fundamentals of the target company's business;
- the company's management team;
- the potential cashflows generated by the company under various projected scenarios;
- the size and dynamics of existing and future markets in which the target company competes; and
- the trading characteristics of the underlying company, in terms of both liquidity and volatility.

In order to secure a steady flow of investment opportunities, the investor should attempt to develop a reputation as an entrepreneurial source of capital with an ability to close a transaction in a timely manner. Also, small-cap companies can often benefit from investors' help and experience in:

- identifying acquisition opportunities;
- developing strategic relationships;
- providing access to additional sources of capital; and
- providing independent advice on how best to execute their business plans.

The more benefits the investor brings to the table, the better deal he will likely be able to negotiate with the company.

## Issues in structuring convertibles

The most attractive security is a convertible with no preset conversion ratio but a fixed dollar amount divided by the price of the stock in the days immediately preceding conversion. While this approach may reduce the potential for straight gains (buy and hold), it should achieve the benefit of being almost fully immunised from market fluctuations.

From the company's perspective, it will get instant equity financing, while keeping the opportunity to ride its share price for a certain amount of time. As mentioned above, if the stock price goes up, it will have optimised its dilution as it will have to issue fewer shares. To protect good-quality companies from an adverse increase in dilution if their stock price goes down, it is customary to include a provision for partial calling of the issued security at a premium.

129

## Exit strategies

Securities purchased will generally be subject to restrictions on transfer, and therefore will be illiquid at the time of purchase. The exit strategy for securities purchased in private placements will generally be the conversion of such securities into the publicly traded common stock of the issuer, pursuant to conversion rights embedded in the private securities or similar rights (registration rights, for example).

Generally, conversion rights or registration rights with respect to private securities generally will not be exercised for a period of time (typically from 60 to 90 days) after the purchase of such securities. During this time, the investor may be precluded from disposing of the securities, or may only be able to sell them at a significant discount. It is therefore of critical importance during the structuring process to emphasise liquidity while seeking to lower risk.

A term sheet from a fairly straightforward private placement should help explain how these structures work (see Exhibit 1). In the example below, the issuer is called Pearl Inc. During negotiations, Pearl said it needed time to execute its business plan, and therefore did not want the investor to sell shares into the market during the initial six-month period. The investor has agreed to a 'six-month lock-up' provision.

We have assumed that the share price was US$10 per share at closing, we then look at two different scenarios after 180 days when the investor is able to convert and sell his shares.

• In Scenario 1, the share price has risen to US$15.
• In Scenario 2, the share price has fallen to US$5.

In either instance the investor is receiving a 7 per cent annual coupon and we will assume that he is able to sell all of his shares on the next trading day after the expiry of the 180-day holding period.

Exhibit 1

### Term sheet for the financing of Pearl Inc

| *Term sheet* | |
| --- | --- |
| **Company:** | Pearl Inc |
| **Financing:** | US$10.0 million |
| **Securities:** | Convertible preferred |
| | Maturity = five years, convertible after 180 days |
| | Coupon = 7% in cash or stock at company's option |
| **Conversion terms:** | Convertible at the lesser of: |
| | • fixed price, set at 120% of closing price; or |
| | • market price, set at 95% of the price at the time of conversion |
| **Floor:** | US$3.50 (subject to milestones) |
| **Warrants:** | 540,000 warrants (cash or cashless exercise, investor's option) |
| | Non-callable, five years, strike price = 120% of closing price |
| **Registration:** | S-3 filing within 45 days of closing the transaction |

## Scenario 1

With the stock at US$15, the investor is able to convert all of his instrument into ordinary shares at the fixed price of US$12 per share (120 per cent of the closing price), thereby receiving 833,333 shares, which he sells at US$15 for a total of US$12.5 million. In addition to this, the investor receives:

- the pro-rata share of the 7 per cent yearly coupon, totalling US$350,000; and
- 540,000 warrants at US$12 per share (US$3 in-the-money), which are now worth US$1.62 million.

In total, the investor has realised US$14.47 million from an initial investment of US$10 million over a six-month period for a 44.7 per cent return.

## Scenario 2

With the stock price at US$5, the investor is able to convert all of his instrument into ordinary shares at the market price of US$4.75 per share (95 per cent of the price at the time of conversion). He receives 2,105,263 shares, which he sells at US$5 each for a total of US$10.52 million. In addition to this, the investor receives the pro-rata share of the 7 per cent yearly coupon totalling US$350,000. The warrants are out-of-the money and are therefore worthless at this time. In total, the investor has realised an 8.7 per cent return: the initial investment of US$10 million has, over a six-month period, risen in value to US$10.87 million.

It is important to note that there is a floor of US$3.50 in this transaction and that if the share price had fallen to US$3 rather than US$5, the investor would have been precluded from converting his shares as the company is under no obligation to convert shares under US$3.50. Although oversimplified, this example nevertheless brings a number of crucial issues (listed below) into focus.

- Trading volume is key for the investor to be able to liquidate his position in a timely manner, particularly when the price of the issuer's stock drops prior to conversion and the investor has to sell far more shares than would otherwise have been the case to recover his investment.
- If the issuer's share price falls, ordinary shareholders will suffer greater dilution than would otherwise have been the case, or that the issuer may have anticipated, and this may anger ordinary shareholders, who might decide to sell their stock in the company, thereby adding further downward pressure to the stock price.
- If the stock price falls below US$3.50, the investor is precluded from selling until the share price rebounds. This may be fine if the fundamentals of the business are sound, and if the floor is contingent on the company having to achieve milestones (since the investor can protect himself from a degradation in the credit quality of the company). If there is a hard floor (not subject to milestones) and the business is deteriorating, however, the investment could be in jeopardy.
- If the issuer squanders the proceeds from the offering or is otherwise unable to execute the business plan, the fundamentals of the business may be severely impacted.
- If the investor is restricted from converting his shares for a period of time (180 days in this example) he will be unable to achieve any liquidity on the investment at precisely the time when the fundamentals of the company's business may be worsening and liquidity shares drying up.

## Credit risk analysis

Since a private placement may have elements of both equity and debt, a two-fold approach to fundamental research is required: traditional equity analysis and credit analysis. One approach is to define what type of economic environment the market is encountering and then determine what sectors should be the best performers. A list of potential investments within the private placement universe is then created that have positive fundamentals. In this fundamental research approach, investors should evaluate each potential investment's:

- management team, business plan, product cycle and competition;
- cashflow, earnings and common stock valuations; and
- interest coverage, bank and indenture covenants, and asset liquidation values.

The outcome of this analysis may be positive, neutral or negative for potential investment. We would recommend discarding the negative candidates but believe that substantial opportunities exist for acting on information with a neutral research opinion while awaiting a more favourable price level.

By using the hedge implicit in the structure of the transaction, it is possible to be invested while waiting for fundamentals or price levels to change. This approach to investing also frees the portfolio manager from the need for market timing.

## Risk management

What are the risks within private placement investing and what are some of the ways these risks can be managed? The primary exposure is the company going bankrupt, and second to that is the liquidity for stock of the company in the public market drying up to the point where it is impossible to unwind a position in a timely manner.

Portfolio managers need to employ a number of methods for managing risk. Among these are:

- allocating a limited amount of investment capital per position;
- making extensive use of fundamental and technical equity and credit research;
- continuous monitoring of event risk, such as bankruptcy;
- analysing and continuing monitoring each position's liquidity; and
- diversifying investment among economic sectors.

If assets become illiquid the investor may not be able to readily sell such investments or may only be able to sell them at substantial discounts. Some portfolio companies may need additional capital to support expansion, or to achieve or maintain a competitive position. There is no assurance that such capital will be available to the company, particularly when liquidity has dried up.

Another significant area of risk, and one that is often overlooked, are the risks associated with the portfolio manager and his business. In our experience these risks are significant and include:

- Funds whose historical performance has been outstanding and which have raised large pools of capital may be unable to replicate historical returns due to their inability to source enough attractive new investment opportunities.

- Although the market for privately placed securities is far more developed than in the early 1990s, it remains comparatively small, and much of this new issuance is below investment grade. Therefore it is crucial not to have too large a pool of assets under management.
- Many fund managers have failed to build the infrastructure needed to process an increasing number of transactions as their assets have grown. Sourcing, analysing and structuring private placements is very time-consuming, and it is crucial to build manpower as well as assets.
- We have witnessed very different valuation methodologies being used for essentially the same instrument and would recommend a thorough review of the portfolio manager's valuation methodology before making an investment.

## Conclusion

We have attempted to illustrate how private placements as an investment strategy pursued with discipline can enhance portfolio returns while reducing downside volatility. We believe that for those investors who are seeking to balance risk and return with a diversified investment portfolio, and who have more than short-term objectives, investing in private placements is an enduring investment strategy during investment cycles. We caution that the strategy is more art than science, and that choosing the right investment manager is crucial in a strategy where both the ethical standards of the managers, in terms of their portfolio-valuation methodology, and their business acumen, are key to their long-term success.

Part IV

# New ventures

Chapter 12

# An introduction to understanding venture capital funds

Joel Press, Senior Partner and Bonnie Kennedy, Principal
*Ernst & Young LLP* [1]

A venture capital fund is basically a vehicle through which high net worth individuals, tax-exempt organisations, and other institutions can invest their capital in start-up companies through a group of unique individuals known as venture capitalists. The terms venture capital fund, venture fund, and investment partnership are used interchangeably in this chapter as these terms are commonly used throughout the industry. Investing in an investment partnership requires a great deal of acumen, patience, and hard work. There are many choices to review and problems to avoid in selecting an investment partnership. Among the issues concerning the appropriate selection of investment vehicles are: investment strategy, tax efficiency and compensations to the general partner.

This chapter addresses these issues along with several others to provide stimulus to ask the right questions in selecting the appropriate venture fund.

## Business considerations and accounting

### Raising capital and marketing

The confidential offering document is one of the principal vehicles through which the venture fund is introduced to potential investors. This document presents a general overview of the fund, including its investment objectives, fees and expenses, risk factors, method of allocating profits and losses, minimum investment and tax status, as well as the biographies and additional information about the key investment-making individuals. The offering document is an overview designed to provide potential investors with a summary of the key elements needed to make an investment decision. The partnership agreement is drafted concurrently and is the governing legal document.

A term sheet, which is an outline of the economic terms of the venture, is generally the first piece of marketing data that is presented to lead investors. At one point the term sheet is very tentative and gives large investors the opportunity to negotiate the terms of the deal.

It is generally a good idea from the fund's marketing standpoint and from an investor's viewpoint that any general partners have a significant amount of personal capital invested in the partnership. Some investment partnerships will require that a general partner commit at least 1 per cent of the total commitments in the partnership.

## Structure

The basic types of investment vehicle are:

- investment partnerships;
- fund of funds;
- offshore funds;
- corporate ventures;
- government affiliated funds.

### Investment partnerships

The traditional venture fund structure in the United States is in the form of a limited partnership with fewer than 100 limited partners. In the last few years, many venture funds have been structured as limited liability companies (LLCs). The difference between these forms of organisation has to do with liability, taxation issues, and management responsibility. The limited partnership still remains the predominant organisational form. As a limited partnership or LLC, the taxable character of all items of income and expenses are passed through to the individual partners at their pro-rata share. A fund with fewer than 100 limited partners or members generally operates without regulation by the Securities and Exchange Commission (SEC) in the United States. Traditional venture funds are closed-end funds which require the participants in the fund to remain in the partnership or LLC until its termination.

The limited partnership or LLC has a general partner(s) or managing member(s) which can be either individuals or some form of legal entity, for example, a LLC or a corporation. The general partner/managing member typically receives an incentive allocation of profits which retains the same tax character as those of the partnership or LLC. In addition, management fees, which are generally 1 to 2 per cent per annum of capital commitments or assets under management, are normally paid by the partnership or LLC either to the general partner(s)/managing member(s) or to an entity controlled by the general partner(s)/managing member(s).

The limited partnership or LLC is typically organised to terminate within a period of seven to 10 years from inception. All partners/members make commitments to the fund at the beginning of the fund. These commitments are 'called' or 'taken down' during the life of the fund, typically at the discretion of the general partner/managing member. A general partner/managing member will typically make a 'capital call' when cash is needed for an investment. When capital calls are made, partners/members need to be able to provide large amounts of cash at very short notice.

If a limited partner/member is not able to provide the cash at the time of a capital call, most partnerships/operating agreements specify that the general partner/managing member may charge the limited partner/member interest on the amount called or take the necessary procedures to ensure that such limited partner does not receive gains related to the investment. In cases where a limited partner/member remains in default on his obligation to meet a capital call, draconian measures may be imposed, including forfeiture of the partner's interest in the fund.

### Fund of funds

In recent times there has been a proliferation of fund of funds, which are a variation of the traditional venture fund. Simply stated, a fund of funds is a venture fund which invests in other venture funds. The principal advantage for an investor in a fund of funds is that it enables the investor to utilise several investment disciplines within one investment vehicle. A fund of funds also allows an investor to gain access to popular fund managers whose funds are no longer accepting investors or have large minimum investment requirements. A fund of funds differs from the traditional venture fund in the structure of the management fees and the incentive allocations paid to the general partners/managing member. Fund of funds fees charged by general partners/managing members are typically a percentage of net assets under management, and, while older fund of funds did not utilise an incentive allocation to the general partner/managing member, the newer ones are using some sort of incentive fee above a hurdle rate (a predetermined level of profit to limited partners/members) before the general partner/managing member receives an incentive fee.

## Offshore funds

US domestic venture funds normally are not marketed to foreign investors because they expose foreign investors to US income tax rules and regulations. To remedy this, many investment managers create offshore funds. Offshore funds provide a mechanism for organising pools of money in an unencumbered regulatory environment. Offshore funds can essentially make the same investments as domestic funds, and indeed their portfolios often are a mirror image of the domestic fund's. Until recently, the Internal Revenue Service (IRS) had determined that an offshore fund could be exempt from US income taxes provided it adhered to a list of rules commonly known as the 'ten commandments'. These rules require that certain activities of the fund be performed offshore. Over the last few years, the IRS and many state legislatures began repealing the ten commandments allowing the activities of offshore funds to be performed domestically.

Recently, the IRS published new proposed regulations which provide that a foreign partnership must file a US partnership tax return if it has gross income derived from sources within the United States (such as interest or dividend income) or it has gross income that is effectively connected with the conduct of a trade or business within the United States. The US source income may also be subject to withholding. To prevent effectively connected income, offshore funds that hold investments in operating entities structured as partnerships (flow-through entities) must be careful to structure the investment through a drop-down entity set up as a corporation. For example, an investment in XYZ Partnership, an operating entity, should be held by the drop down corporation, XYZ Holdings Corporation, and, in turn, XYZ Holding Corporation is held directly by the offshore fund. This limits the offshore fund from trade or business income generated by XYZ Partnership. However, the rate of return on the investment in XYZ Partnership is also affected since the operating income of XYZ Partnership is held by XYZ Holdings Corporation and does not pass down to the offshore fund until XYZ Holdings Corporation is liquidated.

## Corporate ventures

These are typically affiliated with a non-financial corporation or a business development programme. These investment vehicles will typically invest in companies that can provide strategic technologies or cost savings to the investing corporations. In contrast with the other types of investment vehicles that invest primarily outside capital, corporate ventures are organised solely with corporate capital.

### Government affiliated funds

Some venture funds are affiliated with federal, state or local programmes. The affiliation provides additional funding for the partnership provided that the partnership follows the guidelines established by the programmes. One common government programme in the United States, the Small Business Investment Company (SBIC), is administered by the Small Business Administration (SBA). Partnerships affiliated with the SBIC need to prepare and file annually special forms and financial statements with the SBA.

## Investment strategies

The investment strategies of venture funds are different from those of a typical fund primarily because of the illiquidity of the investment. Ordinarily, a venture fund will make an investment in a start-up company and use its own experience and expertise to help the company grow. Naturally, the goal of a venture fund is ultimately to liquidate an investment and realise gains for its partners/members through an initial public offering (IPO) or a merger or sale to another group or a public company. A typical example of the process by which a venture fund invests and subsequently liquidates or exits an investment follows.

Entrepreneurs seeking financing to help grow their business will contact a venture fund and present a business proposal. The venture fund will review the proposal and analyse the potential of an investment in a start-up company. When analysing the potential of an investment, a venture fund will look at the strengths and weaknesses of the company as well as consider the timing and probability of exit strategies. A venture fund will then analyse whether or not it has the necessary expertise to address the needs of the company and determine how much funding is necessary. Frequently, a venture fund will seek co-investments from other venture funds to benefit from their expertise and to spread the risk.

If a venture fund decides that the start-up company has potential, it will invest typically in convertible preferred stock of the company. To address a pressing shortage of cash, a venture fund has the option to finance a company with a bridge loan that will later be converted into preferred stock. The reason a venture fund invests in convertible preferred stock instead of directly in common stock is that preferred stock has liquidation preference over common stock in the event of bankruptcy. A venture fund can also sometimes receive warrants or options as additional consideration for their participation in a financing.

During the course of the next few years after its original investment, a venture fund will help grow and shape the company, putting in place a strong management team, advising on the direction of the company, and helping with additional rounds of financing.

After a few years, a venture fund will begin looking for exit strategies. Is the start-up company ready for an IPO? Is anyone interested in merging or acquiring the company? Is there a future for the company? These are all questions that a venture fund will need to ask itself to determine how to liquidate its investment to obtain the largest returns or whether simply to write-off an investment. The largest returns for an investment typically come from an IPO.

Not all venture funds invest only in start-up companies. Some venture funds are organised more like private equity funds where a fund will buy out a large stake of a more established private company and either try to turn it around or try to find ways to liquidate the company at a profit.

Within the venture capital industry, investments are characterised by their state in the business life cycle. Investments made in start-up companies with ideas only and no products are called 'seed' and could take over 10 years to liquidate. Investments made in companies in the distribution and marketing stages of a product are known as 'early stage' and could take seven to 10 years to liquidate. Finally, investments made in companies trying to attain critical mass to be more successful are known as 'late stage' and are typically expected to liquidate in a few years. A more recent phenomenon of later stage venture funds include investments in portfolio companies after the companies have gone public. Many venture funds are including an option to buy newly issued shares at the public offering in their term sheets.

## Participants in a typical investment partnership

A traditional venture fund, operated as an investment partnership or LLC, is a legal structure consisting of various elements. The following is a summary of those elements. For the purposes of this chapter, we will define the general partner to include managing members of a LLC and limited partners to include non-managing members of a LLC, and partnerships to include both partnerships and LLCs.

### General partner

The general partner interest is the fund manager's participation of his or her capital in the venture fund. The general partner is typically an individual, a limited partnership, an S corporation or an LLC. An attractive element to many investors in a limited partnership is the fact that the fund manager has an amount of capital at risk along with the limited partners. In fact, partnership agreements typically specify a minimum amount of capital that the general partner must maintain in the fund. Additional financial incentive for general partners to manage the partnership comes in the form of a reallocation of gains from the limited partners to the general partner.

General partners are rewarded with an incentive allocation of capital appreciation (as defined in the individual agreements) of typically between 15 and 25 per cent. The use of loss carryforwards, clawbacks, and hurdle rates are common in the structuring of partnerships, since they generally protect investors against an overallocation or overdistribution of incentive allocation to the general partners before an investor has either recovered his original investment or earned a preferential return on his investment.

Loss carryforwards ensure that general partners do not receive an incentive allocation before all the losses of limited partners are recouped. In other words, if a partnership reports net losses in the prior year and net gains in the current year, the general partners can not receive an incentive allocation until the partnership has made up the prior year losses being carried forward.

Similarly, clawbacks ensure that general partners do not receive an overdistribution of gains. If in prior years a partnership distributed to the general partners an incentive allocation on gains, but going forward the partnership only incurs losses, the general partners may need to return any overdistributed incentive allocation to the limited partners to ensure that the limited partners are never at risk for more than their portion of contributed capital.

Hurdle rates ensure that general partners do not receive an incentive allocation before investors either recoup their original investment or make a preferential rate of return on their investment. There are two reasons for hurdle rates. First, they guarantee investors a predetermined return on their investment before the general partners can receive an incentive allocation. Secondly, the hurdle rate can be used as an additional incentive to the general partners. For example, if a partnership makes a predetermined preferential rate of return, the percentage of incentive allocation due to the general partners can be set at a higher amount.

## Limited partners

Investors who wish to enter an investment partnership as limited partners must qualify as 'accredited investors' as defined by SEC rules. In essence, this definition utilises a minimum net worth or a minimum annual income test. SEC rules mandate that the fund limit the number of limited partners (including general partners) to 100. If the number of limited partners exceeds 100, the fund would be come regulated by the SEC under the Investment Company Act of 1940 (the 'Act') rather than a private partnership. As such, the fund would be subject to onerous reporting requirements and very restrictive trading and finance rules. Therefore, it is of vital importance that the partnership make an accurate count of its partners. There are several common pitfalls to avoid when counting the number of investors. A joint investment made by a husband and wife counts as two investors. More importantly, if a fund of fund's limited partnership interest in the fund exceeds 10 per cent of the fund's capital, the 'look-through' rules may apply. If the look-through rules apply, the partnership will be required to count each of the investors in the fund of funds as if they were individual investors in the partnership. It should also be noted that a fund manager is precluded from establishing a sister fund with identical strategies for the principal objective of creating a second group of investor slots.

Another pitfall faced when admitting new limited partners is limitations on employee benefit plan assets. If 25 per cent or more of a fund's partnership interests comprise employee benefit plans, the fund would be subject to the provisions of the Employee Retirement Income Security Act of 1974 (ERISA). The fund's investment strategies may be limited and the fund would be subject to onerous reporting requirements.

The prospective limited partner should be cognisant as to the percentage of the partnership assets his or her capital represents from the standpoint of risk as well as from the standpoint of regulatory issues (for example, ERISA).

Effective 9 June 1997, the SEC has allowed investment partnerships to form under Rule 3 (c )(7) of the Investment Company Act of 1940 which allows partnerships to exceed the '100 limited partner' rule above (up to 499 partners) as long as the limited partners meet the requirements of a 'qualified purchaser' as defined by SEC rules. A qualified purchaser is either a person that owns more than US$5 million in investments, or an institutional investor that owns and invests on a discretionary basis more than US$25 million. By eliminating the cap on the number of investors allowed in an investment partnership, the SEC has opened the door for the expansion of the venture capital industry.

## Management company

The venture fund normally does not have any employees or assets other than those which are investment related. It is the management company that provides the administrative resources for the venture fund. The management company, which is typically owned by the same individuals who are the general partners of the fund, is compensated for these services in the form of a management fee based upon the net assets of the fund or the total committed capital to this fund. This fee, which is computed and paid quarterly, has traditionally been in the range of 0.75 to 2 per cent of the fund's net assets or committed capital. However, there are many variations on this percentage, including a sliding scale percentage dependent upon the total capital raised or the capital invested by each partner.

In addition, because of the advisory role general partners typically have with the startup companies they invest in, a management company can earn advisory or merger and acquisition fees for work performed on behalf of these companies. These fees are typically netted against the aforementioned management fee. These fees may need to be generated through a registered broker/dealer. Attorneys must be consulted in determining the legal structure to receive breakup fees, advisory fees, or other transaction related fees. The management company is usually a corporation or LLC that provides the investment administration and back office support to the venture fund. The management company's operations vary depending upon the size of the fund and the amount of services required. Services provided by management companies may include portfolio and general ledger accounting, operations, cash management, performance calculation, risk management, legal and compliance, systems, tax and administration.

The partnership agreement and the confidential offering document should specify the expenses that will be borne by the partnership. In many cases, legal and accounting fees are paid by and expensed by the limited partnership (not the management company). In addition, the organisational expenses incurred are typically charged to the venture fund. From a marketing perspective, the management company can limit the amount of expenses the partnership will be charged.

## Accounting

As a general rule, the venture fund's investments are recorded at their original cost on the date of purchase. Realised gains and losses on securities sold are recorded on the venture fund's income statement for reporting purposes.

Investments are typically kept at cost unless a better pricing estimate is available from a more recent round of financing (with a new investor) or from the sale or public offering of the underlying company. In those cases, a write-up or a write-down is warranted and recorded as an unrealised gain or loss. Typically the partnership agreement authorises the general partner or an advisory board to determine the valuation of the investments.

Generally, when a stock becomes public, the venture fund does not record it at its full market price. In the United States a 'haircut' is usually taken to reflect the '144 lock-up' under SEC rules or to reflect the fact that the venture fund's holdings are so significant that, if sold, they would affect the price at which the stock trades.

An individual partner capital account is maintained for each partner of the fund. This account is increased and decreased by capital contributions, distributions, and the allocations of profits and losses. Depending upon the structure of the partnership agreement, unrealised gains and losses may or may not be allocated directly to the partners. A venture fund is typically organised with a fixed number of investors. Investors commit a predetermined amount of capital in the venture fund, fixing their pro-rata share of income and losses at the inception of the fund.

## Systems

The investment vehicle must have systems in place not only to account and give accurate information as to its cash balances, but also to be able to control investments, partners' capital accounts, the appreciation/depreciation by accounting period, etc. The complexity of the system is a direct function of the size and complexity of the underlying portfolio. In any event, a prospective investor might be well advised to make inquiry of the general partner as to its accounting systems prior to committing to an investment.

## Reports to partners

Generally, at a minimum, venture funds provide annual audited financial statements to their partners and a K-1. The financial statements are prepared under generally accepted accounting principles (GAAP), as promulgated by the various accounting rule-making bodies and reflect common industry accounting practices. The annual financial statements include a statement of financial condition, an income statement, a statement of changes in partners' capital, a condensed schedule of investments, and related footnotes. GAAP requires that all investments reflected on the balance sheet be shown at fair value. However, some venture funds do not reflect investments on the balance sheet at fair value, and instead reflect private placements at cost, due to a number of the following reasons: (i) simplicity and reduction in administrative burden; (ii) the fund is a closed-end fund, with no new partners being admitted, and there is no need to allocate unrealised gain; (iii) the performance allocation to the general partner is normally calculated on a realised basis; and (iv) valuation of these types of investments can be difficult prior to the ultimate disposition.

## US tax considerations

### Basic principles of partnership taxation

#### Conduit principle of taxation

One of the main benefits of the partnership structure as a form of organisation is the conduit principle of taxation. Under this, a partnership's items of income, expense, gain, and loss flow through to its partners and are taxed at the partner level, rather than at the partnership level. This flow-through approach eliminates the double taxation inherent in the corporate form of organisation. As items of income, expense, gain and loss flow through from the partnership, they retain their tax character timing, and source.

#### Character, timing, and source

Character, timing and source are three basic tenets that govern federal income taxation.

Character refers to the type of income or expense, some examples being ordinary income and expense, capital gains or losses and tax-exempt income. The character of the item will determine how it is treated at the partner level for income tax purposes. For example, in the case of an individual, a long-term capital gain could be taxed at a lower rate than an ordinary gain.

The concept of timing determines when an item of gain, loss, income or expense should be recognised for tax purposes. Under general tax principles, gain or loss is not recognised until it is realised. For example, while unrealised appreciation or depreciation is accounted for on a book (GAAP) basis, it would not be recognised for tax purposes until the position is actually disposed. .

The concept of source is used to determine the origin of partnership income (that is, foreign source, domestic source, unrelated business taxable income). For US partnerships, the source of income, expenses, and withholding are used primarily for the calculation of the foreign tax credit at the partner level. Source may also be used to determine withholding requirements for any foreign partnerships and foreign partners in US partnerships.

### Partner capital accounts and allocations

Tax capital accounts are calculated under specific tax rules and will in many instances be different from book capital accounts calculated under GAAP. Since book income under GAAP includes both realised and unrealised gains and losses, partner's book capital accounts will reflect both realised and unrealised amounts.

### Partnership tax returns and partner Schedule K-1

Form 1065, US Partnership Return of Income, is used to report partnership income, deductions, gains, and losses. For domestic partnerships on a calendar year-end basis, the due date for the return is 15 April, although most investors will prefer to receive K-1s as soon after year-end as possible. Partner K-1s are used to report each partner's share of the partnership income, deductions, gains, and losses. The K-1s should also provide sufficient information to allow the partner to calculate its taxable income for both federal and state purposes. Information such as foreign income, deductions, income from US government obligations, interest expense, and unrelated business taxable income (UBTI) should be listed on the face of the K-1, or provided in supplemental disclosures.

### New tax law developments

Venture funds are the focus of two important tax law developments, which independently or together can provide great opportunities for investors.

Contained in The Revenue Reconciliation Act of 1933 was a provision (Internal Revenue Code Sec. 1202) that allows non-corporate taxpayers to exclude up to 50 per cent of any gain realised on the disposition of 'qualified small business stock' (QSBS) that is issued after 10 August 1993, acquired at original issue and held for more than five years. To a non-corporate taxpayer, this investment incentive translates to an effective maximum tax rate of 14 per cent (50 per cent of the old 28 per cent maximum tax rate) on gain from the sale of QSBS. Note that the lower capital gain rates established by the Taxpayer Relief Act of 1997 (the '1997 Act'), such as the 20 per cent rate, do not apply to the includible portion of the gain on the QSBS. In order to determine whether stock is considered QSBS and entitled to preferential tax treatment, a number of conditions and specific criteria must be met. In general, to qualify as a small business, the issuing corporation must meet a gross asset test, satisfy an active trade or business requirement, and must be a domestic subchapter C (regular) corporation.

The 1997 Act also builds on the favourable treatment of QSBS by providing individuals with the ability to indefinitely defer tax on specified qualified investments. The 1997 Act provides a reinvestment rollover election that allows an investor to sell an appreciated position in QSBS and reinvest the proceeds in replacement QSBS within a 60-day period without presently recognising gain. Thus, the new rollover provision creates an opportunity for those invested in QSBS to adjust their present investment portfolio by rolling over appreciated QSBS to other QSBS with greater potential for capital appreciation.

## Conclusion

Creating and managing a venture fund is not an easy task. Selecting one can be even more complex. As we have described, there are numerous accounting, tax, and business issues that need to be addressed. Although the tasks may seem monumental, they are not overwhelming to the person that seeks out sound professional advice.

---

[1] We would like to thank Ingrid Chen, Hans Allegaert and Kirsi Fontenot for their invaluable contribution to this chapter.

Chapter 13

# Structuring venture capital investments

Jonathan E. Cole, Esq. and Albert L. Sokol, Esq.
*Edwards & Angell, LLP*


An entrepreneur raising capital faces a daunting challenge: keep the research and development, marketing, and sales etc 'show on the road' but also obtain sufficient capital to fund these activities.

This often means running the gauntlet of finding sophisticated venture capitalists (VCs) who like the company's market, business strategy, management team and investment opportunity, and who can be a value-added addition to the stockholder group. It also means dealing with the commonly complex structures that VCs propose for an investment in the company.

For most entrepreneurs who have not been through the process before, such structures often appear confusing, and perhaps overbearing, and involve too much control for the VCs and too little appreciation of the sacrifices and contributions of the founders and other management team members. An entrepreneur receiving such a proposal might feel that the structure of the VC's proposed investment sets back his relationship with the VC.

From the VC's point of view, the basic structure of most investments in entrepreneurial companies is similar, driven largely by the key objectives of the VC fund and its managers. This chapter seeks to help entrepreneurs understand the link between deal structure and the objectives of the VCs.

The discussion below focuses on the structures used most frequently by the institutional VC community, meaning primarily the professionally managed pools of capital listed in *Pratt's Guide to Venture Capital Sources*. In venture capital, as elsewhere, the golden rule ('he who has the gold makes the rules') generally applies, and a VC fund's objectives will influence the structure of its investment.

This chapter does not cover the investment structures used by so-called 'angels' (typically private individuals, such as friends and family; wealthy individuals; suppliers or customers; or other industry contacts). Nor does it cover investment by so-called 'strategic partners' (typically operating companies in the same or allied industry or marketplace, including non-US firms). Those types of structures tend to be more diverse and again, are often driven by different objectives than those which drive VCs.


## Pre-investment considerations

Before approaching the VC community for funding, an entrepreneur should expend the resources to assure that his company's legal and organisational structure does not impede an arms'-length investment by an institutional VC, and that there are no unusual entangling relationships. Examples of pre-investment considerations are:

147

## Business plan

It is *essential* that the management team has developed a coherent, fairly complete and readable business plan. This should contain a clear statement of the business strategy that the company intends to pursue and a relatively complete picture of the resources required (including people, plant, intellectual property and money) to achieve the business strategy.

The business plan is important to the VC investor not only because it describes the business opportunity, but also because it demonstrates the ability of the management team to plan for and organise a successful business venture, taking into account the principal factors that can affect the outcome.

For the purposes of this chapter, however, the business plan is important for three reasons. a) The investment structure may be largely derived on the basis of the predicted results set forth in the business plan. b) The business plan provides the basic set of assumptions on which the entrepreneur and his or her advisers must evaluate the potential impact of the investment structure on the positions of the entrepreneur and the management team. c) The important milestones in the company's development identified in the business plan may become the benchmarks for important aspects of the investment structure. These include conditions to the release of deferred investment commitments, the vesting of management equity, or control of the board of directors. The interrelationship of the business plan with the investment structure is discussed further below.

## Intellectual property rights

The company's rights to its primary intellectual property (patents, copyrights, trade secrets or other rights) must be clear and protected. There should be proper assignments to the company of all patents, inventions or other rights acquired from the third parties (including the entrepreneur and other founders). Structures that provide for the founder or entrepreneur or other related party to retain the rights to the basic patents or other intellectual property under a licence and royalty arrangement are not favoured by the VC community. The following can often be useful:

- conducting patent or trademark searches;
- seeking the opinion of patent counsel; and
- asking other third parties to evaluate the company's basic technology and intellectual property rights.

Key employees should be covered by Non-disclosure and Invention Assignment Agreements, which protect the company from any claims by the employees of individual rights to any of the company's technology or other intellectual property. Where appropriate, key employees should also be covered by Non-competition Agreements. The possibility of entangling relationships between the key employees and their prior employers in relation to the company's intellectual property must also be examined, and where possible, eliminated.

## Prior history of the company

The legal entity to be used as the vehicle for both the investment and the conduct of the business should have no unusual prior history. For example, the company should not have been engaged previously in a business that was closed or sold. These situations present too many opportunities for unknown risks or unasserted claims. In particular, the company must not be a 'public shell', with an attendant diverse and unrelated stockholder group. In most cases, the equity interests should be held by:

- the entrepreneur;
- the key management team; and
- a small group of people who have made investments in the company to support the early development of the business, as described in its business plan.

The company's organisational documents (charter, by-laws and director and shareholder minutes) should be clear, complete and up to date, with no unusual provisions granting special rights to any group of stockholders or others. Provisions giving the stockholders, or a particular group of them, pre-emptive rights to acquire a pro-rata share of new equity issues can be problematic. In some cases, such rights can be implied by law unless specifically denied in the charter documents. If possible, these should be removed.

All prior issuances of equity interests must be properly documented and reviewed for compliance with applicable securities laws. Equity interests include not only common or preferred stock, but also options or warrants to acquire stock, or if applicable, partnership interests or limited liability company member interests. In particular, there should be no exclusive dealing arrangements with finders, brokers or other financial intermediaries, including arrangements providing for equity interests, options or warrants in the event of a successful financing. These arrangements not only restrict the company's ability to raise capital in the future, but also dilute the ownership percentage of the existing stockholder group and, potentially, the VC investors.

In most cases, the equity interests held by minority stockholders, including key employees, should be subject to vesting arrangements; restrictions on transfer, rights of first refusal in favour of the company; and rights for the company to acquire the stock held by the employees upon termination of their employment.

Finally, there should be no litigation of any material nature involving the company.

## Regulatory matters

All regulatory filings required by the company should be up to date and well documented. Any regulatory or governmental restrictions on the transfer of ownership interests should be analysed and the impact of a substantial equity financing should be anticipated.

## US tax matters

The impact of federal and state tax on the probable investment structure should be analysed and understood. At the moment, the institutional VC community still appears to continue to favor the 'C' corporation as the preferred legal entity for the investee company. (C corporations are permitted by the US tax code to use multiple classes of securities, but are subject to double taxation. In contrast S corporations are limited to having voting or non-voting equity, but are treated as pass through entities for tax purposes.) C corporations present the simplest and perhaps most easily understood legal and capital structures and are the preferred vehicle (in fact, practically the exclusive vehicle) for initial public offerings in the United States. Because of the prevalence of C corporations as the preferred investment vehicle for most VC funds, these are the focus of the discussion below.

C corporations can present tricky structuring issues where a substantial net operating loss (NOL) has ben generated from prior operations. While the value of the NOL can be used to shelter future profits, its availability will be severely restricted if there is a change of owner-ship under the tax regulations in any three-year period. Accordingly, the past and predicted future changes in stock ownership must be considered by the company's tax advisers.

'S' corporations are often used by entrepreneurs during the start-up phase and can pro-vide tax deferral opportunities for the initial investors. Conversion from an S to a C corpora-tion is feasible (in fact it is automatic in the case of the issuance of equity interests to non-qualifying investors, such as VC funds). The tax impact of such a conversion must, how-ever, be analysed. Other structures, principally limited partnerships and limited liability com-panies, are sometimes used. For liability reasons, general partnerships are almost never used.

All tax returns and other tax filings must be up to date and well documented.

## Cross-border considerations

For many entrepreneurs and companies, cross-border considerations are important for at least two reasons.

- First, as markets and competition for most products are increasingly global, VCs general-ly expect every company's business plan to evaluate and discuss how the company will deal with international opportunities and threats. Is there a potential competitor with supe-rior technology in another country? How will the company distribute its products outside its home market? Is it necessary to have different versions of the product to account for regional/geographic variances in markets?
- Second, in appropriate cases, a company's global strategy might include arranging that the VCs who invest in the company include one or two VCs from another country. Advantages to be gained for the company include validation of the international part of the business plan by the foreign VC, and assistance in certain cross-border matters. These might include access to the foreign VC's business network and to the VC's financial, business and legal expertise in foreign countries.

The strategy of arranging a cross-border VC syndicate is not without its problems. Some VCs prefer to invest near to home. Also, such deals do involve some extra planning to account for the cross-border effect of various countries' tax and other regulations on VC investments.

Proper attention to these pre-investment structure considerations, as well as to any other unusual aspects of the company or its history, will ease the investment process for VC funds. Inattention may well lead to the rejection of investment interest.

## Typical documentation for a venture capital investment

### Term sheet

The basic terms of the investment structure will typically be set forth in a term sheet prepared by the VC fund and submitted to the entrepreneur and the company as a part of a letter of intent. The letter of intent and term sheet are generally not intended to be binding on the par-ties, with the exception of certain provisions for the payment of expenses (whether or not the transaction closes) or exclusive dealing rights which may be included as legally binding agreements. The term sheet can be, and often is, negotiated in detail, since it sets forth the fundamental terms of the investment structure as well as the financial terms upon which the investment is proposed to be made.

While some VC funds use their outside counsel to prepare the term sheet and letter of intent, many do not. Most VCs deliver the term sheet directly to the entrepreneur with the expectation that it will be discussed and negotiated largely between the business people, without the active participation of counsel on either side.

However, because the term sheet becomes the 'road map' for the preparation of the definitive investment documentation, and since the term sheet is only a summary of the principal terms of the investment, the entrepreneur would be wise to consult with experienced counsel and other financial advisers when the term sheet is being negotiated. Such advisers can give the entrepreneur a more complete explanation of the ramifications of the summary provisions of the term sheet. They can suggest negotiating positions that can move the parties toward an agreement relatively quickly and smoothly. Often, this process can minimise the likelihood of unpleasant surprises arising out of the negotiation of the full-blown investment documentation.

Once the term sheet has been negotiated and the letter of intent executed by the parties, counsel for the VC fund will prepare and circulate drafts of the principal investment documents. These documents will be based upon the provisions agreed in the term sheet, but will be set forth in more complete detail, and include other standard provisions. The set of documents including not only agreements among or between the company, some or all of its existing stockholders and where relevant, its employees, as well as the VC investors. The documents also include provisions to be included in the company's charter and by-laws. A typical set of investment documents is described further below.

## Standard investment documentation

### General

The investment documentation agreed to by the parties at the time the investment is made sets forth the contract and legal rights of the parties governing their future relations. While some of the documentation, or at least certain provisions, will be peculiar to each transaction, depending on the circumstances involved, the VC industry has developed a relatively standard set of documentation that the entrepreneur should expect to see.

Since the documentation is prepared by the VC fund in connection with its investment, it is designed largely to protect the rights of the investors. Again, the terms are for the most part negotiable. However, negotiating positions that vary materially from the principal terms set forth in the term sheet will not generally be accepted, absent unusual circumstances and may result in a breakdown of the investment process. Accordingly, the entrepreneur should address the principal terms when the letter of intent is executed, even though it may not be legally binding.

The standard investment documentation typically includes the following:

- a Securities Purchase Agreement (also called a Preferred Stock Purchase Agreement or Note) and a Warrant Purchase Agreement (or similar designation, depending upon the structure of the investment);
- a form of investment security (including typically the preferred stock terms, or the forms of note and warrant);
- a Registration Rights Agreement;

- an Exit Rights Agreement (or alternatively a Put Agreement, if such terms are not included in the Stockholders Agreement);
- a Stockholders Agreement;
- an Employee Agreement (and Restricted Stock Agreement or similar designation);
- a Non-competition Agreement; and
- an Inventions and Confidentiality Agreement.

This set of documentation taken together governs the legal rights of the parties relating to the investment and the legal aspects of the company's operations after the investment. The principal terms of these documents are described below.

**Securities Purchase Agreement**

The Securities Purchase Agreement (or Preferred Stock Purchase Agreement or note and Warrant Purchase Agreement or similar designation) typically contains the following principal terms:

- The financial commitment of the investors to purchase the newly issued securities of the company, which may be common stock, preferred stock, promissory notes (including convertible notes) and stock purchase warrants, or some combination of these securities. These may be purchased in whole at the initial closing, or over time, depending upon the achievement of certain milestones.
- The representations and warranties of the company as to the material facts relating to its organisation and business, requiring relatively complete disclosure of any material arrangements.
- The representations and warranties of investors as purchasers of the company's securities.
- Affirmative and negative covenants of the company (the breach of which may give rise to contractual claims for damages, or which may result in other consequences, such as changes in the composition of the board of directors, or a default on outstanding indebtedness or the like), including limitations on: debt; mergers and acquisitions; changing the business focus; transactions with affiliates; and changes in compensation for the key managers. They also make provision for certain information rights (financial statements, board participation, inspection rights, and so on).
- Conditions as to the obligations of the VC investors to fund the investment (which will typically include the execution and delivery of the other agreements included in the standard investment documentation);
- Special provisions (covering any special arrangements between the parties); and
- Miscellaneous provisions (often called 'legal boiler-plate').

**Form of investment security**

The investment security will be either an equity security (that is, common stock or preferred stock in the case of corporate issuers), some sort of debt instrument (that is, promissory notes or debentures, which may be convertible into an equity security); or rights to acquire an equity security (that is, stock purchase warrants which may cover either preferred or common stock). The principal terms of the security will be contained in the corporate charter for common or preferred stock, and in the terms of the instrument itself for promissory notes, debentures or warrants.

The terms of equity securities typically cover:

- voting rights;

152

- dividends (including preferential and cumulative dividends);
- liquidation preferences, conversion or exchange rights, and redemption or 'put' rights (usually in favour of the investors); and
- special provisions relating to the board of directors, including rights to assume control.

The terms of debt instruments will include:

- provisions for the payment of interest and principal;
- default provisions;
- provision for collateral or guarantees (which will be more completely set forth in separate documents); and
- if applicable, conversion or exchange rights.

Special affirmative or negative covenants may also be included in the terms of the equity or debt securities as well as in the Securities Purchase Agreement or Stockholders Agreement.

Convertible securities (for example, convertible preferred stock or convertible or exchangeable notes) or warrants will also typically contain anti-dilution protection. This usually gives the investors the right to obtain more common stock, without additional aggregate consideration, in the event that the company subsequently issues new common stock (or common stock equivalents) at a price below the effective 'as converted' common stock price paid by the investors. The anti-dilution provisions can be quite complex and typically will be based on either the so-called 'full ratchet' or 'weighted average' formula.

**Registration Rights Agreement**

The Registration Rights Agreement sets forth the rights of the investors to Securities and Exchange Commission (SEC) registration of their equity securities. These will typically include 'demand' registration rights and 'piggyback' registration rights, as well as related agreements governing the procedures and understandings of the parties as to the implementation of such rights (for example, so-called 'cutback' provisions and indemnity agreements).

**Stockholders Agreement**

The Stockholders Agreement, which will be entered into by the company, the investors and the principal management stockholders of the company, will often contain provisions that are peculiar to each investment transaction or company but will typically include: restrictions on transfer (for example, no transfers for a given period of time or without the approval of the board of directors), rights of first refusal on proposed transfers, voting agreements with respect to the board of directors or other matters, and 'co-sale' rights (sometimes referred to as 'tag-along' or 'drag-along' rights. Co-sale rights set forth the rights of the investors and/or others to participate in certain sales of stock by the entrepreneur or other key management stockholders (the 'tag-along' right) and the right of the investors to require the management to participate in a sale of stock by the investors (the 'drag-along' right).

The Stockholders Agreement (or in some cases, the Restricted Stock Agreement with each key stockholder employee) may also include provision for the purchase of the stock held by the entrepreneur or other key management personnel in the event of death or termination of employment. The Agreement may include a 'call' in favour of the company, or a 'put' in favour of the stockholder or his or her estate, or both with provision for differing valuations applicable to the purchase, depending upon the circumstances.

### Exit Rights Agreement

The Agreement, if there is one, typically replaces the Registration Rights Agreement and may replace the Stockholders Agreement. It will contain the registration rights of the investors as well as any redemption or put rights as to common stock or warrants and any co-sale rights. All of these provide opportunities for the investors to obtain liquidity for, or exit, the investment.

### Employee Agreement

Typically the investors will want the employment duties and responsibilities of the entrepreneur and other key management personnel to be set forth in written agreements, which will provide for duties and responsibilities; compensation (including participation in bonus or other profit-sharing or incentive compensation plans or stock option arrangements); and the rights of the company to terminate the employment arrangements, including severance benefits that may be available.

Often, the VC investors will require that some or all of the common stock or options held by the key management team or issued to them pursuant to equity incentive plans, be subject to Restricted Stock Agreements, providing for a vesting of the rights to the stock or options over a period of three to five years, with restrictions on transfer and call or buy-back rights in favour of the company at death or other termination of employment, at a price depending on the circumstances of such termination.

### Non-compete Agreement

Investors generally want key employees, including the entrepreneur, to enter into Non-compete Agreements in the event of termination of employment (including termination after the investors have assumed control), the term of which may be related to the severance benefits available.

### Inventions and Confidentiality Agreement

The investors may require the key employees to enter into Inventions and Confidentiality Agreements. Such agreements will confirm the rights of the company to any intellectual property developed by the key employees, as well as setting forth the obligation of the key employees to maintain confidentiality as to the company's proprietary information and trade secrets.

## Achieving goals via investment structure

Four key considerations motivate a VC's investment structure:

- maximising financial returns;
- priority protection against loss;
- participation in management and potential control; and
- exit rights.

These objectives seem simple enough, but complexities arise when implementing the goals. For example, although a common stock investment will often be a good form for maximising potential financial returns, common stock will not provide the VC with priority protection against loss or potential control of management, and may provide only limited exit (or rights to obtain liquidity) opportunities.

The entrepreneur who understands the key objectives of his or her prospective investors or how these objectives are then reflected in the documentation will be better able to deal with VCs on an efficient, pragmatic and realistic basis.

## Financial returns

The financial returns to the VC investor come primarily in the form of capital appreciation of the equity securities, and occasionally as a current return (that is, dividends on equity securities or interest on debt securities). In most early-stage investments, there will be no current return, since the company's cashflow (if any) will most often be dedicated toward funding the future growth of the business. Even in these investments, however, the structure may provide for a cumulative dividend on a convertible preferred stock, which will become part of the liquidation preference upon sale or redemption. This has the effect of providing a minimum rate of return to the investors on a priority basis before the common stock held by the entrepreneur and others will receive anything.

In later-stage and expansion financings, where the company's projected cashflow is strong enough to provide some kind of current return, the structure will often include a so-called 'current pay' dividend on preferred stock or current interest payments on debt instruments. Even in those situations, however, the principal financial objective of the VC investors will be capital appreciation of the equity securities associated with the investment.

Standard debt instruments (such as straight promissory notes) or conventional preferred stock provide only for the return of capital through repayment of the principal of the notes or redemption of the preferred stock at its liquidation preference (typically the purchase price plus unpaid cumulative dividends). As a standard debt instrument does not participate in the capital appreciation represented by the company's increase in value, most VC investors will want to obtain their financial return through an equity security that will participate with the common stock in the increased value of the company upon achievement of its business plan.

The most common investment structures that provide the VC investors with participation in the common stock value are: a) convertible preferred stock, which is convertible into common stock at the option of the investors or, perhaps mandatorily upon the occurrence of certain events, such as a public offering; b) a convertible note, which provides for conversion of the principal amount of the note into common stock at the option of the VC investors or mandatorily upon the occurrence of certain events; c) stock purchase warrants (usually issued in conjunction with promissory notes), giving the investors the right to purchase common stock at a fixed price at some future date; and d) common stock purchased directly at the time of the initial investment, usually in conjunction with the purchase of non-convertible preferred stock or debt instruments.

A key VC consideration is the percentage of the company that the investors will hold on a common-stock equivalent basis. Typically, investors will base their investment decision upon an analysis of the risk-adjusted projected value of the company, assuming it achieves its business plan, at a fixed time in the future, such that the VC investors will receive an appropriate percentage of the projected value of the company at that time to provide them with their required rates of return on invested capital. This analysis will take into account the projected dilution of the percentage ownership of the VC investors that will arise from anticipated follow-on equity investments. The investment documentation will typically include both pre-emptive rights to participate in future equity financings as well as the anti-dilution provisions described above.

## Protection against loss

VC investors typically expect that their invested capital will be protected against loss to a greater degree than the capital interests of the founders or other earlier-stage stockholders.

The investment structure is designed to provide this protection in a number of ways. Of course, with respect to debt securities, the investors have a right to the return of the invested capital through repayment of the debt. This right may be secured through collateral interests in the company's assets or guarantees of others.

The principal 'downside' protection for investments in equity securities is typically achieved through the use of preferred stock, which gives the investors the right to receive the liquidation preference (typically the invested capital plus perhaps a guaranteed return through unpaid cumulative dividends) on a priority basis before any other distributions can be made on the common stock or junior preferred stock held by the entrepreneur and other stockholders. In the case of multiple rounds of VC investment, the relative priority of each series of preferred stock or note issue must be negotiated among the investors and the company.

VC investors also seek protection against loss through rights to control or liquidate the company if the business plan is not achieved or other material defaults arise. In the event of such a default, these rights are intended to permit the VC investors to determine the advisability and timing of a sale or liquidation or other material development affecting the company, or a change in management, with maximum flexibility. It is possible that the course of action decided upon may substantially impair the value of the equity securities held by the entrepreneur and other stockholders. The default or change of control provisions for equity investments are typically included in the Securities Purchase Agreement or in the preferred stock terms, or both.

In some situations, the investor will invest funds in installments, depending upon the company's achievement of certain business milestones. This aspect of the structure is intended to reduce the capital commitment of the investors in the event that the company's business does not proceed as anticipated or other developments arise.

## Participation in management and control

Most VC investors expect that the entrepreneur and the management team will control and operate the business without interference from the former, the investment structure will typically provide for the investors to participate in the management and operation of the company a) through representation on the board of directors b) restrictions and limitations imposed by the affirmative and negative covenants in the Securities Purchase Agreement or terms of the equity or debt securities, and c) through stock transfer restrictions on the equity interests held by the management team imposed under the Stockholders Agreement. In addition, the investors will typically insist that the Employee Agreements provide for termination of the employment of the key management upon relatively short notice without cause, but subject to severance and buy-back rights.

In general, the investment structures are designed to permit the entrepreneur and the management team to operate the business without substantial participation by the VC investors (except at board level) so long as the company is operating in accordance with and achieving the objectives set forth in its business plan. However, in the event that the company materially fails to achieve its business plan or certain agreed specific milestones, or the company violates any of the affirmative and negative covenants contained in the Securities Purchase Agreement or the terms of its equity or debt securities held by the VC investors, the VC may have the right to seize control as well as to pay off any debt. These draconian measures are often hotly negotiated. Rights to control the company are typically reserved for situations where the VC investors have acquired a majority ownership position while the put rights are typically reserved for those situations where VC investors hold a minority ownership position. In any event, the incidence of the actual exercise of such rights appears to be fairly low, but the availability of such rights in the investment documentation is a useful negotiating tool in the hands of the VC investors in discussions with the management in those situations where serious problems have arisen.

## Exit rights

As the primary goal of the VC investor is return on the investment, VCs favour a structure that provides a means of liquidity (that is, the realisation of the return through the sale of the investment or sale of the company). VCs use the term 'exits' to refer to these paths to liquidity, and a typical structure will provide at least one and often two or more exit mechanisms.

VC funds generally have a limited life (usually 10 years, with a possible extension of up to two years). Therefore, VCs will favour structures that provide for an agreed exit opportunity within five to seven years, so that an investment made in the third or fourth year of the fund's life will be turned into cash or marketable securities prior to the time that the fund winds up and the fruits of the fund's investments are distributed fully to the VC fund's investors. Entrepreneurs seeking capital from institutional VC funds should be aware of these constraints and prepared to accommodate them. (In this respect, it is advisable for the entrepreneur to enquire about the age and investment horizon of the particular investor funds involved so that there are no surprises about the desired timing of an exit.)

The primary paths to liquidity for venture-backed companies have historically been the public offering and the sale of the company (by merger or otherwise) to another firm, typically an operating company in a similar or allied industry. These tend to produce the highest valuations and accordingly the highest returns to the investors (although the consequences for the entrepreneur and the management team can be markedly diverse). A secondary path for financially successful companies has been the redemption or repurchase of the investment, usually in connection with a refinancing or recapitalisation of the company.

The investment structure advances the exit objectives of the investors through the public marketplace by the rights granted in the Registration Rights Agreement, under which the investors can in theory force the company to go public through the demand registration rights and can participate in company-sponsored registrations though the 'piggy-back' registration rights. Since most entrepreneurs share the investors' view of the desirability of going public the management stays in control and also obtains liquidity opportunities at a high initial valuation, while the company receives substantial capital to fund future growth. Registration Rights are therefore typically willingly accepted.

Exits other than through the public market are typically dealt with in the investment structure and documentation by means of a put, or option to sell, in favour of the investors as to equity securities (generally referred to as a redemption right in the case of preferred stock), usually exercisable after a period of time (five to seven years) if no other liquidity event has occurred (such as a public offering).

The critical issue in the put or redemption structure is the pricing formula. Typically, the investors will be looking for a) no less than the minimum return provided for in the liquidation preference of a preferred stock investment (original purchase price plus unpaid cumulative dividends), and b) if higher, the common stock equivalent value (for example, the 'as converted value' of the preferred stock as if it had been converted to common stock as shared in the value of the company's common equity on a pro-rata basis). Some put or redemption pricing formulae determine common stock equivalent value by reference to 'fair market value' (FMV), usually fixed by appraisal, while others determine such value by reference to a multiple of earnings (usually EBITDA – earnings before interest, taxes, depreciation and amortisation). In some cases, the put or redemption price may be the highest of all three of liquidation preference, FMV or EBITDA.

Other, more exotic, pricing formulae can also be used. Whatever, the formula, however, the ultimate structure will likely contain some form of exit right involving the right of the investors to require the company to 'take them out', and entrepreneurs should be prepared to deal with these issues in the term sheet and definitive investment documentation.

On a practical basis, exercising the put may not give the investors the ability to receive cash upon exercise, since many growing companies, especially those that have experienced bumps in the road to success, will likely not be able to finance a buy-out of a significant equity partner. Rather, a put gives the VCs the power to force the management to find a practical solution to the exit requirements of the investors, the absence of which will give the investors the right to cause the liquidation and forced sale of the company. Also the failure of the company to meet a redemption or put exercise will likely give rise to a shift in the control of the board under the preferred stock terms or Put Agreement or Stockholders Agreement. The put rights set the negotiating table far in advance of the exit date and give a strong incentive to management to plan for a liquidity event for the investors in a timely manner.

Other exit rights that appear in typical investment structures are 'tag-along' rights, which give the investors the right to join (to tag along) in any sale of equity securities by management. In cases where the investors control the majority of the company on a common-stock equivalent basis, it is not uncommon for the structure to contain 'drag-along' rights in favour of the investors. These give the investors the right to require management and other stockholders to join in (to be dragged along) the sale of all or substantially all of the company's stock to a third party, providing yet another full exit opportunity to the investors.

With respect to debt-oriented investments, the repayment of the principal with interest is, of course, the primary means of liquidity, but since VC debt investments are typically paired with a convertibility feature or warrants as means of providing for the upside financial return, the structure will typically provide for a put of the debt or warrants on a formula basis (that is the functional equivalent of the redemption pricing structure discussed above.)

## Conclusion

Entrepreneurs who are new to fund-raising may find VC investment structures unduly complex and at times overbearing. However, while the details may vary from one VC fund to another (or even from one transaction to another), the investment structures used by the VC community tend to fit common patterns and are designed to achieve a few basic objectives.

In our experience, the failure of the entrepreneur and the management team to appreciate the objectives of the investors can lead to early breakdowns in what might otherwise be fruitful discussions and negotiation. Entrepreneurs who wish to be successful in dealing with VCs should spend the time and effort to understand the objectives of their potential investors and to expect proposed investment structures that accommodate those objectives. At that point the entrepreneur, together with knowledgeable and experienced counsel and other advisers, should be in a better position to negotiate a fair and rational investment structure, which can provide the opportunity for all parties to profit from the arrangement.

Chapter 14

# Negotiating the best valuation and terms for early-stage investment[1]

Joseph W. Bartlett
*Partner at Morrison & Foerster LLP in New York and*
*adjunct professor at the New York University School of Law*

A early-stage company seeking to raise capital in the private equity market must contend with the high transaction costs and relative inefficiencies that accompany investments below the US$10 million level. Protracted negotiations, particularly among inexperienced parties or their intermediaries, can consume so much time and resources that the costs rapidly overwhelm the investment proceeds. In a recent article, Steve Vogel and I suggested that entrepreneurs and investors could improve the efficiency of the negotiation process if the parties attempted to 'price' (ie, assign a hypothetical value to) contested deal terms. With a more complete knowledge of the value and consequences, the founder or entrepreneur might be willing to accept a reduced valuation in exchange for more favourable terms.

This article continues our effort to improve the valuation and negotiation process associated with early-stage investments. As part of the earlier study, we conducted a survey of venture capital firms to quantify, from their perspective, the value-specific elements in a typical early-stage financing. This article draws upon those empirical results, as well as this author's more than 35 years of experience in drafting and negotiating venture deals, in evaluating a number of terms common to most early-stage investments from the vantage point of the founder, entrepreneur, or pre-seed money investor.

Despite the widely held view that registration rights and board control should be heavily bargained, we suggest that the business realities of venture investing render these particular terms relatively less important to the founder/entrepreneur. In contrast, we argue that certain other terms – protections against dilution, the form of investment, the definitions of benchmarks and milestones and severance and parachute payments – should not be underestimated when drafting and negotiating a venture deal.

## The process of valuing and financing an early-stage company

Early-stage companies pass through three critical, initial rounds of financing. These can be identified as the 'Rolodex round', the 'angel round', and the 'first venture round'. As the name implies, the Rolodex round constitutes the money raised from the Rolodex file: friends, relatives, and neighbours. These funds, raised from intimates of the entrepreneur, generally add up to US$500,000, and the pre-money valuation of the company at the Rolodex stage is usually (based on some unknown law) US$1 million.

The angel round that follows brings in money from high net worth individuals. This financing, too, precedes the stage at which venture capital and professionally managed asset

159

pools participate. Ordinarily, angels will contribute no more than US$1 million to the company, and the pre-money valuation at this point is no greater than US$3 million.

Experience teaches that entrepreneurial aspirations to angel round valuations in excess of US$3 million are purely romantic, and disappointment awaits an entrepreneur who entertains such idealism.

As a side note, companies in the new media and e-commerce business base have defied the traditional methods of valuation. Early-stage companies in these industries may approach professional venture capitalists (VCs) with absolutely delirious valuations. The VCs willingly examine the data and many – loathe to miss out on the second Industrial Revolution embodied by the Internet – invest. The recent spate of spectacular IPOs in the '.com' sector evidences that nothing from our historical milieu holds true in this area or, at least, that there are no absolute rules for the new game.

The first venture round is the point at which most professional VCs invest. Empirical research, however, confirms what many in the industry know intuitively: there is less and less seed money available from professional asset managers. Many venture capital funds, large numbers of which were formerly seed funds, are now mid- to late-stage funds. The greater ease and lower risk associated with mid- to late-stage ventures make them attractive to a VC with an adequate deal stream of mid- to late-stage investments. Consequently, the pre-money valuation in the first venture round will rarely exceed US$3 million, although in unusual cases it can be as high as US$5 million. In arriving at a valuation, the VCs may use models and discounted cash flows as well as work with the founders' projections to generate a valuation. In almost all cases, however, the valuation in the first venture round approximates US$3 to US$5 million – again the result of some mysterious law.

Valuation of companies in early rounds may appear somewhat artificial or 'canned' because the valuations tend to fall out in patterns lacking fundamental logic. Indeed, professional VCs have become familiar with patterns in an entrepreneur's projections. When a forecast shows no revenues, no earnings, and no EBITDA, there is nothing on which to base an objective valuation. Consequently, a VC must take the projections and integrate them with what the entrepreneur says will happen, as well as why it will happen, over the next four to five years to generate a valuation.

Interestingly, the forecast almost invariably affords a terminal valuation of US$100 million. Not US$99 million, not US$103 million or US$86 million, but always US$100 million – which explains in part the reason why the initial valuation seems to be a canned, formulaic item. What many do not realise, however, is that a terminal valuation of US$100 million is an outdated number. Ten years ago, a US$100 million valuation would have been right in line with a company primed for an IPO. Even today, if a company can reach a terminal valuation of US$100 million, it is not unreasonable to shoot for a US$30 million IPO, selling 30 per cent of the company.

The problem with a US$100 million valuation is that, more often than not, it lands you in the 'orphanage'. The orphanage is home to companies with a market capitalisation – albeit public – under US$300 to US$500 million. Companies of this size simply cannot attract significant interest among analysts or institutional investors. Without the liquidity created by an efficient market, the benefits of a publicly traded stock, such as being a currency for acquisitions, fail to materialise.

The only way for an orphan to generate interest in its stock post-IPO is for the CEO to drop whatever else he or she is doing and promote the company, or alternatively, to pursue a maniacal consolidation play, aka a rollup – an increasingly common occurrence these days.

In short, the CEO of a post-IPO company in the US$100–300 million valuation range is faced with the prospect of a never-ending road show. Today's terminal valuation must be expanded, if only by a consolidation play, because shooting for a US$100 million market cap, in my view, only gets one a number of the negatives.

Once the seed round is completed, and the later rounds stand ahead, there are usually real cash flows and occasionally even earnings. At that point, discounted cash flow methods can be utilised with more precision and the entire valuation process becomes somewhat more elegant. The challenge, from the perspective of the founder as well as the Rolodex and angel participants, is to negotiate one's participation in the initial rounds so that the fruits of later rounds may be enjoyed.

## Empirical results

The exhibits set out a partial summary of an empirical survey of venture capital firms with regard to the value and priority that VCs place on various terms in a venture investment term sheet. In a recent article intended to introduce an element of objectivity to the process of value-based bargaining, Steve Vogel and I discussed the design and methodology of the survey and provided some interpretation of the results. Roughly half the universe of active venture capital firms were surveyed. The response rate of 12 per cent (a reasonable number given the relatively short time span in which the survey was conducted) indicated to us that the VCs who responded shared our view that there was a need for improvement in the negotiation process.

The VCs were asked to rank 11 terms and conditions common to early-stage term sheets with regard to priority, frequency and relative value. The terms and conditions included in the survey questionnaire included: selection of the CEO, board seat, purchase of controlling interest, registration rights pre-IPO, registration rights post-IPO, redemption privileges, antidilution privileges, pre-emptive rights, liquidation preference, drag along rights, and negative covenants. In Exhibit 1, the VC ranked the relative priority, value and frequency of the

Exhibit 1

**Relative priority, value and frequency of terms and conditions reported by venture capital firms**

| Term or condition | Priority | Value | Frequency |
|---|---|---|---|
| Antidilution provisions | 4 | 4 | 1 |
| Board seat | 2 | 1 | 2 |
| Registration rights: post-IPO | | | |
| Liquidation preference | 3 | 3 | 4 |
| Pre-emptive rights | 5 | 5 | 5 |
| Redemption privileges | 9 | 7 | 6 |
| Negative covenants | 6 | 6 | 7 |
| Drag-along rights | 11 | 9 | 8 |
| Registration rights: pre-IPO | 10 | 11 | 9 |
| Selection of the CEO | 1 | 2 | 10 |
| Purchase of a controlling interest | 7 | 10 | 11 |

Exhibit 2

**Value of term or condition expressed as a percentage of value of consideration**

| Term or condition | Percentage of value of consideration |
|---|---|
| Board seat | 4.4 |
| Selection of the CEO | 3.9 |
| Liquidation preference | 3.8 |
| Antidilution provisions | 3.5 |
| Pre-emptive rights | 2.6 |
| Negative covenants | 2.4 |
| Redemption privileges | 2.2 |
| Registration rights: post-IPO | 2.2 |
| Drag-along rights | 1.9 |
| Registration rights: pre-IPO | 1.5 |

11 terms and conditions. Exhibit 2 was generated by asking the respondents to approximate a value for each term as a percentage of the total consideration for the investment.

The motivation for the survey was impatience with the ideological arguments one often sees in this business. In the context of redemption rights, for instance, lenders are likely to insist that they always have redemption rights, or that the market itself personifies redemption rights, or that there is some religious or quasi-religious reason why they should have redemption rights in our convertible preferred security. With our study, we attempt to introduce some rationality, some quasi-codification, into a system of 'rights'. We, the founders, may not want merely to give away redemption rights. Nor do we want the preferred stock to be what is called in trade jargon an 'exploding preferred' – ie, after five years it explodes and comes back as a debt instrument rather than an equity instrument. If the buyer is insistent, however, we will agree to the buyer's terms in exchange for a percentage bump-up in valuation.

More generally, we argue that this system of valuing rights and pricing terms would permit more efficient outcomes, with founders and investors more willing to accept a reduced valuation in exchange for a break in the deal terms. While the empirical results presented in the exhibits should not be taken too seriously, they are illustrative of our attempt to inject some rationality and objectivity into the valuation process, rather than accept what too often becomes a personalised, tedious argument. For the interested founder or entrepreneur, the survey results should inform as to which terms the venture investors consider most important. Only with an informed understanding of the operation and value of each of the deal terms can an entrepreneur distinguish between terms that are relatively unimportant and those that should be heavily bargained.

## Protection against 'cram-down' or burnout financing

The early stages of a firm's existence are the most hazardous for the entrepreneur and the early-round investors. Given the often difficult journey from the firm's inception to a liquidity event, there is a high statistical likelihood that the founders will be forced to surrender control along the way. No less significant is the possibility of a 'cram-down' or burnout round of financing which will reduce the early-round investors to relatively trivial ownership percentages when the liquidity event occurs.

Thus, while many of the terms of venture finance merit discussion, the single most important issue, from the perspective of an entrepreneur or early-stage investor, focuses on the first venture round.

Imagine an inverted, bell-shaped curve – a prototypical trajectory of an early-stage financing. If we consider a healthy valuation in the upper end of the range suggested earlier, say US$5 million, then the VCs invest US$2.5 million on a post-money valuation of US$7.5 million. After the VC investment, the entrepreneurs and the participants in the Rolodex and angel rounds own two-thirds of the company. At this point, we have a pretty good term sheet and everything looks fine. Despite the fact that the company is firing on all cylinders, however, Murphy's Law prevails and bad things happen. For reasons that have held true throughout my many years in this business, all surprises at this point are negative.

Eventually the company, strapped for cash, requires additional financing in the form of a so-called down round or salvage round at the bottom of the inverted, bell-shaped curve. The down round is usually arranged and funded by the VCs, the cash investors, sometimes thought of as the 'vulture capitalists'. The entrepreneurs, angels, and Rolodex investors are invited to participate, but all of their money is tied up in the company. Thus, the golden rule reigns – 'he who has the gold makes the rules' – and a salvage round commences.

It is at this point that the founders as well as the Rolodex and angel investors are said to be crammed-down or burnt-out. These people, who were in at the beginning but had no money to participate in the down round, are diluted through the accumulated weight of antidilution adjustments and purchases of cheap stock to the point where their percentage interest in the company on a fully diluted basis (ie, assuming all derivative securities are exercised or converted) shrinks from perhaps 50 per cent to a mere 2–3 per cent.

In the final act of this all-too-common story, the company's fortunes change as the red ink turns to black, and the company proceeds up the right-hand side of the bell-shaped curve with a sharp increase in valuation. At some point, when the company crosses the US$100 million threshold, there is a liquidity event such as an IPO or a sale of the company, and the VCs are handsomely rewarded. Unfortunately, the other investors, who have put their money or their sweat equity at risk, are rewarded with a rate of return that they could have beaten by going to a trade school and becoming skilled carpenters.

While there is no pat answer regarding how to avoid dilution, entrepreneurs must approach the term sheet with this possibility in mind. Given the struggle of a typical corporate launch, the ability to protect oneself (as an early-round sweat equity or Rolodex-cum-angel investor lacking deep pockets) against dilution in the down rounds is paramount. There are numerous examples of unanticipated burnouts and cram-down rounds ending up in litigation. Founders and other early-stage investors should take a proactive stance when contemplating drafting points, and to the extent possible, insist on language that protects them against subsequent dilutive financings.

As a note of caution, investors on the cheque-writing side should be wary of a trend in the law of fiduciary duty. Up until the last few years, the notion had been that, absent any provision in the contract to the contrary, if the cheque-writers participating in the down round were to offer the founders the opportunity to participate – even though they knew that the founders lacked cash with which to participate – that was the end of the argument as far as the lawyers were concerned. In other words, the mere offer to participate would cut off any challenge on fiduciary duty grounds to the pricing in the down round, which of course is an inside trade with the VCs pricing the transaction to themselves.

Although this reasoning remains an article of faith within the VC culture, it is not good law. VCs are subject to the constraints of fiduciary duty, and VCs would be wise to incorporate those constraints into their contracts rather than rely on the subsequent decision of a judge or jury, which is both expensive and unpredictable. The cheque-writers cannot flippantly dilute the early, cash-poor investors simply by offering them an opportunity to participate.

## Pay or play provisions

Another troublesome issue with regard to antidilution is the problem of the free rider. If we assume that the VC investors are holding a convertible preferred (or its equivalent), we might ask whether they should get more stock in the down round by virtue of doing nothing. By this, I refer to so-called full ratchet or weighted average antidilution protection. It is an article of faith with most VCs that, if there is a salvage or down round, they should get more stock simply because the founder and the management – usually synonymous – are not meeting their plan or forecast. Thus, without investing more, the VCs expect more stock. While the founder and early-round investors might consider dilution to be an equitable result among investors who participate in the salvage round, they may feel quite strongly that preferred holders who refuse to pay their share of the dilutive round should not receive more stock simply by automatic operation of the antidilution provisions.

One solution to the free rider problem is a 'pay or play' provision, requiring each investor to answer the call for funds (play) or suffer a penalty of losing or compromising the conversion privilege (pay). With this in mind, entrepreneurs should consider antidilution provisions as an open negotiation point, albeit one that the entrepreneur is unlikely to win.

While the shortage of early-stage capital gives the VC most of the leverage in the negotiation, there is no principled reason why a VC must get more stock or a higher percentage of the company without investing, simply by virtue of the need for a salvage round. The entrepreneur should recognise, however, that the custom in the trade favours the VC on this point. For example, Exhibit 1 shows that among the VC firms surveyed, the respondents receive antidilution privileges always or often in 93 per cent of all cases. Thus, unless you as an entrepreneur are stronger than most, this is an open negotiation point that you may well lose.

## Form of the transaction

Most of the literature about the first venture round suggests that the form of security VCs will insist upon is a convertible preferred with the amount of the investment established by the conversion price. This valuation presumes that the convertible preferred is merely a waystation toward owning common stock, and the price attached is the exercise price of the conversion privilege. Simple math evidences how much common stock the VCs will own, which, in turn, explains how they have valued the company.

Times are changing, however, and participating preferred stock is rapidly becoming the security of choice among many VCs. Unlike convertible preferred, which converts upon any liquidity event including an IPO, participating preferred gets its money back and participates in the upside through the medium of cheap stock. Depending on the exit value for the company – ie, the termination value at a liquidity event such as an IPO or a sale of the company – the difference between convertible and participating preferred can have profound consequences for the founder as well as the Rolodex and angel participants.

As an illustration, consider the following: assume that the exit value for our company is US$100 million and the original preferred investment was US$3 million. In this scenario, the angels and Rolodex participants take their share, perhaps 50 per cent, of the sale price less the preferred investment of US$3 million. In the context of a high exit value, the entrepreneurs, angels and Rolodex participants are unlikely to cry about the US$3 million not shared. If, however, the termination value is only US$10 million, a very different outcome results. Under those circumstances, if the VCs take not just their half of the US$10 million off the table but also their initial US$3 million, the seed-money investors have precious little to show for their efforts and their risk.

In sum, the choice between convertible and participating preferred is an open point of negotiation in the original term sheet. The form of the transaction is critical to the early-stage investors, and the options should be costed out based on the company's financial forecasts. Depending on where the leverage lies between the entrepreneurs and the VCs, the choice between participating and convertible preferred should be heavily bargained. The form of the transaction is a significant money issue, one that goes directly to the ultimate rate of return.

## Benchmarks and milestones

Another trend in early-stage investing that merits discussion is the so-called benchmark or milestone deal. This means just what the name implies: the founder announces, I've got a company that hasn't done anything yet, but I've got some terrific projections that I really believe in, and I think my valuation pre-money should be US$5 million. The VC responds, I'd love to do business with you, but I think you're pricey, and I think you're romantic about your valuation. Based on my analysis, the pre-money valuation is US$3 million. Under ordinary circumstances, the difference in valuation is unbridgeable; the two parties will say thanks but no thanks and move on.

The virtue of a benchmark or milestone deal is that the VC says instead: Look, let's do business, but I'll make a bet with you. Let's take your forecast. If you hit it, the valuation is US$5 million; if you don't hit it by x per cent, the valuation is US$3 million. Fair enough? The founder agrees, signs up, and then the fun begins. In these deals, the excitement lies in the definition of the benchmarks and milestones. They cannot, from the founder's standpoint, be fuzzy. Because of the imbalance in bargaining power between a rich VC and an impecunious founder, it is imperative that the benchmarks and milestones be defined as precisely as possible. To do otherwise runs the risk that, in subsequent negotiations, the 800-pound gorilla will eat all the bananas in the zoo. The founder should insist upon a precise definition of the milestones and a very conservative plan. The danger to the founder is that the benchmarks and milestones may be perceived later by the VCs not as a forecast but, in effect, as a promise with consequences arising from its breach.

## Registration rights

During 35 years in this business, I have spent close to one full year's time negotiating registration rights. I consider this time to be wasted; never I have seen pre-IPO registration rights exercised in accordance with their terms. And if it has never happened, why talk about it? The right to demand registration rights prior to an IPO is simply a right to make a pest of yourself if you don't like what's going on. No one will register and sell securities unless an underwriter comes forward and gives the go-ahead; and if a legitimate underwriter comes forward and says go, then everyone sells. This reasoning is supported by the survey results: Exhibit 1 confirms that VCs rank pre-IPO registration rights at or near the bottom in each of the priority, value, and frequency categories. Similarly, in Exhibit 2, it is clear that VCs rank pre-IPO registration rights lowest as a percentage of the value of the consideration. Thus, in view of the business realities, it makes no sense for the parties to haggle over the issue of pre-IPO registration rights.

For technical reasons, post-IPO registration rights are more valuable to major investors, including the founder-cum-entrepreneur, because they enable the registrant – if there is to be a secondary offering – to require the company to pay expenses and to indemnify the underwriter. Interestingly, Exhibit 1 indicates that VCs ranked post-IPO registration rights third in frequency but relatively low in both priority and value. This supports the view that although they are somewhat more valuable than their pre-IPO counterparts, post-IPO registration rights remain relatively unimportant.

## Control

The question of control, going forward, is probably the most hotly debated issue in the first venture round. Does the investor get two board seats or three? What about visitation rights or negative covenants? Is there a flip if the entrepreneur fails to meet forecasts? Here again, a somewhat more cynical view may be appropriate. In most instances, the cash investors control the company de facto whether or not they control it de jure, which again is the golden rule of venture investing. Companies frequently require rounds of financing after the first venture round. If a company falls short of its forecasts, for example, it may be forced to return to its capital providers – the cheque-writers – for more money. At that point, the VCs have the power to turn the spigot on or off, and consequently, the power to tell management what to do.

Viewed in this light, whether the VCs receive two board seats or three is relatively less important. Professional asset managers are not looking to change jobs and run the company. Nonetheless, while they do not want the job themselves, they want the ability to replace company management. Even among successful venture-backed companies, over 50 per cent of the time management is replaced somewhere between inception and the exit event. Considering the survey results, while selection of the CEO ranked very highly in both priority and value, it ranked near the bottom in frequency (see Exhibit 1). This may be explained, in part, by recognising that VCs rarely choose the CEO, at least initially, because the CEO is commonly the founder. On the other hand, the decision to retain or replace the CEO is among the most important decisions facing the venture investors. Thus, the ranking of board seat first in value and second in both priority and frequency should surprise no one. It is management oversight, rather than day-to-day control, that venture investors seek in negotiating their terms.

Some VCs will invest only if they have de jure control. This is a so-called 'gating condition', a go or no-go test. Gating conditions are not worth valuing, as a percentage of either the transaction costs or the consideration being paid, or even arguing over in negotiations with VCs who have built gating conditions into their methods of operation. Without receiving certain terms, the VCs simply walk away. Therefore, there is no point in discussing what a particular gating condition is worth to them: it's worth everything or it's worth nothing.

## Severance payments and parachutes

The management changes occurring in those 50 per cent of successful venture-backed companies often are not amicable partings. When the founder-cum-entrepreneur proves not to be the person to take the company where the shareholders would like to see it go, he or she is terminated. Consequently, the notion of severance payments and parachutes, and the issue of what happens to the individuals who represent the management of the company at the stage of the first venture round, should be a significant point of negotiation for the founder or entrepreneur. The founder may consider that, with ownership of 30 per cent of the company, why argue about a two-month versus two- to three-year parachute payment? The answer is: Argue about it. It is important to be able to sustain oneself while awaiting an exit event. Even for an owner of 51 per cent of the company, the employment contract issue should be a significant item.

## No-shop/no-solicit provisions

A seemingly innocuous term-sheet item that does not appear in the definitive documentation is the so-called no-shop or no-solicit provision. While negotiating a deal between a professional asset manager and an issuer or founder, the VC will ask for an exclusivity period in which to bargain. The term of exclusivity may run anywhere from 30 to 90 days. In the throes of due diligence, VCs spend a lot of their own money, tend to be tired and overworked, and are constantly on the road. Understandably, they want some assurance that the target is not going to defect for a better offer during this period. But all too frequently, the founder or issuer agrees to a no-shop/no-solicit clause without much thought. Exclusivity provisions have legal significance, and a requirement to bargain in good faith and exclusively with a particular capital source can lead to an actionable breach if the issuer or founder entertains and eventually accepts a better offer. Increasingly, disappointed capital providers are being awarded a percentage of the exit event valuation on the basis of a breach of a no-shop/no-solicit duty to bargain in good faith obligation written into the term sheet.

## Alternative investors

In the search for private capital, some early-stage companies turn to strategic investors. In particular industries, such as pharmaceuticals and biotech, strategic investments are commonplace. For example, ethical drug companies (commonly called 'big pharmas') frequently invest in a number of start-ups to ensure a steady supply of R&D and new products as their existing product lines come off patent.

From the perspective of an entrepreneur, a strategic investor brings both good and bad news to the table. One advantage comes in the form of an enhanced valuation. Strategic investors may pay as much as a 25 per cent premium over comparable financial partners because of their ability to take advantage of other considerations, including the opportunity to buy out the company and bring the technology in-house. On the downside, the sell cycle for strategic investors is around four to six months from start to closing, as opposed to a two-month average with a financial partner.

Additionally, a strategic investment, even for a big pharma, is not an everyday occurrence – it is the property of a small group of development specialists inside a large corporation who are experienced in making strategic investments. Because these investment specialists are not independent operators, however, and their jobs are on the line if their recommendation later goes bust, the investment decision must percolate through any number of layers of approval.

The issue of control within a strategic investment often falls under the rubric of a joint venture. A well-done strategic investment usually includes both licensing and distribution agreements. An entrepreneur approaches a strategic investor lacking the money, infrastructure or expertise to market and distribute the product successfully. In exchange, the strategic investor wants an exclusive license, or at least a most favoured nation license, on the technology. The complexities generated by licensing, distribution and royalty arrangements make a strategic investment more difficult. Perhaps not surprisingly, approximately 50 per cent of these arrangements fail to meet the parties' expectations. Thus, joint ventures, in many respects, are like mergers, and there should be, in the words of Warren Hellman, a presumption of failure.

## Risks and rewards

In the limited universe of companies at the Rolodex or angel stage, what are the hits, runs, and errors? Many companies at this stage fail to provide returns that will match the stock market or even the Treasury bond rate. VCs have hurdle rates – ie, compounded rates of return – of 25–30 per cent, and companies that have not enjoyed VC participation demonstrate significantly lower rates of return. Indeed, in the late 1980s and early 1990s, even the best venture capital funds struggled to outperform the stock market. What's more, Rolodex or angel stage companies carry enormous risk, and investing at this stage is not for the faint of heart.

Given that the risk/reward percentages in the Rolodex and angel rounds are so formidably in favour of the house and against the player, why would anyone invest in that round? In the first place, pre-seed round investors get a terrific valuation if they hit what is called in the trade a 'portfolio maker'. Second, angel investors and intelligent Rolodex investors are having fun. They invest their so-called fun money because they are retired, they have sold their companies at huge profits, and they derive great satisfaction from investing at this stage. They become directors and guide the company to realise its potential. Although angel and Rolodex investors may not receive a huge rate of return, their participation is somewhat analogous to buying a house: it is an investment but they also live in it. Enjoyment is an important part of the motivation.

On occasion, a company chooses to preserve a larger ownership percentage for early-stage investors by plunging into an IPO early in life, and circumventing VC involvement entirely. Such a premature IPO is likely to be a US$10 million offering underwritten by an obscure and under-powered investment bank. The problem with such a scenario is that it portends a lack of genuine liquidity. The company has undertaken the burdens of public ownership without the benefits. More significantly, however, is the reality that if additional money is required (which is often the case), one must undertake a PIPS (Private Investment in a Public Security) deal, a difficult endeavour and one that is heavily regulated by the SEC. The casualty rate – either through a fire sale of assets or simply going entirely out of business – of such companies reveals that, by and large, this shortcut is not a good idea.

## Conclusion

Both entrepreneurs and investors would benefit from a system that assigned a 'price' to each of the contested terms in an early-stage investment. In the absence of such a system, however, all sides can facilitate the negotiation process by recognising when and where pressure should be applied in the negotiation process. While the survey results we discussed herein are preliminary, they should inform the founder or entrepreneur as to the VC's perspective at the bargaining table. Moreover, entrepreneurs as well as Rolodex and angel investors should never underestimate the potential for things to go wrong, and they should strive to protect themselves by drafting language that anticipates unpleasant contingencies and business realities.

---

[1] This article is based on a presentation made by the author on 20 August 1998 to the New York Venture Group. This article was prepared with the assistance of the author's colleague, Troy E. Wilson.

Chapter 15

# The pricing of successful venture capital-backed high-tech and life-sciences companies

Houlihan Valuation Advisors/VentureOne Study
*San Francisco, California*

## Introduction

### Purpose and scope of the study

This article is the product of 18 months of analysis and research conducted through the joint efforts of Houlihan Valuation Advisors (HVA) and VentureOne undertaken to examine the question: What drives the pricing of venture capital (VC) investments in high-technology and life-sciences companies? In particular, we have attempted to explain changes in the value of venture capital-backed high-technology and life-sciences companies between the initial equity financing round (typically at inception date), interim financing rounds and their initial public offering. The San Francisco-based investment research firm VentureOne has made available its proprietary database of venture capital investments in high-tech and life-sciences companies. HVA, a national securities valuation firm, has used this reliable source of information to examine venture investors' activity and identify key factors involved in the pricing of venture capital investments in these companies.

This study examines the private financings of companies that have successfully completed their initial public offering (IPO) of common stock in the period of January 1993 to June 1997. Given the rapidly increasing number of companies operating in these technology sectors, and the growing venture capital activity, HVA and VentureOne identified the need for developing alternative valuation methodologies to determine market pricing for pension funds (and other non-VC institutional investors), private and corporate investors, joint venturers, 'investment angels' and entrepreneurs. As a result of our analysis, we have developed a methodology that is useful for the valuation of companies in emerging technologies and industries, and the pricing of their securities (ie, equity and stock options). The characteristics below summarize the profile of the companies included in the study:

- completed an IPO on a US stock exchange in the period of January 1993 to June 1997, and therefore, represent only the group of 'winners that achieved enough success' to go public;
- their shareholders are professional, institutional venture capital partnerships investing primarily in the US and hold equity, rather than debt, in the company prior to IPO; and
- produce and develop products (high-tech and life-sciences), rather than providing services.

## Methods

To present our findings in the clearest manner, we have chosen a methodology for segmenting our analysis into subject categories called dimensions. The main dimensions of our analysis are defined as follows:

- *Stage of development:* describes where the company is in its business evolution (startup, product development, product shipping and profitability);
- *Type of financing round:* identifies six different round types which follow chronological order (seed, first, second, third, mezzanine and IPO);
- *Industry type:* six industries are grouped into high-tech (electronics, semiconductors, software and communications) and life-sciences (biotechnology and medical devices).

### Stage of development

The different development stages identify where the company is in the evolution of becoming a viable business. *Startup* represents the earliest stage at which the entrepreneur has the concept or idea and has a team of people willing to work on it with a goal: developing a marketable product. *Product development* follows the startup phase; the company is developing products but has not yet begun to ship or test them with customers. At *product shipping*, the company is shipping at least one product for which it is receiving revenues, regardless of the number of other products still in development or testing. The *profitability* stage assumes that the company is shipping products from which it derives revenues and is profitable at least on an operating basis. These categories and their descriptions are consistent with VentureOne's proprietary database classification of development stages. In addition, the database includes one other stage: Product in beta test/clinical trials. Beta testing is the intermediate stage between development and shipping and constitutes a rather brief interval prior to product rollout, especially for high-tech firms. Although our analysis incorporates this stage, we will not include it in this article since the number of observations is very low compared to that of the four main stages of development.

### Type of financing round

With regard to financing rounds, seed is the initial equity funding by a venture capital investor. For the round to be defined as seed, the amount raised cannot exceed US$2 million, the company has to have been in business for less than two years (it cannot be significantly into product development or shipping) and the development stage must be startup; otherwise it is considered a first round. Because not all companies' initial financing meets these requirements, first round includes some startups. First, second and third rounds follow chronological order and legal documents may refer to the securities issued as Series A Preferred Stock, Series B Preferred Stock, etc.[1] A mezzanine round is usually the last venture round prior to a public offering and typically closes within 12 to 24 months prior to an IPO. The IPO round is an equity financing event whereby the company raises capital in the public equity markets for the first time. In addition to these six rounds, VentureOne tracks other types of financing rounds such as later,[2] Regulation D, restart and leveraged buy-out. These additional rounds have also been included in our analysis but are not presented separately in this article due to their limited number of observations.[3]

### Industry type

The industry name categorizes the company based on its major product during the financing round. For example, the software industry is comprised of those companies for which software development is the core business, regardless of any other activities in which they may be engaged. In addition, we have grouped industries according to the nature of their primary business, resulting in aggregate groups called high-tech (software, communications, electronics and semiconductors) and life-sciences (biotechnology and medical devices) companies.

## Multidimensional analysis

With this understanding of the core dimensions, it is now easier to visualize the multidimensional picture depicted by our analysis. Formatting the data through a dimensional approach permitted us to measure both aggregate and detailed information regarding any combination of categories. For example, we can select information about all life-sciences companies in development stage (aggregate data) or we may just want to look at biotech companies in shipping stage at mezzanine round (crisp detail). The information viewable through this dimensional window can be any of the following: returns on equity, increases in equity value between rounds or development stages (step-ups), invested capital per round (amount raised), price-to-trailing revenues multiples, performance of a particular venture capital firm, measurement of law firms and underwriters by the success of their venture clients at IPO and the like. The underlying purpose of the analysis will dictate the variables that should be considered and evaluated. Our goal is to understand how venture capitalists, in conjunction with entrepreneurs, analyze circumstances to agree upon the price of a company at a particular financing round, in a certain industry, at a specific stage of development, at certain market intervals. The dimensional view was integral to the analysis employed in this study.

## Key definitions

The following terms used throughout the discussion of the results of the study are defined as follows:

- *Pre-money valuation:* post-money valuation of a company at a financing round minus the amount raised at that round. For example, a post-money valuation of US$10 million after raising US$3 million implies a pre-money valuation of US$7 million.
- *Step-up in value:* increase in a company's pre-money valuation between two financing rounds. It is calculated as the pre-money valuation at a round divided by the pre-money valuation at a prior round. For example, a company with a pre-money valuation of US$2 million at the first round and US$10 million at the second round, has realized a step-up in value of five times between these two financing rounds.
- *Return on capitalization (ROC):* annualized change, or growth, in pre-money market capitalization between two rounds. To some extent, it would represent the annualized returns on equity for an investor at a certain financing round, without considering the potential dilution effects caused by the entrance of new investors at subsequent rounds.

## Structure of the study

We have analyzed the data in two distinct but complementary ways: a transactional data analysis and a statistical analysis. First, the transactional approach measures the following key variables: time between financing rounds, time until IPO, amount raised at each round, pre-money valuations, price-to-trailing revenues multiples, step-ups in value between any round and the IPO, step-ups in value between any two rounds or development stages, and returns on capitalization. This kind of analysis provides insights about the determining factors of venture investing in the high-tech and life-sciences industries. Accordingly, we have segregated different companies' profiles and the specific investor returns, valuations and multiples assigned, or attributed, to them – and their respective industries. It also yields general information regarding trends in the financing of these companies over the past four and one-half years. In short, the transactional analysis provides information pertaining to over 1,700 financings (private investments and IPOs) and the known variables most relevant to their pricing.

Our second approach is a statistical analysis, which is a key element in any study that deals with such a large volume of data. Our intention is not only to test the accuracy and validity of the results and conclusions reached at the transactional level but also to go beyond this first layer and add another valuable dimension to the study. With this type of analysis, we have measured the explanatory power of several variables with regard to pricing. Said differently, we tested the variables that may explain why the value of a company increases, or decreases, over time, between rounds of development stages. We observed how these variables were prioritized, identified their weighting in the determination of pricing and analyzed how those weights change over time. The statistical analysis facilitates an understanding of how variables interact with one another. To conduct the analysis, we engaged two experienced statisticians, not to build a model that forecasts or estimates values, but to group and interpret facts and identify trends or commonalties observed in the data.

Our analyses proceeds in the following order. First, we performed an analysis of the transactions at a macro level, that is, we compared high-tech and life-sciences companies, in the aggregate, as two distinct groups in order to compare the differences and commonalities between them. Then, we examined the industries of each group separately to observe their performance. Lastly, we conducted the statistical analysis. The analyses were done by year of IPO (each industry analyzed by each year) as well as in the aggregate (each industry taken in all years together). Because we believe this process to be the most effective way to analyze this volume and variety of data, the sequence of this paper's presentation will follow the same format. We begin with some of the general findings at the transactional level.

## Description of the data

The analysis covers transactional data from 479 companies. All the companies had at least one venture financing, typically seed or first financing round; depending on the amount raised, development stage and company age at the round (see Methodology section for a complete description of financing rounds). Occasionally, a company may have had only a mezzanine round and no prior financings. Not all companies completed a seed or a mezzanine round although most had first and second rounds. The median number of financings per company is approximately three and the company with the most venture financings raised funds on 12 occasions. A breakdown of the data by industry, financing round and development stage can be seen in Exhibit 1.

As Exhibit 1 depicts, most companies received financing during the product shipping (602 transactions) and product development stages (580 transactions).[4] Unlike companies that went public in the period 1993–95 that were primarily funded at product development stage, the IPO years of 1996 and the first half of 1997 were characterized by companies which com-

Exhibit 1

**Transactional data from 479 companies**

| Industry | Financing round | | | | | | Development stage | | | |
|---|---|---|---|---|---|---|---|---|---|---|
| | Seed | 1st | 2nd | 3rd | Mezz. | IPO | Startup | Develop. | Shipping | Profit |
| Electronics | 10 | 37 | 32 | 23 | 10 | 54 | 17 | 29 | 70 | 50 |
| Semiconductors | 11 | 37 | 38 | 26 | 19 | 50 | 19 | 39 | 65 | 58 |
| Software | 23 | 102 | 79 | 49 | 40 | 134 | 34 | 53 | 195 | 145 |
| Communications | 17 | 66 | 53 | 32 | 32 | 78 | 28 | 55 | 125 | 70 |
| Biotechnology | 43 | 89 | 71 | 53 | 42 | 96 | 59 | 271 | 53 | 11 |
| Medical devices | 24 | 63 | 55 | 50 | 31 | 67 | 34 | 133 | 94 | 19 |
| **Total transactions** | **128** | **394** | **328** | **223** | **174** | **479** | **191** | **580** | **602** | **353** |

There are as many companies as IPO rounds (one IPO per company). The number of transactions by development stage includes all six financing rounds from seed to IPO.

Exhibit 2

**Transactional data, 1989–97**

| Industry | 1989 | 1990 | 1991 | 1992 | 1993 | 1994 | 1995 | 1996 | 1997* | Total transactions |
|---|---|---|---|---|---|---|---|---|---|---|
| Electronics | 13 | 10 | 11 | 9 | 24 | 12 | 30 | 8 | 1 | 118 |
| Semiconductors | 14 | 11 | 10 | 13 | 30 | 20 | 23 | 6 | 7 | 134 |
| Software | 17 | 23 | 28 | 39 | 44 | 53 | 88 | 68 | 11 | 371 |
| Communications | 17 | 28 | 29 | 25 | 45 | 38 | 37 | 25 | 5 | 249 |
| Biotechnology | 24 | 26 | 33 | 53 | 66 | 39 | 48 | 52 | 11 | 352 |
| Medical devices | 17 | 14 | 21 | 28 | 42 | 31 | 45 | 42 | 3 | 243 |
| **Total transactions** | **102** | **112** | **132** | **167** | **251** | **193** | **271** | **201** | **38** | **1,467** |

* 1 January through 20 June 1997.

pleted most financings (including the IPO round) at product shipping stage. In order to iden-tify changes in pricing trends, we examined the data according to the year in which the com-panies completed an IPO. Of the 479 companies analyzed, 98 had an IPO in 1993, 65 in 1994, 139 in 1995, 143 in 1996, and 34 through 20 June 1997. The data can also be analyzed according to the year in which venture financings occurred, regardless of what year the com-panies went public. The companies that are the subject of this study had venture financings over a wide period of time (starting in 1973), with most of them clustering in the early to 1990s. Transactional data (excluding IPOs) about the companies by industry and year of financing is summarized in Exhibit 2.

Software and biotech companies registered the greatest number of financings, while elec-tronics and semiconductors companies received the least. The year showing most venture financings is 1995, with 271 transactions, some of which were received by companies that went public during 1996 and the first half of 1997. Note that the financings above refer only to the 479 companies comprising the study and which successfully completed an IPO between January 1993 and June 1997. Companies that completed an IPO in the near past show a decreasing number of venture capital financings compared to those companies that went public in 1993, 1994, and even 1995.[5] An enthusiastic public equity market eager for technology stocks making the public equity market accessible earlier has contributed to the decline in venture financings observed since 1995.

## Transactional analysis

### General findings

Data from the companies and their venture financings was imported from VentureOne's database to an Excel spreadsheet. By using pivot tables, key fields and variables were defined, combined and analyzed. For example, pivot tables enabled us to examine variables such as the step-up in value experienced by software companies from the seed financing round to the IPO round or the price-to-trailing revenues multiple and median pre-money valuation derived from financings of communications companies in the product shipping stage. Observations of this type were also made for the aggregate group of high-tech and life-sciences companies. A summary of key findings is presented below.

**Life-sciences companies are faster to IPO than high-tech companies**
The time between each financing round and the IPO, for companies analyzed in our study, was greater for high-tech than for life-sciences companies. Setting aside semiconductor and electronics companies, however, the results are more even (although, in general, life-sciences firms are still slightly faster in reaching the IPO).

Exhibit 3 demonstrates this relationship by illustrating the time line to IPO for high-tech and life-sciences companies.

The gap between the curves can be explained by the fact that life-sciences companies require higher funding levels than high-tech due to a longer product development period.

Exhibit 3

**Median step-ups from each round to IPO**

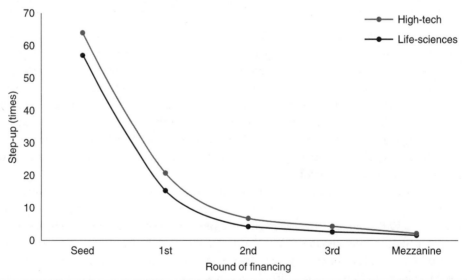

Life-sciences companies can afford to go public at earlier stages of development (ie, product development) than high-tech and raise larger amounts of capital required to fully develop a product or technology and start generating revenues.

Timing affects other variables, as well. The time from financing rounds to IPO shows differences among years, especially when we consider 1996, a year in which many companies rallied to go public taking advantage of a 'wider IPO market window' (an accommodating market with a broad appetite). The period of time between each round and an IPO in 1996 compressed significantly at all rounds. The drop was steeper in high-tech than life-sciences companies – due in large part to the IPO rush in communications and software industries, and even among electronics firms.

**High-tech and life-sciences companies show similar pre-money valuations for earlier rounds, but valuations vary widely in later stages**

Communications companies received the highest pre-money valuations of all six industries at the mezzanine and IPO rounds.

When we observed pre-money valuations on a yearly basis, high-tech companies' valuations have been higher than in prior years for seed to mezzanine rounds and at IPO since early 1996. High-tech companies that went public in 1996 and during the first half of 1997 had higher pre-money valuations at earlier rounds than companies that went public in any other year. One of the reasons for these higher valuations could be the increasing amount of institutional money going into venture funds. Another reason could be that the favorable IPO market since 1995 may have influenced the pricing of venture investments thereafter, driving private financings in 1996 and 1997 to higher levels than in previous years.

The life-sciences group though, showed radically different results: declining valuations in 1996 and during the first half of 1997 (except at IPO) from peaks in 1995 (see Exhibit 4). Potentially, biotech investors may have uncovered a new rationale for pricing these types of

Exhibit 4

**Startups' median step-up to IPO, 1993–97**

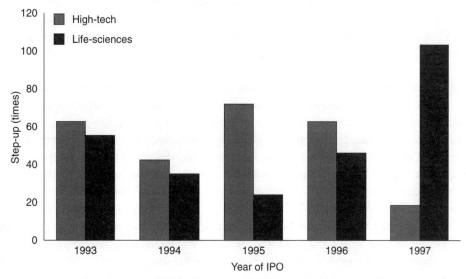

175

Exhibit 5

**Median pre-money valuations by development stage, IPO classes of 1996–97 (US$ million)**

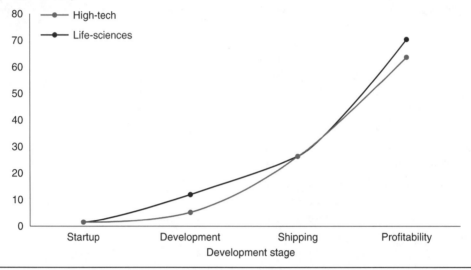

companies during this period. Many in the industry have speculated, that in the height of the biotech craze of the early 1990s analysts used inappropriately low discount rates on projected cash flows and also inadequately estimated the lengthy FDA approval process. Realization of these discontinuities may have come through in the private equity markets for biotech in the 1995 time frame and this new found rationale may be an explanation for our observation.

Exhibit 5 illustrates how both groups show logical increasing pre-money valuations from startup to profitability stage. The most significant difference in value between life-sciences and high-tech firms occurs at product development stage. The spread narrows as companies progress to product shipping and widens again as they approach profitability.

The companies that went public in 1996 and during the first half of 1997 are peculiar in that the value spread between the two groups narrows compared to previous years.

High-tech companies seem to get lower calculations than do life-sciences companies at product development and profitability stages.

**High-tech companies tend to raise less capital than life-sciences companies at all financing rounds except IPO, due in part to a shorter time to IPO (see Exhibit 3) and favorable market appetite for their stock during all years of the study**

Life-sciences firms are observed to raise greater sums than high-tech companies from seed to mezzanine rounds; the closer to IPO, the higher the amounts raised. High-tech firms, on the other hand, raise increasing funds from seed to second rounds, drop slightly at third and increase thereafter, reaching the highest level at IPO. Exhibit 6 illustrates these differences between the two industry groups.

Although not depicted by Exhibit 5, we observed that the closer a company is to the profitable stage of development, the higher the amount of capital raised. Life-sciences companies tend to raise more money than high-tech firms at product development and shipping stages. This reflects the fact that life-sciences companies spend a greater amount of time in the prod-

Exhibit 6

**Median amount raised by round, 1993–97 (US$ million)**

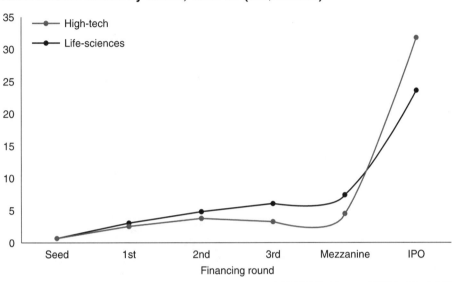

uct development stage than do high-tech companies. High-tech companies, however, attract more capital at startup and profit stages. Communications companies are the leaders in fundraising, followed by biotech companies.

Finally, the amounts raised per round and development stage demonstrate important differences among the years analyzed. Amounts raised by companies that went public in 1996 and during the first half of 1997 have soared at all rounds, particularly mezzanine and IPO.

**On average, both high-tech and life-sciences companies went public at higher price-to-trailing revenues multiples in 1996 than in any other year**

Price-to-trailing revenues multiples are much higher for the life-sciences group than for high-tech firms because most of these companies either have lower revenues than high-tech or only begin to generate revenues near the time of their IPO. Although most high-tech companies primarily seek private funding to finance their growth, life-sciences companies mainly utilize IPO proceeds to fund their research and development efforts. As the description of the data section of this report shows, the majority of high-tech companies completed an IPO during the product shipping stage, that is, they had already started to generate product revenues. Conversely, most life-sciences companies went public during the product development stage, characterized by heavy R&D expenditures and a lack of revenues.[6]

The highest price-to-trailing revenues multiples of high-tech firms are not always observed at the IPO round; this is true in 1995 and 1996 only, as Exhibit 7 depicts. The life-sciences group shows very similar relationships between rounds, with multiples at IPO typically higher than those at earlier financing rounds. High-tech companies that went public in 1996 show the highest multiples, even at pre-IPO financing rounds. This observation indicates that companies that were priced at high multiples by venture capitalists went public at above-average multiples. The poor IPO aftermarket performance of many of these stocks suggests that (private and public equity) investors overpaid for these companies (see 'Initial

Exhibit 7

**Median price-to-trailing revenues by round and IPO year (high-tech companies), 1993–97**

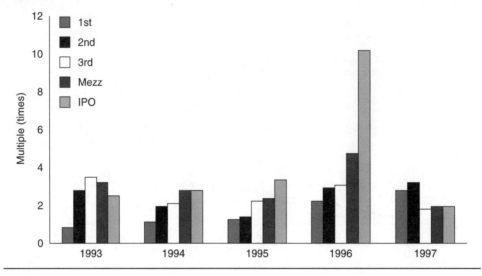

Exhibit 8

**Median price-to-trailing revenues by IPO year, 1993–97**

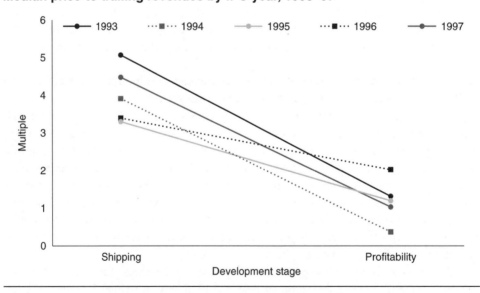

Public Offerings Often Not Letter-Perfect', *Chicago Tribune*, 27 July 1997 and 'Marketwise Perspectives', *News.com*, 20 February 1997).

There are major differences in the price-to-trailing revenues multiple at the product shipping and profitability stages (see Exhibit 8). The companies that went public in 1994 registered lower multiples at both stages of development compared to the IPOs of 1993. The companies that completed an IPO in 1996 exhibited the highest multiples of the period ana-

Exhibit 9

**Median price-to-revenues multiples by stage (IPO classes of 1996–97, high-tech industry comparison)**

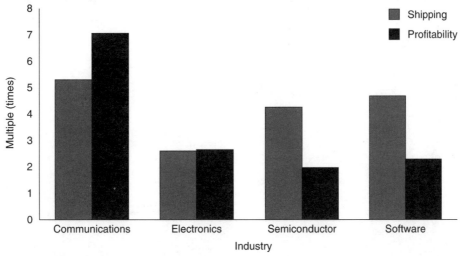

lyzed at profitability stage, while those that went public in 1993 showed top multiples at shipping stage.

We also observed disparities among industries with regard to price-to-trailing revenues multiples. Exhibit 9 shows the relationship for the 1996–97 data.

From a price-to-trailing revenues approach, communications and electronics experience an increase in multiples as companies move from product shipping to profitability. The comparison between software and semiconductor companies shows a surprising similarity: they are priced at almost identical multiples declining from product shipping to profitability stage. Similarly, the two life-sciences industries show declining price-to-trailing multiples from product shipping to profitability stage, and close to those of semiconductor and software companies.

### High-tech companies achieve higher step-ups in value than life-sciences companies, especially from seed and first financing rounds to IPO

Step-ups are increases in company valuations from one point in time to another. VentureOne tracks a company's pricing each time it has a financing round.[7] Therefore, we have a valuation point for each time (round) that a company obtains financing and observed that high-tech firms typically have higher step-ups between rounds and development stages than that of life-sciences companies. This result is attributed to the outstanding performance of two components of the high-tech group: software and communications companies. Exhibit 10 depicts these relationships.

Mezzanine investors obtain higher returns than investors in prior rounds because of the very short time between the mezzanine round and the IPO, and not as a result of a large step-up in market value, which would benefit prior rounds investors as well.[8] In fact, the closer a financing round is to the public offering, the smaller the step-up in value to the IPO.

179

Exhibit 10

**Median step-ups from each round to IPO**

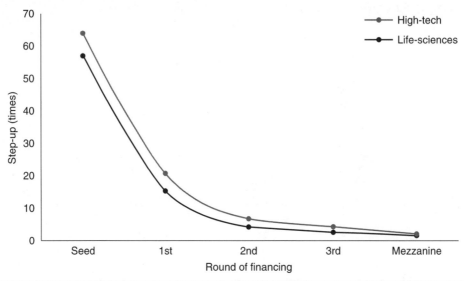

**Step-ups between consecutive financing rounds or development stages vary significantly**

In the high-tech group, the lowest step-up between two consecutive rounds typically occurred between the second and third financing rounds. This means that the value of an investment made at a second round for a high-tech company does not increase significantly (relative to changes between other rounds) at the time of the third round. This is common to all years observed. The life-sciences group shows very similar results although the lowest value creation occasionally takes place between the third and mezzanine rounds.

Regarding step-ups between development stages, both categories of industries display steady or flat step-up multiples between startup and product shipping (approximately four to five times, except high-tech in 1997), as Exhibits 11 and 12 illustrate. Nevertheless, as companies turn to profitability stage, step-up multiples tend to increase.

As shown in the statistical analysis section of this report, the shorter the period from inception to a given round, the higher the step-up in value to IPO. In addition, earlier stage, less profitable companies tended to reach higher pre-money valuations and step-ups in value the closer the financing occurred to 1996. The more quickly a company reaches milestones required for subsequent funding, the greater reason to reward the company with a greater step-up in value.

The explanation for the lower value step-ups in 1994 mirrors the pre-money valuation section of this paper. Just as the strong 1995 IPO market contributed to higher valuations in venture financings, so too did the favorable 1993 IPO market push up valuations of privately-held firms. A 'colder' 1994 IPO market drove venture valuations to only modest increases. Consequently, the step-ups in value – and returns on capitalization, or ROC – were generally lower in 1994 than in any other year. Exhibits 13 and 14 illustrate the timing effect on step-ups and returns.

The highest pre-money valuations were registered by the 'class of 1996'. Valuations in 1993 and 1995 were almost as high and slightly higher in the latter year, particularly at early

Exhibit 11

**Median high-tech's step-ups between development stages**

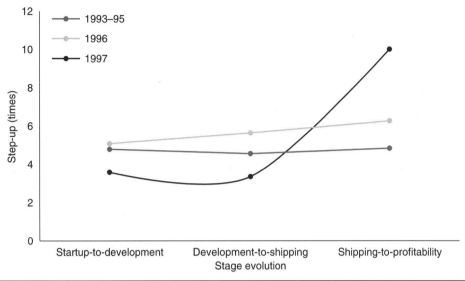

Exhibit 12

**Median life-sciences' step-ups between development stages**

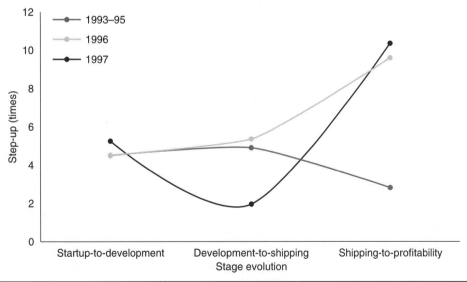

financing rounds. This explains, in part, why step-ups to IPO were lower in 1995 than in 1993 (see Exhibit 13). The 1996 IPOs show the highest ROC, followed by the IPOs of the first half of 1997, particularly for high-tech companies, as Exhibit 14 displays.

Exhibit 15 depicts the overall median ROC obtained at IPO by investors that invested in all financing rounds from seed to mezzanine (assuming equal amounts of funds were invested each time). For example, an investor that invested a fixed amount of dollars (eg, US$1 mil-

Exhibit 13

**Median step-ups to IPO by IPO year, 1993–97**

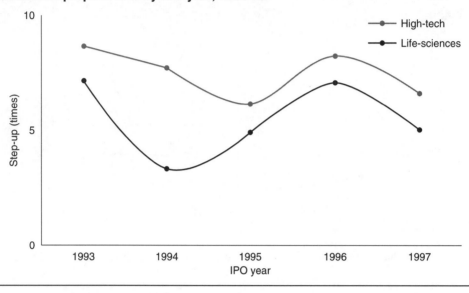

Exhibit 14

**Median ROC by IPO year, 1993–97 (%)**

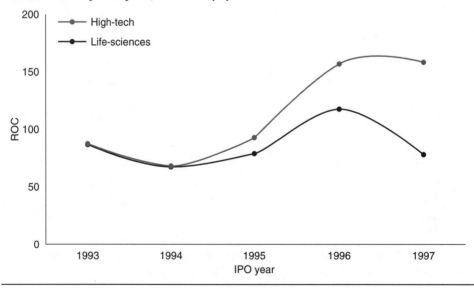

lion) in each financing round of an average communications company would have reached a median ROC of 125 per cent (on a total investment of US$5 million, assuming there were five private financing rounds, and without considering the effects of dilution). The median ROC suggests that, regardless of the pre-money valuations, investors require different returns according to three risk classes represented by the following groups: electronics and semiconductors, software and communications, and biotech and medical devices.

Exhibit 15

**Median ROC to IPO by industry – all rounds, 1993–97 (%)**

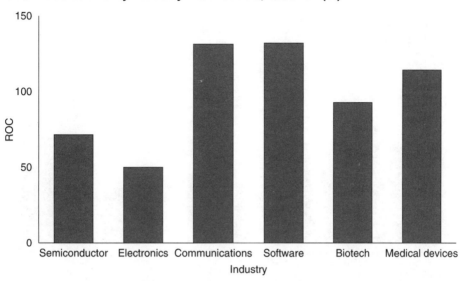

**Both high-tech and life-sciences returns on capitalization to IPO decline in the progression from seed to third rounds and increase significantly at the mezzanine round**

The data shows that seed investors generally realize higher returns than first, second and third round investors. First round investors obtain better results than second and third round investors, and second round investors reach higher returns than third round investors. Mezzanine round investors reach the highest returns, regardless of IPO year or industry. Exhibit 16 illustrates this trend.

Comparing the two groups based on ROC to IPO, high-tech has yielded higher results than life-sciences, due mainly to the strong returns of software and communications companies. Further, we identified a shift from biotech to medical devices: while the former reached a higher ROC during 1993 and 1994, medical devices outperformed in 1995 and repeated higher results in the remaining two years, registering higher returns at every round.

Returns on capitalization measure the required rate-of-return that a venture investor would expect from an investment made in a company with a given risk level. The higher the risk, the greater the required return. Given this generally accepted tenant of finance, the combination of Exhibits 15 and 16 indicates that venture investors perceive software and communications firms as a riskier investment than life-sciences companies, which in turn are riskier than semiconductors and electronics companies.

Exhibit 16 shows how, as a company proceeds to the IPO, returns on capitalization decline at every round except mezzanine. The declining returns suggest that investors consider older, more experienced companies a safer investment.

Step-ups and returns on capitalization at IPO are largely affected by the market conditions under which a company goes public. High-tech and life-sciences companies show the highest returns and step-ups in 1996, and the lowest ones in 1994 (see Exhibits 14 and 15). It cannot be overstated that the IPO market at a specific point in time has a dramatic effect on valuation. The favorable IPO market in 1996 not only increased step-ups in value but also reduced the time

Exhibit 16

**Median ROC from each financing round to IPO (%)**

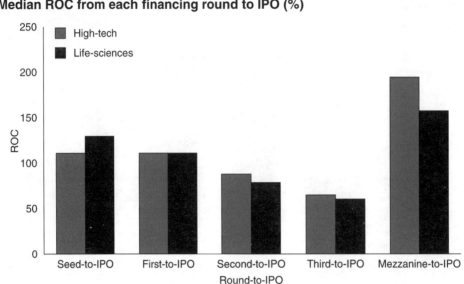

between financing rounds and the IPO, resulting in higher returns on capitalization. Although step-ups to IPO general dropped from 1996 to 1997 (see Exhibit 13), high-tech returns remained at the same level due to a shorter time to IPO (see Exhibit 14). Life-sciences' returns declined with step-ups since their time to IPO did not change significantly from prior years.

In terms of ROC both high-tech and life-sciences show very similar profiles, moving together in the same direction. However, this observation does not mean necessarily that they yield analogous returns, as Exhibit 14 illustrates. High-tech companies have consistently yielded higher median returns than life-sciences' companies since 1995. Step-ups to IPO show also parallel trends for both industries, as Exhibit 13 depicts. Generally, returns and step-ups tend to be higher for high-tech companies than life-sciences' companies for the period analyzed.

As venture capitalists' estimates of potential market for high-tech companies' products increase, they are willing to pay more for these firms. Also, the high prices paid for startups may be caused by the increasing amounts of institutional money committed to venture funds. According to a recent study by Prof. Joshua Lerner and Paul Gompers, two Harvard Business School faculty members, venture capitalists historically have paid 10 to 25 per cent more than they otherwise would for equity stakes in companies when institutional investors pour large sums of money into venture funds. These investments have had increasingly shorter payback periods (or less time to IPO) and higher IPO valuations, resulting in spectacular investor returns, especially between January 1995 and June 1997. A 'colder', or less ebullient IPO market would reduce the market pricing for such stocks. Under this scenario, step-ups in value would decline significantly, resulting in a negative impact on investor returns.

## Statistical analysis

### Objectives and methodology

The above analyses examined relationships between two variables or dimensions, as well as trends within single variables. Additional multivariate analyses were undertaken to examine the relative importance of company characteristics in valuations, as well as to describe significant differences between industries and valuation trends over time. That is, all variables were examined together to discern significance of individual characteristics.

A general linear model employing ordinary least squares was used, regressing the valuation of companies on their characteristics. These independent variables included age at round, round type, year founded, stage of development, industry segment, geographic region, and time to IPO. Revenues and number of employees (as proxy for firm size) were not used, as VentureOne has not historically archived this data.

Pre-money valuation and step-up in value were the dependent variables; their logarithms were regressed on dummy variables created from the categorical variables and on the logarithms of the continuous variables. This model was used to combine categorical and continuous variables, to control for multiplicative relationships (for example, larger/older/later stage companies can attract disproportionately larger valuations), and to control the impact of outliers.

## Results

- *Companies identified as in a profitable stage had significantly higher valuations.*
  Controlling for all other variables, companies which were profitable were more likely to have higher valuations than similar companies in development or shipping product.

- *East Coast/West Coast companies (particularly California) had significantly higher valuations.*
  Controlling for all other variables, a company located in California or Massachusetts was more likely to have a higher valuation than a similar company in another state or region.

- *Communications companies had higher valuations than other companies in the universe studied, as well as significantly higher step-ups.*
  Among companies with similar business stage status, location, and start date, communications and networking companies were more likely to have higher valuations than companies in other industries.

- *The type of financing round is the most significant factor in determining the value increase experienced by companies.*
  Later rounds are associated with higher valuations, even when considering whether a company is in product development, product shipping or profitability stage. The round type is the variable most strongly associated with level of valuation. Generally, earlier rounds tend to have lower valuations than later rounds.

- *Step-ups in value decline from start-up to profitability stages, with the aging of a company and with increases in amount raised at any particular round.*
  That is, start-up companies generally have higher step-ups than developmental stage companies which in turn generally have higher step-ups than profitable companies. Likewise, younger companies have higher step-ups than older companies, and companies raising less money in a round have higher step-ups than their higher funded counterparts.

- *With all other variables considered, specific years were not significant in determining differences in step-ups.*
  That is, after examining round types, business stage, and industry types of companies, the year of IPO was not significant in predicting the valuations of companies. Again, the round

type was most significant, location, type of industry, and business stage of companies were also significant correlates of highly-valued companies.

## Applicability of the study

This study incorporates elements that are key in any security valuation. It examines institutional investors' risk-return profiles of private placements of equity over a $4^1/2$ year period for very young companies in emerging technologies and industries.[9] In addition, it provides indications regarding the importance and prioritized weights of several variables with regard to pricing. Moreover, it demonstrates valuable insights about the differences among distinct stages of development and types of financing rounds under alternative scenarios (which correspond to the cycles observed by IPO year).

HVA has applied certain findings of this analysis to valuations of technology companies in conjunction with generally accepted valuation methodologies; the results are compelling. The methodology, which combines both the fundamental and statistical analysis, deploys a powerful tool for the valuation of technology companies (especially those in very early stages of development), and the pricing of their securities. The valuation of nascent technology firms does not respond to classic pricing methodologies or models. Technological advances are swift and the market's reaction to new products and services is somewhat unpredictable. The discounted cash flow (DCF) analysis may not deal effectively with factors that defy supportable modeling (such as selecting an appropriate discount rate). In these cases, a better indication of value comes from a market approach that is based on an analysis of truly comparable companies. The analytical method presented herein is such an approach, and the resulting valuation methodology conforms to observed and measured private pricing transactions.

## An example

Consider the utility of the study on the valuation of an Internet applications company in a very early stage of development about to negotiate a financing round with investors. The management requested that HVA perform an analysis and determine the investment value of the company. We conducted a thorough analysis of the industry, performed a due diligence of the company and applied various valuation methodologies, including the method presented herein. This method allowed us to examine several variables – pre-money valuations, returns on capitalization, value step-ups, amounts raised, and time to IPO, among others – with regard to the pricing of similar Internet applications companies with respect to age, development stage and fundraising history. Further, it provided us with a range of values for three alternative scenarios (according to the then current 'appetite' of the capital markets, a key element of the study). Finally, and in conjunction with the results derived from more conventional, widely accepted valuation methodologies (primarily discounted cash flow analysis and market approach), we determined a valuation range for the company.

## Implications of the study

This methodology adds much to the overall analysis, and to some extent it provides a superior and unique insight into valuing early stage technology and life-sciences' companies. For instance, it did not require subjective assumptions about a key factor in determining a private

186

company's value: the lack of marketability adjustment, which reduces the value of a marketable security due to the illiquidity of the private firm's stock (since it is not publicly traded). Because the data used in our analysis corresponds to companies that were private during all of their financing rounds, the pre-money valuations implicitly consider the illiquidity factor.[10] Therefore, no subjective assumptions regarding a marketability discount or further adjustment for illiquidity was needed. Furthermore, based on the pre-money valuations of these firms we calculate the illiquidity discounts applied by venture investors to these types of companies at each development stage.

The data and findings presented in this paper demonstrate the important factors necessary for equity allocation and the pricing of a broad variety of assets such as incentive stock options (ISOs) and technology (in the form of allocation of value to technology, products or patents). Finally, this analytical method is not only useful for private, corporate and institutional investors but also for entrepreneurs who require a valuation tool for analyzing their business from inception to IPO.

Address correspondence to Steve Kam, Houlihan Valuation Advisors, 180 Montgomery Street, Suite 2000, San Francisco, CA 94104.

This study and its findings are the product of the collaborative efforts of the following individuals: John Draper; Luis Gutierrez-Roy; Steve Kam; Alice Prager; Greg Robin; Russell Snipes; Dave Witherow; and Jean Yaremchuk. For information on products and services offered in conjunction with this study, please contact Steve Kam of Houlihan Valuation Advisors at 415-392-0888 or at kam@houlihan.com, or Jean Yaremchuk of VentureOne at 415-357-2100.

---

[1] VentureOne's database does not differentiate between common and preferred stock, and therefore, neither does this study.

[2] Later rounds generally include fourth, fifth and subsequent rounds of financing. The round may also be called later when the company has been in business for a few years, is not considered a startup, previous financings are uncertain, and there is no other round categorization that fits.

[3] For inquiries regarding development stages (ie, beta testing/human clinical trial) or financing rounds (ie, later rounds, leveraged buy-outs, restarts and Regulation D) not presented herein, please refer to the end of the article for contact information.

[4] Additional data regarding yearly combinations of financings and development stages is available upon request.

[5] For further information with regard to venture financings that occurred after June 1997, and transactions involving venture capital-backed companies which went public before 1993 or have not completed an IPO yet, you may contact VentureOne.

[6] Of the 34 companies that went public during the first half of 1997, 24 per cent of their venture financings occurred in 1996, 20 per cent in 1995, and 13.5 per cent in 1994. During 1996, 143 companies went public. The concentration of venture financings followed a similar pattern: 27 per cent in 1995; 15 per cent in 1994; and 17 per cent in 1993. In addition, the majority of rounds closed in 1995 and 1996 correspond to high-tech companies, which may explain why this group, not life-sciences, experienced elevated pre-money valuations in those two years.

[7] The return will depend both on the increase of the company's equity value – as a proxy for investment value, without consideration of the effects of dilution – and the time between that financing round and the public offering. Therefore, given a value increase, the shorter the period of time between a round and the IPO, the greater the return received by investors.

[8] To participate in a mezzanine round, investors are often required to participate in prior rounds. By investing in earlier rounds, venture investors have the opportunity to participate in the attractive mezzanine round but also maintain – to some extent – their ownership percentage of the company, thus reducing the dilution effects that the entrance of new investors may cause.

[9] The study does not analyze IPOs that occurred after 20 June 1997.

[10] The adjustment for lack of marketability observed in our data derives from venture capital transactions and may not reflect the adjustment that other types of investors (ie, strategic investors) apply in their valuations.

# Chapter 16

# The evolution of the UK venture capital industry: the dynamics of capital, entrepreneurship, public policy and investors

Vicky Mudford
*Director, Murray Johnstone Private Equity Limited, in charge of Investor Relations (Executive Director of the British Venture Capital Association, 1984–1997)*

In the New Oxford English Dictionary, published in the summer of 1998, venture capital was, for the first time, listed. It is defined as:

> '**venture capital**. *n.* Money put up for speculative business investment'

Whether we agree with the definition is immaterial but what is important is that the UK venture capital industry has matured enough to be seen as part of the financial community, that it warranted inclusion.

Today, the UK venture capital industry is second largest in the world after the United States, and accounts for around half the total European venture capital investment. This is a far cry from the small, nascent industry of the early 1980s. I remember when I first started working in the venture capital industry in 1981 for an independent firm, Alan Patricof Associates (Apax Partners as it is known today), there was definitely a feeling that as an industry we were not to be taken seriously – here today and gone tomorrow. Consequently there was a pioneering spirit on the part of those players in existence in the UK at that time – around 30 firms who between them managed around £300 million – today there are over 120 UK firms managing well in excess of £40 billion. Both 3i and Charterhouse had been in venture capital since World War II, but until the early 1980s had been operating in a fairly static entrepreneurial environment. The arrival of The Rt. Hon Margaret Thatcher MP as the British prime minster in the late 1970s did much to change this. In her Budget in late 1979, she cut the top rate of income tax from 80 per cent to 40 per cent. This, combined with the launch of the Unlisted Stock Market (USM, the secondary market to the main market of the London Stock Exchange) gave huge encouragement to the venture capital industry, as it offered a realisation route.

In 1983, four UK venture capitalists decided to found the British Venture Capital Association (BVCA) with the support of the Bank of England and the Department of Trade & Industry (DTI). Although an association has rather dull connotations, a lobbying forum was needed to encourage politicians, the media, potential entrepreneurs, investors and professional firms to understand what venture capital was and what it could do and the impact it would have on the UK economy. This the BVCA achieved over the following years.

## The evolution of UK public policy

Government *financial* support was not needed but it was important that politicians understood the economic impact of venture capital and the relevant spin-offs. If politicians talked about the industry, this would have a domino effect of encouraging the media to write about venture capital and the entrepreneurs involved. The articles would, in turn, be read by potential entrepreneurs, investors and those setting policy. In order to attract their attention, hard facts were needed. But the industry was new, with only a few years' track record behind it. The numbers we had did not look that convincing as their totals were so small and so could not bring a convincing argument to the table. It took the BVCA about five years to collect the statistical proof which could be used with the key audiences to raise the perception of entrepreneurship and the role venture capital could play.

Political recognition was not necessarily wanted for venture capital firms, but for potential entrepreneurs – the mainstay of our industry. Entrepreneurs were likely to come from a range of professional backgrounds, but there was little financial incentive for them to give up what was a very secure package. The government needed to recognise that entrepreneurs make a vital contribution to the UK economy – they run businesses which in turn create jobs, make substantial contributions to the Exchequer, exports, and so on, and for taking the risk they should be incentivised. Entrepreneurs were, and still are to a lesser extent, penalised for taking the risk of running a business. Until recently, if they sold their equity interest after a number of years, they had to pay a 40 per cent capital gains tax (CGT) rate, one of the highest CGT rates in the western world. This is even more ridiculous when one considers that UK pension funds – those providing some of the capital to the venture capital funds in the first place, do not pay any CGT at all, yet they see the financial upside of a successfully backed entrepreneur. For many years the BVCA lobbied continuously for financial incentives for entrepreneurs, focusing particularly on the abolition or a reduction in CGT. The Conservative government did much to encourage the entrepreneurial culture and introduced a variety of incentives for entrepreneurs: CGT roll-over relief, retirement relief, inheritance tax relief and various other tax initiatives. The Labour government has also taken on the entrepreneurship cause. In 1998 Labour introduced a tapered CGT relief – though there is some scepticism about whether this tapered relief will actually work. And in 1999, at a British Venture Capital Association conference, the prime minister, The Rt Hon Tony Blair MP, stated publicly, 'I want this government to be the champion of entrepreneurs. We need more of you. We need government policy to reflect this. We need society as a whole to applaud you ... We've asked the former chief of Ford, Alex Trottman, to review policies and small business enterprise and entrepreneurship and consider what further steps the government should take.' This public statement from the prime minister shows that at last it would seem that venture capital has come of age in the eyes of politicians. Labour, or rather New Labour, want to be in the front row when it comes to applauding the success of the industry.

One key issue in the early 1980s was to find an onshore investment vehicle that UK venture capital managers could use. Until 1987, many UK venture capital funds were run offshore to avoid double taxation. The administration of these funds was onerous. In 1987, the

Inland Revenue and the DTI agreed to an onshore structure called a 'limited partnership'. The government had realised that they were losing income by not having onshore vehicles. The limited partnership has, to date, proved to be the most popular investment vehicle for independent UK funds, though with the passage of time it might itself become dated unless revised. This is mainly due to the fact that some institutions which invest in limited partnerships find the 10-year life of the fund too long-term and restrictive. On this latter point, there is now an active secondary market for institutions to sell their venture capital positions. Over the past few years, various investment vehicles have been introduced and it would not be surprising, if in 10 years' time, the limited partnership has been replaced or augmented with a more flexible vehicle or vehicles.

## Differences between the UK and US markets

The UK venture capital industry has, for the most part, followed in the footsteps of the US venture capital/private equity industry in terms of its evolution and the problems faced. It is worth mentioning here the various definitional differences between the UK and US industries. The terms venture capital and private equity describe equity investments in unquoted companies. In the UK and much of continental Europe, venture capital is used interchangeably with the term private equity, and in this article I will use the term venture capital. In the US, venture capital usually refers to the provision of funds for young, entrepreneurial businesses, many of which are in technology-related sectors, whereas private equity is mainly associated with the financing of leveraged management buyouts and buyins (MBOs and MBIs). What is interesting to note, however, is that in the last few years, and particularly during 1999, there has been an explosion of interest in new technology and start-up funds throughout Europe, with many venture capital firms now including technology and start-ups in their investment criteria.It would not be surprising to see the gap narrowing between UK and US definitions where venture capital really does mean start-up/expansion finance only.

## Entrepreneurs

The culture and entrepreneurial environments in each country are also very different. In the US, entrepreneurship has been actively encouraged by the government for many years and is an accepted part of society. Entrepreneurs operate in an environment that encourages and celebrates their financial success with many becoming national heroes. Entrepreneurs who have failed are encouraged to go out and try again; there is no stigma attached to failure. In the US, entrepreneurs are also much better qualified. If you meet a managing director or a top executive of a technology firm, it is likely that not only will he/she have a technology degree but will have also been to business school.

In the UK, the growth of entrepreneurship has been slow, though the past 16 years have seen society's perception of entrepreneurship change quite radically, most noticeably in the last few years. The venture capital industry does have some entrepreneur role models but very few are national heroes. There is still a stigma attached to failure, which is not seen as a sign of experience, unlike in the US. Also in the UK, entrepreneurs have been far less qualified than their counterparts in the US, though this too is slowly changing. Business schools and universities are beginning to include courses on entrepreneurship in their curriculum, something that their US counterparts have been doing for many years. There is also some stigma attached to making money, but this too is changing – having money or old money is approved of, but the making of it isn't!

## Early-stage/technology versus management buyouts/management buyins (MBOs/MBIs)

In the early 1980s, most UK venture capital investment was aimed at early-stage and often technology-related businesses following the US format. For many firms this was not a success. The cost of doing these types of investments was high, investments took longer to realise; there were no public markets that they could float on and there was a very high failure rate. At the time, UK venture capital managers had limited investment experience in these sectors and many progressed to making less risky investments in expansion stage situations and by the late 1980s in MBOs and MBIs. This migration highlighted the so-called 'equity gap' for smaller/early-stage companies looking to raise smaller amounts of equity finance.

Exhibit 1

**UK investment by stage, 1984–98 (£ million)**

| | *Early stage* | | | | *Expansion* | | | | *MBO/MBI* | | | *Total amount invested* |
| Year | Start-up | Early | Total | Exp | Ref | 2ndry | Total | MBO | MBI | Total | Grand total |
|------|----------|-------|-------|-----|-----|-------|-------|-----|-----|-------|------|-------|
| 1984 | 25 | 13 | 38 | 62 | n/a | 11 | 73 | n/a | n/a | *29 | 140 |
| 1985 | 32 | 18 | 50 | 104 | n/a | 16 | 120 | n/a | n/a | *107 | 277 |
| 1986 | 58 | 28 | 86 | 104 | n/a | 20 | 124 | n/a | n/a | *174 | 384 |
| 1987 | 75 | 45 | 120 | 278 | n/a | 23 | 301 | 480 | 33 | 513 | 934 |
| 1988 | 70 | 60 | 130 | 402 | n/a | 33 | 435 | n/a | n/a | 733 | 1,298 |
| 1989 | 86 | 129 | 215 | 319 | n/a | 19 | 338 | n/a | n/a | 867 | 1,420 |
| 1990 | 76 | 52 | 128 | 343 | n/a | 53 | 396 | n/a | n/a | 582 | 1,106 |
| 1991 | 35 | 23 | 58 | 261 | 72 | 54 | 387 | n/a | n/a | 544 | 989 |
| 1992 | 43 | 39 | 82 | 279 | 43 | 40 | 362 | 670 | 137 | 807 | 1,251 |
| 1993 | 34 | 35 | 69 | 295 | 12 | 86 | 393 | 585 | 184 | 769 | 1,231 |
| 1994 | 45 | 31 | 76 | 415 | 6 | 59 | 480 | 797 | 315 | 1,112 | 1,668 |
| 1995 | 26 | 59 | 85 | 419 | 5 | 71 | 495 | 1,090 | 470 | 1,560 | 2,140 |
| 1996 | 41 | 90 | 131 | 384 | 31 | 177 | 592 | 1,566 | 517 | 2,083 | 2,806 |
| 1997 | 58 | 101 | 159 | 678 | 8 | 221 | 907 | 1,513 | 487 | 2,000 | 3,066 |
| 1998 | 111 | 177 | 288 | 688 | 3 | 131 | 822 | 2,129 | 536 | 2,665 | 3,775 |
| **Total** | **811** | **904** | **1,715** | **n/a** | **n/a** | **n/a** | **6,225** | **n/a** | **n/a** | **14,545** | **22,485** |

Notes

1. Figures are not strictly comparable as membership changes annually. 3i Investment is not included in the 1984–86 figures.

2. * Includes investment in 'acquisitions' as well as 'MBOs/MBIs'.

3. 1992–date: Secured debt is included where it is concurrent or alongside equity investment or where it is rescue finance. Previously only unsecured debt as part of an equity/quasi-equity package was included.

*Source:* BVCA.

In 1995, the Conservative government introduced venture capital trusts (VCTs), a listed investment vehicle that gives investors dividends and capital gains, free of tax as well as income tax relief on the subscription of new shares. VCTs were designed to encourage funding for smaller UK companies – those that have traditionally found it hard to raise capital. A VCT can only invest up to £1 million a year in any one company. VCTs have to date

Exhibit 2

## UK investment by industry sector, 1984–98 (£ million)

| Year | Consumer related | Computer related | Electronics related | Industrial products | Medical health biotech | Communications | Energy | Transport | Construction | Financial services | Other services | Manufacturing, agriculture and other | Total |
|---|---|---|---|---|---|---|---|---|---|---|---|---|
| 1984* | 26 | 22 | 11 | 6 | 7 | 7 | 5 | 3 | 2 | n/a | 18 | 6 | (*113) 140 |
| 1985* | 33 | 32 | 21 | 12 | 7 | 13 | 2 | 6 | 6 | 10 | 15 | 14 | (*171) 277 |
| 1986* | 39 | 21 | 15 | 13 | 17 | 14 | 1 | 16 | 4 | 19 | 25 | 6 | (*190) 384 |
| 1987 | 260 | 46 | 39 | 101 | 46 | 17 | 8 | 36 | 46 | 46 | 219 | 70 | 934 |
| 1988 | 457 | 56 | 19 | 103 | 23 | 18 | 6 | 40 | 84 | 166 | 72 | 254 | 1,298 |
| 1989 | 605 | 74 | 28 | 112 | 46 | 29 | 18 | 72 | 98 | 38 | 110 | 190 | 1,420 |
| 1990 | 386 | 67 | 25 | 67 | 49 | 17 | 3 | 95 | 77 | 80 | 88 | 152 | 1,106 |
| 1991 | 326 | 65 | 36 | 103 | 23 | 6 | 25 | 78 | 39 | 33 | 156 | 99 | 989 |
| 1992 | 396 | 30 | 19 | 159 | 42 | 23 | 125 | 82 | 53 | 42 | 164 | 116 | 1,251 |
| 1993 | 390 | 109 | 58 | 103 | 101 | 13 | 10 | 129 | 93 | 73 | 70 | 82 | 1,231 |
| 1994 | 482 | 82 | 54 | 238 | 67 | 37 | 18 | 136 | 74 | 88 | 106 | 286 | 1,668 |
| 1995 | 536 | 129 | 84 | 248 | 181 | 101 | 79 | 276 | 94 | 30 | 125 | 257 | 2,140 |
| 1996 | 769 | 96 | 69 | 581 | 183 | 104 | 30 | 104 | 48 | 203 | 315 | 304 | 2,806 |
| 1997 | 899 | 179 | 103 | 414 | 236 | 171 | 73 | 174 | 112 | 79 | 277 | 349 | 3,066 |
| 1998 | 557 | 253 | 103 | 381 | 210 | 506 | 57 | 129 | 101 | 58 | 502 | 918 | 3,775 |
| **Total** | **6,161** | **1,261** | **684** | **2,641** | **1,238** | **1,076** | **460** | **1,376** | **931** | **965** | **2,262** | **3,103** | **\*22,485** |

Notes

1. Figures are not strictly comparable due to annual membership changes.
2. The totals in 1985 and 1986 were restated when 3i plc joined the BVCA in 1987.
3. *These industry sector sub-totals exclude some types of deals, therefore they do not correlate to the final column on the far right.

   *1984: Figures exclude buy-out and acquisitions.

   *1985: Figures exclude buy-ins/outs and acquisitions.

   *1986: Figures exclude buy-ins/outs, acquisitions and secondary purchases.
4. 1992–93: Secured debt is included where it is concurrent or alongside equity investment, or where it is rescue finance. Previously only unsecured debt as part of an equity/quasi-equity package was included.
5. Consumer related = leisure, retailing, food, products, services.
6. Computer related = hardware, Internet, semiconductors, software.
7. Electronics related = components, instrumentation, other.
8. Industrial products = chemicals and materials, services, automation.
9. *£22,485 million: Total investment in the UK includes deals that were omitted in the industry sector investment tables in 1984–86.

*Source:* BVCA.

Exhibit 3

## Key listing requirements for AIM, Easdaq and the LSE

| Name of exchange | AIM (based in London and managed by the London Stock Exchange) | Easdaq (electronic exchange, similar to Nasdaq in the US, based in London) | The main market LSE |
|---|---|---|---|
| Description | Secondary market established in 1985 for young, fast growing businesses, including start-ups, MBOs, MBIs, family owned businesses, former BES (Business Expansion Scheme) companies. | European stock market for high-growth companies, which started trading in November 1996 and modelled on the successful Nasdaq National Market. | One of the largest and oldest stock markets in the world, established in the 18th century, currently trading over 3000 companies (including AIM and overseas companies), with a total market capitalisation of over £3,680 billion (as at 31 December 1997). |
| Company size | No requirement for company to be a certain size. | Must have total assets of at least Ecu3.5 million (US$4 million) and capital and reserves of at least Ecu2 million (US$2.3 million). | Equity capitalisation to be in excess of £700,000 (approx. US$1.15 million). |
| Shareholding | No requirement to have a defined number of shares in public hands or prove a lengthy trading history. | Easdaq expects 20 per cent of the company capital to be publicly held and recommends a minimum number of 100 shareholders. | 25 per cent of shares should normally be held by persons unconnected with the company. |
| Trading period | Normally required to be trading for several years – very short trading records may need closer attention. | No minimum level of profitability is required. | Normal minimum requirement for trading under current management is three years. Exceptions are made to allow a wider range of companies to join. |
| Regulation | Model Code for Directors' Dealings (see LSE). | Companies coming to a public market for the first time are required to undertake that directors will not dispose of any shares for at least six months from admission to trading on Easdaq except through a public offering. | Model Code for Directors' Dealings – Directors are expected to follow the Model Code in all dealings in their company's securities. |
| | | Dual listing is available on Easdaq for companies already listed on certain other exchanges eg, Nasdaq. | |

been very successful, having raised over £700 million. This initiative was followed in 1996 by two studies by the Bank of England and the Confederation of British Industry (CBI) which looked at other ways of encouraging more capital into early-stage and technology-related businesses. Policy-makers were persuaded that in order to encourage early stage and particularly technology investing, the government must be seen to be supporting it, both politically and financially. The Labour government has responded to this by launching in early 1998 The University Challenge – a £50 million venture capital fund directed at getting ideas out of universities – encouraging the link between academics and venture capital managers. This initiative, though small in terms of money, is wholeheartedly supported by the industry. It will highlight the lack of business experience possessed by those with the ideas.

Momentum has been building up in the technology sectors. Over the past two years, a plethora of technology-related funds have been launched in the UK and continental Europe, matched at a pace by the growth in European technology-friendly stock markets.

Exhibits 2 and 3 show the growth of funding the various financing stages and industrial sectors. Although most of the money invested on an annual basis is in MBOs and MBIs, expansion financings dominate in terms of the number of companies backed.

## The development of European IPO markets

Trade sales/strategic buyers have always been, and remain today, the most popular exit route for venture-backed companies, particularly for companies in the mid-sized market. The reasons for this are fairly obvious: it is cheaper than floating a business; it is quicker; it often creates a partnership with a similar business; and the venture capital firm is generally able to get all of its cash out. This exit route is usually always available and is not so affected by the vagaries of economic cycles and the impact these have on IPO markets. Floating a business can take up a lot of management time, taking the team away from the business for several months; it is an expensive process; it brings somewhat onerous responsibilities – both to the City (the UK's Wall Street) and shareholders; and the venture capital firm may well be restricted from realising its investment for a period of time.

That said, the importance of IPO markets for the venture capital industry cannot be overstated, particularly for the larger deals, The growth in the number of IPOs on the London Stock Exchange owes much to the long-term expansion of the UK venture capital industry. Buoyant IPO markets allow venture capital investors to attribute independent values to portfolio companies and facilitate profitable exits, stimulating the inflow of capital into the venture capital industry. An HSBC James Capel MBO Index of MBO flotations capitalised at over £25 million shows that, where venture capital firms were significantly involved in their development 'both in the short and long term, venture capital backed flotations continue to outperform the market by a significant margin [and have] notably outperformed the small companies indices and their sectors by a large margin.'

In the early 1980s, the USM (Unlisted Stock Market) was launched as a secondary market to the main market of the London Stock Exchange. The USM was supported by the venture capital industry but with its various restrictions on the types of companies that it could float, it was replaced in early 1995 by the Alternative Investment Market (AIM). AIM seeks to attract small-cap companies, and, with fewer restrictions than its predecessor, means that more immature companies can join. Since AIM has been trading, nearly 20 per cent of fund-raising flotations have been venture-backed companies,.most of which were expansion-stage businesses at the time of receiving venture capital. The main UK market, the LSE, has seen the flotation of many MBOs and MBIs. In the four years to 31 December 1998, 30 per cent of trading company flotations were venture-backed companies.

The mid-1998 downturn in the UK IPO markets has affected those venture capital firms wishing to exit from some of their larger investments, and it will require some inno-vative thinking to realise their capital within the necessary time-frame. However, a down-turn in IPO markets also creates significant opportunities. In the UK today, public to private transactions (companies quoted on the main market being taken private again) are frequent, with 1999 being the most active year. The downturn has also seen companies that may have thought of raising capital on the public markets looking to the venture capital industry instead.

Technology-related businesses suffered for many years by not being able to raise capital on the public markets. The relaxation in the listing rules for IPO companies in allowing loss-making companies to join the main market was particularly beneficial for biotechnology companies. In November 1999, the LSE launched TechMARK, a market totally dedicated to trading in innovative technology companies.

The last few years have seen the launch of a number of continental European stock mar-kets, some in response to the rapid growth in the venture capital industry. The first was Easdaq, which was launched in 1994. It was set up mirroring Nasdaq in the United States and offers a dual-listing facility with Nasdaq. Easdaq's launch was followed swiftly by the Nouveau Marché (France), the Neuer Markt (Germany) and the Euro NM (a joint market between sev-eral European countries), to name a few. Recently Nasdaq has announced that it will be open-ing up in London, in response, no doubt, to the surge in technology companies in Europe. Some of these public markets are relatively immature, but with the recent growth of venture capital activity in continental Europe, they will have a major role to play in the years to come.

## The economic impact of venture capital

Venture capital plays a crucial role in the financing and creation of successful enterprises in the United Kingdom and these enterprises have been shown to grow faster than companies financed by other means. In 1998, the BVCA and PricewaterhouseCoopers repeated a major survey originally undertaken in 1996 on the economic impact of venture capital in the UK. The 1998 survey found that:

- **Venture-backed companies create more jobs**
  Over the four years to 1998, the number of people employed in venture-backed compa-nies grew by 24 per cent per annum against a national growth rate of less than 1.3 per cent per annum. Over two million people in the UK are estimated to be employed by companies currently using venture capital, a figure that represents 4 per cent of the national workforce.

- **Venture-backed companies boost the UK economy**
  On average, venture-backed companies increased:

  – sales by 40 per cent a year, or twice as fast as FTSE 100 companies;

- exports by 44 per cent per annum compared with a national growth rate of 8 per cent;
- pre-tax profits by 24 per cent per annum; and
- investment by 34 per cent per annum compared with a national increase of 7 per cent.

• All the companies felt that the venture capital firms had made a major contribution besides the provision of money, and rated the venture capital firms as superior in terms of effectiveness and commitment to their commercial banks.

• 95 per cent of venture-backed companies claimed that they would not have existed, or would have grown less rapidly, without venture capital.

What is encouraging about this most recent survey is that the growth rates have grown quite considerably from the previous survey in 1996 and the results of similar surveys carried out in other countries including France, Australia, and the United States show similar results. This kind of data is absolutely vital in maintaining support from governments by demonstrating that venture-backed business, from start-ups to large MBOs, create jobs and wealth for the UK economy.

## Venture capital today

There is no doubt that the venture capital industry today is recognised as playing a key role in the UK economy and can challenge any criticism that it has not performed. The industry has matured and improved, but it would be foolish to pretend that the growth has been without its problems. The excesses of the late 1980s, when there was a lot of cash to invest, had an impact on the venture capital industry. Some UK firms were guilty of engineering financial structures for companies that ultimately could not stand up in a recession.

The regulatory environment for investment has since become much tougher (in the early 1980s, regulation was virtually non-existent), ensuring a high standard of professionalism in the industry. However, there is a feeling that there is a danger of the industry becoming over-regulated, and one result of this could be that it drives the financial services market away from London. Venture capital is a relatively low-risk area of the financial services industry and this should be recognised by the government and the regulators. Business deregulation has created investment opportunities in industry sectors such as telecommunications and financial services. Consumer habits have changed and new retail concepts have enabled venture capital firms to fund substantial companies. Venture capital firms have been able to demonstrate the added value they can bring to businesses. There appears to be a general acceptance by entrepreneurs today that venture capitalists can bring more to the table than money.

## Fund raising

The last few years have seen fund-raising records being set. It should be noted that Exhibit 4 only gives an indication of the funds available. There has been a huge growth in billion-dollar pan-European funds being raised by UK and US managers in the last couple of years (not all are included in the figures in the exhibit). It is estimated that of the funds raised over the last couple of years, less than 50 per cent will be available to UK companies, with the remainder expected to be invested outside the UK. Apart from pan-European funds,

Exhibit 4

## UK funds raised by BVCA member firms for the years ended 31 December 1998 (£ million)

| | 1987 | 1988 | 1989 | 1990 | 1991 | 1992 | 1993 | 1994 | 1995 | 1996 | 1997 | 1998 | Total | % of total |
|---|---|---|---|---|---|---|---|---|---|---|---|---|---|---|
| *Pension funds* | | | | | | | | | | | | | | |
| UK | 221 | 130 | 433 | 175 | 149 | 97 | 113 | 437 | 170 | 734 | 622 | 553 | 3,833 | 16 |
| Overseas | 58 | 59 | 331 | 117 | 95 | 99 | 130 | 359 | 191 | 519 | 1,397 | 1,875 | 5,230 | 23 |
| *Insurance companies* | | | | | | | | | | | | | | |
| UK | 68 | 56 | 167 | 82 | 25 | 72 | 92 | 239 | 131 | 221 | 1,160 | 152 | 2,465 | 11 |
| Overseas | 53 | 71 | 158 | 39 | 12 | 7 | 25 | 128 | 12 | 104 | 505 | 193 | 1,307 | 6 |
| *Corporate investors* | | | | | | | | | | | | | | |
| UK | 5 | 13 | 72 | 40 | 7 | 1 | 12 | 145 | 32 | 29 | 376 | 83 | 815 | 3 |
| Overseas | 35 | 36 | 128 | 105 | 20 | 29 | 69 | 280 | 18 | 51 | 428 | 432 | 1,629 | 7 |
| *Other sources* | | | | | | | | | | | | | | |
| UK | 205 | 127 | 676 | 202 | 82 | 108 | 147 | 683 | 78 | 399 | 640 | 727 | 7,783 | 34 |
| Overseas | | | | | | | | 280 | 117 | 388 | 1,368 | 1,555 | | |
| **Total** | **645** | **492** | **1,964** | **760** | **390** | **413** | **588** | **2,551** | **749** | **2,445** | **6,496** | **5,570** | **23,062** | **100** |
| **Total UK** | **n/a** | **n/a** | **n/a** | **n/a** | **n/a** | **n/a** | **n/a** | **1,504** | **412** | **1,383** | **2,798** | **1,515** | | |
| **Total overseas** | | | | | | | | **1,047** | **337** | **1,062** | **3,698** | **4,055** | | |

Note

Other sources includes primarily banks and private individuals, government agencies, academic institutions and others including investment trusts.

*Source:* BVCA.

firms have been raising sector-specific funds, particularly with regard to technology. It is estimated by Private Equity Europe that in the last two years €12.9 billion have been raised for technology-focused funds across Europe, with the UK taking up about 25 per cent of that amount.

## Performance

Can the venture capital industry provide returns consistently superior to those available from other asset classes? The answer is yes. For many years, the UK industry had no independent means of performance measurement, mainly due to the immaturity of the industry. Performance data (The Performance Measurement Survey 1998, produced by The WM Company for the BVCA) has been available since 1995. In 1998, composite performance since inception showed a net internal rate of return (IRR) of 14.9 per cent. This number covers independent UK funds investing primarily in the United Kingdom in all financing stages. The numbers also show that venture capital has outperformed returns produced by UK pension funds. When making comparisons, it is important to remember that pension funds are measured gross.

Performance figures are available for all types of funds and vintage years and show that superior returns can be obtained across a range of funds. Although better performance can be

Exhibit 5

## BVCA performance measurement survey, 1998

Overall performance by investment stage

**Current year and longer-term return (% per annum)**

|  | No of funds | 1998 | Three years | Five years | Ten years |
|---|---|---|---|---|---|
| Early stage | 23 | 27.8 | 4.0 | 7.3 | 8.4 |
| Development | 44 | 13.9 | 27.4 | 22.9 | 8.9 |
| Mid MBO | 41 | 19.7 | 29.6 | 27.7 | 15.1 |
| Large MBO | 44 | 28.4 | 28.1 | 23.3 | 22.9 |
| Generalist | 37 | 64.8 | 33.8 | 20.7 | 7.1 |
| Total (ex ITs) | 189 | 30.1 | 28.8 | 22.1 | 13.1 |
| UK | 173 | 26.0 | 33.7 | 27.4 | 12.9 |
| Non-UK | 16 | 44.5 | 13.2 | 10.1 | 14.7 |
| Investments trust (ITs) | 17 | 12.2 | 15.1 | 15.9 | 14.5 |

**Since inception return (% per annum)**

|  | No of funds | To Dec-98 | To Dec-97 | To Dec-96 | To Dec-95 |
|---|---|---|---|---|---|
| Early stage | 17 | 8.3 | 8.2 | 6.5 | 4.3 |
| Development | 34 | 9.1 | 8.9 | 8.1 | 6.9 |
| Mid MBO | 27 | 16.5 | 16.6 | 16.2 | 16.2 |
| Large MBO | 28 | 19.2 | 19.7 | 25.4 | 23.8 |
| Generalist | 30 | 13.5 | 11.7 | 9.9 | 9.7 |
| Total (ex ITs) | 136 | 14.9 | 14.0 | 14.2 | 13.0 |
| UK | 125 | 15.5 | 15.0 | 16.4 | 14.4 |
| Non-UK | 11 | 9.8 | 7.6 | 8.2 | 7.0 |

**Principal comparators' return (% per annum)**

|  | 1998 | Three years | Five years | Ten years |
|---|---|---|---|---|
| *UK pension funds (WM All Funds Universe)* |  |  |  |  |
| UK equities | 12.0 | 17.1 | 13.4 | 15.6 |
| Overseas equities | 17.2 | 8.9 | 7.6 | 11.5 |
| Total assets | 14.0 | 13.8 | 11.0 | 13.3 |
| *Indices* |  |  |  |  |
| FTSE All-Share | 13.8 | 17.9 | 13.9 | 15.9 |
| FTSE 100 | 17.5 | 20.9 | 15.8 | 17.5 |
| FTSE SmallCap | -8.1 | 5.1 | 5.2 | 7.2 |
| FTSE Fledgling | -6.7 | 4.1 | n/a | n/a |
| FT/S&P World (ex UK) | 22.3 | 13.9 | 12.4 | 11.1 |
| FT/S&P Europe (ex UK) | 31.5 | 23.1 | 18.0 | 16.8 |

**Other comparators' return (% per annum)**

|  | 1998 | Three years | Five years | Ten years |
|---|---|---|---|---|
| *UK pension funds (WM All Funds Universe)* |  |  |  |  |
| UK bonds | 20.6 | 14.6 | 10.1 | 12.7 |
| Overseas bonds | 11.6 | 3.6 | 5.5 | 10.6 |
| UK index-linked | 20.3 | 13.5 | 8.5 | 10.3 |
| Cash | 7.3 | 6.8 | 6.9 | 9.4 |
| Property | 12.8 | 12.5 | 10.6 | 7.4 |
| *Inflation indices* |  |  |  |  |
| Retail Price Index | 2.8 | 2.9 | 3.0 | 4.1 |
| Average earnings | 4.5 | 4.7 | 4.3 | 5.3 |

*Sources:* BVCA, The WM Company.

seen in the MBO and MBI funds, even early-stage funds, where performance takes longer to come through, are beginning to show better performance year-on-year. In 1999, for the first time, the BVCA produced performance statistics on funds dedicated to, or including, investment in UK technology companies (the returns had historically been hidden within the annual Performance Measurement Survey). To summarise, overall high-technology investments have produced an average return of 23 per cent.

Performance will inevitably be better in some years than in others, and like all industries, venture capital is affected by economic cycles. However, provided that investing institutions understand that venture capital is a medium- to long-term investment, overall superior performance can be achieved. Investing institutions must also learn to diversify among fund managers. They must choose venture capital managers with relevant experience and track records who can prove their competitive edge in their respective sectors.

## Investor participation and lack of it

What is perhaps disappointing in the United Kingdom, and certainly surprising to US institutions, is the lack of participation by UK institutions in this asset class, despite the availability of performance data. US institutions have been, and continue to be, one of the largest single country contributors to UK funds. For many years, UK pension funds have been the largest contributors to UK venture capital funds, but as can be seen from Exhibit 6, this has changed in the last few years.

Exhibit 6

**UK funds raised by source and by country, 1991–98 (£ million)**

|  | 1998 | 1997 | 1996 | 1995 | 1994 | 1993 | 1992 | 1991 |
|---|---|---|---|---|---|---|---|---|
| *By source* | | | | | | | | |
| Banks | 1,023 | 705 | 221 | 49 | 592 | 45 | 10 | 14 |
| Pension funds | 2,428 | 2,019 | 1,253 | 361 | 796 | 232 | 157 | 251 |
| Insurance companies | 345 | 1,665 | 325 | 143 | 368 | 106 | 72 | 34 |
| Corporate investors | 515 | 804 | 80 | 50 | 424 | 37 | 50 | 20 |
| Private individuals | 309 | 306 | 176 | 47 | 96 | 19 | 38 | 22 |
| Government agencies | 439 | 244 | 83 | 17 | 35 | 3 | 5 | 1 |
| Academic institutions | | | 55 | 50 | 10 | 21 | 0 | 6 |
| Others (includes investment trusts) | 511 | 753 | 252 | 32 | 230 | 17 | 14 | 20 |
| **Total** | **5,570** | **6,496** | **2,445** | **749** | **2,551** | **479** | **347** | **368** |
| As restated in 1994 | | | | | | 588 | 413 | 390 |
| *By country* | | | | | | | | |
| UK | 1,515 | 2,798 | 1,383 | 412 | 1,504 | 202 | 221 | 219 |
| Rest of Europe | 815 | 842 | 135 | 78 | 145 | 52 | 30 | 33 |
| North America | 2,865 | 2,359 | 822 | 235 | 723 | 216 | 57 | 111 |
| Asia | 174 | 261 | 55 | 5 | 97 | 2 | 10 | 3 |
| Others | 201 | 236 | 50 | 19 | 82 | 6 | 28 | 2 |
| **Total** | **5,570** | **6,496** | **2,445** | **749** | **2,551** | **479** | **347** | **368** |
| As restated in 1994 | | | | | | 588 | 413 | 390 |

*Source:* BVCA.

The US institutional market is a healthy feeding ground for the UK to raise capital, but it would be positive to see more UK institutions consistently making a significant contribution. In the early 1980s some UK institutions had a bad experience investing in venture capital funds. But the industry has matured and learnt from this experience, as the performance numbers show, and this should encourage UK institutions and their actuaries to reallocate a percentage of their funds under management to this asset class. At the moment, the figure is believed to be around 1 per cent of funds under management. Tony Blair said in 1999, 'I can't make pension funds invest more in venture capital, but I urge them to look at this issue, to examine whether they and other institutional investors are being too cautious when it comes to venture capital...'. The reticence of UK institutions to do so is at odds with their US counterparts who, far from decreasing their allocation to venture capital, have been increasing it, in some cases dramatically, because of excellent returns in recent years, driven by fantastic IPO markets. In the US, the average allocation by tax-exempt organisations to venture capital and private equity funds is 7.3 per cent, although in some cases allocations are much higher (see the Goldman Sachs & Co/Frank Russell Company *Report on Alternative Investing*, November 1999). That said, the recent success and growth of the European venture capital industry has also seen an explosion of interest from European institutions and family offices, with many allocating substantial funds to the asset class. New investors are finding it difficult to get into the top-performing funds and this has led to a large number of funds of funds being available to institutions. These funds are often able to get into the top quartile funds, due to existing relationships. Many investors are having to overcommit in order to reach their allocations, as they are seeing their cash being returned quicker than their total commitments are being drawn down. UK institutions are in danger of being left out of the asset class; it would appear that there are more investors seeking to invest than there are funds available.

## ...And what of the future?

The last few years have seen rapid growth in many European countries' venture capital activity. UK venture capital firms, as well as some large US private equity firms, are transferring their skills to continental Europe to take advantage of the opportunities being created by European economies. Pension fund reform in mainland Europe is giving institutions, which have traditionally invested in the capital markets, the opportunity to invest in venture capital funds.

The arrival of the euro will affect how business is done and the mobility of Europe's people, but will be fraught with difficulties, not least cultural ones. A unified European currency will not create, as some outsiders believe, a 'one-stop shop' overnight. Should this ever materialise, it will not be for some years to come. The growth of venture capital activity in continental Europe is going to create a wealth of opportunities, but there will be problems, perhaps similar to those experienced by the UK venture capital industry in the early 1980s. Attitudes are already changing, encouraging potential entrepreneurs to take a risk, as evidenced by the recent growth in the German venture capital industry. Governments in continental Europe are being persuaded of the benefits of an entrepreneurial culture and many are actively supporting it. Inevitably the learning curve will not be as steep for the continental European managers, they have some mature venture capital markets to learn from.

The UK venture capital industry has gone through some significant changes, particularly in the last few years, which have been record years for money raised and invested, no doubt more records will be set. The UK should retain pole position in terms of experience and track record, and should continue to set an example for the less mature venture capital markets. However, continental Europe is catching up fast. Venture capital is about taking risk and taking advantage of opportunities. The UK is a mature industry and is thus well placed to take advantage of the drivers of change in the economy in both good times and bad.

Part V

# Performance measurement

Chapter 17

# The performance of US buyout funds

Jesse Reyes
*Product Manager, Venture Economics*

Toby Walters
*Publications Manager, Venture Economics*

The following summarises the *1999 Investment Benchmarks Report: Buyouts and Other Private Equity (IBR)*, the 19th performance report on the private equity industry published by Venture Economics, which has published an annual performance report on the venture capital industry for 11 years. This is the sixth comprehensive report published on the performance of investments by the non-venture capital segment of the private equity industry. This alternative private equity segment includes buyout and mezzanine funds and other private equity limited partnerships.

The purpose of the reports is to provide investors, general partners, and the investment public with aggregate investment performance benchmarks for US private equity partnerships engaged in the investment in private companies or in the private acquisition of public companies. The *IBR* volume concentrates on investments in buyout limited partnerships, mezzanine partnerships, and other partnerships that we term 'other private equity', which include funds whose focus is investment in companies, but who do not fit the traditional, venture,

Exhibit 1

**US M&A, buyout commitments, 1980–98 (US$ billion)**

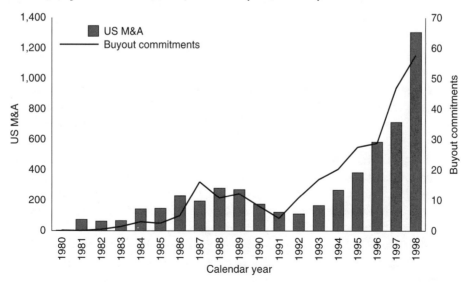

buyouts, or mezzanine model. The primary measure of performance reported is the net investment return to limited partners invested in these limited partnerships.

Venture Economics has researched the performance of the private equity industry for over 10 years and has worked with investors and general partners alike in evaluating current and future needs. The *Investment Benchmarks Report* is a derivative of the work we undertake in developing and maintaining the Venture Economics Private Equity Performance Database, which contains performance information about private equity investing encompassing venture capital, buyout funds, mezzanine funds, and special situation funds. The 1999 edition analyses the aggregate performance of 320 partnerships from that database that were formed from 1976 to 1998.

As we have been involved in extensive research of finding comprehensive and useful ways of presenting private equity performance, we have undertaken the task of including buyouts and other private equity into our traditional venture capital database. During this process, various issues have arisen:

- the inherent structural differences between investments in traditional venture partnerships and in other private equity investments;
- the difference in the private equity industry between the late 1980s, when we first undertook the measurement of private equity industry performance, and the 1990s;
- the difference in the information needs of institutional investors now and in the past;
- the increased level of statistical sophistication of our audience;
- the applicability and suitability of composite portfolio analysis; and
- the differences in time-weighted versus dollar-weighted returns

As the industry has matured and investment horizons have become shorter, there is a need for more information on young funds. In the past, we waited a full year before providing data on the most recent year of fund raising. Even then we waited four years before reporting fund performance. This was primarily because many private equity investments would take years before realised cash flows were generated. Any performance prior to this point would be based on subjective investment valuation and made many practitioners feel that analysis prior to four or five years into the fund's life was premature at best and spurious at worst.

Investment results seem to indicate that, at least for buyout funds, realised performance is often accrued relatively soon in the life of a partnership. In many cases, buyouts partnerships are organised around 'deals' rather than independent aggregate investment pools as in the venture partnership model. This deal structure results in earlier distributions; in many cases, as early as two years after initial investment. In some cases, there have been realised distributions in the same year as the initial investment.

We have spent many hours in the past with industry professionals researching ways of presenting private equity performance metrics that can be compared to that of other asset classes. While we continue to work at finding the best solutions, we still present returns for the industry on an annualised holding period basis for one-, three-, five-, ten-, and twenty-year investment horizons in addition to cumulative returns since inception.

For the time being, much of the discussion about the relative merits of time-weighted versus dollar-weighted returns that has dominated the industry over the past few years has abated.

## Sample composition

This study analyses the performance of 320 funds formed from 1976 to 1998, which represents 30 per cent of the number of funds formed in those years and 51 per cent of the capital raised in those years. The firms whose funds are represented in this edition are listed in Exhibit 2.

## Total capitalisation

Exhibits 3 and 4 compare the universe of funds formed from 1976 to 1998 with the 1999 *IBR* sample by the number of funds and the capital raised, respectively, for each vintage year. Cumulative total comparisons are also shown. Exhibits 5 to 9 provide additional information on annualized cumulative capital committed, average fund size by vintage year, and cumulative investments and cash flow.

## Summary of major findings

### Vintage year results

Exhibit 10 summarises the cumulative interim results as of the end of 1998 by vintage year, ie, the year of the fund's formation.

The data includes sample sizes, average internal rate of return (IRR), capital-weighted IRR, pooled IRR, and median IRRs for each vintage year, cumulative realisation ratios, and quartile performance information.

The summary of the year-end 1998 statistics in Exhibit 10 indicates that older funds formed in the early 1980s have had significantly higher absolute returns when compared to funds formed in the mid-1980s. The evidence also indicates that younger funds have performed remarkably well.

Exhibit 11 presents the cumulative results for each vintage year by age. This provides an overview of:

- the interim averages for each vintage year for each year since inception;
- a comparison by age of how these funds performed throughout their lives; and
- a snapshot of the results that provides an opportunity to compare vintage years and assess the impact of the in-vestment environment on the patterns of interim performance

Among other things, this exhibit indicates that while funds formed in the early 1990s have had significant returns in the upper teens and lower twenties, funds formed in the early 1980s had relatively higher returns earlier in their lives.

Realisation ratio analysis given in Exhibit 11 also indicate that younger funds have had significant realised cash flow as measured by distribution to paid-in capital very early in their lives. In some cases significant cash flow was being generated in their first year of operation! This has been one of the appealing characteristics of buyout funds for limited partners investing in this equity area – the degree of liquidity provided.

## Composite group performance

Venture Economics includes results from its Private Equity Performance Database on aggregate industry results. At one time, the only measurement of returns that we published was on a vintage year basis as we felt that it provided our constituent audience with the best measure of comparable performance.

Vintage year analysis provides investors with a way of benchmarking their individual fund's performance but does not provide a way to benchmark the performance of their portfolios of venture investments. As investors became more analytically sophisticated, we were being asked for benchmarks that mirror the types of analysis that they were being asked to use in comparing private equity performance with that of other asset classes. We have been providing this type of benchmark for some time to our monitoring clients.

We also present aggregate analysis of composites of private equity funds, ie, portfolios of funds made up of funds in different vintage years. Annualised cumulative returns are summarised in Exhibits 12 and 13 and annualised cumulative returns by fund age are summarised in Exhibit 14.

Composite groups were formed for two major reasons:

(1) In order to satisfy sample size constraints, it was often necessary to group vintage years when comparing performance of one fund category (size or type) to another. There were few mezzanine funds formed in the late 1980s, and relatively few large funds formed in the early 1980s. Grouping vintage years allows one to compare buyouts to mezzanine, for example, without running into sample size restrictions; or to compare large fund performance with small fund performance again without being constrained by sample size.
(2) Investors have portfolios of funds and are often constrained by the vintage year approach. An aggregate approach allows them to compare, for example, their portfolio performance with an aggregate portfolio of industry funds.

In order to answer questions about total industry performance, Exhibit 12 aggregates performance by several different composite groups made up of various vintage years. Results in this table are calculated cumulatively since inception. It indicates that for all funds formed from 1976 to 1998, the industry generated a 19.6 per cent cumulative IRR since inception when measured by a pooled average. Funds formed in the mid- to late 1980s appear to have larger relative returns when compared with funds formed in the mid-1990s. This seems to validate the existence of a 'J-curve' effect which describes the logistic curve inherent in long-term private equity investments. It is probably more pronounced in venture investments, but buyouts funds do not seem immune. The only other conclusion that could be drawn if there is no extant J-curve is that returns of funds formed in the mid- to late 1980s dominate later funds.

Exhibit 14 provides historical data by age for various statistical measures for each composite group. This is probably more meaningful than Exhibit 11 in that grouping funds across vintage years tends to hide the effect of the J-curve. This analysis allows one to examine composites by age, which should indicate any life cycle patterns in the returns. It also provides some evidence of the efficiency of the market over time as returns to funds formed later have not had the higher absolute returns of funds formed in the early to mid-1980s when compared at the same points in their life cycles.

Exhibit 13 provides pooled returns for various composite groups for one-year, three-year, five-year, ten-year, and twenty-year investment horizons. This allows one to perform some comparisons with other asset classes for the same investment horizons. It would indicate that

208

for all funds formed from 1980 to 1998, one-year returns were 11.8 per cent while ten-year returns were 16.2 per cent, which are relatively high, but not unexpected returns for this alternative asset group. It indicates one reason why there has been so much money raised in this area and why even in the post-1980s buyout frenzy there continues to be interest in this segment of the private equity industry. However, short-term returns, although still stellar, have declined in recent years from the spectacular returns previously posted. The following additional observations can be made about the data in the report.

Not only did the buyouts and other private equity industry post an 11.8 per cent one-year return as of the end of 1998, it also had returns of 16.4 per cent and 16.2 per cent, respectively, for five- and ten-year investment horizons.

An analysis of the variance of returns in Exhibit 10 indicates that there is quite a wide spread in the returns from high to low performers. This indicates the importance of manager selection. Furthermore, an analysis of upper quartile performance shows that these funds produced double-digit IRRs in every vintage year except 1997 and 1998, indicating that there is opportunity to achieve high returns through this investment vehicle, but again returns appear to have been higher in the past.

The economic environment in which a fund is investing impacts results as much as the experience of the managers. For example, the high returns achieved in the early 1980s were influenced by an excellent investing environment. Conversely, funds investing in later periods were investing in an environment of high valuations and even higher competition, resulting in overall low returns even among the most experienced investors.

In any vintage year, the outstanding performance of the vintage year may be influenced by a few big winners. There is evidence that some funds had spectacular performance of over 100 per cent over short periods of time. These results when compounded by the great variety of fund size can distort any capital-weighted measure or pooled measure. Again, study of the variance of returns as well as percentile performance will provide the reader with information on the relative stability of high returns. A high return with a low variance is the will-o-the-wisp of any investment category. This category is no exception. There is exceptional performance, but at sometime high risk as measured by sample variance.

The data indicate when compared with data from our other analysis on venture performance that these investments are relatively shorter-lived and have higher performance albeit higher risk for these short investment horizons. While the buyouts category appears in absolute terms to dominate other private equity investments, a caveat must be offered to examine both risk and return when comparing performance.

Exhibit 2

## 1999 investment benchmarks composition: private equity firms represented

3i Group PLC
ABRY Partners
ABS Capital Partners
Acland SA Dimeling, Schreiber & Park
Adler & Shaykin
Advent International Corp.
AEA Investors, Inc.
AIG Asian Infrastructure Managers
Alliance Capital
Allied Investment Corporation
Alta Berkeley Associates
Alta Communications
American Acquisition Partners
American Industrial Partners
Apax Partners & Co. Ventures Holdings
Apollo Advisors, LP
Aqua International Partners, LP
Argos Soditic
Bain Capital
Baker Capital Corp.
Banc Funds, The
Bastion Capital Corp.
BC Partners
BCI Partners
Beacon Partners, Inc.
Behrman Capital
Berkshire Partners
Blackstone Group, LP
Boston Ventures Management, Inc.
Bradford Capital Partners
Brentwood Associates Private Equity
Brera Capital Partners
Brown Brothers Harriman
Brynwood Partners LP
Burr, Egan, Deleage & Co.
Butler Capital Corporation
CAI Advisors & Co
Capital Intl Global Emerging Pvt Equity
Capital Partners, Inc.
Capital Resource Partners
Carlyle Group, The
Castle Harlan Inc.
Cedar Creek Partners, LLC
CGW Southeast Partners
Charterhouse Group International, Inc.
Chisholm Private Capital Partners
Churchill Capital, Inc.
CIBC Oppenheimer & Co., Inc.
CID Equity Partners
Cigna Investment Management
Cinven Ltd.
Clayton, Dubilier & Rice, Inc.
Code, Hennessy & Simmons, LLC.
Colonnade Capital LLC
Coniston Partners
Conning & Co.
Conseco Capital Partners
Contrarian Capital Management, LLC
Cornerstone Equity Investors, LLC
Corporate Advisors, LP
Crown Advisors, Ltd.

CVC Capital Partners
Cypress Advisors LP
Desai Capital Midwest Bank Stock, LP
DLJ Capital
DLJ Phoenix Private Equity, Ltd.
ECP
EGI Capital Markets LLC
Emerging Growth Partners
Equus Capital C orp.
Exeter Capital, LP
Fenway Partners, Inc.
Fidelity Venture Associates
First Reserve Corporation
FirstCorp Capital Advisors
Florida Capital Partners
Foothill Group Inc.
Forstmann Little & Company
Founder Court Investors Inc.
Fox Paine & Company, LP
Frazier & Company
Fremont Partners
FS Management Co., LP
Genesis Venture Capital Group, The
Gibbons, Green, Van Amerongen
GKH Partners, LP
Glencoe Capital, LLC
Goldman, Sachs & Co.
Green Mountain Advisors, Inc.
GTCR Golder Rauner, LLC
Haas Wheat & Partners Incorporated
Hamilton Lane Advisors
Hamilton Robinson & Co., Inc.
Hampshire Equity Partners
Harbour Group, Ltd.
Harvest Partners, Inc.
Hellman & Friedman
Heritage Partners
Hicks, Muse, Tate & Furst, Incorporated
HSBC Private Equity Management
Industrial Growth Partners
Integral Capital Management, LP
J.H. Whitney & Co.
J.P. Morgan Capital Corp.
J.W. Childs Associates
Jacobs Investors, Inc.
Joseph, Littlejohn & Levy
KBA Partners, LP
KD (Kellner, Dileo) & Co.
Kelso & Company
Kidd, Kamm & Company
Kirtland Capital Corporation
Kleinwort Benson Development Capital Ltd
Kohlberg, Kravis, Roberts & Co.
Lehman Brothers
Leonard Green & Partners
Lodestar Group
M.D. Sass Investor Services, Inc.
Madison Dearborn Partners, Inc.
Mancuso & Company
Marlborough Capital Advisors
McCown De Leeuw & Co.

Media/Communications Partners
Merrill Lynch Capital Partners
Mesirow Private Equity Investments, Inc.
Morgan Stanley Dean Witter Capital
    Partners, LLC
Morgan, Lewis Githens & Ahn.
Narragansett Capital, Inc.
North American Business Development
    Co., LLC
Oaktree Capital Management, LLC
Odyssey Investment Group
Odyssey Investment Partners, LP
Olympus Advisory Partners, Inc.
Oppenheimer Rennaisance Partners
Peninsula Capital Partners, L.L.C
PENMAN Partners
Pfingsten Partners, LP
Phildrew Ventures
Pilgrim Baxter & Associates
Prime Capital Management Co., Inc.
Prospect Partners LLC
Providence Equity Partners, Inc.
Questor Management Company
Recovery Equity Investors, LP
Reprise Capital Corp.
RFE Investment Partners
Rice, Sangalis, Toole & Wilson
River Capital
Rockefeller & Co., Inc.
Safeguard Scientifics, Inc.
Saratoga Partners LP
Saugatuck Capital Company
SCF Partners
Shansby Group, The
Stolberg Partners
Stonington Partners
Summit Partners
Syndicated Communications Venture
    Partners
T. Rowe Price Threshold Partnerships
TCW Capital
Texas Pacific Group
Thayer Capital Partners
Thomas H. Lee Company
Three Cities Research, Inc.
Torch Energy Advisors, Inc.
Transpac Capital Pte, Ltd.
Triumph Capital Group, Inc.
Trust Company of the West
TSG Capital Group, LLC
Tullis-Dickerson Management Company
Veronis, Suhler & Associates Inc.
Vestar Capital Partners Inc.
Weiss, Peck & Greer Venture Partners, LP
Welsh, Carson, Anderson & Stowe
WestSphere Equity Investors, LP
WHR Management Corp
William Blair & Co.
Willis Stein & Partners
Wingate Partners, LP
ZS Fund, LP

210

Exhibit 3

## 1999 investment benchmarks: sample and universe capitalisation by vintage year

| Vintage year | Universe capitalisation | | | Sample capitalisation | | | Cumulative capitalisation | | | | | |
|---|---|---|---|---|---|---|---|---|---|---|---|---|
| | | | | | | | Universe | | | Sample | | |
| | | US$ million | | | US$ million | | | US$ million | | | US$ million | |
| | Funds | Fund cap | Avg cap | Funds | Fund cap | Avg cap | Funds | Fund cap | Avg cap | Funds | Fund cap | Avg cap |
| 1976–83 | 41 | 2,904.4 | 70.8 | 12 | 1,288.8 | 107.4 | 41 | 2,904.4 | 70.8 | 12 | 1,288.8 | 107.4 |
| 1984 | 20 | 2,932.5 | 146.6 | 6 | 1,628.0 | 271.3 | 61 | 5,836.9 | 95.7 | 18 | 2,916.8 | 162.0 |
| 1985 | 23 | 3,728.3 | 162.1 | 10 | 2,123.4 | 212.3 | 84 | 9,565.2 | 113.9 | 28 | 5,040.2 | 180.0 |
| 1986 | 29 | 5,095.0 | 175.7 | 15 | 2,674.4 | 178.3 | 113 | 14,660.2 | 129.7 | 43 | 7,714.6 | 179.4 |
| 1987 | 42 | 14,908.5 | 355.4 | 24 | 12,151.3 | 486.5 | 155 | 29,568.7 | 190.8 | 67 | 19,865.9 | 296.5 |
| 1988 | 53 | 12,562.4 | 237.0 | 19 | 8,598.1 | 452.5 | 208 | 42,131.1 | 202.6 | 86 | 28,464.0 | 331.0 |
| 1989 | 81 | 12,925.7 | 159.6 | 24 | 4,621.4 | 187.6 | 289 | 55,056.8 | 190.5 | 110 | 33,085.4 | 300.8 |
| 1990 | 71 | 11,154.0 | 157.1 | 14 | 5,718.9 | 408.5 | 360 | 66,210.8 | 183.9 | 124 | 38,804.3 | 312.9 |
| 1991 | 28 | 3,813.6 | 136.2 | 7 | 1,473.5 | 210.5 | 388 | 70,024.4 | 180.5 | 131 | 40,277.8 | 307.5 |
| 1992 | 68 | 12,082.3 | 177.7 | 22 | 5,613.0 | 255.1 | 456 | 82,106.7 | 180.1 | 153 | 45,890.8 | 299.9 |
| 1993 | 77 | 16,652.2 | 216.3 | 23 | 9,296.4 | 404.2 | 533 | 98,758.9 | 185.3 | 176 | 55,187.2 | 313.6 |
| 1994 | 94 | 22,671.6 | 241.2 | 27 | 10,696.7 | 396.2 | 627 | 121,430.5 | 193.7 | 203 | 65,883.9 | 324.6 |
| 1995 | 83 | 26,736.3 | 322.1 | 22 | 15,086.6 | 685.8 | 710 | 148,166.8 | 208.7 | 225 | 80,970.5 | 359.9 |
| 1996 | 85 | 22,583.9 | 265.7 | 30 | 11,552.9 | 385.1 | 795 | 170,750.7 | 214.8 | 255 | 92,523.4 | 362.8 |
| 1997 | 119 | 53,531.3 | 449.8 | 37 | 29,430.7 | 795.4 | 914 | 224,282.0 | 245.4 | 292 | 121,954.1 | 417.7 |
| 1998 | 141 | 71,988.3 | 510.6 | 28 | 30,059.6 | 1,073.6 | 1,055 | 296,270.3 | 280.8 | 320 | 152,013.7 | 475.0 |
| **Total** | **1,055** | **296,270.3** | **280.8** | **320** | **152,013.7** | **475.0** | | | | | | |

Exhibit 4

**1999 investment benchmarks: number of funds by vintage year**

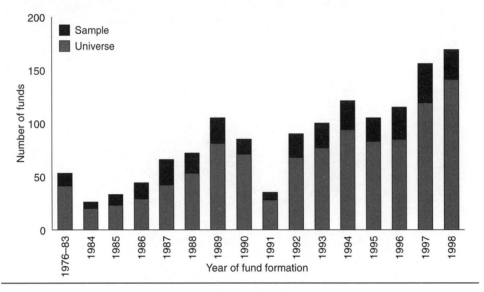

Exhibit 5

**1999 investment benchmarks: capital committed by vintage year (US$ million)**

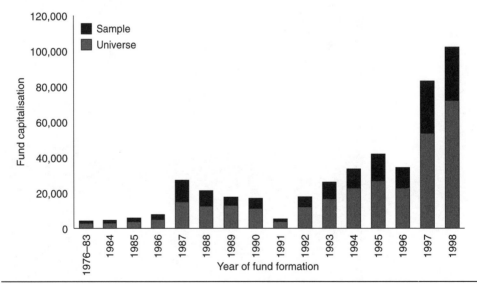

212

Exhibit 6

**1999 investment benchmarks: cumulative capitalisation by vintage year (US$ million)**

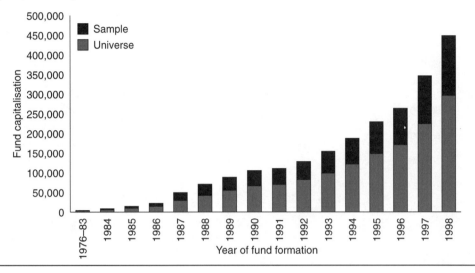

Exhibit 7

**1999 investment benchmarks: average fund size by vintage year (US$ million)**

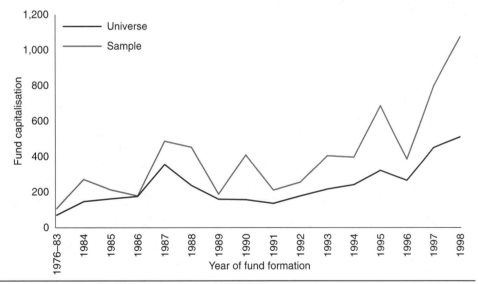

Exhibit 8

**1999 investment benchmarks: cumulative uninvested versus invested capital by calendar year (US$ million)**

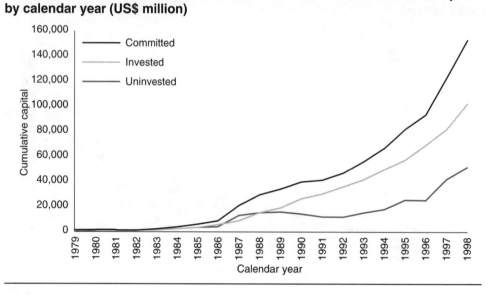

Exhibit 9

**1999 investment benchmarks: cumulative cash flow by calendar year (US$ million)**

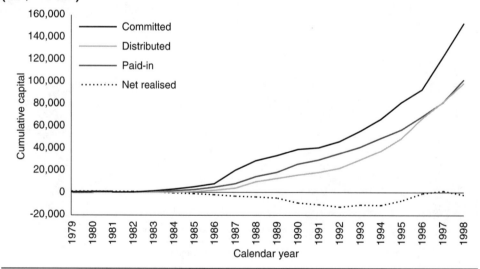

Exhibit 10

## Cumulative benchmark results: overall sample by vintage year as of 31 December 1998

| Description | Year of fund formation | | | | | | | | | | | | | | | |
|---|---|---|---|---|---|---|---|---|---|---|---|---|---|---|---|---|
| | 1976–83 | 1984 | 1985 | 1986 | 1987 | 1988 | 1989 | 1990 | 1991 | 1992 | 1993 | 1994 | 1995 | 1996 | 1997 | 1998 |
| Sample size (no.) | 12 | 6 | 10 | 15 | 24 | 19 | 24 | 14 | 7 | 22 | 23 | 27 | 22 | 30 | 37 | 28 |
| Universe size (no.) | 41 | 20 | 23 | 29 | 42 | 53 | 81 | 71 | 28 | 68 | 77 | 94 | 83 | 85 | 119 | 141 |
| **Sample capitalisation** | | | | | | | | | | | | | | | | |
| (US$ million) | 1,288.8 | 1,628.0 | 2,123.4 | 2,674.4 | 12,151.3 | 8,598.1 | 4,621.4 | 5,718.9 | 1,473.5 | 5,613.0 | 9,296.4 | 10,696.7 | 15,086.6 | 11,552.9 | 29,430.7 | 30,059.6 |
| **Universe capitalisation** | | | | | | | | | | | | | | | | |
| (US$ million) | 2,904.4 | 2,932.5 | 3,728.3 | 5,095.0 | 14,908.5 | 12,562.4 | 12,925.7 | 11,154.0 | 3,813.6 | 12,082.3 | 16,652.2 | 22,671.6 | 26,736.3 | 22,583.9 | 53,531.3 | 71,988.3 |
| **Overall** | | | | | | | | | | | | | | | | |
| Sample size | 12 | 6 | 10 | 15 | 24 | 19 | 24 | 14 | 7 | 22 | 23 | 27 | 22 | 30 | 37 | 28 |
| Avg IRR (%) | 37.5 | 35.1 | 45.4 | 15.1 | 12.4 | 11.2 | 11.7 | 11.4 | 15.5 | 20.3 | 17.0 | 15.6 | 9.7 | 49.1 | 1.4 | -22.6 |
| Cap-wtd IRR (%) | 32.8 | 28.2 | 33.1 | 17.7 | 16.4 | 12.6 | 14.5 | 25.3 | 14.6 | 24.1 | 21.8 | 12.1 | 11.4 | 31.0 | 3.4 | -30.1 |
| Pooled IRR (%) | 34.7 | 26.0 | 45.6 | 17.1 | 15.3 | 13.3 | 15.9 | 26.0 | 15.3 | 21.4 | 19.5 | 12.3 | 9.3 | 22.2 | 5.3 | -25.7 |
| Median IRR (%) | 31.4 | 23.5 | 19.0 | 9.4 | 10.9 | 12.2 | 14.9 | 14.0 | 16.9 | 20.4 | 16.5 | 11.8 | 2.5 | 12.1 | -5.0 | -16.1 |
| Std. dev. (%) | 36.1 | 45.5 | 71.5 | 15.2 | 18.1 | 8.3 | 17.3 | 27.1 | 7.6 | 21.4 | 22.5 | 22.5 | 23.2 | 190.1 | 65.2 | 50.4 |
| Coef. of Var. (%) | 1.0 | 1.3 | 1.6 | 1.0 | 1.5 | 0.7 | 1.5 | 2.4 | 0.5 | 1.1 | 1.3 | 1.4 | 2.4 | 3.9 | 46.6 | -2.2 |
| **Realisation ratios** | | | | | | | | | | | | | | | | |
| Distr/paid-in (times) | 3.23 | 3.95 | 2.68 | 2.37 | 1.40 | 1.44 | 1.66 | 1.81 | 1.28 | 1.24 | 0.76 | 0.53 | 0.23 | 0.21 | 0.13 | 0.03 |
| Res val/paid-in (times) | 0.15 | 0.02 | 0.12 | 0.34 | 0.65 | 0.35 | 0.29 | 0.34 | 0.35 | 0.57 | 0.80 | 0.77 | 0.93 | 1.11 | 0.91 | 0.90 |
| Tot val/paid-in (times) | 3.38 | 3.97 | 2.80 | 2.71 | 2.05 | 1.79 | 1.95 | 2.15 | 1.63 | 1.81 | 1.55 | 1.30 | 1.16 | 1.31 | 1.04 | 0.93 |
| **Percentiles** | | | | | | | | | | | | | | | | |
| Maximum IRR (%) | 146.7 | 124.8 | 243.9 | 64.5 | 67.4 | 29.5 | 32.5 | 58.5 | 27.0 | 63.5 | 60.8 | 91.3 | 84.5 | 472.3 | 330.2 | 163.8 |
| Upper quartile (%) | 40.6 | 30.5 | 39.4 | 16.7 | 17.5 | 14.1 | 22.2 | 19.5 | 19.2 | 24.0 | 22.3 | 24.8 | 14.6 | 29.6 | 9.7 | -2.2 |
| Median IRR (%) | 31.4 | 23.5 | 19.0 | 9.4 | 10.9 | 12.2 | 14.9 | 14.0 | 16.9 | 20.4 | 16.5 | 11.8 | 2.5 | 12.1 | -5.0 | -16.1 |
| Lower quartile (%) | 15.5 | 6.3 | 13.3 | 7.3 | 6.0 | 8.4 | 5.4 | -0.4 | 11.6 | 7.2 | 11.0 | 4.1 | -4.3 | -0.7 | -13.3 | -49.0 |
| Minimum IRR (%) | 13.1 | 2.1 | -0.3 | 3.8 | -33.7 | -6.1 | -45.5 | -55.0 | 3.4 | -23.5 | -61.8 | -30.1 | -13.7 | -31.1 | -100.0 | -100.0 |

215

Exhibit 11

## Vintage year results by fund age (in years) after formation, as of 31 December 1998

| Vintage | | | | | | | | | Fund age | | | | | | | | | |
|---|---|---|---|---|---|---|---|---|---|---|---|---|---|---|---|---|---|---|
| | 1 | 2 | 3 | 4 | 5 | 6 | 7 | 8 | 9 | 10 | 11 | 12 | 13 | 14 | 15 | 16 | 17 | 18 |
| **Sample size** | | | | | | | | | | | | | | | | | | |
| 1976–83 | 11 | 11 | 12 | 12 | 12 | 12 | 12 | 12 | 12 | 12 | 12 | 12 | 12 | 12 | 12 | 5 | 4 | 3 |
| 1984 | 6 | 6 | 6 | 6 | 6 | 6 | 6 | 6 | 6 | 6 | 6 | 6 | 6 | 6 | | | | |
| 1985 | 10 | 10 | 10 | 10 | 10 | 10 | 10 | 10 | 10 | 10 | 10 | 10 | | | | | | |
| 1986 | 15 | 15 | 15 | 15 | 15 | 15 | 15 | 15 | 15 | 15 | 15 | | | | | | | |
| 1987 | 24 | 24 | 24 | 24 | 25 | 25 | 25 | 25 | 25 | 25 | 24 | | | | | | | |
| 1988 | 19 | 19 | 19 | 19 | 19 | 19 | 19 | 19 | 19 | 19 | | | | | | | | |
| 1989 | 24 | 24 | 24 | 24 | 24 | 24 | 24 | 24 | 24 | | | | | | | | | |
| 1990 | 14 | 14 | 14 | 14 | 14 | 14 | 14 | 14 | | | | | | | | | | |
| 1991 | 7 | 7 | 7 | 7 | 7 | 7 | 7 | | | | | | | | | | | |
| 1992 | 22 | 22 | 22 | 22 | 22 | 22 | | | | | | | | | | | | |
| 1993 | 23 | 23 | 23 | 23 | 23 | | | | | | | | | | | | | |
| 1994 | 25 | 26 | 27 | 27 | | | | | | | | | | | | | | |
| 1995 | 22 | 22 | 22 | | | | | | | | | | | | | | | |
| 1996 | 29 | 30 | | | | | | | | | | | | | | | | |
| 1997 | 37 | | | | | | | | | | | | | | | | | |
| **Average IRR** | | | | | | | | | | | | | | | | | | |
| 1976–83 | 4.3 | 12.2 | 39.5 | 41.5 | 39.5 | 38.0 | 38.9 | 38.5 | 38.2 | 38.1 | 37.9 | 37.4 | 37.5 | 37.5 | 37.3 | 31.4 | 36.0 | 34.6 |
| 1984 | 5.1 | 31.2 | 29.2 | 32.2 | 31.8 | 31.8 | 32.7 | 34.3 | 34.6 | 34.6 | 35.0 | 35.2 | 35.2 | 35.1 | | | | |
| 1985 | 7.2 | 18.6 | 42.5 | 54.1 | 49.5 | 49.9 | 47.9 | 47.9 | 46.6 | 46.2 | 46.0 | 45.2 | 45.4 | | | | | |
| 1986 | 8.9 | 12.7 | 13.1 | 7.5 | 8.4 | 14.4 | 14.7 | 15.7 | 14.5 | 15.0 | 15.1 | 15.1 | | | | | | |
| 1987 | 7.8 | 9.0 | 3.7 | 3.8 | 5.1 | 8.1 | 8.7 | 9.3 | 12.5 | 12.2 | 12.4 | | | | | | | |
| 1988 | 10.4 | 3.9 | 4.0 | 5.4 | 7.0 | 8.8 | 10.3 | 10.8 | 11.4 | 11.2 | | | | | | | | |
| 1989 | 2.8 | 4.9 | 4.0 | 7.3 | 7.3 | 10.1 | 11.3 | 11.5 | 11.7 | | | | | | | | | |
| 1990 | -4.8 | 4.7 | 24.7 | 19.3 | 11.3 | 11.9 | 11.3 | 11.4 | | | | | | | | | | |
| 1991 | -3.2 | 16.6 | 9.1 | 15.4 | 14.9 | 16.7 | 15.5 | | | | | | | | | | | |
| 1992 | 3.9 | 10.7 | 18.3 | 19.7 | 20.0 | 20.3 | | | | | | | | | | | | |
| 1993 | 9.6 | 15.7 | 20.9 | 19.9 | 17.0 | | | | | | | | | | | | | |
| 1994 | 5.3 | 18.2 | 15.1 | 15.6 | | | | | | | | | | | | | | |
| 1995 | 2.7 | 8.5 | 9.7 | | | | | | | | | | | | | | | |
| 1996 | 23.5 | 49.1 | | | | | | | | | | | | | | | | |
| 1997 | 1.4 | | | | | | | | | | | | | | | | | |
| **Median IRR** | | | | | | | | | | | | | | | | | | |
| 1976–83 | 0.3 | 14.9 | 28.9 | 27.0 | 34.4 | 33.0 | 30.8 | 30.1 | 29.9 | 30.3 | 29.5 | 30.2 | 31.0 | 30.7 | 30.6 | 31.7 | 35.9 | 31.7 |
| 1984 | 0.0 | 12.6 | 9.8 | 18.0 | 17.9 | 17.7 | 19.7 | 20.1 | 21.5 | 22.0 | 23.3 | 23.8 | 23.7 | 23.5 | | | | |
| 1985 | 0.1 | 7.7 | 16.3 | 34.9 | 25.4 | 23.0 | 20.4 | 20.6 | 19.0 | 18.7 | 18.8 | 18.3 | 19.0 | | | | | |
| 1986 | 3.7 | 11.2 | 12.3 | 7.9 | 8.8 | 9.4 | 10.4 | 11.9 | 9.7 | 9.8 | 9.5 | 9.4 | | | | | | |
| 1987 | 0.0 | 1.1 | 0.0 | 2.3 | 4.3 | 8.4 | 11.0 | 10.9 | 11.5 | 11.2 | 10.9 | | | | | | | |
| 1988 | 6.1 | 1.0 | 2.2 | 5.9 | 8.4 | 11.3 | 11.1 | 11.9 | 11.8 | 12.2 | | | | | | | | |
| 1989 | 0.0 | 3.6 | 4.1 | 5.8 | 6.1 | 12.9 | 12.0 | 14.0 | 14.9 | | | | | | | | | |
| 1990 | 1.8 | 2.8 | 13.8 | 14.5 | 13.4 | 13.8 | 14.7 | 14.0 | | | | | | | | | | |
| 1991 | -4.5 | 22.5 | 8.9 | 17.3 | 14.5 | 17.1 | 16.9 | | | | | | | | | | | |
| 1992 | 2.8 | 8.0 | 14.5 | 18.3 | 22.0 | 20.4 | | | | | | | | | | | | |
| 1993 | 4.2 | 10.9 | 18.4 | 22.8 | 16.5 | | | | | | | | | | | | | |
| 1994 | 3.4 | 14.3 | 15.2 | 11.8 | | | | | | | | | | | | | | |
| 1995 | -8.1 | 2.3 | 2.5 | | | | | | | | | | | | | | | |
| 1996 | 6.2 | 12.1 | | | | | | | | | | | | | | | | |
| 1997 | -5.0 | | | | | | | | | | | | | | | | | |

Exhibit 11 *continued*

## Vintage year results by fund age (in years) after formation, as of 31 December 1998 *continued*

| | | | | | | | | | Fund age | | | | | | | | | |
|---|---|---|---|---|---|---|---|---|---|---|---|---|---|---|---|---|---|---|
| Vintage | 1 | 2 | 3 | 4 | 5 | 6 | 7 | 8 | 9 | 10 | 11 | 12 | 13 | 14 | 15 | 16 | 17 | 18 |
| **Upper quartile IRR** | | | | | | | | | | | | | | | | | | |
| 1976–83 | 3.6 | 18.0 | 33.6 | 38.1 | 41.7 | 38.7 | 42.0 | 41.0 | 40.9 | 40.9 | 40.7 | 40.6 | 40.6 | 40.5 | 40.4 | 40.2 | 40.4 | 36.4 |
| 1984 | 4.5 | 28.0 | 26.3 | 32.0 | 31.2 | 30.0 | 31.6 | 31.3 | 30.9 | 30.6 | 30.5 | 30.5 | 30.5 | 30.5 | | | | |
| 1985 | 8.8 | 23.6 | 47.0 | 51.9 | 47.6 | 45.3 | 42.4 | 47.6 | 46.3 | 40.7 | 39.5 | 39.5 | 39.4 | | | | | |
| 1986 | 8.5 | 17.0 | 16.8 | 9.3 | 13.6 | 17.1 | 16.2 | 17.1 | 15.5 | 16.4 | 16.7 | 16.7 | | | | | | |
| 1987 | 11.4 | 13.5 | 13.3 | 14.3 | 14.9 | 17.1 | 16.1 | 15.4 | 16.8 | 16.8 | 17.5 | | | | | | | |
| 1988 | 14.2 | 6.5 | 8.1 | 8.4 | 11.8 | 12.6 | 13.8 | 14.9 | 14.3 | 14.1 | | | | | | | | |
| 1989 | 4.6 | 17.3 | 23.8 | 22.9 | 17.1 | 19.5 | 21.5 | 22.3 | 22.2 | | | | | | | | | |
| 1990 | 5.5 | 15.6 | 24.9 | 25.6 | 21.0 | 20.9 | 18.3 | 19.5 | | | | | | | | | | |
| 1991 | 4.1 | 27.1 | 13.5 | 20.2 | 19.9 | 23.5 | 19.2 | | | | | | | | | | | |
| 1992 | 14.4 | 21.3 | 22.6 | 27.9 | 24.1 | 24.0 | | | | | | | | | | | | |
| 1993 | 12.4 | 17.5 | 25.8 | 25.1 | 22.3 | | | | | | | | | | | | | |
| 1994 | 7.7 | 27.2 | 29.0 | 24.8 | | | | | | | | | | | | | | |
| 1995 | 3.7 | 20.0 | 14.6 | | | | | | | | | | | | | | | |
| 1996 | 38.0 | 29.6 | | | | | | | | | | | | | | | | |
| 1997 | 9.7 | | | | | | | | | | | | | | | | | |
| **Average distribution to paid-in** | | | | | | | | | | | | | | | | | | |
| 1976–83 | 0.03 | 0.16 | 0.39 | 0.72 | 1.39 | 1.87 | 2.25 | 2.59 | 2.78 | 2.92 | 3.00 | 3.18 | 3.39 | 4.19 | 4.21 | 6.43 | 7.41 | 7.97 |
| 1984 | 0.08 | 1.06 | 1.18 | 1.51 | 1.54 | 2.11 | 2.19 | 2.42 | 2.76 | 2.93 | 3.05 | 3.41 | 3.45 | 3.60 | | | | |
| 1985 | 0.03 | 0.20 | 1.24 | 2.74 | 2.73 | 2.80 | 2.75 | 3.06 | 3.16 | 3.24 | 3.33 | 3.44 | 3.56 | | | | | |
| 1986 | 0.13 | 0.20 | 0.25 | 0.31 | 0.44 | 1.06 | 1.33 | 1.59 | 1.72 | 1.93 | 2.17 | 2.36 | | | | | | |
| 1987 | 0.10 | 0.15 | 0.25 | 0.28 | 0.34 | 0.56 | 0.77 | 1.08 | 1.36 | 1.49 | 1.62 | | | | | | | |
| 1988 | 0.07 | 0.12 | 0.17 | 0.25 | 0.40 | 0.67 | 0.95 | 1.18 | 1.36 | 1.43 | | | | | | | | |
| 1989 | 0.06 | 0.08 | 0.15 | 0.38 | 0.57 | 0.90 | 1.14 | 1.42 | 1.52 | | | | | | | | | |
| 1990 | 0.10 | 0.14 | 0.28 | 0.50 | 0.68 | 0.83 | 1.02 | 1.13 | | | | | | | | | | |
| 1991 | 0.04 | 0.09 | 0.12 | 0.34 | 0.77 | 1.04 | 1.28 | | | | | | | | | | | |
| 1992 | 0.05 | 0.13 | 0.33 | 0.61 | 0.85 | 1.26 | | | | | | | | | | | | |
| 1993 | 0.08 | 0.15 | 0.43 | 0.76 | 0.93 | | | | | | | | | | | | | |
| 1994 | 0.05 | 0.26 | 0.38 | 0.69 | | | | | | | | | | | | | | |
| 1995 | 0.05 | 0.14 | 0.23 | | | | | | | | | | | | | | | |
| 1996 | 0.07 | 0.14 | | | | | | | | | | | | | | | | |
| 1997 | 0.08 | | | | | | | | | | | | | | | | | |
| **Average residual value to paid-in** | | | | | | | | | | | | | | | | | | |
| 1976–83 | 1.01 | 1.08 | 1.30 | 1.56 | 1.42 | 1.12 | 1.08 | 0.85 | 0.72 | 0.72 | 0.80 | 0.86 | 1.02 | 0.25 | 0.19 | 0.10 | 0.11 | 0.02 |
| 1984 | 0.98 | 0.99 | 0.97 | 0.88 | 0.90 | 0.83 | 0.92 | 0.94 | 0.72 | 0.63 | 0.65 | 0.41 | 0.19 | 0.04 | | | | |
| 1985 | 1.03 | 1.07 | 0.96 | 0.99 | 0.95 | 1.09 | 0.97 | 0.80 | 0.56 | 0.41 | 0.34 | 0.21 | 0.14 | | | | | |
| 1986 | 0.96 | 1.01 | 1.05 | 0.95 | 0.93 | 0.93 | 0.80 | 0.70 | 0.57 | 0.51 | 0.32 | 0.18 | | | | | | |
| 1987 | 0.95 | 0.96 | 0.85 | 0.85 | 0.84 | 0.78 | 0.68 | 0.54 | 0.47 | 0.38 | 0.31 | | | | | | | |
| 1988 | 1.01 | 0.93 | 0.89 | 0.88 | 0.82 | 0.75 | 0.60 | 0.45 | 0.37 | 0.31 | | | | | | | | |
| 1989 | 0.97 | 1.01 | 0.98 | 0.91 | 0.79 | 0.69 | 0.63 | 0.47 | 0.39 | | | | | | | | | |
| 1990 | 0.86 | 0.94 | 1.44 | 1.18 | 0.83 | 0.72 | 0.55 | 0.45 | | | | | | | | | | |
| 1991 | 1.03 | 1.19 | 1.12 | 1.23 | 0.89 | 0.81 | 0.55 | | | | | | | | | | | |
| 1992 | 1.01 | 1.02 | 1.02 | 0.89 | 0.82 | 0.60 | | | | | | | | | | | | |
| 1993 | 0.99 | 1.06 | 0.97 | 0.80 | 0.65 | | | | | | | | | | | | | |
| 1994 | 1.03 | 1.02 | 0.98 | 0.72 | | | | | | | | | | | | | | |
| 1995 | 0.96 | 1.00 | 0.96 | | | | | | | | | | | | | | | |
| 1996 | 1.14 | 1.29 | | | | | | | | | | | | | | | | |
| 1997 | 0.96 | | | | | | | | | | | | | | | | | |

Exhibit 12

**Cumulative benchmark results: overall sample by composite portfolio, as of 31 December 1998**

| | 1976 | 1984 | 1985 | 1986 | 1987 | 1988 | 1989 | 1990 | 1991 | 1992 | 1993 | 1994 | 1995 | 1996 | 1997 |
|---|---|---|---|---|---|---|---|---|---|---|---|---|---|---|---|
| | | | | | | | | *Year of fund formation* | | | | | | | |
| **Overall** | | | | | | | | | | | | | | | |
| Sample size | 320 | 308 | 302 | 292 | 277 | 253 | 234 | 210 | 196 | 189 | 167 | 144 | 117 | 95 | 65 |
| Avg IRR (%) | 14.9 | 14.0 | 13.6 | 12.5 | 12.4 | 12.4 | 12.5 | 12.5 | 12.6 | 12.5 | 11.5 | 10.6 | 9.5 | 9.4 | -9.0 |
| Cap-wtd IRR (%) | 5.8 | 5.6 | 5.4 | 5.0 | 4.8 | 3.7 | 3.2 | 2.7 | 1.6 | 1.4 | 0.2 | -1.7 | -3.5 | -6.5 | -14.2 |
| Pooled IRR (%) | 19.6 | 18.4 | 17.5 | 16.0 | 15.9 | 16.2 | 17.5 | 18.0 | 15.5 | 15.5 | 13.9 | 11.3 | 10.7 | 12.0 | -0.3 |
| Median IRR (%) | 11.6 | 10.7 | 10.6 | 10.0 | 10.2 | 9.7 | 9.0 | 8.4 | 8.1 | 7.2 | 4.4 | 0.0 | -0.8 | -2.9 | -9.5 |
| Std. dev. (%) | 68.9 | 69.8 | 70.2 | 70.0 | 71.8 | 74.9 | 77.9 | 82.0 | 84.6 | 86.2 | 91.3 | 98.0 | 108.2 | 119.8 | 60.1 |
| Coef. of var. (%) | 4.6 | 5.0 | 5.2 | 5.6 | 5.8 | 6.0 | 6.2 | 6.6 | 6.7 | 6.9 | 7.9 | 9.2 | 11.4 | 12.7 | -6.7 |
| **Realisation ratios** | | | | | | | | | | | | | | | |
| Distr/paid-in (times) | 0.94 | 0.91 | 0.86 | 0.82 | 0.78 | 0.69 | 0.61 | 0.53 | 0.42 | 0.40 | 0.32 | 0.24 | 0.16 | 0.13 | 0.10 |
| Res val/paid-in (times) | 0.69 | 0.69 | 0.70 | 0.72 | 0.73 | 0.74 | 0.78 | 0.82 | 0.86 | 0.87 | 0.90 | 0.92 | 0.95 | 0.97 | 0.90 |
| Tot val/paid-in (times) | 1.63 | 1.60 | 1.57 | 1.54 | 1.51 | 1.43 | 1.39 | 1.34 | 1.28 | 1.27 | 1.22 | 1.15 | 1.12 | 1.10 | 1.00 |
| **Percentiles** | | | | | | | | | | | | | | | |
| Maximum IRR (%) | 472.3 | 472.3 | 472.3 | 472.3 | 472.3 | 472.3 | 472.3 | 472.3 | 472.3 | 472.3 | 472.3 | 472.3 | 472.3 | 472.3 | 330.2 |
| Upper quartile (%) | 22.7 | 21.4 | 21.3 | 21.2 | 21.3 | 21.3 | 22.6 | 22.6 | 23.0 | 23.4 | 23.0 | 23.0 | 14.6 | 15.7 | 0.0 |
| Median IRR (%) | 11.6 | 10.7 | 10.6 | 10.0 | 10.2 | 9.7 | 9.0 | 8.4 | 8.1 | 7.2 | 4.4 | 0.0 | -0.8 | -2.9 | -9.5 |
| Lower quartile (%) | -0.8 | -1.3 | -1.6 | -2.1 | -3.7 | -4.6 | -6.5 | -7.3 | -8.0 | -8.7 | -9.9 | -12.7 | -13.3 | -16.8 | -25.1 |
| Minimum IRR (%) | -100.0 | -100.0 | -100.0 | -100.0 | -100.0 | -100.0 | -100.0 | -100.0 | -100.0 | -100.0 | -100.0 | -100.0 | -100.0 | -100.0 | -100.0 |

Exhibit 13

**Investment horizon IRRs by composite portfolio, as of 31 December 1998**

| Vintage year | 1-year | 3-year | 5-year | 10-year | 20-year |
|---|---|---|---|---|---|
| 1980–90 | 21.4 | 23.4 | 17.8 | 16.5 | 20.5 |
| 1980–98 | 11.8 | 18.5 | 16.4 | 16.2 | 19.5 |
| 1981–98 | 11.8 | 18.5 | 16.4 | 16.1 | |
| 1982–98 | 11.8 | 18.5 | 16.4 | 16.1 | |
| 1983–98 | 11.8 | 18.5 | 16.4 | 16.1 | |
| 1984–98 | 11.9 | 18.6 | 16.7 | 16.3 | |
| 1985–98 | 11.7 | 18.6 | 16.7 | 15.9 | |
| 1986–98 | 11.4 | 18.5 | 17.1 | 15.5 | |
| 1987–98 | 11.1 | 18.3 | 16.9 | 15.5 | |
| 1988–98 | 10.3 | 16.5 | 15.2 | 15.9 | |
| 1989–98 | 9.6 | 15.1 | 15.1 | | |
| 1990–98 | 8.4 | 15.0 | 14.5 | | |
| 1991–98 | 8.3 | 15.2 | 14.6 | | |
| 1992–98 | 8.2 | 15.0 | 14.5 | | |
| 1993–98 | 7.6 | 13.9 | 12.7 | | |
| 1994–98 | 8.7 | 11.7 | | | |
| 1995–98 | 8.8 | 11.2 | | | |
| 1996–98 | 6.4 | | | | |
| 1997–98 | -0.1 | | | | |

Exhibit 14

## Summary of cumulative results of buyout and mezzanine partnerships, by composite portfolio, by fund age, as of 31 December 1998

| Vintage | 1 | 2 | 3 | 4 | 5 | 6 | 7 | 8 | 9 | 10 | 11 | 12 | 13 | 14 | 15 | 16 | 17 | 18 |
|---|---|---|---|---|---|---|---|---|---|---|---|---|---|---|---|---|---|---|
| **Sample size** | | | | | | | | | | | | | | | | | | |
| 1976–98 | 288 | 253 | 225 | 203 | 177 | 154 | 132 | 125 | 111 | 87 | 67 | 43 | 28 | 18 | 12 | 5 | 4 | 3 |
| 1984–98 | 277 | 242 | 213 | 191 | 165 | 142 | 120 | 113 | 99 | 75 | 55 | 31 | 16 | 6 | | | | |
| 1985–98 | 271 | 236 | 207 | 185 | 159 | 136 | 114 | 107 | 93 | 69 | 49 | 25 | 10 | | | | | |
| 1986–98 | 261 | 226 | 197 | 175 | 149 | 126 | 104 | 97 | 83 | 59 | 39 | 15 | | | | | | |
| 1987–98 | 246 | 211 | 182 | 160 | 134 | 111 | 89 | 82 | 68 | 44 | 24 | | | | | | | |
| 1988–98 | 222 | 187 | 158 | 136 | 109 | 86 | 64 | 57 | 43 | 19 | | | | | | | | |
| 1989–98 | 203 | 168 | 139 | 117 | 90 | 67 | 45 | 38 | 24 | | | | | | | | | |
| 1990–98 | 179 | 144 | 115 | 93 | 66 | 43 | 21 | 14 | | | | | | | | | | |
| 1991–98 | 165 | 130 | 101 | 79 | 52 | 29 | 7 | | | | | | | | | | | |
| 1992–98 | 158 | 123 | 94 | 72 | 45 | 22 | | | | | | | | | | | | |
| 1993–98 | 136 | 101 | 72 | 50 | 23 | | | | | | | | | | | | | |
| 1994–98 | 113 | 78 | 49 | 27 | | | | | | | | | | | | | | |
| 1995–98 | 88 | 52 | 22 | | | | | | | | | | | | | | | |
| 1996–98 | 66 | 30 | | | | | | | | | | | | | | | | |
| 1997–98 | 37 | | | | | | | | | | | | | | | | | |
| **Average IRR** | | | | | | | | | | | | | | | | | | |
| 1976–98 | 6.5 | 15.9 | 15.3 | 16.8 | 15.9 | 17.6 | 17.5 | 18.1 | 19.4 | 21.5 | 24.6 | 31.1 | 39.8 | 36.7 | 37.3 | 31.4 | 36.0 | 34.6 |
| 1984–98 | 6.6 | 16.1 | 14.0 | 15.2 | 14.2 | 15.8 | 15.4 | 15.9 | 17.2 | 18.8 | 21.7 | 28.7 | 41.5 | 35.1 | | | | |
| 1985–98 | 6.6 | 15.7 | 13.5 | 14.7 | 13.5 | 15.1 | 14.5 | 14.8 | 16.1 | 17.5 | 20.1 | 27.1 | 45.4 | | | | | |
| 1986–98 | 6.6 | 15.5 | 12.0 | 12.4 | 11.1 | 12.4 | 11.3 | 11.4 | 12.4 | 12.6 | 13.5 | 15.1 | | | | | | |
| 1987–98 | 6.5 | 15.7 | 12.0 | 12.9 | 11.4 | 12.1 | 10.7 | 10.7 | 11.9 | 11.8 | 12.4 | | | | | | | |
| 1988–98 | 6.3 | 16.6 | 13.2 | 14.5 | 12.9 | 13.3 | 11.5 | 11.2 | 11.6 | 11.2 | | | | | | | | |
| 1989–98 | 6.0 | 18.0 | 14.5 | 15.9 | 14.1 | 14.6 | 12.0 | 11.5 | 11.7 | | | | | | | | | |
| 1990–98 | 6.4 | 20.2 | 16.6 | 18.2 | 16.6 | 17.0 | 12.7 | 11.4 | | | | | | | | | | |
| 1991–98 | 7.3 | 21.9 | 15.5 | 18.0 | 18.0 | 19.5 | 15.5 | | | | | | | | | | | |
| 1992–98 | 7.8 | 22.2 | 16.0 | 18.2 | 18.5 | 20.3 | | | | | | | | | | | | |
| 1993–98 | 8.4 | 24.7 | 15.3 | 17.6 | 17.1 | | | | | | | | | | | | | |
| 1994–98 | 8.2 | 27.4 | 12.7 | 15.6 | | | | | | | | | | | | | | |
| 1995–98 | 9.0 | 31.9 | 9.7 | | | | | | | | | | | | | | | |
| 1996–98 | 11.1 | 49.1 | | | | | | | | | | | | | | | | |
| 1997–98 | 1.4 | | | | | | | | | | | | | | | | | |
| **Median IRR** | | | | | | | | | | | | | | | | | | |
| 1976–98 | 0.1 | 8.2 | 9.8 | 11.3 | 12.4 | 13.9 | 13.8 | 13.9 | 14.0 | 13.6 | 15.5 | 17.7 | 28.4 | 29.8 | 30.6 | 31.7 | 35.9 | 31.7 |
| 1984–98 | 0.1 | 7.9 | 9.3 | 10.6 | 11.9 | 13.1 | 12.5 | 12.6 | 12.6 | 12.2 | 12.6 | 15.5 | 19.1 | 23.5 | | | | |
| 1985–98 | 0.2 | 7.8 | 9.3 | 10.6 | 11.9 | 13.1 | 12.5 | 12.6 | 12.5 | 11.5 | 12.3 | 13.2 | 19.0 | | | | | |
| 1986–98 | 0.3 | 7.8 | 9.0 | 9.4 | 11.7 | 12.7 | 11.8 | 11.9 | 11.7 | 11.4 | 10.7 | 9.4 | | | | | | |
| 1987–98 | 0.1 | 7.7 | 8.7 | 10.7 | 11.8 | 12.8 | 11.8 | 12.1 | 12.1 | 11.5 | 10.9 | | | | | | | |
| 1988–98 | 0.1 | 8.2 | 9.3 | 11.8 | 13.5 | 12.9 | 12.3 | 12.7 | 12.5 | 12.2 | | | | | | | | |
| 1989–98 | 0.0 | 8.6 | 12.2 | 15.3 | 15.2 | 16.3 | 13.9 | 14.0 | 14.9 | | | | | | | | | |
| 1990–98 | 0.2 | 9.7 | 14.0 | 17.3 | 18.1 | 18.4 | 15.6 | 14.0 | | | | | | | | | | |
| 1991–98 | 0.1 | 10.0 | 14.0 | 17.6 | 18.5 | 20.3 | 16.9 | | | | | | | | | | | |
| 1992–98 | 0.3 | 9.8 | 14.4 | 17.6 | 18.7 | 20.4 | | | | | | | | | | | | |
| 1993–98 | 0.1 | 10.8 | 14.3 | 16.3 | 16.5 | | | | | | | | | | | | | |
| 1994–98 | 0.0 | 9.9 | 9.3 | 11.8 | | | | | | | | | | | | | | |
| 1995–98 | -1.0 | 9.1 | 2.5 | | | | | | | | | | | | | | | |
| 1996–98 | -0.4 | 12.1 | | | | | | | | | | | | | | | | |
| 1997–98 | -5.0 | | | | | | | | | | | | | | | | | |

Exhibit 14 *continued*

## Summary of cumulative results of buyout and mezzanine partnerships, by composite portfolio, by fund age, as of 31 December 1998 *continued*

| Vintage | 1 | 2 | 3 | 4 | 5 | 6 | 7 | 8 | 9 | 10 | 11 | 12 | 13 | 14 | 15 | 16 | 17 | 18 |
|---------|---|---|---|---|---|---|---|---|---|----|----|----|----|----|----|----|----|----|
| **Upper quartile IRR** | | | | | | | | | | | | | | | | | | |
| 1976–98 | 10.6 | 21.3 | 24.1 | 23.9 | 22.1 | 22.5 | 21.2 | 21.8 | 23.1 | 23.1 | 28.9 | 31.4 | 39.6 | 38.2 | 40.4 | 40.2 | 40.4 | 36.4 |
| 1984–98 | 10.8 | 21.5 | 23.2 | 23.7 | 21.3 | 20.9 | 18.9 | 19.5 | 20.0 | 19.0 | 21.4 | 29.3 | 36.8 | 30.3 | | | | |
| 1985–98 | 10.8 | 21.4 | 23.0 | 23.4 | 21.2 | 20.7 | 18.5 | 19.0 | 19.5 | 17.7 | 19.7 | 20.0 | 38.5 | | | | | |
| 1986–98 | 10.9 | 21.0 | 22.7 | 22.7 | 20.9 | 20.6 | 17.2 | 18.2 | 17.9 | 15.5 | 17.3 | 16.6 | | | | | | |
| 1987–98 | 11.8 | 21.4 | 22.8 | 22.9 | 21.0 | 20.7 | 18.0 | 18.4 | 17.9 | 15.0 | 17.1 | | | | | | | |
| 1988–98 | 11.8 | 22.3 | 23.1 | 23.8 | 22.1 | 20.9 | 18.1 | 19.0 | 19.0 | 14.1 | | | | | | | | |
| 1989–98 | 10.8 | 23.1 | 24.7 | 24.7 | 22.8 | 22.6 | 20.3 | 20.5 | 21.5 | | | | | | | | | |
| 1990–98 | 12.2 | 23.5 | 24.9 | 24.8 | 23.2 | 23.3 | 18.3 | 19.4 | | | | | | | | | | |
| 1991–98 | 14.2 | 23.9 | 25.0 | 24.8 | 23.4 | 24.0 | 19.2 | | | | | | | | | | | |
| 1992–98 | 14.3 | 23.5 | 26.3 | 25.5 | 23.6 | 23.6 | | | | | | | | | | | | |
| 1993–98 | 14.9 | 24.1 | 26.9 | 25.2 | 22.4 | | | | | | | | | | | | | |
| 1994–98 | 20.0 | 26.6 | 27.9 | 24.8 | | | | | | | | | | | | | | |
| 1995–98 | 21.9 | 25.5 | 14.0 | | | | | | | | | | | | | | | |
| 1996–98 | 28.1 | 29.1 | | | | | | | | | | | | | | | | |
| 1997–98 | 9.7 | | | | | | | | | | | | | | | | | |
| **Average distribution to paid-in** | | | | | | | | | | | | | | | | | | |
| 1976–98 | 0.07 | 0.17 | 0.35 | 0.64 | 0.82 | 1.13 | 1.33 | 1.60 | 1.83 | 2.05 | 2.37 | 2.98 | 3.47 | 3.99 | 4.21 | 6.43 | 7.41 | 7.97 |
| 1984–98 | 0.07 | 0.17 | 0.34 | 0.63 | 0.77 | 1.07 | 1.24 | 1.49 | 1.72 | 1.91 | 2.23 | 2.91 | 3.52 | 3.60 | | | | |
| 1985–98 | 0.07 | 0.15 | 0.32 | 0.60 | 0.75 | 1.02 | 1.19 | 1.44 | 1.65 | 1.82 | 2.13 | 2.79 | 3.56 | | | | | |
| 1986–98 | 0.07 | 0.15 | 0.27 | 0.48 | 0.61 | 0.88 | 1.04 | 1.27 | 1.47 | 1.58 | 1.83 | 2.36 | | | | | | |
| 1987–98 | 0.07 | 0.14 | 0.27 | 0.50 | 0.63 | 0.86 | 0.99 | 1.21 | 1.42 | 1.46 | 1.62 | | | | | | | |
| 1988–98 | 0.07 | 0.14 | 0.28 | 0.54 | 0.70 | 0.94 | 1.08 | 1.27 | 1.45 | 1.43 | | | | | | | | |
| 1989–98 | 0.06 | 0.15 | 0.29 | 0.58 | 0.76 | 1.02 | 1.13 | 1.32 | 1.52 | | | | | | | | | |
| 1990–98 | 0.07 | 0.16 | 0.32 | 0.63 | 0.83 | 1.08 | 1.11 | 1.13 | | | | | | | | | | |
| 1991–98 | 0.06 | 0.16 | 0.33 | 0.66 | 0.87 | 1.20 | 1.28 | | | | | | | | | | | |
| 1992–98 | 0.06 | 0.16 | 0.34 | 0.69 | 0.89 | 1.26 | | | | | | | | | | | | |
| 1993–98 | 0.07 | 0.17 | 0.35 | 0.73 | 0.93 | | | | | | | | | | | | | |
| 1994–98 | 0.06 | 0.18 | 0.31 | 0.69 | | | | | | | | | | | | | | |
| 1995–98 | 0.07 | 0.14 | 0.23 | | | | | | | | | | | | | | | |
| 1996–98 | 0.07 | 0.14 | | | | | | | | | | | | | | | | |
| 1997–98 | 0.08 | | | | | | | | | | | | | | | | | |
| **Average residual value to paid-in** | | | | | | | | | | | | | | | | | | |
| 1976–98 | 0.99 | 1.04 | 1.01 | 0.93 | 0.86 | 0.80 | 0.72 | 0.59 | 0.50 | 0.45 | 0.43 | 0.41 | 0.53 | 0.18 | 0.19 | 0.10 | 0.11 | 0.02 |
| 1984–98 | 0.99 | 1.04 | 1.00 | 0.89 | 0.82 | 0.77 | 0.69 | 0.56 | 0.47 | 0.41 | 0.35 | 0.23 | 0.16 | 0.05 | | | | |
| 1985–98 | 0.99 | 1.04 | 1.00 | 0.90 | 0.82 | 0.77 | 0.67 | 0.54 | 0.45 | 0.39 | 0.32 | 0.19 | 0.14 | | | | | |
| 1986–98 | 0.99 | 1.04 | 1.00 | 0.89 | 0.81 | 0.74 | 0.65 | 0.52 | 0.44 | 0.39 | 0.31 | 0.18 | | | | | | |
| 1987–98 | 0.99 | 1.04 | 1.00 | 0.88 | 0.79 | 0.72 | 0.62 | 0.48 | 0.41 | 0.35 | 0.31 | | | | | | | |
| 1988–98 | 1.00 | 1.05 | 1.02 | 0.89 | 0.78 | 0.70 | 0.60 | 0.46 | 0.38 | 0.31 | | | | | | | | |
| 1989–98 | 1.00 | 1.07 | 1.03 | 0.89 | 0.78 | 0.68 | 0.59 | 0.46 | 0.39 | | | | | | | | | |
| 1990–98 | 1.00 | 1.08 | 1.04 | 0.89 | 0.77 | 0.68 | 0.55 | 0.45 | | | | | | | | | | |
| 1991–98 | 1.01 | 1.09 | 0.99 | 0.83 | 0.75 | 0.65 | 0.55 | | | | | | | | | | | |
| 1992–98 | 1.01 | 1.09 | 0.98 | 0.80 | 0.73 | 0.60 | | | | | | | | | | | | |
| 1993–98 | 1.01 | 1.10 | 0.97 | 0.76 | 0.65 | | | | | | | | | | | | | |
| 1994–98 | 1.02 | 1.12 | 0.97 | 0.72 | | | | | | | | | | | | | | |
| 1995–98 | 1.02 | 1.17 | 0.96 | | | | | | | | | | | | | | | |
| 1996–98 | 1.04 | 1.29 | | | | | | | | | | | | | | | | |
| 1997–98 | 0.96 | | | | | | | | | | | | | | | | | |

Table header spanning columns 1–18: *Fund age*

Chapter 18

# The performance of US venture capital funds

Jesse Reyes
*Product Manager, Venture Economics*

Toby Walters
*Publications Manager, Venture Economics*

The *1999 Investment Benchmarks Report: Venture Capital (IBR)* is an annual performance report of the US venture capital industry and the 18th in a series of reports on the private equity industry conducted by Venture Economics. The purpose of the report is to provide investors, general partners, and the investment public with aggregate benchmarks for US private limited partnerships investing in venture-backed companies. The following, which is excerpted from the 1999 edition, analyses the aggregate performance of 775 venture capital limited partnerships formed from 1969 to 1998.

It is now easy to characterise the venture capital industry as a legitimate alternative investment vehicle for the institutional investor as the industry appears to be in the second large cycle of its long life. The first major cycle since venture capital became an investable asset class for pension funds was in the early 1980s and was characterised by the record vol-

Exhibit 1

**Venture capital industry statistics, 1970–98 (US$ million)**

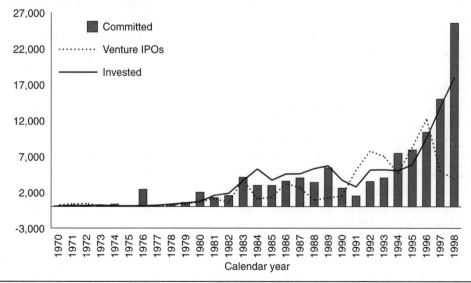

ume of capital raised, investments made, and the first significant wave of venture-backed technology stocks resulting from investments made in the late 1970s and early 1980s. Companies like Lotus, Apple, and Compaq were among the darlings of the industry and of the press.

After a long spell of below-average performance, relatively low amounts of money invested and increased market efficiency, the industry appears now to be well into what some have termed 'the second golden age of venture capital'. While the names have changed – Netscape, eBay, About.com – and much of the venture industry's participants changed their focus from start-up and early-stage investing in the 1970s and 1980s to later-stage and expansion financing, the game is still the same: venture capital investors trying to invest in companies that will provide extraordinary growth opportunities.

It is evident from Exhibit 1 that the industry's health is tied closely to the availability of exit opportunities whether through merger, acquisition or through that most glamorous vehicle – the initial public offering. The period from 1991 to 1998, except for 1994, saw increasingly larger amounts of capital being raised and invested. Furthermore, IPO activity eventually increased to record volume as the industry was finally able to harvest the fruits of its labour of the huge investments made in the first half of the 1980s.

We shall examine the performance results that have accrued to the industry from this investment. Only a few short years ago, it appeared that the industry would not be able to live up to its performance expectations. As the first volume of this report series went to press in 1988, many in the industry were afraid that publishing the single-digit returns of that time would have a devastating effect on the industry on and the ability of the industry to raise capital. However, in a few years, the fortunes of the industry have changed dramatically as the industry has been able to take advantage of the current investment boom and stock market cycle that began in 1991.

While the industry focuses on long-term performance, it is the short-term performance of the past few years that has garnered attention as the industry has been able to post +30 per cent annual periodic returns from 1995 to 1997 (though the industry posted a 17.7 per cent return for the 12 months ending 31 December 1998 for funds formed from 1969 to 1998). These stellar performance levels have not been seen in over a decade and the industry is making the most of it.

It is ironic to the authors of this chapter that when this report series was first published many in the industry cautioned us against publishing the returns of 'young funds' with little realised performance results (funds less than about four years old). It was felt the returns were too low and not indicative of 'true performance' as much of the performance to date was unrealised. Many thought publishing the results of these funds would drive investors away from investing in this asset class.

Now, even young funds are turning in impressive early year interim results as the industry rides on the robust small-cap and new issues market driven by the technology sector. Currently, it is not unusual to see firms going back to raise capital for a new fund some 18 to 24 months after the close of their previous fund on the basis of these 'preliminary' results.

Some members of our constituent audience have indicated that we should not publish the results of young funds because the returns of some of the funds formed between 1995 and 1998 are turning in interim performance of +30–40 per cent and publishing such high returns could (1) raise expectations to an unsustainable level similar to the period 1980–84 or (2) bring 'too much capital' into the industry. What remains to be seen is whether the industry can continue to invest profitably the record capital raised over the past few years and be able to learn from the last major cycle how to sustain their investors' performance expectations.

## Sample composition

This study analyses the performance of 775 funds formed from 1969 to 1998, which represent 39 per cent of the number of funds formed in those years and 52 per cent of the capital raised.

## Total capitalisation

Exhibits 3 and 4 compare the statistics from the universe of funds formed from 1969 to 1998 to the 1999 *Investment Benchmarks* Sample by the number of funds and the capital raised respectively for each vintage year.

Exhibit 5 details the number and capitalisation of funds formed in each year which we call the universe and compares the Investment Benchmark sample with that of the universe. Capitalisation is provided both in terms of funds raised and by the cumulative amount of funds raised. Exhibit 6 provides the historical representation of the sample by cumulative fund capitalisation. It indicates that the sample has continued to track the growth of capital in the industry and from 1989 until 1996 consistently contained about 75–80 per cent of total capital.

## Average capitalisation and sample bias

Exhibit 7 compares the average fund size in the *IBR* sample to the universe by vintage year. This figure indicates that fund size has increased substantially since the early to mid-1980s when analysing by vintage year and that the sample average fund size closely tracks the universe average fund size in each vintage year. The average fund size for the universe is now US$63.1 million while the average fund size for our sample is US$83.1million. If the sample is at all biased, it is biased towards larger funds. This is due to our client constituency and is representative of the significantly larger investments favoured by mainstream institutional investors.

## Cash flow investment cycle

Exhibit 8 compares the cumulative cash flow investment life cycle of the sample with the universe, while Exhibit 9 shows the net cash flow. As Exhibit 8 shows, fund raising and the amount of capital invested, while flat for a decade, have dramatically increased since the early 1990s. This is particularly evident in the 1990s. However, investment opportunities continue to increase as the amount of uninvested capital has not increased as much and has, at certain times, decreased, particularly in boom periods when returns were high. Exhibit 9 shows that beginning in 1995, limited partners as a group started receiving positive inflows of capital. As a result, cumulative distributions almost equalled the cumulative amount of capital raised. This is a dramatic difference from around 1990, when negative net cash flow was at its lowest point, a testament to the long entrepreneurial investment process.

## Summary of major findings

### Vintage year results

Exhibit 10 summarises the cumulative interim results by vintage year, ie, the year of the fund's first investment as of the end of 1998, and Exhibit 11 represents results by fund age to compare fund life cycles.

The following observations can be made about the data in the report.

The economic environment in which a fund is investing impacts results as much as the experience of the venture capital managers. For example, the high returns achieved in the period 1976–80 were in large part due to the excellent investing and exiting environment. Conversely, the 1982 funds were investing in an environment of high valuations and even higher competition, resulting in overall low returns even among the most experienced investors. As we are in the second investment cycle for the industry as defined earlier, it appears that funds formed since 1990 will again be superior performers.

Funds formed in recent years have demonstrated strong overall returns buoyed in part by what has been a strong IPO and therefore exit market.

The data confirm that venture capital is a long-term investment process. The analysis of distributions to paid-in capital in Exhibit 11 suggests that most funds experience a significant increase in distributions around their fifth year of operation. The trend of the past few years indicates that original committed capital will be returned between the seventh and eighth year of operation. However, it does appear that funds formed in 1987 and 1988 have accelerated distributions and thus increased their relative returns when compared to other funds formed in the 1980s.

### Top quartile performance

The real key to judging the success of the venture capital industry overall may lay in the analysis of the funds in the top quartile. In a market such as venture capital, where there is a wide dispersion of returns, the averages may not be reliable indicators of the potential returns. Exhibits 12 and 13 provide statistics for funds in the top quartile and upper half, respectively. We have included funds that have been formed in recent years as they have begun to have realisation early in their life. Exhibit 12 indicates that most top quartile funds formed since 1988 have had returns in excess of 30 per cent. One would have to go back to the late 1970s to early 1980s to see results in that range. There are a few aberrations – funds in certain vintage years had some spectacular performances due to short-term investment in companies that have gone public.

### Cumulative results by fund characteristics

Exhibit 14 is a summary of statistics for all funds formed between 1969 and 1998 by fund characteristics: stage, size, and sequence. These statistics must be viewed with care as averages can be distorted by outliers. For example, the results within each vintage year may differ from results for the entire industry.

Analysis by size of funds indicates that the largest funds (US$100 million) have historically outperformed funds under US$100 million in size. As of recently, there has been a definite bias towards larger funds. In prior editions of the *IBR* there was a U-shaped performance curve, with smaller funds and large funds dominating the others. As of 1998, large funds have clearly begun to pull away. When the large funds were first starting to be formed in the early 1980s, there was some scepticism about their ability to produce returns that would be equivalent to those of smaller partnerships. It appears that through their depth of experience, different investment strategies, and enhanced resources they are generally as successful or more successful than small funds of the same vintage. Even median returns of large funds have outpaced those of smaller funds. It is no surprise that the average fund has become larger and larger (see Exhibit 7), but at the same time the industry has become more later-stage focused with commensurate shorter investment horizons as indicated by the performance of the latest vintage years.

One of the reasons that investors have become active in private equity/venture capital is diversification due to long-term investment horizons. However, as the average investment horizon has decreased, has diversification also decreased? It is not surprising to find significant correlation of venture capital returns with public market returns, especially small-cap markets. However, there is evidence that would indicate that there is significantly less correlation of smaller early-stage focused funds companies with the public markets – bringing forth the classic asset allocation risk/return question: invest for higher, quicker returns with later-stage/ large funds or invest with less risk with smaller/early-stage focused funds?

## Composite portfolio performance

While vintage year analysis provides investors with a way of benchmarking their individual funds' performance, it does not provide a way to benchmark the performance of their portfolios of venture investments. As the industry has become analytical, we were asked by investors for benchmarks that mirrored the types of analysis that they were being asked to present to compare with other asset classes. We have been providing this type of benchmark for over five years to our monitoring clients.

Composite portfolio holding period returns are presented in Exhibit 15 and cumulative benchmark results for composite portfolios are shown in Exhibit 16.

Highlights of the composite analysis include:

- The venture industry (funds formed from 1969 to 1998) posted a 17.4 per cent one-year return as of 31 December 1998 and has returns of 27.3 per cent and 17.4 per cent, respectively, for five- and ten-year investment horizons.
- Funds formed more recently (1991–97) have performed very well over a one-year period. It is also important to keep in mind that returns wane over a 10-year period, as Exhibit 15 shows.

## Exhibit 2

# 1999 investment benchmarks composition: venture capital firms represented

Abacus Ventures
Abingworth Management, Ltd.
ABS Ventures
Acacia Venture Partners
Accel Partners
Acorn Ventures, Inc.
Adams Capital Management, Inc.
Adler & Co.
Advanced Technology Development Fund
Advanced Technology Ventures
Advent International Corp.
Aegis Venture Funds
Allegra Partners
Allen & Co., Inc.
Allied Capital Advisers, Inc.
Allsop Venture Partners
Alpha Capital Venture Partners, L.P.
Alpine Technology Ventures
Alta Berkeley Associates
Alta Communications
Alta Partners
Ampersand Ventures
AMT Venture Partners, Ltd.
Apac Holdings
Apax Partners & Co. Ventures Holdings Ltd.
Apex Investment Partners
Applied Technology
Artesian Capital
Asset Management Associates, Inc.
Atlantic Venture Partners
Atlas Venture
August Capital Management
Austin Ventures, L.P.
AVI Capital, L.P.
Axiom Venture Partners, L.P.
Bass Associates
Batterson, Johnson & Wang, L.P.
Battery Ventures, L.P.
BAY Partners
BCI Advisors, Inc.
Becker Technological Associates
Benchmark Capital
Beta Partners
Boston Capital Ventures
Brantley Venture Partners
Brentwood Associates Private Equity
Brentwood Venture Capital
Burr, Egan, Deleage & Co.
Cable & Howse Ventures
Calvert Social Venture Partners, L.P.
Campbell Venture Management
Capform Partners
Centennial Funds, The
CEO Venture Fund
Cerulean Fund/WGC Enterprises
Charles River Ventures
Cherry Tree Investments, Inc.
Chicago Capital Fund
Chisholm Private Capital Partners
CID Equity Partners
CMEA Ventures

Coleman Swenson Hoffman Booth Inc.
Collinson, Howe & Lennox, LLC
Colorado Venture Management
Columbine Venture Funds, The
Communications Ventures
Connecticut Seed Ventures, L.P.
Connecticut-Greene Ventures, L.P.
Conning & Co.
Consumer Venture Partners
Continental Capital Ventures
Copley Venture Partners
Coral Ventures
Cornerstone Equity Investors, LLC
Cornerstone Ventures
Costine Associates, L.P.
Crescendo Venture Management LLC
Crosspoint Venture Partners
Crown Advisors, Ltd.
Cullinane & Donnelly Venture Partners, L.P.
CW Group, Inc.
Cygnus Venture Partners
Davis Venture Partners, L.P.
Delphi Ventures
DeMuth, Folger & Wethrill
Deucalion Venture Partners
Doll Capital Management
Domain Associates
Dominion Ventures, Inc.
Dougery Ventures
DSV Partners
E.M. Warburg, Pincus & Co., LLC.
Eastech Management Co., Inc.
Edison Venture Fund
EG&G Venture Partners
El Dorado Ventures
EnerTech Capital Partners, L.P.
Enterprise Development Fund
Enterprise Partners
Entertainment Media Venture Partners
Essex Venture Partners
Essex Woodlands Health Ventures
Fairfield Venture Partners
First Analysis Venture Capital
First Century Partners
First Chicago Investment Advisors
Fleet Equity Partners
Foothill Group Inc.
Foreign & Colonial
Fortis Private Capital. Inc.
Fostin Capital Partners
Foundation Capital
Frazier & Company
Frontenac Co.
Galen Associates
Gateway Associates, L.P.
Geocapital Partners, L.L.C.
Glenwood Management
Grace Ventures Corp. & Horn Venture
  Partners
Greylock
Grotech Capital Group

H&Q Asia Pacific, Ltd.
Halpern, Denny & Co.
Hambrecht & Quist Private Equity
Hambrecht & Quist Venture Associates
Hambro International Equity Partners
Hancock Park Associates
Healthcare Ventures LLC
Heartland Capital Fund, Ltd.
Highland Capital Partners
Hill, Carman Ventures
HLM Partners
HMS Capital Partners
Hook Partners
Houston Venture Partners
HSBC Private Equity Management
Hummer Winblad Venture Partners
Inco Venture Capital Management
Inman & Bowman
InnoCal, L.P.
Institutional Venture Partners
Intermountain Technology Management L.P.
Intersouth Partners
InterVen Partners
InterWest Partners
InvestAmerica Venture Group, Inc.
J.P. Morgan Capital Corp.
Japan/America Ventures, Inc.
Julian, Cole & Stein
Keystone Venture Capital Management Co.
Kingsbury Associates
Kitty Hawk Capital
Kleiner Perkins Caufield & Byers
Lambda Funds, The
Lovett Miller & Company
M/C Venture Partners
MarketCorp Ventures L.P.
Marquette Venture Partners
Massey Burch Capital Corp.
Matrix Partners
Mayfield Fund
MBW Management, Inc.
MedCorp Development Fund
Media/Communications Partners
Medical Innovation Partners
Medical Science Partners
MedVenture Associates
Menlo Ventures
Meridian Venture Partners
Merrill, Pickard, Anderson & Eyre
Mesirow Private Equity Investments, Inc.
Mid-Atlantic Venture Funds
Minnesota Seed Capital, Inc.
MK Global Ventures
Mohr, Davidow Ventures
Montgomery Bridge/Pathfinder
Montgomery Medical Ventures, L.P.
Morgan Stanley Dean Witter Capital
  Partners, LLC
Morgenthaler Ventures
N.Y. State Business Venture Partners
Nazem & Co.

Exhibit 2 *continued*

## 1999 investment benchmarks composition: venture capital firms represented *continued*

| | | |
|---|---|---|
| New Enterprise Associates | R. Chaney & Co., Inc. | Telecom Management, LLC |
| Newtek Ventures | RFE Investment Partners | Telos Venture Partners |
| Noro-Moseley Partners | Roanoke Capital, Ltd. | Ticonderoga Capital, Inc. |
| North Atlantic Capital Corp. | Robertson Stephens & Company, LLC | TL Ventures |
| North Bridge Venture Partners | Roser Ventures Limited Liability Company | Toronto Dominion Investments, Inc. |
| Norwest Venture Partners | Rothschild Ventures, Inc. | Triad Investors Corp |
| Oak Investment Partners | Schroder Ventures | Triad Ventures, Ltd. |
| Olympic Venture Partners | Seidman, Jackson, Fisher & Co. | Trident Capital |
| Omega Venture Partners | Sequel Venture Partners | Trinity Ventures |
| OneLiberty Ventures | Sequoia Capital | Trinus Partners, L.P. |
| Onset Ventures | Sevin Rosen Management Co. | TVM Techno Venture Management |
| Orien Ventures | Shaw Glasgow Partners | U.S. Venture Partners |
| OSCCO Ventures | Sierra Ventures | Utah Ventures II, L.P. |
| Oxford Bioscience Partners | Sigma Partners | Vanguard Venture Partners |
| Pacific Venture Partners | Silver Creek Technology Investors | Vector Fund Management, L.P. |
| Palmer Partners, L.P. | SOFTBANK Technology Ventures | Ventana Growth Funds |
| Paragon Venture Partners | Sorrento Associates, Inc. | Venture Capital Fund of New England, The |
| Partech International | South Atlantic Venture Funds, L.P. | Venture First Associates |
| Pathfinder Venture Capital Funds | Southern California Ventures | Venture Founders Corp. |
| Patricof & Co. Ventures, Inc. | Southwest Enterprise Associates, L.P. | Venture Growth Associates |
| Peregrine Ventures | Southwest Venture Partnerships, The | Venture Management Associates, Inc. |
| Philadelphia Ventures, Inc. | Spectrum Equity Investors, L.P. | Ventures Medical Associates |
| Phillips-Smith Specialty Retail Group | Sprout Group | Venturtech Management |
| Phoenix Partners, The | Summit Partners | Vista Group, The |
| Pittsburgh Seed Fund Partners | Sunwestern Investment Group | Walden International Investment Group |
| Plant Resources Venture Funds | Sutter Hill Ventures | Weiss, Peck & Greer Venture Partners, L.P. |
| Point Venture Partners | T. Rowe Price Threshold Partnerships | Welsh, Carson, Anderson & Stowe |
| Polaris Venture Partners | T.V.P. Associates | Western Technology Investment |
| Poly Ventures | TA Associates, Inc. | Weston Presidio Capital |
| Primus Venture Partners, Inc. | Taylor & Turner | William Blair Venture Partners |
| Prince Ventures | TDH Capital | Wind Point Partners |
| Princeton/Montrose Partners | Technology Crossover Ventures | Woodside Fund |
| Prism Venture Partners | Technology Funding | Worldview Technology Partners |
| Prospect Street Ventures | Technology Partners | Zero Stage Capital Co., Inc. |
| Quest Ventures | Technology Venture Investors | |

Exhibit 3

**1999 investment benchmarks: number of funds by vintage year**

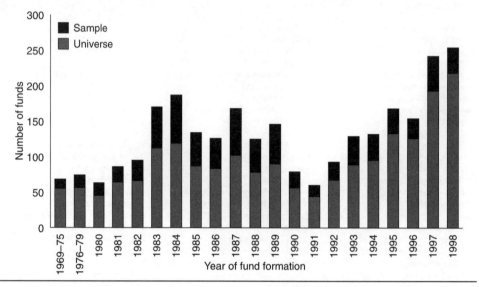

Exhibit 4

**1999 investment benchmarks: capital committed by vintage year (US$ million)**

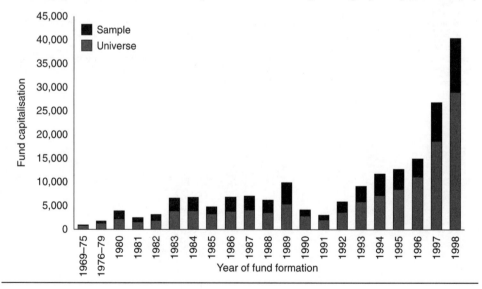

Exhibit 5

## 1999 investment benchmarks: sample and universe capitalisation by vintage year

| Vintage year | Universe capitalisation US$ million | | | Sample capitalisation US$ million | | | Cumulative capitalisation Universe US$ million | | | Sample US$ million | | |
|---|---|---|---|---|---|---|---|---|---|---|---|---|
| | Funds | Fund cap | Avg cap | Funds | Fund cap | Avg cap | Funds | Fund cap | Avg cap | Funds | Fund cap | Avg cap |
| 1969-75 | 55 | 814.8 | 14.8 | 13 | 116.6 | 9.0 | 55 | 814.8 | 14.8 | 13 | 116.6 | 9.0 |
| 1976-79 | 56 | 1,314.6 | 23.5 | 18 | 442.9 | 24.6 | 111 | 2,129.4 | 38.3 | 31 | 559.5 | 33.6 |
| 1980 | 45 | 2,222.8 | 49.4 | 18 | 1,690.2 | 93.9 | 156 | 4,352.2 | 87.7 | 49 | 2,249.7 | 127.5 |
| 1981 | 64 | 1,571.4 | 24.6 | 22 | 910.5 | 41.4 | 220 | 5,923.6 | 112.3 | 71 | 3,160.2 | 168.9 |
| 1982 | 66 | 1,890.6 | 28.6 | 29 | 1,247.8 | 43.0 | 286 | 7,814.2 | 140.9 | 100 | 4,408.0 | 211.9 |
| 1983 | 112 | 3,915.0 | 35.0 | 58 | 2,696.7 | 46.5 | 398 | 11,729.2 | 175.9 | 158 | 7,104.7 | 258.4 |
| 1984 | 119 | 3,920.0 | 32.9 | 68 | 2,841.5 | 41.8 | 517 | 15,649.2 | 208.8 | 226 | 9,946.2 | 300.2 |
| 1985 | 87 | 3,263.0 | 37.5 | 47 | 1,513.9 | 32.2 | 604 | 18,912.2 | 246.3 | 273 | 11,460.1 | 332.4 |
| 1986 | 83 | 3,824.2 | 46.1 | 43 | 3,008.7 | 70.0 | 687 | 22,736.4 | 292.4 | 316 | 14,468.8 | 402.4 |
| 1987 | 102 | 4,113.9 | 40.3 | 66 | 2,937.6 | 44.5 | 789 | 26,850.3 | 332.7 | 382 | 17,406.4 | 446.9 |
| 1988 | 78 | 3,587.5 | 46.0 | 47 | 2,618.4 | 55.7 | 867 | 30,437.8 | 378.7 | 429 | 20,024.8 | 502.6 |
| 1989 | 90 | 5,395.6 | 60.0 | 56 | 4,493.3 | 80.2 | 957 | 35,833.4 | 438.7 | 485 | 24,518.1 | 582.8 |
| 1990 | 56 | 2,872.2 | 51.3 | 23 | 1,295.2 | 56.3 | 1,013 | 38,705.6 | 490.0 | 508 | 25,813.3 | 639.1 |
| 1991 | 44 | 2,080.3 | 47.3 | 16 | 971.9 | 60.7 | 1,057 | 40,785.9 | 537.3 | 524 | 26,785.2 | 699.8 |
| 1992 | 67 | 3,643.9 | 54.4 | 26 | 2,226.9 | 85.7 | 1,124 | 44,429.8 | 591.7 | 550 | 29,012.1 | 785.5 |
| 1993 | 89 | 5,886.9 | 66.1 | 40 | 3,255.1 | 81.4 | 1,213 | 50,316.7 | 657.8 | 590 | 32,267.2 | 866.9 |
| 1994 | 95 | 7,197.9 | 75.8 | 37 | 4,541.2 | 122.7 | 1,308 | 57,514.6 | 733.6 | 627 | 36,808.4 | 989.6 |
| 1995 | 133 | 8,510.4 | 64.0 | 35 | 4,254.1 | 121.5 | 1,441 | 66,025.0 | 797.6 | 662 | 41,062.5 | 1,111.1 |
| 1996 | 126 | 11,111.3 | 88.2 | 28 | 3,850.0 | 137.5 | 1,567 | 77,136.3 | 885.8 | 690 | 44,912.5 | 1,248.6 |
| 1997 | 193 | 18,681.7 | 96.8 | 49 | 8,161.2 | 166.6 | 1,760 | 95,818.0 | 982.6 | 739 | 53,073.7 | 1,415.2 |
| 1998 | 218 | 29,067.6 | 133.3 | 36 | 11,351.5 | 315.3 | 1,978 | 124,885.6 | 1115.9 | 775 | 64,425.2 | 1,730.5 |
| **Total** | **1,978** | **124,885.6** | **63.1** | **775** | **64,425.2** | **83.1** | | | | | | |

231

Exhibit 6

**1999 investment benchmarks: cumulative capitalisation by vintage year (US$ million)**

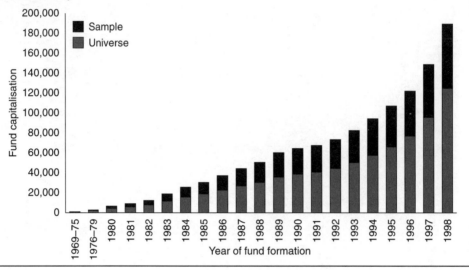

Exhibit 7

**1999 investment benchmarks: average fund size by vintage year (US$ million)**

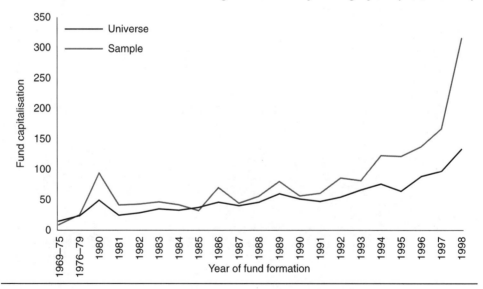

Exhibit 8

**1999 investment benchmarks: cumulative uninvested versus invested capital by calendar year (US$ million)**

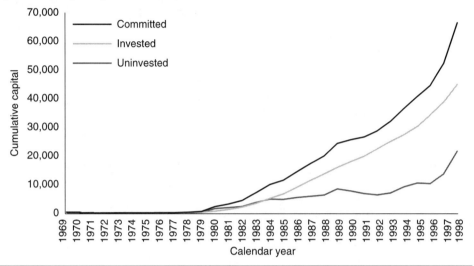

Exhibit 9

**1999 investment benchmarks: cumulative cash flow by calendar year (US$ million)**

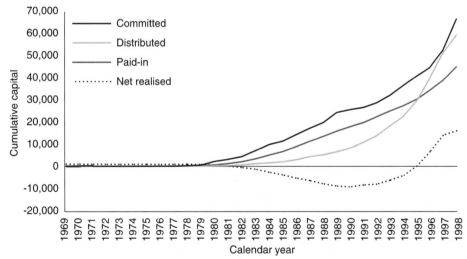

Exhibit 10

## Cumulative benchmark results: overall sample by vintage year, as of 31 December 1998

| | 1969–75 | 1976–79 | 1980 | 1981 | 1982 | 1983 | 1984 | 1985 | 1986 | 1987 | 1988 | 1989 | 1990 | 1991 | 1992 | 1993 | 1994 | 1995 | 1996 | 1997 | 1998 |
|---|---|---|---|---|---|---|---|---|---|---|---|---|---|---|---|---|---|---|---|---|---|
| **Overall** | | | | | | | | | | | | | | | | | | | | | |
| Sample size | 13 | 18 | 18 | 22 | 29 | 58 | 68 | 47 | 43 | 66 | 47 | 56 | 23 | 16 | 26 | 40 | 37 | 35 | 28 | 49 | 36 |
| Avg IRR (%) | 19.3 | 30.2 | 13.5 | 7.2 | 3.3 | 6.2 | 4.9 | 7.1 | 8.2 | 8.4 | 11.5 | 12.2 | 17.7 | 14.3 | 23.3 | 20.4 | 22.6 | 27.8 | 44.6 | 13.7 | -7.2 |
| Cap-wtd IRR (%) | 18.9 | 29.9 | 22.2 | 10.1 | 4.4 | 7.0 | 5.5 | 8.6 | 12.2 | 13.2 | 18.5 | 17.7 | 25.0 | 19.7 | 26.4 | 26.7 | 26.7 | 29.6 | 42.8 | 14.2 | -18.6 |
| Pooled IRR (%) | 19.8 | 28.4 | 18.6 | 9.9 | 4.6 | 7.9 | 6.1 | 9.7 | 13.5 | 14.1 | 18.8 | 19.1 | 28.2 | 20.3 | 30.4 | 31.1 | 31.0 | 38.8 | 45.6 | 24.6 | 30.2 |
| Median IRR (%) | 19.9 | 29.3 | 13.4 | 9.2 | 4.2 | 5.8 | 4.3 | 7.9 | 7.1 | 7.9 | 8.4 | 10.0 | 10.6 | 13.0 | 14.6 | 11.1 | 21.0 | 17.3 | 15.0 | 1.0 | -12.5 |
| Std. dev. (%) | 8.3 | 19.5 | 9.2 | 8.4 | 6.7 | 9.1 | 8.3 | 12.6 | 5.8 | 13.4 | 13.0 | 16.4 | 22.0 | 18.5 | 26.9 | 24.9 | 24.9 | 45.9 | 99.3 | 45.6 | 60.4 |
| Coef. of var. (%) | 0.4 | 0.6 | 0.7 | 1.2 | 2.0 | 1.5 | 1.7 | 1.8 | 0.7 | 1.6 | 1.1 | 1.4 | 1.2 | 1.3 | 1.2 | 1.2 | 1.1 | 1.6 | 2.2 | 3.3 | -8.4 |
| **Realisation ratios** | | | | | | | | | | | | | | | | | | | | | |
| Distr/paid-in (times) | 4.48 | 3.16 | 2.36 | 1.81 | 1.34 | 1.66 | 1.38 | 1.77 | 2.30 | 1.91 | 2.02 | 1.63 | 2.27 | 1.30 | 1.68 | 1.09 | 0.53 | 0.49 | 0.38 | 0.11 | 0.00 |
| Res val/paid-in (times) | 0.03 | 0.07 | 0.06 | 0.04 | 0.07 | 0.09 | 0.15 | 0.16 | 0.43 | 0.35 | 0.32 | 0.69 | 0.48 | 0.80 | 0.71 | 0.93 | 1.26 | 1.25 | 1.23 | 1.09 | 1.08 |
| Tot val/paid-in (times) | 4.50 | 3.22 | 2.42 | 1.85 | 1.41 | 1.75 | 1.53 | 1.92 | 2.73 | 2.27 | 2.34 | 2.32 | 2.75 | 2.10 | 2.39 | 2.03 | 1.78 | 1.74 | 1.62 | 1.20 | 1.08 |
| **Percentiles** | | | | | | | | | | | | | | | | | | | | | |
| Maximum IRR (%) | 36.2 | 74.1 | 31.8 | 25.4 | 13.5 | 41.5 | 25.5 | 28.3 | 25.6 | 41.8 | 42.9 | 56.1 | 75.2 | 62.2 | 102.8 | 83.4 | 99.7 | 252.3 | 472.3 | 156.7 | 262.1 |
| Upper quartile (%) | 24.5 | 45.7 | 18.2 | 13.6 | 8.5 | 10.6 | 11.4 | 14.9 | 12.1 | 17.2 | 19.2 | 22.0 | 29.8 | 24.4 | 23.8 | 31.9 | 34.6 | 35.8 | 39.0 | 31.8 | 0.0 |
| Median IRR (%) | 19.9 | 29.3 | 13.4 | 9.2 | 4.2 | 5.8 | 4.3 | 7.9 | 7.1 | 7.9 | 8.4 | 10.0 | 10.6 | 13.0 | 14.6 | 11.1 | 21.0 | 17.3 | 15.0 | 1.0 | -12.5 |
| Lower quartile (%) | 12.5 | 12.4 | 8.8 | -0.2 | 0.1 | 1.5 | 1.1 | 1.6 | 3.4 | 0.8 | 2.2 | 0.8 | 0.7 | -0.8 | 8.0 | 3.7 | 4.6 | 4.8 | 3.0 | -7.5 | -39.5 |
| Minimum IRR (%) | 7.8 | 6.0 | -1.9 | -5.9 | -19.1 | -11.4 | -18.4 | -41.5 | 0.0 | -37.8 | -9.7 | -28.0 | -8.8 | -11.2 | -6.4 | -6.6 | -23.6 | -32.9 | -19.1 | -88.7 | -81.7 |

*Year of fund formation*

Exhibit 11

## Vintage year results by fund age (in years) after formation, as of 31 December 1998

| | *Fund age* | | | | | | | | | | | | | | | | | | |
|---|---|---|---|---|---|---|---|---|---|---|---|---|---|---|---|---|---|---|---|
| *Vintage* | *1* | *2* | *3* | *4* | *5* | *6* | *7* | *8* | *9* | *10* | *11* | *12* | *13* | *14* | *15* | *16* | *17* | *18* | *19* |
| Sample size | | | | | | | | | | | | | | | | | | | |
| 1969–75 | 13 | 13 | 13 | 13 | 13 | 13 | 13 | 13 | 13 | 13 | 13 | 13 | 13 | 13 | 13 | 13 | 13 | 13 | 13 |
| 1976–79 | 18 | 18 | 18 | 18 | 18 | 18 | 18 | 18 | 18 | 18 | 18 | 18 | 18 | 18 | 18 | 18 | 18 | 18 | 18 |
| 1980 | 18 | 18 | 18 | 18 | 18 | 18 | 18 | 18 | 18 | 18 | 18 | 18 | 18 | 18 | 18 | 18 | 18 | 18 | |
| 1981 | 22 | 22 | 22 | 22 | 22 | 22 | 22 | 22 | 22 | 22 | 22 | 22 | 22 | 22 | 22 | 22 | 22 | | |
| 1982 | 29 | 29 | 29 | 29 | 29 | 29 | 29 | 29 | 29 | 29 | 29 | 29 | 29 | 29 | 29 | 29 | | | |
| 1983 | 58 | 58 | 58 | 58 | 58 | 58 | 58 | 58 | 58 | 58 | 58 | 58 | 58 | 58 | 58 | | | | |
| 1984 | 68 | 68 | 68 | 68 | 68 | 68 | 68 | 68 | 68 | 68 | 68 | 68 | 68 | 68 | | | | | |
| 1985 | 47 | 47 | 47 | 47 | 47 | 47 | 47 | 47 | 47 | 47 | 47 | 47 | 47 | | | | | | |
| 1986 | 43 | 43 | 43 | 43 | 43 | 43 | 43 | 43 | 43 | 43 | 43 | 43 | | | | | | | |
| 1987 | 66 | 66 | 66 | 66 | 66 | 66 | 66 | 66 | 66 | 66 | 66 | | | | | | | | |
| 1988 | 47 | 47 | 47 | 47 | 47 | 47 | 47 | 47 | 47 | 47 | | | | | | | | | |
| 1989 | 56 | 56 | 56 | 56 | 56 | 56 | 56 | 56 | 56 | | | | | | | | | | |
| 1990 | 23 | 23 | 23 | 23 | 23 | 23 | 23 | 23 | | | | | | | | | | | |
| 1991 | 16 | 16 | 16 | 16 | 16 | 16 | 16 | | | | | | | | | | | | |
| 1992 | 26 | 26 | 26 | 26 | 26 | 26 | | | | | | | | | | | | | |
| 1993 | 40 | 40 | 40 | 40 | 40 | | | | | | | | | | | | | | |
| 1994 | 37 | 37 | 37 | 37 | | | | | | | | | | | | | | | |
| 1995 | 35 | 35 | 35 | | | | | | | | | | | | | | | | |
| 1996 | 28 | 28 | | | | | | | | | | | | | | | | | |
| 1997 | 49 | | | | | | | | | | | | | | | | | | |
| Cumulative average IRR | | | | | | | | | | | | | | | | | | | |
| 1969–75 | 2.0 | 2.9 | -0.2 | 3.4 | 5.5 | 9.6 | 13.2 | 16.7 | 18.2 | 19.4 | 19.4 | 19.3 | 19.3 | 19.3 | 19.2 | 19.2 | 19.2 | 19.2 | 19.2 |
| 1976–79 | 38.0 | 29.1 | 32.2 | 38.8 | 36.0 | 33.1 | 32.3 | 31.6 | 31.3 | 30.9 | 30.8 | 30.3 | 30.4 | 30.4 | 30.3 | 30.3 | 30.3 | 30.2 | 30.2 |
| 1980 | 2.4 | 11.1 | 24.6 | 19.6 | 15.8 | 16.3 | 14.7 | 15.2 | 14.3 | 14.0 | 13.9 | 13.5 | 13.6 | 13.6 | 13.7 | 13.5 | 13.6 | 13.5 | |
| 1981 | 8.1 | 20.0 | 10.3 | 7.4 | 7.2 | 8.4 | 7.2 | 6.7 | 6.3 | 7.3 | 7.2 | 7.1 | 7.1 | 7.2 | 7.2 | 7.2 | 7.2 | | |
| 1982 | 9.8 | 3.0 | 0.0 | 1.5 | 2.2 | 2.8 | 3.3 | 2.8 | 3.5 | 2.3 | 2.5 | 2.5 | 2.7 | 3.0 | 3.1 | 3.3 | | | |
| 1983 | 0.6 | 2.4 | 4.2 | 5.3 | 4.9 | 4.8 | 4.6 | 5.8 | 6.1 | 6.2 | 6.4 | 6.4 | 6.4 | 6.3 | 6.2 | | | | |
| 1984 | -2.8 | -0.2 | 2.4 | 2.2 | 2.7 | 2.0 | 3.1 | 4.0 | 4.3 | 4.1 | 4.7 | 5.0 | 4.9 | 4.9 | | | | | |
| 1985 | -2.8 | 1.1 | 2.2 | 3.0 | 4.0 | 7.4 | 6.7 | 6.9 | 6.9 | 7.4 | 7.1 | 6.9 | 7.1 | | | | | | |
| 1986 | -2.7 | 0.5 | 1.9 | 1.8 | 3.8 | 4.5 | 6.4 | 6.4 | 7.6 | 8.1 | 8.2 | 8.2 | | | | | | | |
| 1987 | -3.9 | -1.2 | -0.8 | 2.5 | 2.7 | 4.7 | 5.5 | 7.2 | 8.0 | 8.1 | 8.4 | | | | | | | | |
| 1988 | -4.0 | -0.7 | 4.4 | 5.9 | 8.7 | 8.9 | 11.2 | 12.2 | 11.9 | 11.5 | | | | | | | | | |
| 1989 | -8.3 | -1.3 | 2.1 | 6.8 | 8.3 | 12.7 | 13.5 | 13.0 | 12.2 | | | | | | | | | | |
| 1990 | -2.0 | 0.9 | 4.0 | 9.5 | 15.3 | 19.3 | 18.3 | 17.7 | | | | | | | | | | | |
| 1991 | -7.7 | 3.1 | 6.4 | 13.6 | 13.8 | 11.8 | 14.3 | | | | | | | | | | | | |
| 1992 | -2.4 | 5.9 | 19.6 | 26.7 | 25.9 | 23.3 | | | | | | | | | | | | | |
| 1993 | -0.7 | 18.0 | 22.7 | 22.3 | 20.4 | | | | | | | | | | | | | | |
| 1994 | 22.3 | 23.3 | 24.1 | 22.6 | | | | | | | | | | | | | | | |
| 1995 | 17.7 | 27.1 | 27.8 | | | | | | | | | | | | | | | | |
| 1996 | 32.3 | 44.6 | | | | | | | | | | | | | | | | | |
| 1997 | 13.7 | | | | | | | | | | | | | | | | | | |
| Cumulative median IRR | | | | | | | | | | | | | | | | | | | |
| 1969–75 | 0.0 | 1.5 | 0.0 | 4.5 | 5.8 | 6.5 | 11.6 | 14.5 | 19.0 | 20.4 | 20.1 | 20.0 | 20.0 | 19.9 | 19.9 | 19.9 | 19.9 | 19.9 | 19.9 |
| 1976–79 | 10.1 | 23.4 | 26.6 | 32.9 | 36.6 | 32.3 | 30.8 | 30.2 | 29.8 | 29.6 | 29.4 | 29.3 | 29.2 | 29.2 | 29.3 | 29.3 | 29.3 | 29.3 | 29.3 |
| 1980 | 3.3 | 10.0 | 26.5 | 18.3 | 14.8 | 14.2 | 14.4 | 14.1 | 13.8 | 13.4 | 13.4 | 13.1 | 13.2 | 13.2 | 13.3 | 13.3 | 13.4 | 13.3 | |
| 1981 | 4.4 | 21.2 | 9.7 | 8.5 | 7.7 | 9.0 | 7.6 | 6.3 | 5.9 | 9.2 | 9.2 | 10.6 | 10.4 | 10.3 | 9.9 | 9.7 | 9.2 | | |
| 1982 | 7.6 | 1.1 | -1.2 | 0.6 | 2.3 | 2.2 | 3.5 | 2.1 | 3.2 | 2.3 | 2.5 | 1.8 | 2.6 | 3.4 | 4.2 | 4.2 | | | |
| 1983 | 0.0 | 1.1 | 2.7 | 4.9 | 5.1 | 5.4 | 4.5 | 5.9 | 6.2 | 5.8 | 6.3 | 6.0 | 6.4 | 6.4 | 5.8 | | | | |
| 1984 | -0.8 | 0.0 | 1.7 | 1.2 | 2.7 | 2.6 | 4.4 | 4.7 | 3.7 | 3.4 | 4.3 | 4.6 | 4.4 | 4.3 | | | | | |
| 1985 | 0.0 | 0.0 | 0.6 | 2.3 | 3.3 | 7.8 | 8.4 | 7.1 | 6.2 | 8.6 | 8.0 | 7.8 | 7.9 | | | | | | |
| 1986 | -2.3 | 0.5 | 1.2 | 0.2 | 3.9 | 5.3 | 6.4 | 5.5 | 6.1 | 6.5 | 6.7 | 7.1 | | | | | | | |
| 1987 | -1.9 | 0.0 | 0.0 | 0.3 | 2.5 | 3.1 | 3.6 | 6.9 | 8.9 | 7.5 | 7.9 | | | | | | | | |
| 1988 | 0.0 | 0.0 | 0.9 | 4.1 | 7.7 | 6.4 | 8.7 | 10.2 | 8.7 | 8.4 | | | | | | | | | |
| 1989 | -9.0 | -0.3 | 1.6 | 3.8 | 5.6 | 8.9 | 10.2 | 9.5 | 10.0 | | | | | | | | | | |
| 1990 | 0.0 | 0.0 | 0.0 | 5.3 | 6.5 | 14.2 | 13.2 | 10.6 | | | | | | | | | | | |
| 1991 | -7.0 | 0.0 | 6.8 | 12.3 | 14.8 | 13.7 | 13.0 | | | | | | | | | | | | |
| 1992 | -5.3 | 1.9 | 13.7 | 20.1 | 17.4 | 14.6 | | | | | | | | | | | | | |
| 1993 | -0.8 | 12.9 | 14.4 | 13.2 | 11.1 | | | | | | | | | | | | | | |
| 1994 | 0.0 | 17.4 | 18.2 | 21.0 | | | | | | | | | | | | | | | |
| 1995 | 4.9 | 20.5 | 17.3 | | | | | | | | | | | | | | | | |
| 1996 | 5.0 | 15.0 | | | | | | | | | | | | | | | | | |
| 1997 | 1.0 | | | | | | | | | | | | | | | | | | |

Exhibit 11 *continued*

## Vintage year results by fund age (in years) after formation, as of 31 December 1998 *continued*

**Fund age**

| Vintage | 1 | 2 | 3 | 4 | 5 | 6 | 7 | 8 | 9 | 10 | 11 | 12 | 13 | 14 | 15 | 16 | 17 | 18 | 19 |
|---|---|---|---|---|---|---|---|---|---|---|---|---|---|---|---|---|---|---|---|
| **Cumulative upper quartile IRR** | | | | | | | | | | | | | | | | | | | |
| 1969–75 | 3.2 | 7.5 | 4.7 | 7.7 | 9.2 | 21.3 | 20.8 | 22.6 | 23.9 | 24.5 | 24.5 | 24.5 | 24.5 | 24.5 | 24.5 | 24.5 | 24.5 | 24.5 | 24.5 |
| 1976–79 | 34.9 | 42.8 | 43.8 | 51.7 | 46.7 | 44.4 | 45.6 | 45.1 | 45.0 | 44.8 | 44.8 | 44.7 | 44.7 | 44.7 | 44.7 | 44.7 | 44.7 | 44.8 | 44.8 |
| 1980 | 8.5 | 17.5 | 34.2 | 30.4 | 22.6 | 20.3 | 17.9 | 17.1 | 16.0 | 15.7 | 16.5 | 17.2 | 18.2 | 17.1 | 17.8 | 17.7 | 18.2 | 17.7 | |
| 1981 | 12.4 | 30.9 | 13.5 | 11.4 | 14.8 | 14.6 | 14.0 | 13.5 | 13.4 | 13.8 | 13.8 | 13.6 | 13.7 | 13.5 | 13.4 | 13.4 | 13.3 | | |
| 1982 | 18.2 | 6.0 | 6.4 | 4.2 | 6.4 | 7.0 | 6.1 | 7.9 | 7.1 | 7.9 | 8.2 | 8.5 | 8.4 | 8.4 | 8.4 | 8.5 | | | |
| 1983 | 3.3 | 6.7 | 9.9 | 10.7 | 10.0 | 10.7 | 8.2 | 9.8 | 10.2 | 10.0 | 9.8 | 9.9 | 10.3 | 10.2 | 10.5 | | | | |
| 1984 | 1.7 | 4.5 | 5.7 | 7.1 | 7.7 | 7.7 | 7.6 | 9.1 | 9.3 | 7.8 | 10.0 | 11.3 | 11.3 | 11.4 | | | | | |
| 1985 | 2.1 | 4.2 | 5.3 | 7.4 | 7.4 | 13.5 | 13.5 | 14.3 | 14.3 | 15.3 | 15.0 | 15.0 | 14.9 | | | | | | |
| 1986 | 3.6 | 3.2 | 4.4 | 6.3 | 8.2 | 10.6 | 13.5 | 10.7 | 10.9 | 12.0 | 12.0 | 12.1 | | | | | | | |
| 1987 | 0.0 | 2.1 | 2.2 | 5.3 | 6.8 | 10.2 | 11.5 | 15.4 | 16.3 | 17.1 | 17.1 | | | | | | | | |
| 1988 | 1.9 | 3.5 | 8.3 | 12.3 | 13.4 | 13.6 | 18.6 | 20.4 | 20.0 | 19.2 | | | | | | | | | |
| 1989 | 0.0 | 1.9 | 8.1 | 11.1 | 14.5 | 20.1 | 22.7 | 23.0 | 21.4 | | | | | | | | | | |
| 1990 | 7.1 | 12.2 | 10.1 | 14.7 | 19.2 | 32.7 | 31.6 | 29.8 | | | | | | | | | | | |
| 1991 | 0.0 | 8.1 | 11.9 | 25.4 | 24.0 | 23.9 | 24.0 | | | | | | | | | | | | |
| 1992 | 13.7 | 15.4 | 23.3 | 32.9 | 26.0 | 23.8 | | | | | | | | | | | | | |
| 1993 | 13.0 | 28.9 | 30.1 | 29.3 | 31.9 | | | | | | | | | | | | | | |
| 1994 | 12.9 | 31.2 | 35.2 | 34.6 | | | | | | | | | | | | | | | |
| 1995 | 31.1 | 34.2 | 35.8 | | | | | | | | | | | | | | | | |
| 1996 | 16.4 | 37.9 | | | | | | | | | | | | | | | | | |
| 1997 | 31.8 | | | | | | | | | | | | | | | | | | |
| **Cumulative average distribution paid-in** | | | | | | | | | | | | | | | | | | | |
| 1969–75 | 0.00 | 0.05 | 0.11 | 0.11 | 0.21 | 0.30 | 1.28 | 1.99 | 2.84 | 3.45 | 3.86 | 3.92 | 4.13 | 4.18 | 4.18 | 4.24 | 4.25 | 4.27 | 4.42 |
| 1976–79 | 0.00 | 0.04 | 0.30 | 0.98 | 1.76 | 2.10 | 2.41 | 2.72 | 2.93 | 2.99 | 3.07 | 3.11 | 3.23 | 3.24 | 3.25 | 3.25 | 3.27 | 3.35 | 3.36 |
| 1980 | 0.01 | 0.08 | 0.31 | 0.40 | 0.60 | 0.93 | 1.14 | 1.21 | 1.37 | 1.50 | 1.59 | 1.70 | 1.82 | 1.86 | 2.05 | 2.10 | 2.18 | 2.19 | |
| 1981 | 0.01 | 0.03 | 0.10 | 0.18 | 0.39 | 0.65 | 0.80 | 0.92 | 1.01 | 1.28 | 1.39 | 1.45 | 1.51 | 1.53 | 1.55 | 1.57 | 1.58 | | |
| 1982 | 0.00 | 0.02 | 0.05 | 0.13 | 0.26 | 0.37 | 0.55 | 0.68 | 0.84 | 0.94 | 1.00 | 1.05 | 1.10 | 1.17 | 1.18 | 1.21 | | | |
| 1983 | 0.01 | 0.02 | 0.13 | 0.24 | 0.31 | 0.44 | 0.59 | 0.78 | 0.93 | 1.07 | 1.23 | 1.35 | 1.47 | 1.52 | 1.53 | | | | |
| 1984 | 0.01 | 0.03 | 0.06 | 0.12 | 0.22 | 0.34 | 0.48 | 0.62 | 0.77 | 0.92 | 1.07 | 1.22 | 1.29 | 1.33 | | | | | |
| 1985 | 0.00 | 0.02 | 0.06 | 0.14 | 0.23 | 0.51 | 0.66 | 0.85 | 1.05 | 1.28 | 1.46 | 1.60 | 1.65 | | | | | | |
| 1986 | 0.01 | 0.02 | 0.07 | 0.13 | 0.23 | 0.41 | 0.58 | 0.77 | 0.99 | 1.24 | 1.38 | 1.49 | | | | | | | |
| 1987 | 0.01 | 0.02 | 0.05 | 0.11 | 0.24 | 0.43 | 0.61 | 0.95 | 1.24 | 1.42 | 1.56 | | | | | | | | |
| 1988 | 0.00 | 0.02 | 0.08 | 0.17 | 0.35 | 0.53 | 0.79 | 1.13 | 1.36 | 1.49 | | | | | | | | | |
| 1989 | 0.01 | 0.03 | 0.09 | 0.22 | 0.36 | 0.67 | 1.00 | 1.28 | 1.42 | | | | | | | | | | |
| 1990 | 0.01 | 0.06 | 0.11 | 0.24 | 0.64 | 1.11 | 1.38 | 1.50 | | | | | | | | | | | |
| 1991 | 0.01 | 0.02 | 0.09 | 0.29 | 0.51 | 0.64 | 1.02 | | | | | | | | | | | | |
| 1992 | 0.00 | 0.03 | 0.20 | 0.56 | 1.44 | 1.69 | | | | | | | | | | | | | |
| 1993 | 0.01 | 0.14 | 0.42 | 0.68 | 0.83 | | | | | | | | | | | | | | |
| 1994 | 0.01 | 0.10 | 0.34 | 0.61 | | | | | | | | | | | | | | | |
| 1995 | 0.04 | 0.29 | 0.43 | | | | | | | | | | | | | | | | |
| 1996 | 0.29 | 0.40 | | | | | | | | | | | | | | | | | |
| 1997 | 0.08 | | | | | | | | | | | | | | | | | | |
| **Cumulative average residual value to paid-in** | | | | | | | | | | | | | | | | | | | |
| 1969–75 | 1.03 | 1.03 | 0.94 | 1.05 | 1.13 | 1.47 | 1.06 | 1.27 | 1.05 | 0.81 | 0.51 | 0.43 | 0.25 | 0.14 | 0.11 | 0.10 | 0.11 | 0.11 | 0.11 |
| 1976–79 | 1.35 | 1.52 | 1.68 | 1.92 | 1.42 | 1.04 | 0.89 | 0.64 | 0.48 | 0.41 | 0.34 | 0.27 | 0.19 | 0.17 | 0.16 | 0.16 | 0.19 | 0.14 | 0.12 |
| 1980 | 1.01 | 1.11 | 1.35 | 1.31 | 1.08 | 0.92 | 0.76 | 0.77 | 0.59 | 0.49 | 0.42 | 0.32 | 0.26 | 0.25 | 0.23 | 0.12 | 0.08 | 0.07 | |
| 1981 | 1.08 | 1.28 | 1.15 | 1.08 | 0.94 | 0.82 | 0.64 | 0.53 | 0.43 | 0.36 | 0.25 | 0.20 | 0.16 | 0.15 | 0.12 | 0.11 | 0.10 | | |
| 1982 | 1.12 | 1.04 | 0.98 | 0.94 | 0.86 | 0.81 | 0.67 | 0.54 | 0.45 | 0.29 | 0.24 | 0.20 | 0.17 | 0.14 | 0.13 | 0.12 | | | |
| 1983 | 1.01 | 1.03 | 0.99 | 0.95 | 0.91 | 0.84 | 0.71 | 0.66 | 0.56 | 0.48 | 0.38 | 0.30 | 0.21 | 0.16 | 0.14 | | | | |
| 1984 | 0.96 | 0.98 | 0.99 | 0.97 | 0.91 | 0.79 | 0.75 | 0.70 | 0.60 | 0.44 | 0.39 | 0.29 | 0.24 | 0.19 | | | | | |
| 1985 | 0.97 | 1.00 | 1.01 | 0.97 | 0.97 | 1.02 | 0.86 | 0.76 | 0.59 | 0.50 | 0.35 | 0.22 | 0.19 | | | | | | |
| 1986 | 0.97 | 0.99 | 0.98 | 0.93 | 0.97 | 0.88 | 0.86 | 0.70 | 0.62 | 0.47 | 0.37 | 0.29 | | | | | | | |
| 1987 | 0.96 | 0.98 | 0.94 | 0.96 | 0.90 | 0.85 | 0.79 | 0.71 | 0.58 | 0.48 | 0.40 | | | | | | | | |
| 1988 | 0.97 | 0.98 | 1.03 | 1.01 | 0.99 | 0.89 | 0.88 | 0.74 | 0.51 | 0.39 | | | | | | | | | |
| 1989 | 0.92 | 0.95 | 0.97 | 0.99 | 0.93 | 0.98 | 0.86 | 0.64 | 0.51 | | | | | | | | | | |
| 1990 | 1.10 | 1.09 | 1.10 | 1.17 | 1.22 | 1.13 | 0.86 | 0.73 | | | | | | | | | | | |
| 1991 | 0.95 | 1.02 | 1.04 | 1.10 | 1.04 | 0.92 | 0.87 | | | | | | | | | | | | |
| 1992 | 0.98 | 1.06 | 1.23 | 1.33 | 1.07 | 0.76 | | | | | | | | | | | | | |
| 1993 | 0.99 | 1.14 | 1.12 | 1.03 | 0.96 | | | | | | | | | | | | | | |
| 1994 | 1.18 | 1.31 | 1.28 | 1.21 | | | | | | | | | | | | | | | |
| 1995 | 1.10 | 1.15 | 1.23 | | | | | | | | | | | | | | | | |
| 1996 | 1.13 | 1.26 | | | | | | | | | | | | | | | | | |
| 1997 | 1.03 | | | | | | | | | | | | | | | | | | |

Exhibit 12

## Statistics for funds in top quarter, cumulative results by vintage year, as of 31 December 1998

| Vintage | Sample size (no.) | Avg IRR (%) | Cap-wtd IRR (%) | Pooled IRR (%) | Max IRR (%) | Median IRR (%) | Min IRR (%) | Distr/ paid-in (times) | Res val/ paid-in (times) | Tot val/ paid-in (times) |
|---------|-------------------|-------------|-----------------|----------------|-------------|----------------|-------------|------------------------|--------------------------|--------------------------|
| 1969–75 | 3 | 30.3 | 27.6 | 27.4 | 36.2 | 28.0 | 26.6 | 8.50 | 0.00 | 8.50 |
| 1976–79 | 5 | 54.3 | 52.7 | 55.1 | 74.1 | 50.3 | 45.7 | 5.40 | 0.10 | 5.50 |
| 1980 | 5 | 24.5 | 28.0 | 24.4 | 31.8 | 23.8 | 18.2 | 3.30 | 0.20 | 3.50 |
| 1981 | 5 | 17.8 | 17.5 | 16.7 | 25.4 | 16.5 | 14.8 | 2.60 | 0.00 | 2.60 |
| 1982 | 7 | 10.5 | 10.4 | 10.4 | 13.5 | 10.3 | 9.3 | 1.80 | 0.10 | 1.90 |
| 1983 | 15 | 17.1 | 12.6 | 12.7 | 41.5 | 15.0 | 10.6 | 2.40 | 0.40 | 2.80 |
| 1984 | 17 | 15.6 | 15.3 | 15.3 | 25.5 | 14.0 | 11.4 | 2.40 | 0.70 | 3.10 |
| 1985 | 12 | 20.6 | 19.4 | 19.5 | 28.3 | 19.7 | 15.4 | 3.00 | 0.50 | 3.50 |
| 1986 | 11 | 15.9 | 17.4 | 17.9 | 25.6 | 15.2 | 12.6 | 3.60 | 0.60 | 4.20 |
| 1987 | 16 | 24.7 | 24.6 | 24.0 | 41.8 | 23.2 | 17.2 | 3.30 | 1.00 | 4.30 |
| 1988 | 12 | 29.9 | 30.5 | 30.2 | 42.9 | 29.0 | 19.7 | 3.20 | 0.80 | 4.00 |
| 1989 | 14 | 34.7 | 35.7 | 38.7 | 56.1 | 33.0 | 23.1 | 3.80 | 1.00 | 4.80 |
| 1990 | 6 | 47.9 | 43.9 | 45.4 | 75.2 | 47.9 | 30.2 | 3.60 | 1.00 | 4.60 |
| 1991 | 4 | 35.8 | 36.9 | 35.6 | 62.2 | 27.9 | 25.1 | 2.70 | 1.40 | 4.10 |
| 1992 | 6 | 64.8 | 58.9 | 62.3 | 102.8 | 61.5 | 34.5 | 3.50 | 1.40 | 4.90 |
| 1993 | 10 | 56.9 | 53.4 | 56.3 | 83.4 | 60.4 | 32.0 | 2.30 | 1.40 | 3.70 |
| 1994 | 10 | 53.3 | 64.9 | 64.0 | 99.7 | 47.1 | 34.6 | 2.10 | 1.40 | 3.50 |
| 1995 | 9 | 78.1 | 68.9 | 81.4 | 252.3 | 54.2 | 38.2 | 1.10 | 1.90 | 3.00 |
| 1996 | 7 | 150.1 | 127.8 | 116.1 | 472.3 | 68.6 | 41.2 | 0.80 | 2.10 | 2.90 |
| 1997 | 13 | 73.2 | 79.0 | 82.5 | 156.7 | 76.0 | 31.8 | 0.10 | 1.50 | 1.60 |
| 1998 | 11 | 48.9 | 33.3 | 42.8 | 262.1 | 27.7 | 0.0 | 0.00 | 1.20 | 1.20 |

Exhibit 13

**Statistics for funds in the upper half, cumulative results by vintage year, as of 31 December 1998**

| Vintage | Sample size (no.) | Avg IRR (%) | Cap-wtd IRR (%) | Pooled IRR (%) | Max IRR (%) | Median IRR (%) | Min IRR (%) | Distr/ paid-in (times) | Res val/ paid-in (times) | Tot val/ paid-in (times) |
|---|---|---|---|---|---|---|---|---|---|---|
| 1969–75 | 7 | 25.2 | 24.0 | 24.1 | 36.2 | 24.5 | 19.9 | 6.10 | 0.00 | 6.10 |
| 1976–79 | 9 | 46.9 | 46.4 | 48.6 | 74.1 | 45.7 | 34.3 | 4.60 | 0.10 | 4.70 |
| 1980 | 9 | 20.2 | 26.4 | 22.0 | 31.8 | 18.2 | 13.6 | 2.50 | 0.10 | 2.60 |
| 1981 | 11 | 14.4 | 14.8 | 15.0 | 25.4 | 13.6 | 9.5 | 2.30 | 0.00 | 2.30 |
| 1982 | 15 | 8.2 | 7.6 | 7.3 | 13.5 | 8.5 | 4.2 | 1.70 | 0.10 | 1.80 |
| 1983 | 29 | 12.8 | 10.4 | 10.7 | 41.5 | 10.6 | 6.4 | 2.00 | 0.10 | 2.10 |
| 1984 | 34 | 11.0 | 10.3 | 10.3 | 25.5 | 11.4 | 4.4 | 1.90 | 0.20 | 2.10 |
| 1985 | 24 | 15.9 | 14.7 | 14.8 | 28.3 | 14.9 | 7.9 | 2.30 | 0.20 | 2.50 |
| 1986 | 22 | 12.7 | 15.4 | 15.8 | 25.6 | 12.1 | 7.1 | 3.00 | 0.60 | 3.60 |
| 1987 | 33 | 18.7 | 19.8 | 19.8 | 41.8 | 17.2 | 8.0 | 2.70 | 0.70 | 3.40 |
| 1988 | 24 | 21.4 | 24.7 | 24.6 | 42.9 | 19.2 | 8.4 | 2.60 | 0.50 | 3.10 |
| 1989 | 28 | 24.5 | 21.8 | 22.5 | 56.1 | 22.0 | 10.0 | 1.90 | 0.90 | 2.80 |
| 1990 | 12 | 33.5 | 32.8 | 36.5 | 75.2 | 29.8 | 10.6 | 2.70 | 0.90 | 3.60 |
| 1991 | 8 | 28.4 | 29.3 | 29.4 | 62.2 | 24.4 | 13.8 | 1.80 | 1.30 | 3.10 |
| 1992 | 13 | 39.9 | 40.6 | 44.9 | 102.8 | 23.8 | 15.0 | 2.50 | 1.00 | 3.50 |
| 1993 | 20 | 38.2 | 46.5 | 48.3 | 83.4 | 31.9 | 11.4 | 1.60 | 1.30 | 2.90 |
| 1994 | 18 | 40.8 | 47.6 | 49.7 | 99.7 | 34.8 | 21.2 | 1.20 | 1.40 | 2.60 |
| 1995 | 17 | 53.7 | 56.4 | 62.9 | 252.3 | 38.2 | 17.8 | 0.80 | 1.40 | 2.20 |
| 1996 | 14 | 88.0 | 76.6 | 77.6 | 472.3 | 39.0 | 17.1 | 0.40 | 1.60 | 2.00 |
| 1997 | 25 | 44.7 | 51.3 | 52.2 | 156.7 | 31.8 | 1.0 | 0.10 | 1.30 | 1.40 |
| 1998 | 18 | 27.5 | 13.4 | 26.1 | 262.1 | 0.0 | -11.9 | 0.00 | 1.11 | 1.11 |

Exhibit 14

## Statistics of cumulative results by fund stage, size and sequence, as of 31 December 1998

| Vintage | Sample size (no.) | Avg IRR (%) | Cap-wtd IRR (%) | Pooled IRR (%) | Max IRR (%) | Upper quartile (%) | Median IRR (%) | Lower quartile (%) | Min IRR (%) | Distr/ paid-in (times) | Res val/ paid-in (times) | Tot val/ paid-in (times) |
|---|---|---|---|---|---|---|---|---|---|---|---|---|
| Overall | 775 | 12.9 | 12.9 | 14.9 | 472.3 | 18.6 | 8.4 | 0.6 | -88.7 | 1.31 | 0.67 | 1.98 |
| **Fund stage** | | | | | | | | | | | | |
| Seed | 48 | 7.2 | 7.6 | 12.2 | 41.2 | 15.0 | 6.2 | 1.2 | -65.9 | 1.83 | 0.25 | 2.08 |
| Early | 237 | 16.5 | 21.5 | 17.4 | 472.3 | 23.1 | 9.4 | -0.3 | -88.7 | 1.31 | 0.82 | 2.13 |
| Balanced | 412 | 11.7 | 14.3 | 14 | 156.7 | 17.0 | 7.8 | 1.0 | -81.7 | 1.37 | 0.60 | 1.97 |
| Later | 78 | 11.7 | 1.5 | 16.3 | 67.8 | 19.5 | 10.4 | -0.8 | -72.4 | 0.99 | 0.78 | 1.77 |
| **Fund size (US$ million)** | | | | | | | | | | | | |
| 0–25 | 238 | 9.3 | 8.3 | 11.6 | 472.3 | 14.3 | 5 | -0.8 | -41.5 | 1.27 | 0.41 | 1.68 |
| 25–50 | 202 | 12.5 | 13 | 10.4 | 262.1 | 16.2 | 8.4 | 1.8 | -40.6 | 1.35 | 0.41 | 1.76 |
| 50–100 | 184 | 13.7 | 13.7 | 13.4 | 252.3 | 21.1 | 9.8 | 2.3 | -88.7 | 1.53 | 0.52 | 2.05 |
| 100+ | 151 | 18.1 | 13.1 | 18.8 | 268.6 | 31.7 | 13.9 | 0.0 | -75.8 | 1.20 | 0.83 | 2.04 |
| **Fund sequence** | | | | | | | | | | | | |
| New | 165 | 11.1 | 14.6 | 11.6 | 93.1 | 16.1 | 9.3 | 1.8 | -28 | 1.45 | 0.41 | 1.85 |
| Follow-on | 582 | 13.9 | 12.5 | 15.4 | 472.3 | 19.9 | 8.6 | 0.1 | -88.7 | 1.25 | 0.73 | 1.99 |
| Sole | 28 | 2.9 | 19.8 | 19.3 | 41.8 | 7.0 | 3.5 | -6.1 | -37.8 | 2.00 | 0.20 | 2.19 |

Exhibit 15

## Investment horizon IRRs by composite portfolio, as of 31 December 1998

| Vintage year | 1-year | 3-year | 5-year | 10-year | 20-year |
|---|---|---|---|---|---|
| 1969–75 | 4.2 | 10.7 | 100.4 | 28.6 | 56.1 |
| 1969–98 | 17.4 | 27.9 | 27.3 | 17.4 | 14.9 |
| 1976–79 | -8.8 | 1.7 | 1.5 | 1.5 | 29.4 |
| 1980–98 | 17.5 | 27.9 | 27.4 | 17.5 | |
| 1981–98 | 17.5 | 29.7 | 28.3 | 17.5 | |
| 1982–98 | 17.5 | 29.8 | 28.3 | 17.6 | |
| 1983–98 | 17.5 | 29.8 | 28.4 | 17.8 | |
| 1984–98 | 17.7 | 30.2 | 29.1 | 18.6 | |
| 1985–98 | 18.0 | 30.6 | 30.3 | 19.8 | |
| 1986–98 | 18.1 | 31.0 | 30.9 | 20.3 | |
| 1987–98 | 19.5 | 31.2 | 32.3 | 21.9 | |
| 1988–98 | 19.7 | 31.2 | 32.0 | 23.8 | |
| 1989–98 | 20.1 | 31.6 | 32.0 | | |
| 1990–98 | 23.1 | 33.0 | 34.8 | | |
| 1991–98 | 23.9 | 33.0 | 33.0 | | |
| 1992–98 | 23.2 | 33.9 | 34.0 | | |
| 1993–98 | 26.6 | 32.9 | 33.8 | | |
| 1994–98 | 30.1 | 33.9 | | | |
| 1995–98 | 42.9 | 38.6 | | | |
| 1996–98 | 47.0 | | | | |
| 1997–98 | 32.6 | | | | |

239

Exhibit 16

## Cumulative benchmark results: overall sample by composite portfolio, as of 31 December 1998

| Portfolio vintages | 1969 1998 | 1969 1994 | 1980 1998 | 1981 1998 | 1982 1998 | 1983 1998 | 1984 1998 | 1985 1998 | 1986 1998 | 1987 1998 | 1988 1998 | 1989 1998 | 1990 1998 | 1991 1998 | 1992 1998 | 1993 1998 | 1994 1998 | 1995 1998 | 1996 1998 | 1997 1998 |
|---|---|---|---|---|---|---|---|---|---|---|---|---|---|---|---|---|---|---|---|---|
| **Overall** | | | | | | | | | | | | | | | | | | | | |
| Sample size | 775 | 662 | 744 | 726 | 704 | 675 | 617 | 549 | 502 | 459 | 393 | 348 | 292 | 269 | 253 | 227 | 187 | 149 | 113 | 85 |
| Avg IRR (%) | 12.9 | 12.6 | 12.3 | 12.3 | 12.5 | 12.9 | 13.5 | 14.6 | 15.3 | 15.9 | 17.2 | 17.9 | 19.0 | 19.1 | 19.4 | 19.0 | 18.7 | 17.7 | 14.7 | 4.9 |
| Cap-wtd IRR (%) | 12.9 | 18.6 | 12.8 | 12.5 | 12.6 | 12.8 | 13.0 | 13.4 | 13.6 | 13.6 | 13.7 | 13.4 | 12.9 | 12.5 | 12.3 | 11.4 | 9.9 | 7.1 | 3.0 | -4.9 |
| Pooled IRR (%) | 14.9 | 14.6 | 14.1 | 13.8 | 14.0 | 14.6 | 15.8 | 17.8 | 18.8 | 21.0 | 23.6 | 25.1 | 30.2 | 30.8 | 33.0 | 33.8 | 35.0 | 37.8 | 36.8 | 25.4 |
| Median IRR (%) | 8.4 | 9.0 | 7.9 | 7.6 | 7.5 | 7.9 | 8.0 | 9.2 | 9.5 | 10.0 | 10.1 | 10.9 | 11.0 | 11.0 | 11.0 | 9.6 | 8.6 | 5.3 | 0.1 | -3.7 |
| Std. dev. (%) | 31.9 | 19.6 | 32.3 | 32.7 | 33.1 | 33.8 | 35.2 | 37.0 | 38.5 | 40.1 | 42.9 | 45.3 | 48.9 | 50.5 | 51.9 | 54.0 | 58.5 | 64.3 | 69.2 | 53.1 |
| Coef. of var. (%) | 2.5 | 1.6 | 2.6 | 2.7 | 2.6 | 2.6 | 2.6 | 2.5 | 2.5 | 2.5 | 2.5 | 2.5 | 2.6 | 2.6 | 2.7 | 2.8 | 3.1 | 3.6 | 4.7 | 10.8 |
| **Realisation ratios** | | | | | | | | | | | | | | | | | | | | |
| Distr/paid-in (times) | 1.31 | 1.54 | 1.28 | 1.24 | 1.23 | 1.22 | 1.19 | 1.18 | 1.16 | 1.05 | 0.97 | 0.87 | 0.72 | 0.64 | 0.61 | 0.47 | 0.34 | 0.27 | 0.18 | 0.07 |
| Res val/paid-in (times) | 0.67 | 0.57 | 0.68 | 0.70 | 0.72 | 0.73 | 0.77 | 0.82 | 0.85 | 0.89 | 0.94 | 0.99 | 1.05 | 1.09 | 1.10 | 1.15 | 1.19 | 1.17 | 1.14 | 1.09 |
| Tot val/paid-in (times) | 1.98 | 2.11 | 1.96 | 1.94 | 1.94 | 1.95 | 1.97 | 2.00 | 2.00 | 1.93 | 1.90 | 1.86 | 1.77 | 1.72 | 1.71 | 1.62 | 1.54 | 1.43 | 1.32 | 1.16 |
| **Percentiles** | | | | | | | | | | | | | | | | | | | | |
| Maximum IRR (%) | 472.3 | 252.3 | 472.3 | 472.3 | 472.3 | 472.3 | 472.3 | 472.3 | 472.3 | 472.3 | 472.3 | 472.3 | 472.3 | 472.3 | 472.3 | 472.3 | 472.3 | 472.3 | 472.3 | 262.1 |
| Upper quartile (%) | 18.6 | 18.0 | 17.8 | 17.8 | 18.1 | 18.8 | 20.6 | 22.5 | 23.6 | 24.6 | 26.2 | 29.0 | 30.0 | 29.8 | 31.8 | 31.8 | 31.1 | 30.4 | 29.5 | 25.6 |
| Median IRR (%) | 8.4 | 9.0 | 7.9 | 7.6 | 7.5 | 7.9 | 8.0 | 9.2 | 9.5 | 10.0 | 10.1 | 10.9 | 11.0 | 11.0 | 11.0 | 9.6 | 8.6 | 5.3 | 0.1 | -3.7 |
| Lower quartile (%) | 0.6 | 2.0 | 0.3 | 0.1 | 0.3 | 0.3 | 0.3 | 0.1 | 0.0 | -0.3 | -0.5 | -0.8 | -1.7 | -1.8 | -1.9 | -2.7 | -4.3 | -7.5 | -13.3 | -20.5 |
| Minimum IRR (%) | -88.7 | -41.5 | -88.7 | -88.7 | -88.7 | -88.7 | -88.7 | -88.7 | -88.7 | -88.7 | -88.7 | -88.7 | -88.7 | -88.7 | -88.7 | -88.7 | -88.7 | -88.7 | -88.7 | -88.7 |

Chapter 19

# Historical performance of European private equity

Alan Doran
*Bannock Consulting*

## Introduction

Investors, external analysts and private equity practitioners probably feel a sense of frustration at the lack of data on private equity performance in Europe, compared with what is available for the US industry. In the United States, annual performance benchmarks, based on net internal rate of return (IRR) to investors, including analysis by fund vintage year, and within stage-focus groups, have been published since 1988 in the *Investment Benchmarks Reports* series. These reports provide good, though not comprehensive, coverage, and are widely respected as authoritative. They include cumulative returns from inception, as well as investment horizon returns for one, three, five and 10 years. Quarterly performance data and portfolio benchmarking services are also available for investors.

More recently, time-weighted returns have been produced that are directly comparable to those of other asset classes. In all the US numbers, due emphasis is placed on measures of dispersion of returns, appropriate for an asset class that is fundamentally opaque, where risk cannot be easily diversified by buying the index, and where headline numbers are much less relevant.

The situation on the other side of the Atlantic is improving, but slowly. Methodological difficulties have still to be overcome as well as the continuing reluctance on the part of some players to provide their own data for aggregation in performance studies. A third difficulty is the increasing amount of cross-border investment, which can fall between nationally based studies. Particular methodological issues arise when funds based in more than one currency are included in a performance measurement set, and when results need to be interpreted by investors based in different currency areas. Before discussing results, we review progress in the performance measurement process.

## Progress in performance measurement

Annual Europe-wide performance numbers using methodology comparable to the US standard, and based in Ecus, were first issued in 1996 as a pilot exercise. The coverage was broadened and updated in 1998 in the first edition of the *Investment Benchmarks Report: European Private Equity*, produced and published by Bannock Consulting in partnership with Venture Economics (the producer of the US *Investment Benchmark Reports*). Two further editions have now been produced. The European report provides:

- returns from inception;

241

- investment horizon returns; and
- analysis by stage focus within vintage year.

Captive and evergreen investor structures are included within its scope, which in total covered Ecu47 billion of funds to the end of 1998. Bannock Consulting and Venture Economics are committed to further improvements in the *European Investment Benchmarks Reports* (EIBR) in successive annual editions, which will be euro-based.

## The United Kingdom, the Netherlands, France and Finland

National-level historical performance data has so far appeared for four countries, published by national venture capital associations.

- In the United Kingdom, the British Venture Capital Association (BVCA) first published results in 1995, with four updates since.
- In the Netherlands, Nederlan. Verenig. van Part. Mijen (NVP) first published results in 1991 and has issued five updates.
- In France, Association Francaise des Investisseurs en Capital (AFIC) first published results in 1994, with updates in 1995 and 1996.
- In Finland, the Finnish Venture Capital Association (FVCA) carried out its first study in 1998.

In the preparation of these reports, only the UK and Finnish numbers are on the same methodology as US benchmarks, that is using net returns to investors as the measure. This basis is appropriate for fixed-life funds raised from external investors and managed by independent teams, where cashflows between external investors and the fund can be monitored and analysed.

However, in the United Kingdom, as in the rest of Europe, other types of investor structures (with evergreen or captive characteristics, or both) undertake a substantial proportion of private equity activity. Indeed, historically, these structures have accounted for a clear majority of such activity. This is the main reason why the French and Dutch performance studies have used gross returns on investment in portfolio companies, based on cashflows between the investing entity and the portfolio companies, as the key performance measure.

The costs of the performance measurement process are higher at the gross returns level in the sense that data on many more transactions, and of a wider variety, has to be captured and analysed. Despite this, the Netherlands data set has a very high coverage of private equity activity in that country (an estimated 88 per cent of realised investments and 74 per cent of unrealised investments). The studies have not, however, calculated returns for individual investment structures, except for a crude analysis by quarters of the distribution of returns with an aggregate return for each. There is still apparently great concern about confidentiality.

The French studies have been restricted to realised investments only, but are intended to include failures and write-offs. Even so, they have covered under half of the total divestments at cost over the period surveyed, because many players have been unwilling to participate. Allowing for unrealised investments, the coverage is around 20 per cent of the total. The only data by investment structure is a frequency distribution of the number of such structures within bands of overall gross returns. No gross returns data is available for the United Kingdom, by far the largest single private equity market in Europe, though the BVCA's net returns coverage of 'independent fund' activity with a UK investment focus is estimated at over 90 per cent, considerably higher than is achieved in the United States.

## The rest of Europe

In other European countries with sizeable private equity activity and active national associations, such as Germany, Italy, and Spain, there has been even less willingness on the part of the players to participate in national performance studies. There are probably three main reasons for this.

- First, there is a feeling that their industries are immature, and that results would be depressed both because too few investments have been harvested and because conservative accounting traditions and regulations will depress interim valuations.
- Second, captive and evergreen structures, including those with government participation, are even more dominant, making for extra methodological problems. Performance data is of less value to those managing structures not fully dependent on external fund-raising.
- Third, there is less widespread confidence that the availability of historical performance measurement benchmarks on balance will be commercially beneficial, despite calls for it from investors and others. Some players maintain that publicly available performance benchmarks would excessively reduce opacity of information (which they see as an essential and desirable feature of a private professional market).

A fourth reason, for which there is anecdotal evidence only, is a fear that confidentiality would be breached, highlighting the identity and damaging the current public reputation of historically poor performers. This fear may outweigh the argument that poor performers gain by pooling their data, bringing down the benchmark, and thus reducing their relative underperformance.

## Gross versus net returns approaches

Ideally, performance measurement in Europe should report at both the gross and net levels, because both have advantages. In practice, as both the resources and enthusiasm for performance measurement are limited, one or the other method has dominated in each area.

As dedicated software packages for private equity management information systems, accounting, and electronic data capture increase their penetration, the costs of data handling will come down. Over the next four or five years we can expect to see substantial progress on both fronts (assuming that the basic demand for more and better quality performance measurement both at the individual investor structure level and benchmarking across structures overcomes the remaining reluctance of those holding the data).

The gross returns approach can allow coverage of the returns performance generated across the full deal flow of private equity investment in portfolio companies within a particular territory, by all types of private equity players. Further advantages are that returns can be analysed by any characteristic of the portfolio companies, including, for example, the date in which they received investment, their industry sector, geographical location or the development stage of the business. The final return from realised investments can also be calculated and analysed separately, with no dependence on subjective valuation of unrealised holdings.

On the other hand, from an external investor's viewpoint, the gross return reveals nothing about the costs of private equity investment management, including fees and profit share, or the efficiency with which the investing entity manages uninvested monies. Both of these are captured by the net returns measure.

However, it is possible to convert actual gross returns performance measures to an implied net returns result. This is done by applying a set of model assumptions about the costs and operating behaviour of a notional fund, which is then credited with the portfolio transactions for the period and territory under review. This has been done by the authors of the French national studies using a single set of assumptions for the entire data set 1978–95, which resulted in a reduction of five percentage points in the IRR.

Clearly, the technique has serious limitations, given that there is in fact wide variation of investment structures and behaviour. In particular, the efficiency and cost-base of many earlier investor structures used in France did not justify the application of the model assumptions.

It is also possible to move in the opposite direction, from net returns to gross, at least in respect of management fees and carried interest. However, the accounting treatment of fees and the rules about when carried interest may be credited to managers vary greatly from fund to fund, so that each fund needs to be dealt with individually, rather than a single model being applied. The difference between gross and net in terms of IRR percentage points can vary widely from fewer than five to as many as 10 percentage points.

## Results

Turning now from methodology to results, no performance data for Europe has yet been published that excludes:

- UK-focus funds; or
- funds managed from the United Kingdom, irrespective of their geographical investment focus.

The data set available to Bannock Consulting and Venture Economics is approaching the point that will allow this in future editions of the *Investment Benchmarks Report*. The company is mindful, though, that there is also an extraordinary sensitivity within Europe, born out of social and political considerations to international performance comparisons. At present non-UK results can be discussed only by cautiously comparing the Europe-wide figures from the *Investment Benchmarks Report* with UK numbers produced for the BVCA's performance measurement survey, and with reference to the French and Dutch nationally based studies already mentioned. These are the sources for the figures quoted in the following paragraphs. Comparisons need to be cautious and broad-brush rather than detailed, due to currency differences, coverage gaps and overlaps, and timing differences.

Certain broad features of historical performance are clear enough to be summarised below without concern about methodological consistency.

- On a long-term comparison for the last 10–15 years, whether using a 10-year investment horizon or returns to inception across all vintage years, the pooled return for funds specialised to early stage has been moderate, throughout Europe, at around 10–11 per cent. Broadly speaking this should be set against equivalent numbers of 8–10 per cent for later stage funds, and 15–17 per cent return for buy-out funds.

- On a direct comparison between the pooled returns from inception to 1998 of early-stage funds formed between 1980 and 1994, 17 UK investment-focus funds, all sterling-based, returned 7.2 per cent IRR. This should be set against a return of 9 per cent (Ecu-based) from 40 funds with an investment focus anywhere in Europe, either single or multi-country, and including those managed from the United Kingdom. The dispersion of returns within both these groups was very high at both ends of the distribution.

- One difference that does emerge is that the upper quartile point of the European distribution was 15.2 per cent, while the corresponding figure for the UK focus group was 13.3 per cent. A tentative inference is that the wider European canvas has allowed more opportunities over this period for early-stage specialists to achieve exceptional results. Of course, a proportion of early-stage investment is carried out by non-specialised funds.

## Returns from France and the Netherlands

The results on a gross returns basis from the Netherlands and France support the view that early-stage investments taken as a whole have historically been less profitable than other private equity categories. In France, the composite results for *capital risque* realisations up to the end of 1995, of investments made between 1978 and 1995 produced a gross IRR of 5.8 per cent. In the Netherlands, early-stage investments realised between 1987 and 1996 produced a gross IRR of minus 1 per cent, with unrealised early-stage investments at valuation producing 7 per cent. The combination of these two segments would result in an early-stage return of around 4 per cent. These pooled figures say nothing about the dispersion of returns by vintage or by fund structure.

## An improving picture for early-stage

Investment horizon return numbers suggest that returns to early-stage funds have been improving, particularly outside the UK. Europe-wide, pooled returns on an Ecu basis for three years and five years up to the end of 1998 were 21.4 per cent and 15.2 per cent respectively. A subset of UK-focus funds on the same measure in pounds sterling returned 13.2 and 7.3 per cent. The detailed analysis of composite portfolio results contained in the *Investment Benchmarks Report* shows that Europe-wide, early-stage funds formed in the years 1990to 1998 had the best result of any cohort, with a pooled IRR to end-1998 of 17.6 per cent.

## Development funds

Sixty-two funds specialised to development, including expansion and other later-stage investments, formed between 1980 and 1994 produced an average IRR (Ecu-based) across Europe on the returns-to-inception measure of 7.0 per cent. The corresponding number for a subset of 34 funds with a UK investment focus, based in sterling, was 9.3 per cent. The dispersion among the underlying individual IRR results for the best funds was smaller than for early-stage funds. The top quarter of funds Europe-wide produced a pooled IRR of 17.4 per cent, with a similar result in the UK-focus subset (range from the 25th to the 10th percentile 14.9 to 17.1 per cent).

Investment horizon pooled returns for development funds Europe-wide to the end of 1998 were 13 per cent for three years and 14.6 per cent for five years. The corresponding figures for UK-focus funds were 29 per cent and 22.9 per cent. The superior result for UK-focus funds may well reflect the greater maturity of the subset, but it seems that the upward trend is present throughout. Direct comparisons between UK-focus funds and Europe-wide funds are not available by vintage year.

The French gross IRR for investments made at the development stage of portfolio companies between 1978 and 1995 and realised by the end of 1995 was 14.1 per cent on a pooled basis. For the Netherlands, the gross IRR was 13 per cent – both on realised and unrealised investments made between 1987 and 1996.

## Buyout funds

For funds specialised to buyouts, the long-term pooled IRR, Europe-wide, for 108 funds formed from 1980 to 1996, was 16.3 per cent (Ecu-based) on returns from inception to 1998. The strong showing of the bulk of this fund set is demonstrated by its median IRR of 12.8 per cent, and the pooled IRR of the upper quarter of the distribution being 36.6 per cent. The upper quartile entry point was 23.5 per cent.

## UK-focus funds

In one study, 55 UK-focus buy-out funds formed between 1980 and 1994 were divided into two groups for performance measurement: mid-sized deal funds, typical equity investment range of £2–£10 million, and funds specialising in larger deals. Combining these two groups, and allowing for the much larger weight of capital in the second group, suggests a pooled IRR, in sterling, of about 18.5 per cent, and an upper quartile entry point of around 27 per cent. The implication is that buy-out funds focused outside the UK have not performed as well in this period.

The same inference can be drawn from the investment horizon returns. Pooled returns for Europe-wide funds for three years and five years to the end of 1998 were 22.8 per cent and 18.9 per cent respectively, against average IRRs of 32 per cent and 25 per cent for UK-focus funds.

The French and the Dutch studies of portfolio gross returns broadly support these conclusions. Returns on buy-out investments between 1987 and 1996 were 22 per cent realised and 21 per cent unrealised. In France, the buy-out results included in the self-selected sample of realised investments (1978–95) were very profitable: a pooled IRR of 31.8 per cent, which rose to 35.6 per cent when failed investments were excluded. Of the 521 companies in the sample, no less than 122, or just under a quarter, provided gross IRRs of more than 50 per cent per annum.

Although there are European funds that specialise in turnarounds, bridge finance and the purchase of secondary positions from other investors, the small weight of activity and the problems of data comparability make it impossible to discuss representative performance results.

## Generalist funds

The final category dealt with in the respective studies Europe-wide and for UK focus funds is generalist funds, which in principle cover all classes of deal. Here the long-term pooled

IRR, Europe-wide, for 79 funds formed between 1980 and 1994, was 8.8 per cent (Ecu-based) on returns from inception to 1998. By comparison, the group of 30 UK-focus funds had an average result in sterling of 11.7 per cent. Upper quartile figures were 12.8 per cent Europe-wide and 12.3 per cent for UK-focus funds.

## Generalist funds

If the historical performance of private equity as a whole is considered, then both UK-focus and Europe-wide funds show a similar cyclical pattern by vintage in overall returns measured to the end of 1998, with a strong recent upswing. There are peaks for 1985 UK funds and 1986 funds Europe wide, and again for 1990-92 and 1994 vintages. The non-UK cycle may differ in detail, but data available at the time of writing do not allow this to be analysed.

Overall, composite IRRs (Ecu-based) from inception were 12 per cent per annum pooled across 263 funds for all vintages between 1980 and 1994. The 125 UK-focus funds considered alone returned a pooled sterling result of 15.5 per cent. When the Europe-wide fund set, including funds denominated in a variety of currencies, is considered from the point of view of a sterling investor (an analysis included in the *Investment Benchmarks Report*), the pooled return rises to 12.6 per cent. However, from the above discussion about large variations between and within the component parts of the fund set, it is clear that no worthwhile inference can be drawn from these slight differences in the overall pooled results.

## Prospects

Reliable data on the historical performance of a relatively new and still maturing asset class is clearly of value, but hard to interpret as a guide to the present, let alone the future. Even when the European private equity industry is more mature, it will retain to some degree its essential characteristics of privacy and illiquidity. Together with the underlying investment risks, this will ensure that a substantial dispersion of returns persists both over time (volatility) and across the market segments where fund managers operate. The cyclic features brought about by economic as well as financial-market cycles, affect entry as well as exit prices and overlay secular trends associated with increasing competition and higher levels of professionalism within the industry. Opportunities to outperform benchmarks, however, will certainly remain.

In the United States, where private equity has been established longer, the correlation between 'hot' IPO markets and venture fund returns has been demonstrated in a number of studies. It is recognised that returns to buy-out funds, which typically have much shorter holding periods, are differently affected by stock market cycles and are subject to other short-term influences. The two components are considered as separate asset classes. This separation is much less evident in Europe, where, historically, the volume of buy-out activity, mainly based in the United Kingdom, has tended to dominate the whole European market. Markets such as France, Germany, Italy, the Netherlands and Spain have been more venture-oriented, although buy-out activity in these areas is increasing in relative importance. The new generation of large buy-out funds (typically over Ecu1 billion) raised in recent years and designed with large multi-country and cross-border deals in mind will accentuate the need to separate out performance measurement components.

Comparisons of private equity performance with that of publicly quoted asset classes brings in a new set of issues, since the latter as liquid assets use time-weighted returns, which are expressed per unit of capital invested for a particular time period. The private equity performance measure, the IRR, allows for the time value of the particular amount of capital held during the lifetime of each illiquid fund, and is thus a money-weighted measure. To make valid comparisons, either IRRs have to be calculated for notional funds that invest in public asset indices using the same pattern of cashflows as private equity, or time-weighted returns have to be calculated for private equity.

The advent of the euro will make more acceptable performance comparisons of multi-currency private equity fund-sets with publicly quoted asset classes, a process that has been initiated in the *Investment Benchmarks Report*. The latter requires at least quarterly or more frequent data capture, and even then slight imprecision can lead to large margins of error, as short-period results are compounded to generate longer-period measures. To date, there have been no time-weighted returns estimated for private equity in Europe.

The twin spurs to more and better quality performance measurement activity are the internal needs of the industry for benchmarking to understand their performance, and the requirements of investors, actual and potential, and their advisers.

The process of gathering data for analysis and presentation will continue to rely on the confidence and voluntary cooperation of the players, although this can be bolstered by the support of trade associations, individual investors and investor circles. We at Bannock Consulting, together with our partners Venture Economics, are committed to making data release easier, and to improvements in the provision of independent and authoritative performance benchmarking and monitoring services for the industry and its funders.

Chapter 20

# The challenge of performance assessment

Paul A. Gompers
*Associate professor at the Harvard Business School and faculty research fellow of the National Bureau of Economic Research*

Josh Lerner
*Professor of Business Administration at the Harvard Business School and research associate of the National Bureau of Economic Research*

Despite advances during the past decades in the pricing and risk adjustment of return in public markets, the measurement of risk and return in private equity has advanced relatively little. This is surprising, given the importance of return measurements for both fund managers and private equity investors. Private equity organisations need to document the performance of their earlier investments when raising new funds.

The benchmark chosen to measure performance is critical in determining an institutional investor's decision to allocate funds across various asset classes, as well as the choice of individual managers within an asset class.

Universities and foundations that spend a certain percentage of their endowments must be able to calculate the change in valuation of their private equity portfolios from year to year. Investment officers at pension funds whose bonuses are tied to the performance of their portfolios must similarly be able to measure accurately how well these funds are performing on a risk-adjusted basis in a timely manner.

At the same time, the relatively slow pace of innovation in assessing riskiness and returns for private equity investments is understandable. Firms receiving capital from private equity funds very often remain privately held for a number of years after the initial investment. These firms have no observable market price. In order to present a conservative assessment of the portfolio valuation, private equity managers often refrain from marking to market portfolio firm values, preferring to maintain the investments at book value. Thus, the stated returns of private equity funds may not accurately reflect the true evolution of value.

The problem is severe for both venture capital and buyout investments. In fact, current practices may substantially understate the true volatility of buyouts because they rarely have follow-on investments when the firm can be revalued.

This chapter describes efforts to address this issue. In particular we outline a method for addressing this problem by 'marking to market' the returns of a private equity group. We next discuss the calculation of risk-adjusted returns. We then apply these concepts in an illustrative calculation of the returns of a private equity group that has been an active investor over the past three decades. The analysis and methodology used here represent a substantial improvement in the measurement of risk and return in private equity. The tool is potentially useful for addressing portfolio allocation and fund assessment in a rigorous and coherent manner.

## The problem

Two primary approaches have been taken in earlier efforts to assess the returns of private equity investment. The first has been to examines the change in the prices of firms backed by private equity investors that have recently gone public. A long-standing example of such an index is the Venture Capital 100 reported each month in Venture Economics' *Venture Capital Journal*. Merrill Lynch has taken a similar approach in the construction of its private equity index: It uses the prices of the least liquid listed public firms with the smallest market capitalisation.[1]

While such an index is relatively easy to construct in a timely manner (the prices of publicly traded firms can be obtained at the end of each trading day), it has several limitations.

First, the valuation of private equity investments will be affected by a variety of factors that do not affect public firms. For instance, a considerable inflow of funds into venture funds may create an environment where 'too many funds are chasing too few deals'. It seems unlikely that such a problem will affect the pricing of public firms, as public investors can readily move their capital across industries and securities.

Second, the market for recently public firms has certain institutional features that affect the pricing of firms. For instance, smaller firms that go public frequently drop in value in their first few years, which may reflect over-optimism, at least by some subset of investors.[2] These institutional changes once again reduce the value of public firms as indicators of private valuations.

Finally, the public firms that make up the indexes may not be good proxies for the current mix of private equity-backed firms. Many of the new private firms may have no public comparables.

The second approach has been to calculate the internal rates of return (IRR) of private equity funds. Among others, Venture Economics and Cambridge Associates collect data from institutional investors on the flow of capital into and out of private equity funds. These data are used to calculate annual and quarterly return series for private equity funds as a whole. These calculated returns are then used to compare the returns of private equity with small-capitalisation stocks and other securities, as well as to determine the relative performance of particular private equity organisations.

Unfortunately, this methodology also has two major problems, which limit its usefulness. The first is the inconsistency in how private equity groups value their investments. Established private equity organisations are usually conservative in their approach to valuing their investments, often holding investments at cost until they are taken public. Less established private equity organisations are often not as conservative in their valuation practices. Inexperienced private equity groups are often under tremendous pressure to raise follow-on funds.[3]

Raising an initial private equity fund is frequently very difficult. Many institutional investors and investment advisers refuse, as a matter of principle, to invest in first-time funds, often on the grounds that they believe these funds have lower returns than other partnerships. As a result, many first-time funds are so small that the management fees generated cannot cover the travel, office and salary expenses that the partnerships incur.

Alternatively, the lead investor in the fund (and perhaps even the placement agent who helped in the fund-raising) may be given a substantial share of the management fees and carried interest. The general partners of the private equity fund are nonetheless willing to accept these terms, because they expect that subsequent funds will be raised on more attractive terms. A major focus of these organisations is consequently on raising such a follow-on fund.

It is not surprising, then, that these private equity organisations are very aggressive in presenting their investment results during fund-raising. Among the behaviours encountered are:

- aggressively valuing still-private firms in their portfolios above cost;
- neglecting to discount firms in the portfolio that have encountered difficulties; and
- failing to discount for the illiquidity of the shares of publicly traded firms still held in the private equity group's portfolio.

These problems may not always be identified by institutional investors, who often are surprisingly willing to accept such claims at face value. Because a much larger fraction of established private equity organisation investments are likely to have been liquidated, these problems are much less likely to have a material impact on their results. Differences in valuation methodology can give the appearance that certain groups have superior performance when interim returns are compared, while in actuality their long-term performance is no different (or even lower) than that of other organisations.

The inconsistency has been the subject of attention by institutional investors in the United States and elsewhere. Efforts in the United States, such as the initiative launched in 1989 by the Institutional Limited Partners Association (ILPA), have made only modest progress.[4] In the United Kingdom, however, the British Venture Capital Association (BVCA), in conjunction with a group of major limited partners, has taken an aggressive approach in addressing this problem. In 1991, it introduced a consistent set of valuation standards that its members must follow.[5] The aim is to standardise the valuation of privately held firms in the private equity organisation portfolios. In particular, it seeks to prevent incidents where private equity investors raise follow-on funds (often from retail investors) based on inflated valuations of still private firms.

These standards were made more specific in 1993 in response to claims that private equity organisations were exploiting 'loopholes' in the standards. Many observers have criticised the revised standards as well, arguing that they still allow too much room for manoeuvre. For example, the distinction between early- and late-stage firms is not precisely defined. Thus, despite the much greater progress made in the United Kingdom than in the United States or elsewhere, it is unclear whether or not the BVCA's efforts have succeeded in curbing many problematic instances of aggressive valuations by less-established private equity organisations.

Even is this problem can be addressed, however, there is a second issue. The practices of the established venture groups, as well as the reform efforts, such as the BVCA initiative, emphasise the computation of returns using conservative assumptions. While these procedures allow investors to compare the performance of different private equity funds and to avoid being misled by overly aggressive organisations, they make it difficult to compare private equity returns to those in other asset classes. Thus, while it may be possible for private equity organisations to demonstrate that their funds have outperformed other partnerships formed around the same time, it is very difficult for them to show that they have produced positive risk-adjusted returns for their investors relative to the equity market *as a whole*.

A key obstacle to such comparisons is what can be termed the 'stale price' problem. While the movements of public market indices can be observed on a daily basis, increases in

251

the value of private firms can only be observed by outsiders after a great deal of delay. Typically, there is a sudden jump in the valuation of a firm reported by a private equity group associated with its initial public offering or a third-party follow-on investment, rather than a gradual increase in value as the company builds up its sales and profitability.

As a result of this problem it is very difficult to compare public and private equity prices. An illustration of this difficulty is to think about a hypothetical setting where:

- the valuation of private equity portfolios exactly mirrors the movements of the Standard & Poor's 500 (S&P 500); but
- returns from private equity funds are observed with a one-day delay.

If we try to relate the observed daily private and public equity returns, we would find virtually no correlation. (The S&P 500's movements on a given day have little predictive power for its movement on the following day.) This might lead us to conclude falsely that there is no relationship between these two asset classes.

This problem has been acknowledged by experienced observers of the private equity industry. To cite one discussion from the *Venture Capital Journal*:

> 'Venture Economics has often been asked in the past to comment on the performance of venture capital relative to other asset classes. It is imperative that any asset classes being compared be measured on the same basis [but] market prices for private venture capital partnerships don't exist ... Therefore, objective comparisons of risk and reward relative to other public markets are difficult to justify.'[6]

Despite the widespread acknowledgement of this problem, few efforts have been made to date to address this concern. In the remainder of this chapter we discuss an approach that we have developed and used to examine the returns of one private equity group.

## A proposed solution

A solution to this problem is to 'mark to market' the portfolio of the private equity organisation. Rather than waiting until there is a 'material' event (such as an initial public offering) to revalue the firm, we re-examine the valuations of all firms in the portfolio on a periodic basis. The quarterly or annual assessments can incorporate a wide variety of information about the changes over this period:

- the change in the public market valuations of comparable firms;
- the change in the relative prices of private and public equity markets as a whole;
- the change in the profitability of the portfolio firm;
- the degree of leverage of the portfolio company; and
- the change in any other firm characteristics commonly used for valuation purposes by equity market analysts to value similar publicly traded firms (for example, for young biotechnology firms, the number of patents awarded).

By undertaking such a calculation, the 'stale price' problem can be addressed; the entire portfolio has been revalued. These revised valuations can be compared with the returns from the public market during the same time interval. A standard approach is to run a regression that seeks to explain the fund's returns using one or more measures of public market performance, as well as a constant. The key item of performance measurement is the constant term. The analysis seeks to determine whether, once the movements in the market have been controlled for, the coefficient on the constant is positive, negative or indistinguishable from zero (that is, whether the market-adjusted performance superior to the appropriate benchmark, inferior to that measure or too close to the measure of market performance to discern).

A second feature of this analysis is that it yields a precise measure of the riskiness of the private equity portfolio. The coefficients on the public market return measures capture the level of riskiness of the portfolio. Risk, in modern theory and the practice of finance, is measured by the correlation of an investment's return with the overall market return. The higher the level of correlation with the public market factors, the greater the riskiness of the portfolio. To put it another way, a large investor should only worry about how the investment affects the riskiness of their entire portfolios, not the riskiness of the individual investment.

In this way, analysts can avoid drawing false conclusions about the success of investment managers. For instance, consider two mutual funds, one that holds equities of small high-technology firms, and one that holds securities issued by utilities. While the high-technology fund may have higher absolute returns over a given period, it may not be a superior performer once one controls the greater riskiness of its portfolio.[7]

The first model of risk-adjusting returns was the capital asset pricing model (CAPM). In measuring risk of an investment, and therefore its required return, investors should care about how the investment's returns co-vary (or move) with general market returns. For instance, while a highly variable stock that moves with the market (for example, a designer clothing company) would need to have a high return, a highly volatile stock that does not move with the market (such as that of a gold-mining firm) would not. In order to determine whether a given portfolio earns positive or negative risk-adjusted returns, a regression is run using the market return and a constant. In this context, the regression coefficient on the market return is the 'beta' of the stock – its measure of riskiness. The coefficient on the constant (also known as the intercept), commonly referred to as Jensen's alpha,[8] is a measure of the abnormal return on the portfolio. A positive alpha implies positive excess risk-adjusted returns.

In recent years, there has been extensive discussion in finance literature about what measures of market performance should be used as control variables in these regressions. A consensus has emerged around the view, first articulated by Fama and French,[9] that there are three crucial measures that should be used in such analyses. The Fama-French model is consistent with previous financial theory by Merton[10] on what factors should affect the expected return on an investment. The intuition of the Fama-French model is that a firm's correlation with the market does not capture the full riskiness of a company. Fama and French propose using a size factor that will control for the fact that small firms are riskier than big firms and a book-to-market factor that captures the differential riskiness between value and glamour stocks.[11]

In the regressions that follow, we use the Fama-French model as well as the CAPM. Their three factors are:

- **RMRF**– the return over Treasury bills on the value-weighted market portfolio;
- **SMB** – the return on an investment portfolio formed by subtracting the return on a large-firm portfolio from the return on a small-firm portfolio; and
- **HML** – the return on an investment portfolio calculated as the return on a portfolio of high book-to-market stocks minus the return on a portfolio of low book-to-market stocks.

The intercept from the regressions is once again an indicator of risk-adjusted performance. The intercepts in these regressions have an interpretation analogous to Jensen's alpha in the CAPM framework. A positive intercept implies positive risk-adjusted performance. The three-factor model has been used by many researchers[12] to explore investment performance.

## A representative calculation

We now illustrate these calculations through an examination of the returns from a single private equity group, E.M. Warburg, Pincus & Co (hereafter referred to as Warburg, Pincus), one of the few firms that has more than 20 years of data. We obtain quarterly data on portfolio companies back to 1972 from this group.

First we have taken the portfolio values in the Warburg, Pincus database as accurate reflections of the value of the underlying investments. In subsequent analyses we 'mark to market' investments that are held at cost are  to get a better assessment of the changes in portfolio value from quarter to quarter.

The quarterly return on the investment portfolio is calculated by taking the ending portfolio value, less investments during the quarter plus any disbursements, divided by the beginning portfolio value. (This is the manner in which returns are calculated for public stocks.) In this way we create a quarterly series of returns from the underlying data.

The return series provides a picture of the performance of Warburg Pincus over the past 25 years. When we use the Warburg, Pincus data, starting with the first quarter of 1972 and ending with the third quarter of 1997, we find an arithmetic average annual return (weighting each year equally and ignoring the amount of money invested) of 30.5 per cent.[13]

In Exhibit 1, we examine the correlation of Warburg, Pincus' returns with other asset classes.

The correlations of Warburg, Pincus' returns with both private and public market asset classes are relatively modest. Clearly, from the viewpoint of a large institutional investor, the diversification benefits of Warburg, Pincus are quite large. One caveat must, however, be kept in mind. We are only looking at the stated returns on the portfolio values, as recorded by Warburg, Pincus. To the extent that the valuations are not 'marked to market,' many of these correlations will be biased downward.

Exhibit 1

**Correlation of unadjusted Warburg, Pincus private equity returns with returns on other assets**

| | |
|---|---|
| Venture capital | 0.5182 |
| Seed-stage | 0.2585 |
| Early-stage | 0.7127 |
| Balanced fund | 0.6900 |
| Later-stage | 0.4520 |
| buyouts | 0.4201 |
| Mezzanine | 0.3154 |
| S&P 500 | 0.5982 |
| Small-cap stocks | 0.6784 |
| Corporate bonds | 0.1003 |
| T-bills | 0.2214 |
| Treasury bonds | 0.0683 |

Exhibit 2

**Risk-adjusted performance of unadjusted Warburg, Pincus private equity portfolio**

| Independent variable | CAPM results | Fama-French results |
|---|---|---|
| Intercept | 2.677 | 2.637 |
| | [1.92] | [1.88] |
| Excess market return (RMRF) | 1.0849 | 0.8950 |
| | [6.06] | [4.11] |
| Excess return on high book-to-market firms (HML) | | 0.0237 |
| | | [0.08] |
| Excess return on small firms (SMB) | | 0.7061 |
| | | [2.38] |
| Adjusted $R^2$ | 0.281 | 0.302 |
| Number of observations | 96 | 96 |

Note

The dependent variables are the quarterly returns on the private equity portfolio of Warburg Pincus from the first quarter of 1972 to the fourth quarter of 1995. RMRF is the value-weighted market return on all NYSE/Amex/Nasdaq firms (RM) minus the risk-free rate (RF), which is the one-month Treasury bill rate. SMB (small minus big) is the difference each month between the return on small firms and the return on big firms. HML (high minus low) is the difference each month between the return on a portfolio of high book-to-market stocks and the return on a portfolio of low book-to-market stocks. (T-statistics are in brackets.)

Exhibit 2 presents the calculation of risk-adjusted returns. As discussed earlier, we present the results from both CAPM regression models and the Fama-French three-factor regressions.[14] In these regressions, the intercept represents the quarterly excess return earned by Warburg, Pincus relative to the model. In the simple CAPM regression (first column), the intercept is 2.68, indicating that relative to the CAPM, Warburg, Pincus has earned an excess quarterly return of 2.68 per cent on a risk-adjusted basis. This coefficient is significant at the 10 per cent confidence level: in other words, we are 90 per cent certain that the result is indeed positive.

It is noteworthy that Warburg, Pincus' portfolio has a beta of slightly greater than one (1.08). This means that the Warburg, Pincus portfolio is only slightly riskier than the market. As a reference, most small-stock portfolios would have betas above 1.5. Again we assess the impact of marking the portfolio to market on the risk adjustments in the next section.

The Fama-French results (second column) continue to show that the Warburg, Pincus returns are positive on a risk-adjusted basis. The magnitude of the excess returns is similar to the CAPM results, a positive 2.64 per cent per quarter. On an annualised basis, the positive risk-adjusted performance of Warburg, Pincus is over 10 per cent. It is also worth noting that the correction for small firms seems important. The Warburg, Pincus portfolio, indicates that the portfolio returns move with the returns on small firms. This is not surprising, given the importance of venture investments in the Warburg, Pincus portfolio.

## The impact of marking to market

As discussed above, accounting conventions in private equity make portfolio evaluation and asset allocation difficult. The infrequency with which portfolio values are adjusted reduces calculated correlations and makes risk adjustment difficult. In this section, we explore one method of marking portfolio values to market that can aid in the evaluation of performance. In determining long-term performance, such an exercise is extremely valuable.

We undertake one methodology although many others could be implemented in a similar manner. From the data on individual Warburg, Pincus investments, we match each portfolio company to a particular three-digit SIC industry. For each of the industries we calculated an equal-weighted industry index from the public market values of all the firms in that industry. In this way we know the relative public market values of firms in the same industry. We can calculate changes in the public market index from quarter to quarter and use these changes to adjust the portfolio value of each company.

In the quarter of any investment or distribution by Warburg, Pincus, we adjust the portfolio value to the stated value in the Warburg, Pincus data. If the company is written down by Warburg, Pincus, we similarly adjust the value to the marked-down value. In quarters in which there is no investment, distribution or write-down, we adjust the portfolio value by the change in the matched industry public market index. In this way, a computer hardware company that is in the private equity portfolio will increase in value by 10 per cent if similar public computer hardware companies rise in value by 10 per cent. We use the equal-weighted index to give more weight to small, public firms because of the nature of private equity investments.

In some ways, marking the portfolio value to changes in the public market will give the most conservative assessment of performance. By construction, we are maximising the possible correlation with the public market returns. This will give the impression of riskier investments (because of the higher correlation), even though private equity valuations are not perfectly correlated with the public markets. It has been shown[15] that while the valuations of public and private markets are correlated, the correlation is much less than one. The estimated risk-adjusted performance should be seen as a lower bound on the true risk-adjusted performance.

In Exhibit 3 we re-estimate the correlations of Warburg, Pincus' marked-to-market returns with various private equity and public market indices. Notice that while the correlations with most private markets decline from Exhibit 1, the correlation with public market returns (such as the S&P 500 and small-cap stocks) increases. This is not unexpected given our adjustment to portfolio values.

We repeat the risk adjustment of returns using both the CAPM and the Fama-French models in Exhibit 4. The regressions are run for Warburg, Pincus marked-to-market quarterly returns from the first quarter of 1972 until the fourth quarter of 1995.

The explanatory power of the these regressions is much higher than in Exhibit 2. The adjusted $R^2$ is nearly twice as high in these new regressions. The CAPM regression

---

Exhibit 3

**Correlations of marked-to-market Warburg, Pincus private equity annual returns with private equity and other benchmarks**

| | |
|---|---|
| Venture capital | 0.4846 |
| Seed-stage | 0.3240 |
| Early-stage | 0.6047 |
| Balanced fund | 0.5985 |
| Later-stage | 0.5188 |
| buyouts | 0.5709 |
| Mezzanine | 0.2262 |
| S&P 500 | 0.7367 |
| Small-cap stocks | 0.7836 |
| Corporate bonds | 0.1872 |
| T-bills | 0.1319 |
| Treasury bonds | 0.1449 |

---

Exhibit 4

**Risk-adjusted performance of marked-to-market Warburg, Pincus private equity portfolio**

| Independent variable | CAPM results | Fama-French results |
|---|---|---|
| Intercept | 1.9731 | 1.714 |
|  | [1.82] | [1.77] |
| Excess market return (RMRF) | 1.4399 | 1.2699 |
|  | [9.64] | [7.16] |
| Excess return on high book-to-market firms (HML) |  | 0.1393 |
|  |  | [0.56] |
| Excess return on small firms (SMB) |  | 0.7557 |
|  |  | [3.14] |
| Adjusted R$^2$ | 0.492 | 0.536 |
| Number of observations | 96 | 96 |

Note

The dependent variables are the quarterly returns on the private equity portfolio of Warburg Pincus from the first quarter of 1972 to the fourth quarter of 1995, marking the portfolio value to market. RMRF is the value-weighted market return on all NYSE/AMEX/Nasdaq firms (RM) minus the risk-free rate (RF), which is the one-month Treasury bill rate. SMB (small minus big) is the difference each month between the return on small firms and the return on big firms. HML (high minus low) is the difference each month between the return on a portfolio of high book-to-market stocks and the return on a portfolio of low book-to-market stocks. (T-statistics are in brackets.)

in the first regression shows that the beta on the Warburg, Pincus returns series has increased significantly, to 1.44. Clearly, marking the portfolio values to market using public indices increases the correlation with the market. The intercept, however, is still positive and significant. The results indicate that relative to the CAPM, Warburg, Pincus earns positive risk-adjusted returns of 2 per cent per quarter, or roughly 8 per cent per year.

As a comparison, Venture Economics has published the betas on 175 mature venture capital funds. Exhibit 5 reports these calculated betas for various types of venture capital funds. The betas calculated by Venture Economics suffer from the bias of not being marked to market (that is, they are based on stated valuations) and therefore should probably be considered as analogous to the non-marked to market beta calculations that we have undertaken using the Warburg, Pincus data in Exhibit 3 (that is, the estimate of 1.08 in the non-marked to market returns data).

Except for later-stage funds, the beta of Warburg, Pincus is substantially lower than all the other classifications of venture capital funds. In addition, because beta measures the level of risk that investors cannot diversify away, a combination of venture capital funds cannot have a lower beta than Venture Economics reports, that is, the betas in Exhibit 5 represent a lower bound on the estimated beta of a portfolio of venture capital funds. The low beta on Warburg, Pincus' investments is likely to be the product of the flexible investment strategy practised. This allows the organisation to take advantage of investments across many industries and many stages of development.

The Fama-French results confirm the CAPM results. Once again, the coefficient on the market return has increased due to marking to market. Similarly, the importance of small-firm risk has increased as well; that is, the coefficient on SMB is significantly higher. Even after

Exhibit 5

**Beta estimates for various classifications of venture capital funds**

|  |  | Beta | Standard deviation |
|---|---|---|---|
| Overall venture capital | (1974–1989) | 1.86 | 5.10 |
| Overall venture capital | (1983–1989) | 3.82 | 5.68 |
| Early stage | (1983–1989) | 2.92 | 9.19 |
| Balanced | (1983–1989) | 1.76 | 5.80 |
| Later stage | (1983–1989) | 1.07 | 3.73 |

Note

The value of beta from the CAPM regressions for the returns of 175 mature venture capital funds compiled and reported by Venture Economics.[16]

controlling for the three factors, however, Warburg Pincus still earns significantly positive risk-adjusted returns. The magnitude in the Fama-French results is similar to the CAPM results: that is, 1.7 per cent excess returns per quarter, or about 7 per cent annual excess performance over a 24-year period.

## Conclusions

Our analysis has two goals. First, we explore the calculations for one private equity organisation. The regression results from asset-pricing models including the CAPM and Fama-French three-factor models indicate positive and significant abnormal returns. On an annualised basis, the excess risk-adjusted return is between 7 per cent and 10 per cent. In other words, Warburg Pincus has earned 7–10 per cent higher returns per year than a portfolio of similar-risk public stocks. These returns are not only significant, but they are also large in economic terms. While these excess returns are calculated using the gross results of Warburg Pincus, the size of the abnormal excess performance leaves a substantial return for limited partners given current fund terms.

Second, we hope to encourage a more general discussion in the private equity industry about risk adjustment and benchmarking. We believe that the issues discussed here open the door to future work on improving the understanding of private equity returns. Innovations in this chapter are important for global asset allocation decisions across various asset classes, as well as the choice of individual portfolio managers. Our results indicate that these techniques can be fruitfully applied to the private equity arena.

This chapter is an amended and updated version of an article that originally appeared in, and is reprinted with permission from:
*The Journal of Private Equity* Volume 1, Number 1, Fall 1997.
© Euromoney Institutional Investor plc. All rights reserved.

---

[1] See Galante, S.: 'Merrill Weighs in with its Own Index for Private Equity', *Private Equity Analyst,* 5, 1 (August 1993), pp. 11–12.

[2] See Ritter, J.: 'The Long-Run Performance of Initial Public Offerings', *Journal of Finance*, 46 (1991), pp. 3–27. See also Brav, A., and Gompers, P.: 'Myth or Reality? The Long-Run Underperformance of Initial Public Offerings: Evidence from Venture and Non-Venture Capital-Backed Companies', *Journal of Finance*, 52 (1997), pp 1791-1821.

[3] See Gompers, P.: 'Grandstanding in the Venture Capital Industry', *Journal of Financial Economics*, 42 (1996), pp. 133–156.

[4] *Proposal for a Standard Industry-Wide System for Measuring Interim Performance of Venture Capital Partnerships, ILPA* (May 1990). The persistence of such problems is discussed, for instance, in Mercer, W.: *Key Terms and Conditions for Private Equity Investing*, William Mercer Inc., New York (1996), and Cain, W.: *LBO Partnership Valuations Matter: A Presentation to the LBO Partnership Valuation Meeting*, Mimeo (February 1997).

[5] See *Guidelines for the Valuation and Disclosure of Venture Capital Portfolios*, BVCA, London (1993).

[6] Reyes, J.E.: 'Industry Struggling to Forge Tools for Measuring Risk', *Venture Capital Journal*, 30 (September 1990), pp. 23–27.

[7] One subtle issue associated with applying the marked-to-market approach to the private equity setting is that we are looking at the gross returns of the fund. Because investors (limited partners) frequently get their capital back before the general partners receive a share of the profits, the riskiness of the investors' investment is likely to be lower than that of the entire portfolio. Thus, the calculations are likely to overstate the riskiness of the portfolio.

[8] This type of regression was first introduced by Michael Jensen in 1968, and is now widely employed by fund evaluation services to evaluate mutual and hedge fund managers. Of course, because mutual funds calculate net asset value daily, they do not generally face these types of valuation problems. See Jensen, M.C.: 'The Performance of Mutual Funds in the Period 1945–64', *Journal of Finance*, 23 (1968), pp. 389–416.

[9] See Fama, E.F., and French, K.R.: 'The Cross-Section of Expected Stock Returns' *Journal of Finance*, 47 (1992), pp. 427–465 and 'Common Risk Factors in the Returns of Stocks and Bonds', *Journal of Financial Economics*, 33 (1993), pp. 3–55.

[10] See Merton, R.: 'An Intertemporal Capital Asset Pricing Model', *Econometrica*, 41 (1973), pp. 867–87.

[11] See Lakonishok, J., Shleifer, A., and Vishny, R.: 'Contrarian Investment, Extrapolation, and Risk', *Journal of Finance*, 49 (1994), pp. 1541–78.

[12] See Barber, B., and Lyon, J.: 'Detecting Long-Run Abnormal Stock Returns: The Empirical Power and Specification of Test Statistics', *Journal of Financial Economics*, 43 (1997), pp. 401–432. See also Brav, A., and Gompers, P.: 'Myth or Reality? The Long-Run Underperformance of Initial Public Offerings: Evidence from Venture and Non-Venture Capital-Backed Companies', *Journal of Finance*, 52 (1997), pp 1791-1821. See also Kothari, S., and Warner, J.: 'Measuring Long-Horizon Security Price Performance', *Journal of Financial Economics*, 43 (1997), pp. 301–339.

[13] The calculated returns in this article are the gross returns of Warburg, Pincus. The large positive performance of the gross returns on a risk-adjusted basis would indicate that net results still leave substantial performance premiums for investors. Other analyses might include looking at the time trend in excess returns, as well as weighting observations by fund size.

[14] The time period for the regression is the first quarter of 1972 to the fourth quarter of 1995. Data for 1996 was unavailable.

[15] See Gompers, P., and Lerner, J.: 'Money Chasing Deals? The Impact of Fund Inflows on the Valuation of Private Equity Investments', *Journal of Financial Economics* (2000) forthcoming.

[16] Reyes, J.: 'Industry Struggling to Forge Tools for Measuring Risk', *Venture Capital Journal*, 30 (September 1990), pp. 23–27.

Chapter 21

# LBO returns in the United States: what will it take to succeed in the new era of LBOs?

Karen Gordon Mills
*Managing Director and Founder, Solera Capital, LLC[1]*

Times have changed in the leveraged buy-out (LBO) industry in the United States. The days when buying smart and selling high could generate returns in excess of 40 per cent (the pattern since the mid-1980s) seem to be over. A recent survey conducted by the Lucas Group indicates that most LBO firms are predicting a narrowing of the spread between average LBO returns and the Standard & Poor's (S&P) 500 average.

Three factors have together altered the outlook for future returns:

- a reduction in allowable debt-to-equity ratios;
- an increase in purchase multiples; and
- the potential for stagnating exit multiples.

Consequently, it appears that different levers will be required to obtain exceptional returns in the future.

## The three eras of LBOs

Looking back, the history of the LBO industry can be divided into three eras roughly defined by the unique factors which determined the components of their returns. The first – the Leverage Era – began with the rise of the leveraged buy-out as a financial tool in the early to mid-1980s, and concluded as we exited the recession of the early 1990s. The second era – the Multiple Expansion Era – began with the rise of the bull market in the early 1990s and appears to be ending as the decade draws to a close.

Looking forward to the third – the Earnings Growth Era – different factors will define who succeeds and who fails going forward in the LBO industry. To give some context for our discussion we will describe each of the eras in some detail and discuss the levers which we believe will be the keys to success in the third era.

### Era one: the Leverage Era

Although people have been doing deals for decades, the rise of the LBO industry as we know it today began in earnest at the beginning of the 1980s, when early entrants in the field discovered the magic behind the original LBO formula. That is, if you identified a relatively stable company that spun off a reasonable amount of cash, bought out the existing owners using an extremely high percentage of debt financing, then paid off the debt with the cashflow pro-

Exhibit 1

**Typical LBOs mid-1980s to early 1990s**

|  |  |
|---|---|
| Purchase: | 4 to 5 times earnings |
| Sale: | at a similar multiple |
| Debt-to-equity ratio high: | 90/10 |
| Interest rate: | 11% |
| Levers: | • High debt-to-equity |
|  | • Strict cost control |
|  | • Strip out, sell assets |
|  | • Cut costs to increase operating income |

duced by the company and sold the company a few years further on even at the same multiple, a significant return could be generated.

The formula worked well during the leverage era because of the character of the financial market at the time. During the mid-1980s, the average LBO was purchased at a multiple of between four and five times its earnings, and sold for a similar multiple three to five years later. Debt-to-equity ratios averaged 90/10 (although after fees it was not unusual for the investor to have little or no money in the deal soon after closing). (See Exhibit 1.)

On the negative side, interest rates were high, averaging around 11 per cent cash interest for the whole capital structure. Subordinated debt (usually provided by insurance companies) bridged the gap between asset-based lenders (generally 50 per cent of the capital structure) and the small slice of equity. The providers of such subordinated debt demanded warrants on top of cash interest of 13 per cent or 14 per cent, bringing their total returns to well above 20 per cent.

After the appearance of Drexel Burnham and the creation of the 'junk bond' market, the unsecured portion of the capital structure became cheaper and larger. This allowed investors to begin to bid up multiples, because they could pay more for a deal (all other factors being equal) and still net the same returns.

LBO investors during this period typically looked for companies with two basic attributes:

• hard assets that they could use as collateral to support financing; and
• business sub-segments that they could strip out and sell.

In addition, there was often a focus on under-performing companies where it was possible to cut costs in order to increase operating income. As a result, the classic buy-out was a manufacturing company with little expected real growth. This company and its management would be left alone by the LBO investor to generate the cashflow necessary to pay off debt. By 'riding' the capital structure, the reduction of leverage could give a 35 per cent return (or greater) to the investor.

The combination of these factors eventually produced enough success stories that the industry won increasing favour with the investment community. The resulting influx of capital, along with the favourable returns generated by the average LBO fund compared to the S&P 500 index at the time, led to a change in industry dynamics. Soon firms that initially raised funds of between US$10 million and US$30 million came to the market to raise second and third funds of US$100 million or more. Thus began the transition to the second era of LBOs.

## The multiple expansion era

The huge influx of capital into the industry during the early 1990s, combined with the bull market in stocks, created a new situation for the LBO industry. After living with high leverage through the recession of 1990–92, investors and bankers began to use higher levels of equity, lowering average debt-to-equity ratios from 90/10 to 75/25. Greater use of available capital and rising equity markets pushed multiples from four or five times earnings to six or seven times.

However, these factors were offset by an expansion in exit multiples. This important development allowed investors to generate substantial returns, despite the fact that a much smaller relative portion of the return was coming from debt reduction, the predominant tool of the first era.

The following profile is typical of the average LBO during the second era.

---

Exhibit 2

**Typical LBOs early to late 1990s**

| | |
|---|---|
| *Purchase:* | 6 to 7 times earnings |
| *Sale:* | at a higher multiple |
| *Debt-to-equity ratio reduced:* | 75/25 |
| *Interest rate:* | 9% |
| *Levers:* | • Buy smart, sell at higher multiple |
| | • Exit into strong IPO market |
| | • Create roll-ups |
| | – Multiple arbitrage |
| | – Operating leverage |

---

- The average company was purchased at a multiple of between six and seven times its earnings, and sold for a multiple that was, on average, two points higher after the usual three- to five-year holding period. This rising tide lifted all boats during the holding period, allowing the seller to benefit in most transactions.
- The debt-to-equity ratio in deals declined over the years, but was on average 75/25, with the debt component at an interest rate of approximately 9 per cent (see Exhibit 2).

Top-quartile IRR returns during the second period were again very attractive, still in excess of 40 per cent, according to most sources, with fortunate buyers and sellers able to generate some higher returns. The ability to buy a company at a low multiple and sell it for a higher multiple was the most important factor in generating returns in this period. Often, the availability of a strong initial public offering (IPO) or public market as an exit strategy made this possible.

One notable characteristic of the second era was the creation of the 'roll-up' strategy to take advantage of multiple arbitrage and operating leverage in fragmented industries. In a roll-up, an LBO firm buys a so-called 'platform' company in a highly fragmented industry. It then uses the platform as a base on which to add acquisitions, thereby consolidating the industry and creating a much larger company. This company is then, at least in theory, worth a higher multiple and has a better market position than the platform company had on its own.

Again, firms that took advantage of the economic trends prevalent during this era were able to produce very strong returns for their investors. These same firms have now raised funds of US$1 billion or more. Can multiple expansion continue in the coming years? With investors accustomed to booming stock market returns in excess of 20 per cent annually, and with private equity investors pouring even more money into the industry, what will it take to succeed in the next era of LBOs?

## The earnings growth era

As the year 2000 begins, the industry is faced with a new set of market conditions. Purchase multiples have risen to eight to 10 times earnings, while future exit multiples are uncertain. Debt/equity ratios are trending down again, approaching 70/30. Interest rates remain low and, apart from the dislocation in the autumn of 1998, the high-yield and bank markets have been providing ample sources of financing (see Exhibit 3).

As will be demonstrated later in this chapter, these circumstances make it much harder for the LBO investor to achieve high returns. Only real increases in sales and/or operating earnings will drive strong LBO returns in the future.

The firms that would seem to be in the best position to succeed in the earnings growth era are those that are able to:

- analyse potential deals from a strategic perspective;
- expand the business in terms of both sales and profits;
- continually develop strong exit opportunities.

Exhibit 3

## Typical LBOs late 1990s and beyond?

| | |
|---:|:---|
| *Purchase:* | 8 to 10 times earnings |
| *Sale:* | at uncertain exit multiple |
| *Debt-to-equity ratio further reduced:* | (70/30 or less) |
| *Interest rate:* | 9% or less |
| *Levers:* | • Increase real top-line revenue |
| | • Increase margins/ quality of earnings |

## Sources of LBO returns

LBO returns come from three sources: debt repayment, multiple expansion and earnings growth. In each era returns have come largely from one particular source, as shown below.

- In the first era, returns came mainly from debt repayment (the use of excess cash to pay off debt).
- In the second era, returns were generated largely by multiple expansion (selling the company for more than was paid for it).

Exhibit 4

## Changing composition of returns – investors' views (% of return)

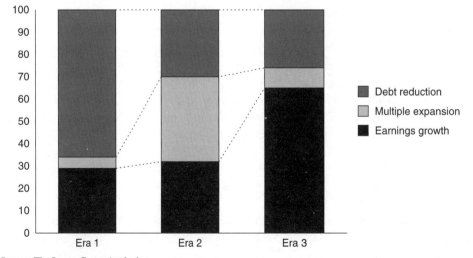

*Source:* The Lucas Group Analysis.

- In the third era, it is earnings growth (improving the operating performance) that is generating profits.

In the course of this analysis The Lucas Group, a strategy consulting firm, surveyed principal investors in the LBO industry. These investors were asked what they thought had been the source of their own portfolio returns.

Looking back at the 1980s (the first era), the investors said that 65 per cent of their returns came from debt reduction (see Exhibit 4). In the early to late 1990s, the returns were perceived to have been evenly split, with 30 per cent coming from debt repayment, 40 per cent from multiple expansion and 30 per cent from earnings growth. The consensus among investors was that most of their future internal rate of return (IRR) will need to come from growth in real sales and earnings.

In order to illustrate what has been happening, a simplified example is helpful. Exhibit 5 delineates a 'typical' LBO company. Using these figures, various mathematical calculations, 'IRR math' can be carried out in order to forecast possible returns.

---

Exhibit 5

**Fundamentals of a 'typical' LBO**

*Assumptions:*

| | |
|---|---|
| Sales: | US$100 million |
| EBIT margin: | 15% |
| Tax rate: | 32% |
| CapEx: | US$1 million |
| Growth: | None |
| Hold period: | 5 years |

*Source:* Solera Capital, LLC.

---

## The effect of lower leverage

What would happen if you acquired this hypothetical company for a six times multiple, paid 9 per cent interest on acquisition financing and sold the company after five years at the same six times multiple? The results would vary significantly depending on the leverage used. With

---

Exhibit 6

**The impact of debt-to-equity ratios on IRR (%)**

Lower debt-to-equity ratios cause average LBO IRRs to drop

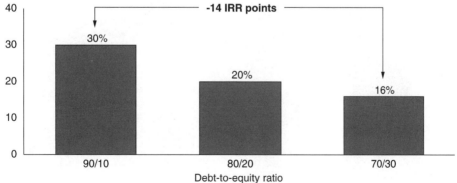

**Assumptions:**
- 6× purchase/sale multiple
- 9% interest rate
- 0% revenue/margin growth

*Source:* Solera Capital, LLC.

---

a 90/10 debt-to-equity ratio, this scenario yields a very respectable IRR of 30 per cent, achieved without any growth of the company. With a debt-to-equity ratio of 80/20, the IRR drops sharply to 20 per cent, and at 70/30 it levels off at 16 per cent (see Exhibit 6).

This means that in the time period from the early 1980s to present, the more conservative leverage structure alone would have taken 14 percentage points of IRR out of the basic LBO economics.

## The effect of higher deal prices

The other dynamic discussed above, which is more generally associated with the success of Era 2, is the effect of rising multiples. However, some quick IRR calculations show that, in fact, an increase in transaction multiples also creates downward pressure on returns. As the transaction multiple rises (all else being equal) the IRR drops. This is because at a higher purchase price there is less cash available to repay debt, thus reducing returns available from the leverage or debt reduction engine.

In our example, if you buy a company at a six times multiple, and sell it at the same multiple, debt reduction alone produces a 17 per cent IRR. This assumes no company growth. The same company bought and sold at a 10 times multiple only gives you a 5 per cent IRR from debt reduction. This means a loss of 12 IRR points due only to higher purchase prices (see Exhibit 7).

Many LBO firms still console themselves with the notion that the solution to higher transaction multiples is to exit at an even larger multiple. Even though this does result in significantly better IRRs, our research shows that, over time, returns will still suffer. Exhibit 8 shows that as transaction prices continue to rise, even if you can 'sell smart' the IRR still drops. For instance, in Exhibit 8 we are comparing the same company purchased at five times and sold at seven times, with the purchase of that company at eight times and a subsequent

---

Exhibit 7

**The impact of purchase multiples on IRR (%)**

Rising purchase multiples will also cause average LBO IRRs to drop (exit multiple = purchase multiple)

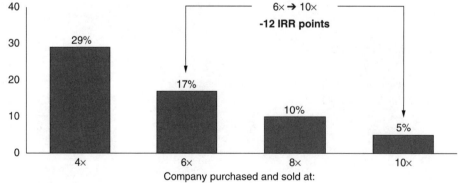

**Assumptions:**
- 75/25 debt-to-equity ratio
- 9% interest rate
- 0% revenue/margin growth

*Source:* Solera Capital, LLC.

---

266

Exhibit 8

**The impact of rising prices on IRR (%)**

As prices continue to rise, even if exit multiples are higher, IRRs will decline

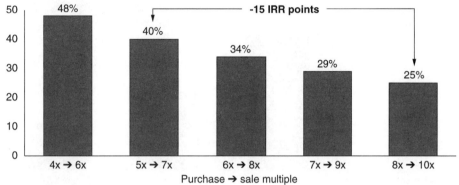

**Assumptions:**
- 75/25 debt-to-equity ratio
- 9% interest rate
- 0% revenue/margin growth

*Source:* Solera Capital, LLC.

exit at 10 times. At the higher purchase and sale combination the IRR is 15 points lower, even though the sale multiple still rose by two points.

The result of all this analysis is that, in recent years less and less of the return for the average LBO fund is coming from debt repayment. For example, in the following chart we cover typical LBO scenarios across Era 1 and Era 2. In Era 1, a company could be bought and sold at a six times multiple using the standard 90/10 debt-to-equity ratio. With this approach, the debt reduction engine could create a healthy 30 per cent IRR mainly due to the high leverage position. In the beginning of Era 2, the company is still bought and sold at a six times multiple, but instead uses the far less aggressive 75/25 debt-to-equity ratio. In this scenario, the debt reduction engine produces a lower return of approximately 17 per cent. Finally as the end of Era 2 approached, a company could be bought and sold at an eight times multiple (again using the 75/25 debt-to-equity ratio), but this time the return drops to 10 per cent IRR due to the increase in purchase and sale multiples (see Exhibit 9).

In addition, more return is beginning to come from other sources, such as multiple expansion (for Era 2/3) and earnings improvement (for Era 3). Exhibit 10 illustrates the impact on returns from these sources. The base case is the beginning scenario for Era 2 in the previous chart, where the company is bought and sold at a six times multiple using a 75/25 debt-to-equity ratio, and produces a 17 per cent IRR. This scenario does not account for top or bottom line growth, but illustrates the effect of debt on the math behind the IRRs. The second scenario shows the effect of multiple expansion on the model, displaying the trends of the mid-1990s when multiples rose for all transactions. Buying the company at six times and selling at eight times five years later produces a very healthy 34 per cent IRR, an increase of 17 percentage points.

Finally, by adding the effect of growth or earnings improvement, Exhibit 10 shows how LBO firms were able to maintain their returns during the second era without the leverage of the past. Adding a conservative 5 per cent growth rate for the company increases five-year IRR to 46 per cent, a further increment of 12 per cent for an LBO with these characteristics.

267

Exhibit 9

## The decline in debt repayment returns (%)

In recent years, less and less of the return is coming from debt pay down

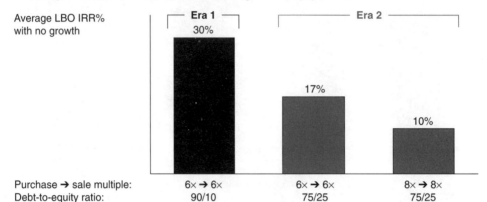

Average LBO IRR% with no growth

| Purchase → sale multiple: | 6× → 6× | 6× → 6× | 8× → 8× |
| Debt-to-equity ratio: | 90/10 | 75/25 | 75/25 |

Note: US$100 million sales, 15% EBITDA margin, no revenue growth, no margin growth, 9% interest rate, 32% tax rate, US$1 million annual capital expenditures, US$500 working capital.

*Source:* Solera Capital, LLC.

Exhibit 10

## How returns were generated during the second era, early to late 1990s (average LBO IRR%)

More return is coming from other sources, such as multiple expansion or earnings improvement

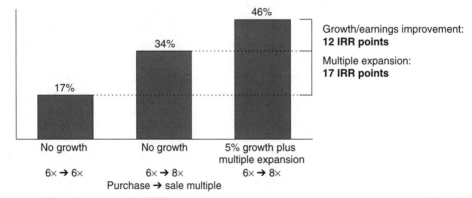

| No growth | No growth | 5% growth plus multiple expansion |
| 6× → 6× | 6× → 8× | 6× → 8× |

Purchase → sale multiple

Growth/earnings improvement: **12 IRR points**

Multiple expansion: **17 IRR points**

Note: US$100 million sales, 15% EBITDA margin, no margin growth, 9% interest rate, 32% tax rate, US$1 million annual capital expenditures, US$500 working capital.

*Source:* Solera Capital, LLC.

Exhibit 11, looks at the prospect for returns during the third era, the period in which we are now. As mentioned earlier, the main problem with an Era 3 LBO transaction is the potential for a levelling or decrease in transaction multiples, particularly in traditional low-tech industries. The exhibit reflects the fear of many investors by outlining scenarios for transactions in the current era. The first scenario is the base case for Era 3. It shows that a company bought and sold at eight times multiple using a 75/25 debt-to-equity ratio, will produce a fair-

Exhibit 11

**The importance of growth in the third era, late 1990s and onwards (average LBO IRR%)**

At today's prices a 1× multiple decline will wipe out returns...meaning significant EBITDA growth is required

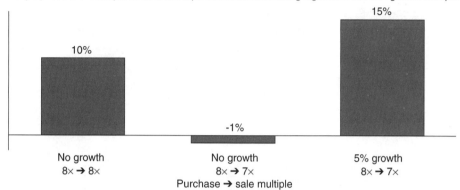

Note: US$100 million sales, 15% EBITDA margin, no margin growth, 9% interest rate, 32% tax rate, US$1,000 annual capex, US$500 working capital.

*Source:* Solera Capital, LLC.

ly unsatisfying 10 per cent five-year IRR without any growth. However, investor anxiety is mainly characterised by the middle scenario, where a company is bought at an eight times multiple using a 75/25 debt-to-equity ratio, but sold at a seven times multiple in the future. This scenario, predicted by many in our survey, generates a negative 1 per cent five-year IRR. Obviously, in this instance, growth of the business after purchase will be of critical importance, but, as Exhibit 11 shows, even with a 5 per cent annual growth, a drop of one multiple in the exit transaction will result in only a mediocre 15 per cent return.

These analyses indicate that the future returns will be less predictable, and less dependent on the traditional skills of LBO firms. Financial engineering in structuring the deal and due diligence in determining the correct price to pay for acquisitions will still be important, but it will be strategic business insights at the time of the investment and the operating decisions that increase revenues and profits that will separate the winners from the losers.

## What are the options for future success?

The following options present ways that firms could increase their IRRs from acquisitions. They also shed more light on our hypothesis that growth will be the most important tool for successful LBOs.

### Option 1: change interest rates

Several respondents to our survey noted that debt was becoming increasingly cheap, and that this would help to increase returns. Therefore, one option would be to count on lower interest rates for debt, or to negotiate for cheaper types of debt. What effect would this have on overall returns? Based on our original model, reducing the interest rate by 200 basis points (ie, from 9 per cent to 7 per cent), would generate a 2 percentage point difference in the five-year IRR for the investment. Surprisingly, the model is not very sensitive to interest rate changes.

## Option 2: change the capital structure

The second, intuitively appealing option would be to use one of a plethora of creative financial instruments available, allowing the firm to lower the percentage of equity in the transaction. How sensitive is the model to changes in the capital structure?

- Using the same model, increasing the debt-to-equity ratio to 80/20 from 75/25 would result in a five-year IRR increase of 3.5 percentage points.
- Similarly, decreasing the debt-to-equity ratio from 75/25 to 70/30 would cause a drop of 2.5 percentage points.

Again, the model proves itself not highly sensitive to important changes in a key variable.

## Option 3: change purchase or sale multiples

Another option often mentioned as being a key differentiator between firms was the ever present 'proprietary' deal flow. By leveraging contacts to develop 'first looks' at deals, and by avoiding auctions, many firms felt they would be able to 'buy cheaper' than the competition and therefore generate higher returns. Though the idea of a private flow of deals may be realistic in some cases, the changing industry dynamics outlined earlier in the chapter point to an increasingly open market for deals. If this is in fact the case, buying cheaper will become significantly more difficult.

Nevertheless, if you could generate ways to 'buy smarter', how sensitive is the model to changes in purchase and sale multiples? Buying one multiple cheaper – at seven times instead

Exhibit 12

**The impact of changes in key variables on IRRs (% change)**

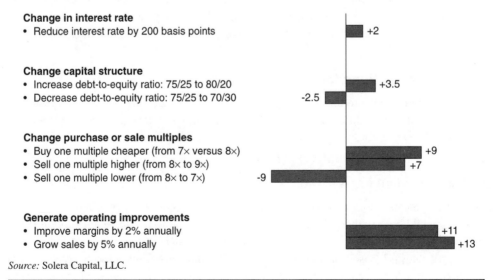

*Source:* Solera Capital, LLC.

of eight times – would generate a 9 percentage point increase in IRR. Selling at one multiple higher (at nine times instead of eight) would generate a 7 percentage point increase in IRR. Certainly these are attractive additional returns for any fund, but far too difficult to count on in the current environment.

Of more interest to most investors in today's LBO world is the very deleterious impact that a one multiple decrease in the sale price would have. As mentioned earlier, the change in IRR wrought by a decrease in sales multiple is significant, in this case selling one multiple lower (ie selling a seven times instead of eight times) causes a 9 percentage point deterioration in the five-year IRR (see Exhibit 12).

## Option 4: generate operating improvements

The most powerful impact on IRRs comes from improved sales or profit margins. For example, improving margins by 2 per cent annually (not two percentage points) generates an 11 point improvement in IRR. Similarly, 5 per cent revenue growth results in a 13 point increase in annual IRR. These are by far the levers with most impact on future LBO returns.

## Implications for LBO firms in the coming era

The levers for sustaining high IRRs growth in the current era have changed significantly from the early days of the industry. The firms that appear best-positioned for this era of LBOs are those that have two new areas of expertise:

- a tough-minded, research-based informed perspective on the industry and company before the investment is made; and

---

Exhibit 13

**Strategic imperatives: the levers for sustaining IRR growth have changed**

| Opportunities | Capabilities |
|---|---|
| **1. Increase topline revenue** | **1. Market expertise** |
| • Develop new markets<br>• Penetrate existing markets | • Know your customers<br>• Know your competitors |
| **2. Increase earnings** | **2. Understand where you make your money** |
| • Focus on profitable customers and products<br>• Move quickly to institute cost improvements | • Organise by profit centre<br>• Have change management expertise |
| **3. Acquire new revenue** | **3. Maximise use of financial instruments and markets** |
| • Use company as a platform for add-on acquisitions<br>• Take out competitor in key markets | • Use increased size for multiple arbitrage and/or access to lower cost financing |

**What does this mean for the organisation and focus of LBO firms in the coming era?**

*Source:* Solera Capital, LLC.

---

271

- a hands-on operating and strategic involvement with the portfolio company, focusing on attaining the necessary revenue and profit growth.

Early expertise in industries and market niches is increasingly important as competition for deals increases. To respond quickly and to pay the prices necessary to win, an LBO firm needs to go into the process with a point of view on the growth potential and competitive dynamics of the business. This is leading firms to some interesting new alliances, such as with strategic consulting firms, with networks of industry experts and with venture capital firms. Others are developing areas of expertise in house and are positioning themselves in the target industry segment to attract early deal flow.

Once the investment is made, the hands-on work begins. In contrast to early eras, the successful buyout firms will help their portfolio companies increase revenues and profits.

## Increase topline revenue

The most obvious lever for increasing the profitability of the portfolio company is to generate new revenues. Increasing sales can come from two main routes:

- deeper penetration of existing markets and/or customers; or
- the development of new markets and/or customers.

Traditionally, the key capabilities required to implement these strategies have been expertise in market segmentation and development, and insight into customers and competitors. These days, expertise in electronic business can provide important incremental revenue opportunities.

## Increase earnings

The next lever for increasing company value is increasing earnings within existing sales, thereby creating a profitable plan for future growth. This is an area where most LBO firms are fairly comfortable, in that the ability to manage an income statement was a key tool for success in the first era. Firms going down this route have to be able to:

- focus resources on the most profitable customers and products; and
- institute cost-reduction initiatives quickly.

To do this, managers and investors must understand where the portfolio company makes its money. This suggests a focus on clearly defining profitable product lines, customers and geographical markets. Once these have been identified, expertise in change-management and project implementation are required to optimise the savings gained from the analysis.

## Acquire new revenues

The final lever for success in the current era is the acquisition of new revenues. This approach is most popular in highly fragmented industries where a roll-up strategy can be used to consolidate the industry. However, an additional advantage of revenue acquisition could be the elimination of key competitors or the opening up of a hitherto unavailable market segment. This strategy would also allow LBO investors to use the increased size or market positioning of the portfolio company to generate higher exit multiples or cheaper financing.

## Conclusion

Are we predicting that the firms of the past will no longer be successful? No. Are we saying that they will need to revamp their skill sets? Probably. The implication, in our view, is that the best way to adapt to the new environment for LBOs will be to develop the required strategic insights and operating expertise to generate growth.

---

[1] The author wishes to thank Iain Michel of the Lucas Group for his contributions to this article.

Part VI

# Investor perspectives

Chapter 22

# The rationale for private investments from an institutional perspective

Betty M. Sheets[1]
*Senior Investment Manager, Private Investments, I.B.M. Retirement Fund*

## Introduction

Private investment is perhaps the oldest asset class, but in recent years it has become one of the hottest investment phenomena. If the ability to raise money quickly and easily signals a hot market, then private equity sizzles. What is this phenomenon and why has it attracted so much attention?

In modern parlance, the term private investment covers a broad range of approaches, from venture capital, growth and expansion financing, to mezzanine debt, to leveraged buy-outs and industry funds, through distressed debt and turnaround investing. Other approaches sometimes included in the term are investing in various physical assets, such as timber, farmland, or oil and gas reserves, and some approaches to real estate. Certain event-driven styles of investing such as risk arbitrage, 'Reg D' hedge funds or other specialised opportunities arising in traded markets are less frequently included, and these latter approaches are not the focus of this chapter.

Although diverse, these forms of private investing do share common characteristics. They entail equity-like risks and promise equity-like returns. They are generally carried out through commingled vehicles like limited partnerships instead of separate accounts. These partnerships are private securities – not registered with securities authorities and not traded on securities exchanges – as are the investments made by the partnerships themselves. And they are inherently long-term investments, with limited and expensive liquidity prior to maturity.

Private investing also involves active investment styles – not active in the sense of public equity managers choosing which stocks to buy or sell, but active in the fundamental corporate processes and management of investee companies. Their objectives are usually stated in terms of absolute returns, not returns relative to a market index. And finally, they are expensive strategies to pursue, with fees that include both ongoing management fees equal to or greater than those of active equity managers, plus a substantial portion of profits.

Even a quick look at statistics compiled by Asset Alternatives Inc.[2] indicates just how large the recent surge in popularity of private investing has been. After struggling for five years to top the US$15 billion peak set in 1989, annual commitments to all types of US private equity partnerships rose steadily, taking a big step up to US$56 billion in 1997, and then surging past even that high-water mark with over US$85 billion raised in 1998. Preliminary results for 1999 indicate yet another record year, perhaps even topping US$100 billion. Since commitments made in any year are available for investing over the next five or six years, the increase in 'dry powder' has been even sharper. The overwhelming bulk of the money comes from institutions. Although recent data are unavailable, Asset Alternatives found that in 1995 financial institutions accounted for 80 per cent of the fund commitments, and public and corporate pensions together represented half the total. Perhaps the surge of the past two years should not have been a surprise, because the 1997 Goldman Sachs–Frank Russell[3] survey of private investing by large, North American, tax-exempt organisations showed that they did intend to increase commitments: allocations to private investments increased from 6.2 per cent of assets in 1995 to 7.6 per cent in 1997, a 23 per cent increase. The absolute dollar increase is even larger as total assets also increased – private equity has become a bigger slice of a bigger pie. The 1999 follow-up Goldman-Russell survey reports that these institutions plan a further increase in allocation to 8 per cent.

## Of risks and returns

Various reasons for the increase in private investing are cited: diversification, low correlation with public market returns, hedging inflation in the case of physical assets such as timber, oil and gas reserves, or farm land, and generating ancillary business for banks and insurance companies. But the strongest reason is the belief that private investing can generate excess risk-adjusted returns relative to public market alternatives, even net of the higher costs. In the Goldman Sachs–Russell study, 75 per cent of respondents cited outperforming traditional investments as their key reason for making private investments. Pension funds and other institutional investors such as endowments and foundations have long time horizons. With most of their assets in liquid securities, they can afford to trade liquidity for higher returns in a portion of their portfolios.

However, substantiating the belief that private investing will meet that objective is more difficult than the rush of dollars into the asset class would indicate. Each part of the phrase 'excess risk-adjusted returns' is problematic. 'Returns' are difficult to measure, 'risk' is an undefined concept, and 'excess' implies beating an alternative.

Unlike public securities, the returns and risks of which can be measured, reported, analysed and compared on a quarterly basis, or daily if you prefer, private market returns in the short term (where 'short term' can stretch to three to five years) are not meaningful. Nor are private equity returns readily comparable between managers, or for that matter, even available. They are not even measured in the same way as public returns. Time-weighted returns are appropriate for managers of public securities, because cash flows in and out of the account are not controlled by the manager. Dollar-weighted measures (internal rates of return and returns on investment) are suitable for general partners of private funds who most definitely do control the timing of cash flows. Finally, the difference in the returns earned by top and bottom quartile private investment managers is probably far wider than among public managers, so that 'just being there' in the asset class may not suffice to capture the anticipated benefit. And in private investing, access to top general partners is episodic and limited. Investors can make allocations to a particular manager only when that manager is offering a fund, and are subject to the fund's size limit.

While the concept of private investment returns exists – and returns can eventually be measured – the concept of risk in private market investing is undeveloped. Since final returns are not known until termination of the partnership, usually between years 10 and 12, use of interim valuations is unavoidable. Most interim valuations are either reported at cost or generated by the fund manager itself. Either does fatal damage to a concept of risk borrowed from public markets based on price volatility and correlation with market indices. Some institutions have developed their own conception of risk in private investing, but as yet there is no generally accepted definition nor any standard risk measurement.

278

If measuring return and risk is the first step in determining whether results are attractive, then comparing them to 'benchmarks' is the second. Benchmarks for public asset classes usually measure passive investment alternatives – ie, results in an asset class as a whole which could be duplicated, net of minor transaction costs, by indexing. Such benchmarks have two functions. They indicate the contribution an asset class makes to the performance of a policy-weighted portfolio – ie, are the risks and returns of the asset class attractive in the entire portfolio? But they also measure the contribution specific active managers make to asset class returns – ie, does this manager contribute anything in excess of the asset class return? Both questions are useful for decisions an institution can make about asset deployment, to either a class or a manager.

However, indexing, or passive management, is not an option for private investing. In private investing, no measure of asset class returns independent of manager performance exists. And the range of actions that could be taken in response to comparisons of actual to benchmark results is quite limited, at least in the time frames normal for investment decisions.

Thus private investment benchmarks are somewhat artificial. Typical benchmarks might be a flat absolute number, maybe 15 per cent, or a spread over some measure of portfolio returns, perhaps 400 basis points over the actuarially assumed returns. The premise is that the alternative to making private investments is to redeploy the assets into either the entire portfolio or some portion of it, typically equities. Such benchmarks are often viewed as floors on expected returns rather than as targets. Used this way, benchmarks only address the first question: is the asset class allocation contributing 'excess' returns to the entire portfolio? They are not much help in determining how a given manager (or private investment portfolio) is doing relative to the asset class as a whole.

With these caveats in mind, consider the following private investment returns compiled by Cambridge Associates[4] for US venture capital, US private equity, and European private equity funds, formed between 1981 and 1997. The data are pooled time-weighted returns net to limited partners as of 30 September 1998. A thorough comparison of private and public markets returns is considerably beyond the scope of this chapter. However, despite all the measurement problems inherent in these numbers, comparing them with public benchmark returns

## Exhibit 1

### Time-weighted returns net to limited partners as of 30 September 1998 (%)

|  | 1 year | 3 years | 5 years | 10 years |
|---|---|---|---|---|
| US venture | 13.9 | 35.4 | 31.9 | 21.4 |
| Russell 2000 | −19.0 | 6.9 | 9.1 | 11.1 |
| US private equity | 18.4 | 24.0 | 20.5 | 16.1 |
| S&P 500 | 9.1 | 22.6 | 19.9 | 17.3 |
| UK private equity | 63.5 | 42.8 | 40.1 | 18.1 |
| Continental Europe private equity[a] | 37.5 | 21.9 | 21.6 | 13.9 |
| MSCI Europe | 8.3 | 18.8 | 17.2 | 14.5 |

[a] Excluding United Kingdom.

*Note:* Based on data compiled from US venture capital, US private equity, and European private equity funds, including fully liquidated partnerships, formed between 1981 and 1997. Pooled time-weighted returns, net of fees, expenses and carried interest.

*Source:* Cambridge Associates.

over the same period is instructive. Generally, they show attractive results, especially in venture capital (which is probably the sector whose returns are most volatile and vulnerable to large inflows of capital). The returns of US private equity, the largest sector, are attractive but not hands-down winners over the S&P index, even before considering risks and illiquidity.

## How the process works

Measurement difficulties are not incidental to private investment, but arise from its essential nature. An institutional private investment programme has three layers: the investments the partnerships make in specific portfolio companies, the commitments the institution makes to specific partnerships, and the resulting aggregation of partnerships. Since the first layer, portfolio company investment, has a multiyear life cycle, the partnership layer, which consists of a series of portfolio company investments made over several years, is inherently longer. The programme level cycle frequently exceeds the tenure of either the staff implementing the programme or the fiduciary boards setting asset allocation policy.

At the partnership level the process starts with general partners seeking commitments from institutions willing to become its limited partners. That process may be instantaneous, in the extreme case of certain successful venture capitalists who basically allocate a scarce and highly desirable resource – entree to their funds – among their coterie of prior investors and a few select others. More typically, it takes a year or more for general partners who are either less successful or less well known or whose fund raising goals exceeds the appetites of prior investors. For all but the most successful venture capitalists, some amount of haggling over partnership terms will slow the advance of even the most prominent general partners in closing their funds.

Once the fund is closed, the process of building the portfolio begins, with sourcing, negotiating, and making portfolio company investments. The initial investment is followed by a period of ownership during which, hopefully, the general partner implements a strategy to create value, culminating in an exit from the investment at exceptional returns. In the classic formulation, portfolio companies are held at cost if there are no third-party transactions validating a higher price, such as an initial public offering. However, practices vary. At one extreme, general partners have even held at cost portfolio companies trading publicly at large profits. Others mark up still private companies based on discounts to comparable public or private valuations. Still others value companies recently gone public at full market price, although the public float may be limited, the stock volatile, and the partnership's shares restricted. These differing valuation policies make it difficult to compare interim results between partnerships based on reported financials.

At the institutional level, the slow ramp-up of each partnership's assets repeats for each year's partnership commitments, because private investment programmes must be built over several years. Thus the emerging results of partnership commitments made in the early years can be overwhelmed by the weight of more recent, immature commitments. Remember that these partnerships typically charge management fees on total commitments, not on invested assets during the five-year active investment period. The 'J-curve' phenomenon (ie, negative partnership returns in early years due to the drag of management fees against low levels of assets held at cost) and the delayed measurement of results is exacerbated at the institutional level as the programme builds annual layers of fund commitments. (Thus the quickest way to increase annual returns in a private investment programme is simply to stop making new commitments.)

280

As a result, private investment programme returns measured and compared to other asset class returns on a time-weighted, quarterly or annual basis are meaningless until the programme reaches some degree of maturity, and even then are fundamentally different in nature. In addition, due to the long time lags, the measured returns may not be the result of the current staff's decisions.

## Why the process works

Given the difficulty of 'proving' the proposition that private investing produces higher risk-adjusted returns, why should an investor expect, or hope, that it can deliver incremental value? Several plausible reasons for optimism do exist.

First, private investing can access a broader range of opportunities than publicly traded markets offer. Even in the United States or the United Kingdom, where the ratios of stock market capitalisation to GNP are among the highest in the world, the overwhelming majority of companies are private. Naturally, many of these, such as the dry cleaner in the High Street, are not suitable for institutional investing, but a surprisingly large percentage of total corporate sales or of the capitalisation of the largest businesses is represented by private companies. Outside the United States and the United Kingdom, the market share of private companies is even greater, and the divergence between the industry profile of the overall economy and of stocks available in the public markets can be large.

Second, private investing can occur in all phases of the corporate life cycle, and especially in those phases that public markets do not readily accommodate. Venture capital is an obvious example. The entrepreneur with only an idea or a plan usually cannot access public markets (the current Internet mania notwithstanding). Companies executing strategic plans that penalise short-term earnings for the sake of greater long-term profitability may also find public markets unaccommodating. Even a mature company might benefit from a capital structure that public markets would consider over-leveraged. Finally, public markets are ill suited for the final phase of Schumpeterian 'creative destruction' when companies desperately need restructuring or liquidation. Enticing new investors into companies in these phases may require far more information and influence than public securities offer.

Third, private investors can target inefficient market segments, where better information can generate a buying advantage. The explosion of pension and institutional assets looking for attractive investments over the past several decades has shifted large portions of public companies' ownership from individual investors to large, professionally managed institutions. These institutions have resources to devote to the search for higher returns, and their need for information has stimulated a further explosion of financial organisations dedicated to serving their needs. The often noted effect is that markets for large corporate securities have become increasingly efficient. However, private investors can range beyond the limits of efficient public markets. Private companies generally trade at discounts to similar public companies. Investment banks do strive to emulate the efficiency of public markets when selling private companies or divisions. Yet the private sale process still offers more opportunity for extensive, direct due diligence and discussions with management about the company, its business and prospects. It also offers the opportunity to negotiate terms with the seller, which can lead to better values for both sides of the transaction.

Finally, and most importantly, the private investment process itself can add value in several ways. Public markets are extremely good at mobilising the investment capital of the economy for managers of corporate assets while preserving liquidity for owners. But the magic has been achieved by fragmenting and dispersing ownership until the interests of owners and managers are not necessarily aligned, the time frames of corporate strategies and capital market evaluation no longer coincide, and avenues for constructive involvement by owners are limited. At its best, private investment aligns the interests of owners and managers, facilitates long-term corporate strategies, and allows owners to influence corporate behaviour to increase value.

Private investment has the potential to 'add value' because private investors generally own at least a significant minority stake but usually a controlling position. At a minimum, they have a seat on the board of directors, but typically they dominate the board and the important committees. Often they select management and direct or approve important corporate policies, such as strategy, budgets and planning, capital structure, acquisitions and divestitures, and capital expenditures. Since they have made similar investments before, they have relevant experience in matters of board governance, especially in capital markets and financing issues. In addition, they may have particular expertise in the company's industry and a wide range of contacts among potential customers, suppliers or management candidates. Sheltered from the short-term dictates of public markets, private investors can focus on the true driver of economic value, cash flow, rather than reported earnings.

The typical private equity investor ensures that management's interests are genuinely aligned with those of investors through direct equity ownership. In addition to grants of performance-based options, top management is generally required to invest significant amounts of their own resources in the company. Typically performance options will extend further down the corporate hierarchy than before the private investor took control. Compensation throughout the organisation may be revamped to reward achievement of value-enhancing goals, such as reducing debt from cash generated by tighter working capital management. When management's potential gains on stock far exceed the value of salaries and 'perks', behaviour changes.

In achieving the high returns investors expect, capital structure plays an important role. Debt is cheaper than equity, of course, and a leveraged capital structure will increase equity returns, if the basic results are positive. But perhaps more fundamental is the role of debt as a disciplinarian in implementation of the investment thesis. The relentless pressure of debt maturities and bank covenants forces careful attention to the initial investment plan, to the timing and scale of improvements to be generated, and to the prompt achievement of those commitments. Such discipline would probably not be acceptable if management did not expect to share in the upside. As John Childs, a veteran private equity investor, recently remarked, common equity ownership is what makes 'these things with their horrible balance sheets work out'.

When the time comes to exit an investment, private investors again have a far greater range of options and degree of influence on the process. Investors in public stocks can choose when to sell and only at the market price. Private investors can choose the avenue of exit, whether through public market sales or through sale to strategic or financial buyers, and by their actions and strategies can substantially influence the outcome and value achieved. Private investors can even sell to themselves via a leveraged recapitalisation and start the value creation and debt reduction process over again, after recouping their prior investment with an adequate return.

## Will the process work?

Not surprisingly, the experience gained in enhancing returns between private investors and portfolio companies is reflected in the relationship between limited partners and general partners in these partnerships. The general partner's ability to create or add value and the commitment to an adequate time frame to allow development of strategies that add value are essential in private investing. But most fundamentally, the economic interests of general partners and limited partners should be aligned. In the classic formulation, that alignment was achieved by having the general partner risk money in the partnership and by deferring significant upside for the general partner until delivery of returns to limited partners. The ongoing management fee was designed to provide sufficient resources to implement the strategy but not to generate profit. The standard split of investment profits is 80/20 between limited and general partners, with or without a preferred return to limited partners. Experience, sometimes hard, has led to innumerable refinements of the formula, but the goal is 'heads, we both win; tails, we both lose'.

However, a division of economics appropriate for US$100 million venture funds whose increased value came from the individual expertise of the general partners – their understanding of technology, their personal contacts, their credibility with entrepreneurs – has now been adopted by a completely different scale and type of fund. As economic incentives change, so may behaviours. Management fee levels established when funds were small – typically 1.5–2 per cent of committed capital – applied to multibillion dollar funds generate substantial income for sponsors, regardless of the success of the portfolio investments. Annual management fees can reach US$50 million or more to support organisations of a few dozen people. In addition, some sponsors also charge other fees, such as management fees to portfolio companies or transaction closing fees, which generate additional income and may incline them to act other than in the best interest of limited partners. Participants in the huge move into real estate in the 1980s through structures that gave incentives to managers to be asset gatherers rather than profit maximisers may recognise the dangers.

However, the profit from excess management fees is dwarfed by the potential windfall from the 20 per cent carry on 'mega' funds. A US$3 billion fund that realised twice its commitments would generate US$600 million in carry distributions to the general partners, although the return to limited partners may or may not be attractive, depending on the time investments were outstanding and competing returns. The absolute dollar size of the carry earned by the sponsor from even marginal returns drives a wedge between the interests of general partners composed of relatively few individuals and limited partners, who must be concerned with bettering competing rates of return. In most funds, an annual 10 per cent incremental return on US$1 billion of assets generates US$20 million for the general partner and a net 8 per cent return to limited partners.

In today's robust market, general partners are strongly motivated to maximise results for limited partners by the hope of raising an even bigger fund. (And limited partners derive negotiating leverage and influence from their continued presence in the market for new funds.) If that inducement were to disappear, the general partner's economic incentives could change. Maximising their cash flow from existing portfolios could matter more. So far, performance in the larger fund sector has been strong enough that few funds have faced the possible demise of their sponsor organisations. Venture partnerships have been around long enough that some funds have faced this situation and its troublesome implications, but they were so small that the problem has not been significant.

Another emerging trend is for sponsors to raise multiple funds either pursuing different strategies or operating in different geographic areas. The premise is that either the investment discipline is transferable to new areas or that synergies such as information flows exist between the different areas. Some organisations have made such structures work, others will be tested over time. One consequence of these developments is that the success and longevity of the sponsor is divorced from the results of any particular partnership. Such a divide undercuts one of the most fundamental drivers of value creation in this asset class – the alignment of interest between investors and investment managers.

## Parting thoughts

Now we have come full circle, to the phenomenal recent success of private investing, at least in fund raising. Some caveats are in order. Successful investment opportunities create demand, and demand creates its own supply. Demand for private investment partnerships has created a plethora of general partners eager to supply them. Part of the surge in commitments has gone to established general partners. 'Follow-on' funds are frequently two or three times the size of their predecessors, and yet are not able to accommodate all interested investors. Part of it has gone to successor general partners, as successful sponsors have split into two or more new partnerships. Part has gone to 'second generation' general partners, as talented junior partners have left well-known firms to set up their own operation. Other funds have been raised by sponsors new to private investment or implementing new strategies, or both.

Has the ramp-up in fund raising simply outpaced the maturation rate of investment organisations and strategies? While the industry has undoubtedly grown and deepened over the past decade and a half (since the pioneering large pools of institutional capital were raised), time will tell whether, at its present maturity, it is adequate to deploy this avalanche of capital at adequate rates of return. Most of today's individual practitioners are experienced in private investing – albeit in the generally benign capital markets of recent years – but some investment teams and strategies have not been tested through the full cycle to cash returns to limited partners. In addition, the quickened pace of fund raising forces the evaluation of general partners on increasingly preliminary results. Successor funds are being raised before the prior portfolio has been harvested (or in some cases even fully invested). In this asset class, lemons ripen late. In such an environment, ranking general partners by performance is obviously difficult. Before performance quartiles can be determined, the next 10-year fund has already been committed.

On the other hand, perhaps the surge in fund raising is not as meaningful as the absolute increase in dollars implies. Economies have grown, stock market capitalisations have increased, and available leverage is lower compared to a decade ago. While the lower leverage ratios available today mean that today's seemingly record levels of private equity commitments have less purchasing power than in previous years, the numerical consequence of lower leverage is also that equity returns must fall.

While data on the sources of the recent surge in funding is not yet available, some of it may come from inexperienced investors rushing to fill recent uncommitted allocations. The recent broadening of the investor base also means some partnerships lack a core of sizable and experienced investors able to influence the partnership's terms and conditions during the negotiation phase or its direction later if difficulties arise. New investors in this asset class may not appreciate how decidedly one-sided these limited partnership agreements are. They can be summarised as: general partners have the right to demand money and limited partners have the obligation to provide it. Any investor considering entering this asset class should read through one of these documents and contemplate the following scenarios: four years from now, when the dollar commitment is fully invested, the limited partners discover that the general partner is incompetent, dishonest, or unsuccessful (as in, will never raise another fund), has lost its talented staff, or is being sued by the investors or its former partners.

In summary, institutions invest privately to achieve returns in excess of those available in liquid markets, since generally they have adequate resources to forego intermediate-term liquidity. Despite measurement and conceptual problems in determining adequate risk-adjusted returns for private investments, experience and anecdotal evidence appear to support the expectation of superior returns. Theoretically, private investors have more avenues to create and to realise value in portfolio companies than are available to public market investors. However, the scale of commitments in this area now dwarfs the size base on which those attractive, preliminary returns were earned, and the speed of the explosion may surpass the rate at which existing investment organisations can expand their capabilities or spawn successful imitators. Finally, the scale of assets deployed has also weakened one of private investing's fundamental success factors, the alignment of interest between investor and investment manager that makes the fortunes of general partners depend on delivering superior returns to limited partners.

---

[1] The author would like to thank Stephen Can, Steven W. Goldmark, Robert F. Ploder and George D. Smith for their helpful comments.

[2] *The Private Equity Analyst*, Volume IX, Issue 1, January 1999.

[3] 'Report on Alternative Investing by Tax-Exempt Organisations', Goldman, Sachs & Co. and Frank Russell Capital Inc., December 1997.

[4] *The Private Equity Analyst*, June 1999.

Chapter 23

# Down and dirty due diligence

Steve Brockman
*Great Lakes Consulting Group, Inc.*

## My gig in a nutshell

After the pitchmen give their spiel in the executive suite and my clients are salivating over another ground-floor Microsoft-like opportunity, I go to work. I don't carry a badge, a gun, a cell phone, or a financial calculator. I holster an unhealthy dose of cynicism. My only stage prop is feigned stupidity.

I treat everything as a hair-brained scheme that must be proven otherwise. I trust no one to be honest or competent. Credentials mean nothing. Convictions mean nothing. Facts? What facts? Faulty misguided assumptions masquerade as facts.

Still interested in why I feel that way and why anyone would want to invite me to rain on their parade? Here's a typical assignment.

## The case of the not-ready-for-prime-time players

### Act I: The passion of opportunity

My client was the president of a store fixtures manufacturing company, serving very large retail chains. He has a tough business, with his customers clearly in a position of power over him. He engaged my firm to evaluate an investment in a company which invented a new sophisticated machine to increase store productivity of a certain retail segment – *if it worked*.

There are two other actors in this real-life drama: The first is Mr. Trusted Advisor, a retired operations and marketing executive from the retail segment which the new invention would service. Mr. Advisor's insights and input over the past years had proven extraordinarily valuable to the president. From my own investigation, his name carried considerable recognition and clout in the executive suites of major retail firms.

Mr. Advisor had recently joined the board of Acme Inventors, a small engineering firm which developed the machine. Thanks to his close ties, Mr. Advisor had been instrumental in assembling a number of executives from the retail sector to view a demonstration of an early prototype. They were enormously impressed and eager to install this exciting innovation as soon as it became available.

Enter our next character, Mr. Pocket Protector, the highly motivated, dictatorial and paranoid leader of Acme Inventors. It seems he had staked most everything he had into his invention over the past year or two of development.

Pocket Protector was prone to temper tantrums that kept everyone on edge and didn't do a lot to promote open communication with his staff. There were two versions of tantrums. The easiest to tolerate was the *Mount St. Helens eruption*. The *corked volcano tantrum* was much more unnerving and manifested by grimacing, long pauses, and slow speech as he tried desperately to keep the lid on his rage. I'm sure everyone wished he would just blow and get it over with. I, however, was not fazed by either version. Let the games begin.

An engineer by training and interest, the inventor recognised his weakness in marketing and industry contacts. After an introduction to Mr. Advisor, the two painstakingly worked out an agreement. Nevertheless, Mr. Advisor admitted that their relationship was a continuously tenuous one. Mr. Pocket Protector hated to cede authority or defer to anyone else's expertise.

As I was brought in, the company was running out of money. Acme claimed that the product design was complete and the customers were lining up at their door. With an infusion of working capital, they could set up manufacturing and begin to fill orders. Each of the players – president, advisor and inventor, in addition to the retail executives – was highly emotional about this opportunity. The president in particular relished not only the notion of a significant financial return, but also being in a position of power over his customers, at whose hands he had suffered considerable bashing in the past. He would be in control for the first time, dealing with high-level executives and yanking their chain for change.

As we close Act I, I suggest that the president was lucky to have this investment opportunity cross his path and smart enough to recognise it. Fortunately, the president was also circumspect enough to realise that he had crossed the Rubicon of objectivity. Sometimes the will to believe becomes belief itself. And in this unsettled emotional environment, he made the wise decision to hire an unemotional, sceptical, cross-check-every-assertion, dour sort of person like me.

## Act II: Demos for Dummies

Mr. Trusted Advisor explained the importance of the device performing flawlessly on rollout. The industry had been had before with overhyped technology, and if this invention stumbled, it might never get a real chance again. In addition, he was understandably concerned about his own reputation and credibility, sticking his neck out by calling his contacts and presenting the product with his stamp of approval. Mr. Advisor had other projects up his sleeve, and if Acme's device underperformed, it would reflect poorly on those projects' future.

It seemed to me that while Mr. Advisor was too honest to hide some of his concerns (through body language as well as words), he was also too excited and too intimidated by Mr. Pocket Protector to face those qualms head on. He was happy to have me involved and anxious for reassurance that he would not regret his involvement with Acme. This was not a reassuring sign for me.

I visited the Acme facility, met with the staff, and saw a demonstration of the prototype. It worked pretty well. But in another lifetime, I, too, had given an orchestrated demo to a prospect...

I had Acme rig up one of their units in the lab area, and I put it through several trial runs of what it might encounter in the real world. It failed several of my impromptu tests. Clearly the product needed further design cycles and testing before it would make sense to order tooling and set up manufacturing. Mr. Pocket Protector, however, would have none of it. While he could not deny the unit's flaws, made obvious by its performance before of us, he steamed that he knew what engineering was still needed and that it would be taken care of. There would be no delays in displaying a market-ready unit at an upcoming trade show! (This show was supremely important to his ego. People who had slighted his efforts and wronged him in the past would be present, and his need to impress them with his invention was obvious.)

To prove his case, he began to outline an impromptu plan to correct the problems I discovered. Trouble was, he couldn't do the math 5 steps ahead so he ended up with a plan to meet his self-imposed deadline requiring more man hours than he had men. When this became obvious to the two of us, he would not acknowledge it. He still maintained it was do-able. He said he was used to working hard.

In addition to product failing, I encountered one of the most difficult entrepreneurs to deal with. He could not be questioned, set or meet reasonable deadlines, or take advice (let alone criticism). He was secretive, not just to a potential investor under non-disclosure but also with his own key employees and board members (many were family). Other than that, he was a great candidate for a partner who presented a great investment you could manage from your recliner at home.

Mr. Trusted Advisor was embarrassed by both the unit's poor performance and Mr. Pocket Protector's behaviour. This was a wake-up call and reality check for him. I inquired as to whether any of the retail executives who had witnessed a demo had examined the unit like I had. 'No', he said. Were there no operations people among them? There were, he asserted. Then why had they not put the unit through more rigorous testing? They must have assumed that he – Mr. Trusted Advisor, himself – had done so. I suspect that all were boondoggled by the same orchestrated demo.

## Epilogue

Mr. Inventor eventually found an investor who did not test the machine. A prototype was constructed and displayed at the trade show, brandishing a brilliantly orchestrated demo. In subsequent testing, the device failed after the equivalent of four months' usage. The inventor is still at work and may yet succeed before he runs out of money and capable staff who will put up with his behaviour. Stranger things have happened.

## Lessons

Never be so intimidated by someone's credentials and convictions that you fail to verify their claims. Respect everyone; be intimidated by no one.

I don't care how successful someone has been or how many articles they published or where they obtained their PhD. Assuming an entrepreneur's beliefs and track record are genuine, he still can make a mistake, get careless, get over his head, or have poor subordinates who don't perform (unbeknownst to him).

### Auto-by-tell-me-a-lie

An auto enthusiast, James Carrnutt, was ready to invest in a new invention – a simple hydraulic actuated system to replace rocker arms and push rods on an internal combustion engine. The benefits were claimed to be better valve timing and range of valve opening and closing patterns resulting in lower emissions, better gas mileage, and more horsepower. The inventor was a race car engine builder with a credible reference. The investor was very excited and ready to fund further testing of the device to prove its utility.

Mr. Carrnutt was entranced not only with the financial potential but also with lapping his competitors during his weekend racing avocation. He was too excited for his own good in more ways than one.

It seemed unlikely that a one man shop can invent something so revolutionary given the internal combustion engine has 100 years and billions of dollars of development behind it. But the upside was too big to ignore and worthy of a low cost reality check.

My client told me Kopikatz engaged him in frequent hour long telephone calls, where the hardy inventor would wax eloquently on the seemingly limitless financial reward for the investor with enough guts to take a swing. Kopikatz also talked about other potential investors and claimed to visit one group while we were in the middle of our own review. He had Mr. Carrnutt climbing the walls with anticipation.

Two weeks of arduous negotiations with the inventor, Dan Kopikatz, transpired to set the conditions for a demonstration and explanation of the device. While the demo was hardly a rigorously controlled test – there was no diagnostic equipment involved – I was somewhat encouraged to continue the evaluation. There was a device, several interesting version in fact. Its principles of operation made sense to me, though more rigorous analysis would be required. I had never seen a *seemingly unmodified* 350 Chevy engine respond and sound as this one did with the invention installed.

The key question in any new technology model is: 'Does it really work?' I did not know and it would take lots of funds to really find out. If it did work, would it be too costly to produce? Was it reliable? Would it only be viable as a modification for auto enthusiasts? Would it be useful on a modern engine and not just benefit an 'ancient' 1970's 350 V8? Would our client have the funds for us to answer all these questions? Some yellow and red flags surfaced on the way to the finish line.

Kopikatz told our client to send someone knowledgeable about automotive engines. He characterised himself as 'a valve event guy' and wanted someone with similar detailed expertise. Feeling intimidated, I brought along a few books on engine design and theory to review on the long plane ride. Curiously, I did not see a single such book in Kopikatz's home or workshop. *Hmmmmm*?

I learned enough on the plane to understand what an engine valve timing curve was – it relates the cycle of piston movements with other mechanical cycles and combustion events. Kopikatz struggled with the concept when I sat down with him to sketch one to help illustrate the difference between his invention and traditional systems? *Hmmmmm*?

Kopikatz said he submitted a patent. I was disappointed to find he had done it himself rather than use a patent attorney. It weirdly began like a will: 'I, Dan Kopikatz, being of sound mind and body, do hereby state, that I have invented....' *Hmmmmm*?

Before I involve a patent attorney I see what I can come up with myself. Based on the most vague description, I scanned patents before my visit and no red flags popped up. But it wasn't until after seeing the device that I understood enough to do a better search. Then, I located several extremely similar sounding devices. After obtaining the complete patents on paper with drawings, there it was, staring me in the face: a patent drawing that looked exactly, and I mean identical, to what our back-woods inventor showed us. The patent (there were several similar ones actually) was also old enough to make you wonder why the device was not already in production if it worked so well.

I wrote the inventor a brief note and asked for his opinion on how his device compared to the (identical) patented device. I also called to get his opinion. He never returned phone calls or letters. My client never broke out of the pack on race weekends but at least I saved him enough money to let him keep trying.

## Lessons

Make sure you're dealing with the original back-woods inventor and not a Kopikatz.

## The case of the in-sourcer

I was taking a plant tour led by the president of Standard Medical Device Company, an established, well-run, profitable firm up for sale. The president took us into a large room to show us the processing of one component of their medical device. He touted the company's cleverness and the savings to be made in taking the process away from their supplier and bringing it in-house.

The process seemed pretty labour-intensive to me. Was it so inefficiently run by their supplier that Standard was better off making the component themselves? Was Standard's labour rate that much lower than the supplier's? What else could explain how Standard benefited by doing it in house?

In another incarnation, I had to cut prices to the bone for one large customer who made a convincing case that he would be better off without me. If I hadn't, my business might have been ruined. Minimally, I needed his volume to make money on the rest of my customers. With this in mind, I asked the president of Standard if he really saved that much. Hadn't the supplier, once he understood that threats to make the product in house were real, cut the price to keep the business? How much did Standard really save after the supplier came back with a better price?

The president responded that the supplier was one unit of a big conglomerate. There was too much bureaucracy at the corporate level for them to cut a special deal for Standard. Me thinks, 'Huh?'. I asked the name of the company. It was AAA Sourcing, a unit of AAA Conglomerated.

I knew AAA Conglomerated as a diversified multi-billion dollar corporation where the division managers are given great autonomy from the corporate office, and I suggested this to the president. (I probably would have said this even if I wasn't sure, but in this case I was.) The president responded, 'Have you ever tried to get a nickel out of Jim Day?' the CEO of AAA, as if he had personal experience of doing so. I challenged again. 'Would Jim Day really get involved in this matter?' I asked as if I had personal experience of doing so.

Ultimately, the president relented and told me the truth. AAA was eliminating the process. They did not have enough volume on the machine to justify running it even if AAA raised their price, let alone lowered it. AAA was also concerned about liability issues in supplying a part used in a medical device. Standard had no choice but to bring the process in house.

## Lessons

Don't let anything pass by your eyes and ears that doesn't make sense. When I inspect a suit, I'll give a tug on every loose thread. It is the same in due diligence: I look for the loose thread and yank it. Time and time again, my boss hands me a new Brooks Brothers-like suit of an opportunity to review, and I give him back a K-Mart vest.

I don't know what is important and what might kill a deal, so I challenge everything that doesn't fit. Get the seller trained to tell you the truth for fear he'll look stupid or get caught in a lie. Sellers and representatives will learn to tell you the truth, decide there are dumber investors available and quit talking to you, or you will decide there are more intelligent, honest managers and quit talking to them. In the case of Standard Medical Device Company, management began revising their forecasts downward as I became more involved, and we submitted a bid lower than we first expected.

## Are they liars, stupid, careless, or just can't read?

I was evaluating an early-stage medical device company, Phoenix Medical Equipment, which was brought out of bankruptcy and was now seeking new funding to begin US clinical trials. Prior to the bankruptcy, the company had marketed the product outside the United States and sold a few units. Some peer-reviewed articles had been published lauding the therapeutic results of the device. I asked what had changed since the bankruptcy that would make an investor interested. Several other medical companies had looked at the company prior to the bankruptcy but then showed no interest. These companies would know more about the technology and the market than me.

The president of Phoenix, an academic researcher who had a long-term role in the product's development, claimed that a foreign clinical investigator had developed a new technique in the use of the device. This new technique improved the results dramatically. His paper had been published quite recently, and the president was exuberantly optimistic about the new prospects for this device. He went on to describe in detail how the new technique works and why it results in better therapy. It seemed to make sense and sounded very promising. He claimed the device previously had been proven to produce fewer complications than competitive devices. With the new technique, it was sure to be the winner in the marketplace.

I analysed all the published clinical results from medical centres in the United States, Europe and Asia. The paper that described the new technique was published in an obscure journal, was rather brief, and dealt with a relatively small number of patients. Other papers offered similar anecdotal evidence of the quality of the device. The results of the therapy were stated in varying terms. Some papers used one method to quantify and qualify symptoms; other papers used different measures. Some papers described improvement in relative terms; other papers described improvement in absolute terms.

After I normalised all the data to a single standard, I could see that the results of the new technique employed by this lone clinician were really no better than those of another investigator who had published a year prior to the bankruptcy of Phoenix. Further, when examining the complication rates of competitive devices with those of Phoenix, Phoenix proved no different. It seems the claims of lower complications were based on taking excerpts of medical articles out of context or measuring them against complication rates from an earlier generation of competitive but non-equivalent devices. Finally, the new technique was more aggressive, and it seemed reasonable that the complication rates could increase with its practice. The near-term and long-term complication data provided by the clinician who had developed the technique were scant. When I went over the data with the president, this genuinely seemed to be news to him.

## Lesson

Get face to face with the raw data – not a summary, not an abstract, not a graph. Sorry, but there is no quick way to do this. It takes a lot of time.

If I had a dollar for every time I found in a business plan something taken out of context, blown out of proportion, or misinterpreted from the ultimate sources and references, I would have retired after three months on this gig.

292

A recurring favourite of mine is the claim that some new government mandate (perhaps OSHA or EPA), or some new association directive or position paper, will make a market for a new service or product. Every time I examine the mandate, it is far less specific and threatening and much more subject to interpretation than was represented by the venture company. The highlight of my day is to watch management squirm and back-pedal when I call them on it.

Do not be surprised that when you call on a business association to explain the data that supports their new position, or to cite a couple of the best references that most strongly make the case for their position, they fail miserably. It is not unusual for a small contingent of well-meaning board members of an association to influence (read hijack) the rest of the directors to support a poorly substantiated position without looking into the details. In some cases, the board is yielding to our media-conscious societal value to appear politically correct rather than being factually correct. But, hey, what can it hurt society by being too cautious or too compassionate? Well, all your money, if that is what you're invested in.

## Why dumb can be smart

In my favourite episode of the Columbo TV series, my hero finds himself in the company of a potential suspect among a group of people. From his previous inspection of a wound on a murder victim, he believes the murderer to be left-handed and to wear a ring with two grooves on the its face. He could simply ask if anyone in the group is left-handed, but would he get an honest answer out of the murderer? He doesn't like to make the suspect sweat in the early stage of the investigation because Columbo is not sure he has his man; and nothing is served by raising the defenses of the suspect.

Instead Columbo goes into a spiel about his superstitious nature and that he has learned something about palm reading. He imposes himself to read the palms of those in the room and provides a ridiculous and incomprehensible reading of each person's personality and future. Everyone reacts with incredulity and some are embarrassed for him. When he nears the suspect, but still faces another person, Columbo extends an open hand to the suspect without looking directly at him, without favouring the suspect's left or right side. The suspect reaches out his left hand and Columbo takes it. While reading his palm, Columbo feels the two-groove pattern in the man's ring. He has confirmed the prime suspect.

## A humble state of mind

Little is served by presenting a capable image to the target company – even in an industry or technology that I know something about. In most cases, I am evaluating the words and deeds of people with decades of experience in industries and technologies I know little about. While some would consider my credentials and experience substantial, and I should be flattered, I believe in maintaining a humble profile.

If I went into a project with a big head, I might worry about looking stupid by questioning a fundamental fact or asking for a down-to-earth explanation that everyone else might see as obvious or trite. I might want to avoid potential embarrassment. But I am not going to the target company to show the managers how smart and successful I am. This is not a job interview. I am there to find out how smart and successful the entrepreneurs and managers are. There is no reason to tell them much, if anything, about my own credentials and experience. There is no reason to present a capable image in either dress or speech.

In my experience, the exact opposite image can be useful. If you appear helpless and confused, it is amazing how much people will want to help you (especially the lower staff). If you're evaluating something technical, you can get people to talk in terms you can understand. My stumbling approach can lower defenses and permit me access to materials and staff I might not have got to otherwise. When speaking to staff (which is very important because they know what is really going on) you'll get better information from them if they feel comfortable with you.

Most importantly, putting myself in the 'green analyst' mode helps me to not be intimidated by credentials and allows the target managers to not be intimated by me. Detective Columbo is always deferential but never intimidated. Such a presentation can avert confrontations with the target managers and protect their egos when I ask them questions that get to the heart of whether they really know what they are talking about.

The downside of this approach is that it may take longer to get answers when you don't ask questions head-on. Columbo would have saved a lot of time if he had asked whether anyone in the room was left-handed, but would he have been given the right answer? Another problem: this approach takes a lot of patience and concentration to stay in character. The more time you work in this field the less patience you have left.

## Lesson

In a previous lesson, I encouraged you to not be intimidated so that you'll ask the right questions rather than avoid them for fear of looking dumb. Now I'm telling you to not intimidate so that you'll get the right answers. The meek shall in inherit the earth and avoid all bad deals.

## Ten down and dirty tactics for your on-site visit

### 1. The written list of questions

You are often asked put your questions in writing, list the items you would like to examine and who you would like to speak to, etc. This is a fair question for the seller to ask, assuming he wants to have all the material prepared and ready for you so that your visit is as productive as possible.

But I like to limit my response to that question. First of all, I don't follow checklists anymore; they get in the way of my nose. Second, giving the target company advance notice will give them time to get their story straight. I'd rather hear an impromptu response than something coordinated and fudged. Someone is more likely to sweat on a question that he hasn't practiced fudging on. I'm pretty good at picking up body language and Freudian hedges.

Third, management may say they don't have the data I'm seeking or an answer to a question, when in fact they do but it will make them look bad. By not giving advance notice of my particular interests, I hope to be speaking to someone who does not know he is not supposed to provide me with the data or that it may be injurious to his cause.

### 2. Initial meeting etiquette

There is not much point in challenging the honchos in the initial meeting. Listen but don't inhale the intoxicating smoke of riches-to-be. Listen for what is not being said, nod, respond with amazement and admiration. Feeding their egos will make them feel comfortable and will increase your access.

Get out of the executive suite silently sceptical and talk to the staff. They know what is really going on. Why is it that employees say the darndest things? Why would they tell you something that is not in the best interest of their company? There are lots of reasons:

- They may not know what story management has told you.
- They may assume you have been told already.
- They haven't been coached on what to say, how to say it, or what data to provide.
- No one may have asked for their opinions before (including management). Now they have someone to talk to, and you're the lucky one.
- They may assume it is a done deal, so why shouldn't they talk to you. They want to get off on the right foot with the new owner.

## 3. Smile, you are on candid camera

Get personable with the staff. It helps them feel comfortable with you and will get them to open up. Don't present yourself as a high-muck-a-muck. Dress down and speak casually. The latest Dilbert cartoon can be an icebreaker. Bone up on the local news by reading the town's newspaper. Ask the secretary what word processor she uses. Help her with a computer problem. Talk shop with the staff so that they see you at their level and they'll open up to you. Start off taking their side in the stereotypical office dynamic.

If I'm talking to the engineers, for example, I might tell a funny story about the difficulty in training sales people to use a technical product. If I'm talking to an accountant, I might say it must be tough to rein in a president with an engineering background to stop developing a product just long enough to sell it. If I'm in the marketing department, I always tell the staff how happy I am to get away from the boring numbers guys and that I'm looking forward to hearing about their most exciting greatest sale story. I hope I can learn something about sales and negotiating from them.

## 4. Get out of your own way

Sit in the back seat. There are times when it serves you to be in the background. When I have a couple of managers or investment bankers shuttle me about town, I always sit in the back seat. Half forgetting I'm there, they sometimes begin to talk shop.

In one case, I started a conversation about activity-based costing and got one manager who was driving to explain it to his front seat passenger, his officious investment banker. I kept my mouth shut as the curious investment banker began asking questions about it, and the manager became more specific about his company and products. In this deal, a large corporation was spinning off a division. However, some products would continue to be manufactured by the large corporation for the newly freed division under a five-year contract, with pricing consistent with historical transfer pricing. Their conversation corroborated my suspicions that the division's premier product was an under-costed resource hog that the large corporation was eager to get rid of. They were willing to subsidise it another five years if it would help unload the division on a sucker (read financial buyer). I didn't have to ask any questions. The investment banker did the work for me.

## 5. It is not what you know, but who you speak to

What is the difference between an engineer and a salesman? An engineer would rather make a better product for tomorrow than sell a lousy product today.

The lesson is to speak to the engineers and technical people. They don't know how to lie, they're too analytical. They can't say $1 + 1 = 3$. It just does not compute. Time and time again, I kill deals or lower valuations by getting the straight story from the engineers. It helps to have an engineering background like me, to practice this tip.

## 6. Make the fog your best friend

Never tell anyone you are sceptical and doubting. Explain it as confusion. 'I am way over my head on this assignment. Sorry, I'm such a bother. I really appreciate your patience with me.' People will try to help you. Give them enough rope to hang themselves.

## 7. See if everyone is on the same page

Cross-check the stories you are told by staff and management with other staff and management and outside experts. Ask questions you know the answers to in order to judge the competency and honesty of staff, management, venture capitalists and bankers.

On a visit to a high-tech company which had a lot of R&D invested prior to its formal incorporation, I asked the three principals individually how much was invested to date in the project. I received three grossly different answers and learned from this test who was the most accurate with the facts.

## 8. Make them keep their commitments

Make a list of everything they said they would provide to you and every question they said they would have to research and answer later. They will do no such thing if the data makes them look bad. You have to hound them.

In preparation for a visit, I asked one company to provide me with their market research on a new product line that was key to their budget. I was told it was much too copious to send. When I arrived at the facility, I asked again. I was told it was locked away in the file cabinet of someone who was away on business. Eventually, I learned the research was negligible and they must have been too embarrassed to show me what little they had.

## 9. Never assume the detail agrees with the summary

Get the next level of detail and the next level below that. It is better to be the filterer of details than the filteree. You might find the company has no details or that the details do not support the higher-level analysis. Check the references.

On one assignment, I examined hand-written inventory logs and compared them to the balance sheet ledger. Although the gross numbers matched, I could see clearly the erasure marks and fudges on the hand-written sheets (eg, make a 7 look like 9). This firm was fudging inventory to avoid default on their loan covenants. On another case, I reviewed lab notebooks in an engineering department and found unfavourable product durability data omitted from a summary report.

## 10. When is as important as who and how

Come in at off-hours and on weekends, even unannounced. There will be fewer bosses around and everything will be at a lower key. Excuses can include forgetting a file, needing to use a PC, or needing to review an accounting binder too big to carry to the hotel. Bring some doughnuts with you to share with the weekend warriors, in particular the clerical folks. You'll be amazed at what you'll learn.

On one assignment, during a weekend, the accounting clerks pointed to a stack of old payables they were just starting to input. This department was severely understaffed and they had fallen way behind. It was unexplained why some invoices were several months old. The total amount was significant. Top management was not really aware how far things were out of whack.

## Bonus down and dirty tactic

## 11. The dumber you look, the smarter you are

If your challenge of some fact or assumption is met with an insulting put-down, charge! I'm not worried about looking stupid so I am not going to retreat. I am not there to look smart. I cannot think of an instance when I pushed forward after an insult that I did not find the manager was flat wrong or had exceedingly little to back him up.

## Afterword

Down and dirty due diligence is an archeological dig, excavating truths embedded in the lower levels of data and staff alike. You must consciously put all assumptions aside and challenge every fact as fiction. No 'truth' is too obvious to be immune from further scrutiny. As a result, your behaviour may be considered to range from imbecilic to hostile.

This is hardly work for the feint-hearted. You may worry about looking dumb. Only a callused and licensed professional can do this safely and still keep his ego intact.

This chapter is an amended and updated version of an article that originally appeared in, and is reprinted with permission from:
*The Journal of Private Equity* Volume 1, Number 3, Spring 1998.